THIRD EDITION

Understanding Arguments

AN INTRODUCTION TO INFORMAL LOGIC

THIRD EDITION

AUNDERSTANDINGS RGUMENTS

AN INTRODUCTION TO INFORMAL LOGIC

Robert J. Fogelin
Dartmouth College

HARCOURT BRACE JOVANOVICH, PUBLISHERS

San Diego   New York   Chicago   Austin

London   Sydney   Tokyo   Toronto

ISBN: 0-15-592862-7
Library of Congress Catalog Card Number: 85-82635

Printed in the United States of America

Illustrations by Eric G. Hieber, eh Technical Services

To Eric, John, and Lars
and the colleges of their choice

An argument isn't just contradiction.

Can be.

No it can't. An argument is a connected series of statements intended to establish a proposition.

No it isn't.

Yes it is.

Argument Clinic,
From MONTY PYTHON'S PREVIOUS RECORD

Preface

This book is about arguments. It considers arguments not in the narrow sense of quarrels or squabbles, but in the broader, logician's, sense of giving reasons in behalf of some claim. Viewing arguments in this way, we see that they are a common feature of daily life, for we are often involved in giving reasons or evaluating reasons given by others. These are not only common but important activities. Deciding what to believe, how to act, how to judge others, and the like are all, in the end, questions to be settled by weighing reasons. Traditionally, logic has been considered the most general science dealing with arguments.

For certain purposes, arguments are best studied as abstract patterns. Logic is not concerned with particular arguments—for example, your attempt to prove that the bank, not you, has made a mistake. The task of logic is to discover the fundamental principles for distinguishing good arguments from bad ones. The study of those general principles that make certain patterns of argument reasonable (or valid) and other patterns of argument unreasonable (or invalid) is called formal logic.

A different, but complementary, way of viewing an argument is to treat it as a *particular use of language:* arguing is one of the things that we do with words. This approach places stress upon arguing as a linguistic activity. Instead of studying arguments as abstract patterns, it takes them "in the rough," as they occur in actual argumentation. It raises questions of the following kind: What is the place of argument within language as a whole? In a given language (say, our own), what words or phrases are characteristic of arguments? What task or tasks are arguments supposed to perform? When an approach to arguments has this form, the study is called informal logic. As its subtitle indicates, *Understanding Arguments* is primarily a text in informal logic.

The Third Edition of this book has been influenced by my own teaching experience with the first two editions and by the generous and helpful suggestions I have received from other instructors. As the result of that classroom experience and those suggestions, this edition involves a number of fundamental changes from the previous two. Since many instructors found the discussion of speech-act theory in the opening chapters too abstruse for some of their students, I have eliminated it. I now try to convey the same ideas about the diversity and richness of the uses of language without introducing technical apparatus. A second important change is that I have added two new chapters, one on inductive reasoning, the other on probability and decision making. This should mitigate the deductive chauvinism that some instructors found in the earlier editions.

Throughout I have tried to update material. Specifically, in Part Two, the discussion of legal reasoning (Chapter 11) has been completely rewritten and now contains, with running explanation, substantial portions of the *Bakke* decision. The discussion of abortion (Chapter 12) contains two new essays, more or less from opposite ends of the spectrum, by Ronald Reagan and Barbara Ehrenreich. The discussion of scientific arguments (Chapter 13) now includes an exchange on the scientific status of creation science. Finally, the chapter on philosophical arguments (Chapter 14) uses a lively exchange, between Douglas R. Hofstadter and Daniel C. Dennett on one hand and John R. Searle on the other, on the subject of machine intelligence.

Throughout Part One, new exercises have been added. The more difficult exercises are now marked with a ♦. Part One also includes a feature new to this edition: discussion questions at the end of each chapter which are intended to encourage students to reflect on the significance of the techniques they are learning. Finally, Chapter 10 contains a number of puzzles concerning probability that deeply perplex most students, and, for that matter, most instructors as well.

Beyond these structural changes, much of the text has been rewritten to avoid obscurity and inelegance. Here my colleagues have been more than generous, indeed, sometimes gleeful in their comments and criticisms. In this regard, I wish to thank Mark Bedau and Susan Brison, Dartmouth College; David J. Luban, University of Maryland; Susan Russinoff, Massachusetts Institute of Technology; and Carl Wolf. Special thanks go to Walter P. Sinnott-Armstrong, also of Dartmouth, who has taught from the text and then made a great many detailed suggestions for its improvement. I am indebted as well to the following reviewers: Sharon Bishop, California State University, Los Angeles; Josiah B. Gould, State University of New York at Albany; and James Edward Magruder, Stephen F. Austin State University. I have also received splendid help from Bill Teague of Harcourt Brace Jovanovich and Florence Fogelin of Plain English at every stage in the preparation of this Third Edition.

ROBERT J. FOGELIN

Contents

PART
TWO

Fields of Argumentation

Part
ONE

The Analysis of Argument

1

The Web of Language

As an introduction to our study of informal logic, this chapter will survey the general nature of language. In doing so, it will stress three main ideas. First, language is *conventional*. Words acquire meaning within a rich system of linguistic rules. An understanding of language demands an understanding of these rules. Second, language is *diverse*. We sometimes use it to communicate information, but we also use it to ask questions, issue orders, write poetry, keep score, formulate arguments, and perform an almost endless number of other tasks. Third, meaning is often conveyed *indirectly*. In order to understand the significance of many utterances, we must go beyond what is literally said to examine what is conversationally implied.

LANGUAGE AND ARGUMENT

This book is about arguments. The word "argument" may suggest quarrels or squabbles, but here it is used in the broader, logician's sense of giving reasons for or against some claim. Viewing arguments this way, we see that they are a common feature of daily life, for we are often involved in giving reasons for things we believe or in evaluating reasons given by others for things they want us to believe. Trying to decide which way to vote in an election, what play to use on third down and long, where to go to college, whether to support or oppose capital punishment—all involve weighing and evaluating reasons. Logic bears on all of these issues because it is the general science of argument; its goal is to lay down principles for distinguishing good arguments from bad arguments.

Arguing is also an activity, in particular, a *linguistic* activity. Arguing is one of the many things that we can do with words. In fact, unlike fighting, it is something that we can *only* do with words. Thus, in order to understand how arguments work, it is important to understand how language works. Unfortunately, our understanding of human languages is incomplete, and linguistics remains a young science where disagreement abounds. Still, there are certain facts about language that are beyond dispute, and recognizing them will help us understand how arguments work.

Language and Convention

As everyone who has bothered to think about it knows, language is conventional. There seems to be no reason why we, as English speakers, use the word "dog" to refer to dogs rather than to cats, trees, or anything at all. Any word might have been used to stand for anything. Beyond this, there seems to be no reason why we put words together in the way that we do. In English we put adjectives before the nouns they modify. We thus speak of a *green salad*. In French adjectives usually follow the noun, and so instead of saying *verte salade* the French say *salade verte*. The conventions of our own language are so much with us that it strikes us as odd when we discover that other languages have different conventions. A French diplomat once praised his own language because, as he said, it followed the natural order of thought. This strikes us English speakers as silly, but in seeing what is silly about it, we see that the word order in our own language is conventional as well.

It is important to realize that our language is conventional, but it is also important not to misunderstand this fact. From the idea that language is conventional, it is easy to conclude that language is *arbitrary*, so that it really doesn't matter which words we use. It takes only a little thought to see that this is not true. If I wish to communicate with others I must follow the system of conventions that others use. To put matters simply, conventions do not destroy meaning by making it arbitrary; conventions bring meaning into existence.

A misunderstanding of the conventions of language can lead to pointless disputes. Sometimes, in the middle of a discussion, someone will declare that "the whole thing is just a matter of definition." Now there are times when definitions are important and arguments turn upon them, but in general this is not true. Suppose someone has fallen off a cliff and is heading toward certain death on the rocks below. Of course, it is a matter of definition (of convention) that we use the word "death" to describe the result of the sudden stop at the end of the fall. We might have used some other word—perhaps "birth"—instead. But it certainly will not help the person who is falling to change the meaning of the word "death" in the middle of his plunge. It will do no good for him to yell out, "By birth I mean death." It will not help even if *everyone* agrees to change the meaning of the words in this way. If we all decided to adopt this new convention, we would then say, "He fell from the cliff to his birth" instead of "He fell from the cliff to his death." But speaking in this way will not change the facts. It will not, for example, make those who care for him feel better.

The upshot of this simple example is that the truth of what we say is rarely just a matter of definition. The words we use are governed by conventions, and in the process of learning our language we learn to follow these conventions in speaking. (Only later do we develop some understanding of these conventions.) We then go on to make certain claims about the world. Others can understand what we say because we follow the ordinary conventions that give meaning to our words. Whether what I have said is true or not will depend, for the most part, on how things stand in the world. For example, if a German wishes to say that snow is black, then he will use the words "Schnee ist schwartz." Other Germans will *understand* his words, but unless snow is different in Germany than every place else, they will also think that he has said something false, and may wonder how he could make such a mistake. In general, then, the truth of what we say is not merely a matter of definition or convention, and when someone uses this ploy in the middle of an argument we can usually assume that he or she is in desperate shape.

In the last sentence I have used two qualifying phrases: "in general" and "usually." To say that something holds *in general*, or *usually*, is to admit that there may be exceptions. Such a qualification is needed in this case because *sometimes* the truth of what we say is simply a matter of definition. Take a simple example. The claim that a triangle has three sides is true by definition, because a triangle is defined as "a three-sided closed plane figure." Again, if someone says that sin is wrong, he has said something that is true by definition, for a sin is defined as, among other things, "something that is wrong."

Consider a more complicated case. Suppose someone argues that the only true democracies exist in communist states. He admits that in such states there are no general elections where a large portion of the population is allowed to choose between competing parties, but he goes on to say that a genuine democracy exists only when the party in power reflects the interests of the masses. Here we might challenge the definition of a democracy that he is using and then be met by the following reply: Why should everyone in the world be bound by the capitalist definition of a democracy? Alternatively, we can accept his definition and argue that communist parties do not reflect the interests of the masses. We might then be told that no democracy is perfect, especially those in newly emerging nations. Here the only way to stop our heads from swimming is to return to common sense and reject both the definition and the facts. Historically, in a democracy the people *choose* the policies that govern them, or at least the representatives who formulate these policies. When this choice is absent, democracy does not exist. A despotism, however benevolent, is not a democracy. We should advise our opponent to be candid enough to admit that he is against a democracy and if he is in favor of another form of government, to give it another name and defend it on its own terms. If he is misrepresenting the facts, we can say that too. In short, we need not be driven to silence by a person who distorts the meaning of words and tampers with the facts. We can simply point out that he is distorting and tampering.

Sometimes, then, it is important to ask a person to define his terms. We should do this whenever we think that someone is distorting the meaning of words to win an argumentative point. We can also ask for a definition in order to clarify, if we think that someone is speaking in a vague and loose way. But it makes no sense to ask that every word be defined. This would prove an endless task and we would never get around to saying anything in particular. Beyond this, asking for definitions is often just silly. If someone says "Pass the butter," it does not usually cross our minds to ask him to define "butter."

In sum, people are able to communicate with each other because they share certain linguistic conventions. These conventions could have been very different and in this sense they are arbitrary. But it does not follow from this that the truth of what we say is also merely arbitrary. In general, the truth of what we say is settled not by an appeal to definition, but by a look at the facts. Sometimes, however, the conventions of our language are misused or even abused. Here it makes sense to call for a definition in order to restore mutual understanding. It would be absurd to ask that every word be defined.

KINDS OF CONVENTIONS

In the previous section we saw that a language is a system of shared conventions that allows us to communicate with one another. If we pause to look at language, we see that it contains many different kinds of conventions. We have seen that words have meanings conventionally attached to them. The word "dog" is used conventionally to talk about dogs. Proper names are also conventionally assigned, for Harry Jones could have been named Wilbur Jones. (There are, of course, social limits involved in giving meanings to words. You cannot name your son John D. Rockefeller unless you happen to be named Rockefeller. But setting aside limitations of this kind and others, the assignment of meanings to words is conventional.)

Other conventions concern the way in which words can be put together to form sentences. These are often called *grammatical* rules. Using the three words "John," "hit," and "Harry," we can formulate sentences with very different meanings. For example, "John hit Harry" and "Harry hit John." We recognize that these sentences have different meanings because we understand the grammar of our language. This grammatical understanding also allows us to see that the sentence "Hit John Harry" does not mean anything at all—even though the individual words possess meaning. (Notice that "Hit John, Harry!" does mean something: it is a way of telling Harry to hit John.) Grammatical rules are very important, for they play a part in giving a meaning to a sentence as a whole. Admittedly, some of our grammatical rules play only a small role in this important task because they are largely stylistic. If I say "Hopefully he will be here tomorrow," I have uttered an ugly and ungrammatical sentence (yet I still make sense since *hopefully* is an adverb literally meaning *full of hope*). If I violate deeper and more fundamental grammatical rules, I speak nonsense. It is worth noting, however, that some grammatical rules which seem only stylistic at first sight do make important contributions to the meaning of a sentence. The subjunctive mood is an example.

There are, then, at least two kinds of conventions that give meaning to what we say. The ones that assign meanings to individual words are commonly called *semantic* conventions. The conventions that lay down rules for combining words into meaningful wholes are called grammatical or *syntactical* conventions. The study of semantic conventions and syntactical conventions is largely the job of linguistics. Although important advances have been made in this field, every linguist will acknowledge that the amount unknown far outweighs the amount known. For this reason, linguistics is one of the most exciting fields of scientific investigation.

Later on we shall look more closely at semantic and syntactical conventions, for at times they are a source of fallacies and other confusions. In particular, we shall see how these conventions can generate *fallacies of ambiguity*. But before we examine the defects of our language, we should first appreciate that language is a powerful and subtle tool. We will next examine the wide variety of jobs that language can perform.

THE USES OF LANGUAGE

When asked about the function of language, it is natural to reply that we use language to communicate our ideas. But this is only *one* of its uses. This becomes obvious as soon as we set aside our prejudices and take a look at the way our language actually works. Adding up a column of figures is a linguistic activity, but it does not communicate any ideas to others. When I add the figures I am not even trying to communicate anything to myself: I am trying to figure something out.

Writing a poem is a more interesting example. Sometimes poems convey factual information, and at other times they express philosophical truths. Poems also express emotions. Yet often the most important fact about a poem is that it is an artistic creation in the same way that a painting or a sculpture is an artistic creation. A poem is a linguistic artifact. We get a bad theory of poetry, and may even lessen our appreciation of poetry, if we think of a poem as a mere device for conveying the poet's thoughts and emotions to others. Consider one example:

Upon Julia's Clothes
ROBERT HERRICK

Whenas in silks my Julia goes,
Then, then, methinks, how sweetly flows
The liquefaction of her clothes.

Next when I cast mine eyes, and see
That brave vibration each way free,
O, how that glittering taketh me!

Using a modern idiom, Herrick might have said "Julia's terrific figure turns me on." This second way of speaking leaves little doubt about what Herrick thinks and how he feels about Julia. The poem, by comparison, may fail to some extent in communication, but the chief difference lies elsewhere. Herrick's emotions are, after all, fairly common. His mode of expressing them, however, produces one of the most perfect poems in the English language. A poem is not simply a news broadcast with fancy frills.

Poetry provides an example of language used for purposes other than communication, but beyond that it is a complicated linguistic phenomenon that defies easy analysis. A look at our everyday conversations produces a host of other examples of language being used for different purposes. Grammarians, for example, have divided sentences into various moods:

(1) Indicative
(2) Interrogative
(3) Imperative
(4) Expressive (and some others)

For example:

(1) He is in England now that spring is here.
(2) Is he in England now that spring is here?
(3) Go to England now that spring is here!
(4) Oh to be in England, now that spring is here!!

The first sentence states a fact; we can use it to communicate information about a person's location. If we use it in this way, what we say will be either true or false. Notice that none of the other sentences can be called either true or false.

PERFORMATIVES

The different types of sentences recognized by traditional grammarians indicate that we use language to do more than convey information or express emotions. But this traditional classification of sentences gives only a small idea of the wide variety of things that we can accomplish using language. Sometimes, for example, in using language, we actually *do* things in the strong sense of bringing about a change, sometimes a fundamental change, between individuals. In one familiar setting, if one person says "I do" and another person says "I do," and finally a third person says "I pronounce you husband and wife," the relationship between the first two people changes in a fundamental way: they are thereby married. With luck, they begin a life of wedded bliss, but they also alter their legal relationship. For example, they may now file joint income tax returns and may not marry other people without first getting a divorce.

Sentences of this kind, those that can be used to *bring something about* rather than merely *stating something,* were labeled *performatives* by the philosopher J. L. Austin (see Appendix A to this book). He called them performatives because they involve the *performance* of an action rather than a mere description of an action. For example, if an umpire shouts, "You're Out!" then the batter is out. The umpire is not describing the situation, but applying a rule and *thereby* declaring the batter out. The word "thereby" supplies a rough and ready test for performatives. *If in saying something I thereby do it,* then the utterance is usually a performative. Thus, in standard situations, in saying "I promise to see you tomorrow," I *thereby* promise to see you tomorrow. By way of contrast, in saying "I am the best tennis player in Tennessee," I am not *thereby* the best tennis player in Tennessee. Becoming the best tennis player in Tennessee is something that you do with a tennis racket, not simply with words.

To avoid complications, we shall concentrate on what Austin called *explicit* performatives. A sentence expresses an explicit performative if it is in the first person singular indicative present and yields a true statement when it is plugged into the following pattern:

In saying "I _____," I thereby _____.

Thus, "I congratulate you" expresses an explicit performative, because it is true that in saying "I congratulate you," I thereby congratulate you. Here a quoted expression occurs on the left side of the word "thereby," but not on the right side. This reflects the fact that the *saying,* which is referred to on the left side of the pattern, amounts to the *doing,* referred to on the right side of the word "thereby." Applied to the following pairs of sentences, this test (we will call it the *thereby test*) shows that the sentences on the left formulate performative (P) expressions whereas the sentences on the right formulate nonperformative (NP) expressions:

I order you to leave. (P)   I am six feet tall. (NP)
I apologize. (P)   I feel sad. (NP)

Notice that with the last pair, in saying "I apologize," I thereby apologize, but *saying* I am sad no more makes me sad than saying I am six feet tall makes me six feet tall. Apologizing, like promising, is something that you can accomplish using words; feeling sad is something that goes on inside you. Finally, questions, imperatives, and exclamations are not explicit performatives since they cannot be sensibly plugged into the pattern at all (as in the question "Is there a washroom on this floor?").

Using the thereby test, as described above, decide which of the following sentences express performatives (P) and which express nonperformatives (NP):

(1) I resign from this rotten club.
(2) Pierre is the capital of South Dakota.
(3) I order you to leave.
(4) I own the World Trade Towers.
(5) I claim this land for Queen Victoria. (Said by an explorer)
(6) I'm out of gas.
(7) Get lost!
(8) I bring you official greetings from the Socialist Party of Finland.
♦ (9) Ask not what your country can do for you, but what you can do for your country.
♦ (10) I ask you, are you better off now than you were four years ago?

EXERCISE 2

Using a college dictionary, find ten verbs that can be used to construct sentences (in the first person singular indicative present) that pass the thereby test.

There are two reasons why we should pay attention to performatives. First, being aware of performatives helps us to see that language can be used to achieve a great many different and important ends. Second, performatives occur often in arguments—the central topic of the field of logic—and to understand arguments, it is important to understand these performatives as well.

Argumentative Performatives

The performatives we have examined thus far concern either interpersonal relations or the relationships between persons and institutions. We can now look at a different kind of performative, which Austin called *expositives*.[1] We will call them *argumentative performatives*. Here are some examples, using the thereby test:

> If I say, "I deny the charge," I thereby deny the charge.
>
> If I say, "I claim he's lying," I thereby claim he is lying.
>
> If I say, "I concede the point," I thereby concede the point.
>
> If I say, "I allow such and such," I thereby allow such and such.
>
> If I say, "I conclude that such and such," I thereby conclude that such and such.
>
> If I say, "I stipulate that such and such," I thereby stipulate that such and such.

These performatives are obviously concerned with arguments. In particular, they are used to *make moves* in arguments. Furthermore, they are not statements about arguments, since they are not even statements. If the lawyer finishes his speech to the jury by saying, "I conclude that the evidence merits acquittal," it makes no sense for someone to say, "No you don't!" We may disagree that the evidence merits acquittal and go on to challenge this, but we cannot disagree that the lawyer has drawn this conclusion.

There are other argumentative moves that are not expressed as performatives. I can challenge someone's claim by saying "I doubt that," but "I doubt that" does *not* express an explicit performative. This is shown by applying the thereby test. If I say "I doubt that" I do not thereby doubt it. Whether I doubt something or not is a fact about me. There are some interesting intermediate cases that change with contexts. Sometimes if I say that I agree I do not *thereby* agree, for again, whether I agree or not is typically considered a fact about me. But in other contexts, saying that I agree amounts to entering into or making an agreement. Here the utterance is performative. Usually "I agree to . . ." is a performative, whereas "I agree that . . ." is not. In a court of law, however, saying "I agree that . . ." is often performative. It is one way of stipulating facts that will not be contested, and by it I waive my right to contest certain facts later on.

Why does our language contain argumentative performatives? What useful purpose do they serve? We have already noticed that argumentative performatives allow us to make moves *in* an argument. By saying "I conclude . . . ," I draw a conclusion. By saying, "I acknowledge what has been said," I thereby acknowledge what has been said. Yet our language provides other means for making argumentative moves. We can mark a conclusion by using a word like "therefore." I can say some-

---

[1] J. L. Austin, *How to Do Things with Words* (New York: Oxford University Press, 1965), pp. 161 ff.

thing like this: "It has been shown that my client was in Detroit on the night in question; therefore, he could not have committed this crime." Here I draw a conclusion without using the phrase "I conclude." Again, I can disagree with someone by saying "That's not so" or by saying the opposite of what he has said. In fact, we can imagine a society where arguments are carried out *without* the use of argumentative performatives. They would simply use words like "therefore" instead of phrases like "I conclude."

So the question remains: Why do we have argumentative performatives at all? Part of the answer is that argumentative performatives make our argumentative moves explicit. If I want to make it perfectly clear that I am concluding something, I can signal this by saying "I conclude. . . ." I will probably reserve this expression for the *final* conclusion, thus leaving little doubt what the argument is intended to show. At other times during an argument it is important not only to disagree but also to make it clear that we are disagreeing. In this way we point explicitly to the part of our opponent's argument we wish to reject. We usually reserve argumentative performatives for the *important* parts of opposing arguments.

Performatives also allow *subtle* moves to be made in the course of an argument. Sometimes an arguer will say, "I grant the point for the sake of argument" (thereby granting the point for the sake of argument). This is a powerful move if it can be carried off, for nothing is better than refuting an opponent on his own grounds. This device also contains an escape hatch, for if our efforts go badly, we can still challenge the statement previously granted just for the sake of argument. Somewhat differently, we can say, "I reserve comment" (thereby reserving comment). Here we neither reject a claim nor accept it (even for the sake of argument); we let it pass until we see what is made of it. This is a useful tactical device. If we are arguing from a strong position, it is a good idea to keep the line of the argument clean. By reserving comment we can avoid being drawn into irrelevant discussions that will cloud the issue. At other times we do not know what we want to say in response to a particular point or we are not quite sure what the person is going to make of it. Reserving comment is a way of not sticking our necks out prematurely. Argumentative performatives are, then, powerful and subtle tools for making moves in an argument.

CONVERSATIONAL RULES

A: What did you think of Jay's performance as Hamlet?
B: Well, he certainly knew all his lines.

Anyone overhearing this conversation would assume that B does not think well of Jay's performance. B seems to be engaged in a verbal practice known as damning with faint praise. By examining this interesting phenomenon closely, we can explore a system of important rules that governs our use of language.

To begin with, getting all the lines right while acting Shakespeare's *Hamlet* is no small achievement—the role has a lot of them. Yet we do not usually praise actors for remembering their lines, for this is the least they are expected to do. On the other hand, we usually criticize actors who forget their lines. One thing that B's remark indicates is that there is criticism that cannot be leveled against Jay: he forgot his lines. How does an acknowledgment of this positive feature take on the negative force of criticism? The answer is not hard to find. A has asked B to give a *general* evaluation of Jay's performance. To do this fairly, B must take into account all of the positive features of Jay's performance and balance them against the negative features. Now if the only positive comment that B makes in behalf of the performance is that Jay remembered all of his lines, this plainly suggests that there is nothing else good to say about it, or at least nothing of importance. If that is so, Jay's performance must have been pretty rotten.

This simple example illustrates a number of important points. First, although the significance or import of a remark is obviously related to its literal meaning, import is not always completely determined by literal meaning alone. Second, understanding the import or significance of a remark usually requires understanding the purpose of the conversational exchange in which the remark occurs. The purpose of the exchange between A and B was to have B give a general assessment of Jay's performance. We all have some idea of the qualities that make up a good performance, for example, the ability to portray a character in a realistic and compelling manner. We assume that B took these possible qualities into account and, moreover, that they formed the central part of his evaluation of Jay's performance. His failure to mention them explicitly suggests that he could find nothing good to say about them. This silence on features of Jay's performance, features that B should have mentioned if he thought well of them, plainly indicates that he did not think well of them at all.

Now if we change the conversational setting, B's remark can have a wholly different import even though its *literal* meaning is unchanged. Suppose that Jay is a very gifted, but flamboyant, young actor. He is difficult to direct and often takes liberties with the script. In fact, there are those who have suggested that he is too lazy or too arrogant to memorize all his lines. Given this background B's remark takes on a wholly new significance; it no longer amounts to damning with faint praise. Rather, its point is to defend Jay. Thus the example illustrates another important point: that understanding the import or significance of a remark often depends upon knowing the *beliefs* shared by those involved in the conversation.

In sum, the significance or import of a remark will usually depend upon at least three factors: (1) the literal content of what it said, (2) the purposes of those involved in the conversational exchange, and (3) the shared beliefs and understandings that the participants bring to the conversational setting. Later in this work (in Chapter 6), we will look closely at this third factor, the background assumptions or presuppositions that structure conversational exchanges. Here we shall concentrate on the second factor and, in particular, examine some of the rules that allow us to achieve our purposes in a conversational setting. This subject was first explored in detail by the philosopher H. P. Grice.[2]

Grice begins with a very general principle, one that he calls the Cooperative Principle (CP):

> Make your conversational contribution such as is required, at the stage at which it occurs, by the accepted purpose or direction of the talk exchange in which you are engaged.

This, of course, is *very* general. It considers a standard case where conversation is a cooperative venture—that is, where all parties have some common goal in talking to each other. (A witness being cross-examined does not accept this principle.) The principle states, quite simply, that in such a context, what we say should contribute toward achieving this goal. This general principle gets more content when we examine other principles that fall under it. One such principle is the rule of *Quantity* or the rule of *Strength*. Grice states it in these words:

(1) Make your contribution as informative as is required (for the current purposes of the exchange).

and possibly

(2) Do not make your contribution more informative than is required.

Here is an application of this rule: A person comes rushing up to you and asks, "Where is a fire extinguisher?" You know that there is a fire extinguisher five floors away in the basement, and you also know that there is a fire extinguisher just down the hall. Suppose you say that there is a fire extinguisher in the basement. Here you have said something that is *true,* but you have violated the rule of Quantity. You have held back an important piece of information that, under the rule of Quantity, you should have produced. A violation of the second version of the

---

[2] H. P. Grice, "Logic and Conversation," in Donald Davison and Gilbert Harman, eds., *The Logic of Grammar* (Encino, California: Dickenson Publishing Company, 1975), p. 67. Reprinted in Appendix B to this book.

rule would look like this: Starting with the basement, you say where a fire extinguisher is located on each floor.

There is another cluster of rules that Grice calls rules of *Quality*. In general:

Try to make your contribution one that is true.

More specifically:

(1) Do not say what you believe to be false.
(2) Do not say that for which you lack adequate evidence.

In a cooperative activity, you are expected not to tell lies. Beyond this, you are expected not to talk off the top of your head either. When we make a statement, we can be challenged in the following ways:

Do you really believe that?
Why do you believe that?
How do you know that?
Are you sure?

That a person has the right to ask such questions shows that statement-making is governed by this rule of *Quality*. (In a court of law, we are expected to tell the truth, the whole truth, and nothing but the truth. The demand for the *truth* and *nothing but the truth* reflects the rule of Quality; the demand for the *whole truth* reflects the rule of Quantity.)

The next rule is called the rule of *Relevance*. Simply stated, it says: Be relevant! Though easy to state, the rule is not easy to explain, because relevance itself is a difficult notion. It is, however, easy to illustrate. If someone asks me where he can find a fire extinguisher, I might reply, among other things, that there is a fire alarm box just down the hall. Though not a direct answer to his question, it is obviously relevant to this person's concerns. Perhaps a violation of the second version of the rule of Quantity, i.e., giving too much information, should be treated as a violation of the rule of Relevance. But the clear-cut violations of this principle are stronger than this. They involve *changing the subject*. Interruptions are typically violations of the rule of Relevance.

Another rule concerns the *Manner* of our conversation. We are expected to be clear. Under this general rule come various special rules:

(1) Avoid obscurity of expression.
(2) Avoid ambiguity.
(3) Be brief.
(4) Be orderly.

In obvious ways, all these rules contribute to the business of conveying information.

There are probably many other rules that should govern our conversations. *Be polite!* might be one of them. *Be charitable!* is another. That is, we should put the best construction on what others say and our replies should reflect this. We should avoid quibbling and unnecessary challenges. There are also rules that govern linguistic performance. Speak clearly, loudly enough to be heard, in a language the other person understands, and so on. For the most part, however, we will not worry about them.

If we look at basic rules we notice that they sometimes overlap. The rule against offering too much information, as we have seen, could be treated as part of the Relevance rule. More important, these rules sometimes clash, or at least push us in different directions. The rule of Quantity encourages us to give as much information as possible, but this is constrained by the rule of Quality, which restricts our claims to things we believe to be true and can back with good reasons. The demands of the rule of Quantity can also conflict with the demand for brevity. Again, in order to be brief, we must sometimes simplify and even falsify, and this can come into conflict with the Quality rule that we have good reasons to support the truth of what we have said. An ongoing conversation is a constant series of adjustments to this background system of rules.

Conversational Implication[3]

We have seen that conversational exchanges are governed by a system of rules that help those involved in the exchange achieve their purposes. Statement making, for example, is governed by conventions concerning quantity, quality, relevance, and manner. Of course, when people make statements they do not always follow these rules. People withhold information, they lie, they talk off the tops of their heads, they wander off the subject, they talk vaguely and obscurely. Yet in a normal setting where people are cooperating toward a shared goal, they conform quite closely to these rules. If, on the whole, people did not do this, we could not have the linguistic practices we do. If we thought, for example, that people very often lied (even about the most trivial matters), the business of communicating would be badly damaged.

But not only do we follow these conventions, we also (1) realize that we are following them, and (2) expect others to assume that we are

---

[3]The notion of conversational implication was also developed by Paul Grice. What follows borrows heavily from his discussion, but there are some important modifications as well. These differences become obvious by comparing this section with his essay, "Logic and Conversation," which is reprinted in Appendix B of this text. Most of the changes are simplifications rather than attempted improvements on his original work.

following them. These points are obvious. If I say that there is a fire extinguisher down the hall, I realize that I am supposed to believe what I say. This explains why it would be odd to say this: "There is a fire extinguisher down the hall, but I do not believe it." This statement, after all, could be true. I might not believe that there is a fire extinguisher down the hall, and there might actually be one there (one, perhaps, that I never noticed). Even so, I am not supposed to state that there is a fire extinguisher down the hall unless I believe it. The person I speak to is *entitled* to assume that I believe it. He too understands these conventions, and, unless he doubts my integrity, he *expects* that I will follow them.

Here, we have to be careful. If I am a pathological liar and my listener knows this, he may doubt that I believe what I say. He has a right to criticize me for abusing linguistic conventions, but since he knows that I lie he is not trapped into believing that I am, in fact, following them. Yet in normal cooperative situations people make assumptions like these:

People follow conventions.
People realize that they are following conventions.
People realize that others assume that they are following conventions.

This leads to the following important result: *In a standard conversational setting, saying something conversationally implies that all the normal rules governing such conversations are being followed.* So if a person says that there is a fire extinguisher in the lobby this will conversationally imply *at least* all of the following.

(1) That this is the nearest or most accessible fire extinguisher.
(2) That the speaker believes this to be true.
(3) That the speaker has good reason for believing this, and is not merely guessing.
(4) That this information is relevant to the listener's interests.
(5) That the remark is intelligible to the listener.

It is important to realize that conversational implication is a pervasive feature of human discourse. It is not something we employ only occasionally for special effect. In fact, virtually every conversation relies upon these implications, and most conversations would fall apart if those involved in them refused to go beyond literal meaning to take into account the implications of what is being said. In the following conversation B is literal-minded in just this way:

A: Do you know what time it is?

B: Not without looking at my watch.

B has answered A's question, but it is hard to imagine that A received the information he was looking for. Presumably he wanted to know what time it was, not merely whether B, at this very moment, knew the time. Finding B rather obtuse, A tries again:

A: Can you tell me what time it is?

B: Oh yes, I have only to look at my watch.

Undaunted, A gives it another try:

A: Will you tell me what time it is?

B: I suppose I will as soon as you ask me.

Finally:

A: What time is it?

B: Two o'clock.

Notice that in each of these exchanges B gives a direct and accurate answer to A's question, yet, in all but the last answer, he does not provide what A wants. Here we might say that B is taking A's question too literally, but we might better say that the problem is that B is doing nothing *more* than taking A's remarks literally. In a conversational exchange, we expect others to take our remarks in the light of the obvious purpose we have in making them. We expect them to share our commonsense understanding of why people ask questions. People often want to be told the time, but only rarely, for example, when they are trying to synchronize their activities, do they care whether others know what time it is. In his replies, B is totally oblivious to the point of A's questions and, like a computer in a science-fiction movie, gives nothing more than the literally correct answer to the question he has been asked.

Violating Conversational Rules

We can next look at a set of conversational implications that attracted Grice's attention. Sometimes our speech acts *seem* to violate certain conventions. On the assumption that the conversation is good-willed and cooperative, the listener will then attempt to make sense of this in a way that overcomes this appearance.

Here is one of Grice's examples:

A: Where does C live?

B: Somewhere in Southern France.

If A is interested in visiting C, then B's reply is not adequate and thus seems to violate the rule of Quantity. We can explain this departure on the assumption that B does not know exactly where C lives and would thus violate the rule of Quality if he said anything more specific. In this case, B's reply conversationally implies that he does not know exactly where C lives.

In a more extreme case, a person may even flout one of these conventions—that is, obviously violate it. Here is Grice's example and his explanation of it: [4]

> A is writing a testimonial about a pupil who is a candidate for a philosophy job, and the letter reads as follows: "Dear Sir, Mr. X's command of English is excellent, and his attendance at tutorials has been regular, Yours, etc." (Gloss: A cannot be opting out, since if he wished to be uncooperative, why write at all? He cannot be unable, through ignorance, to say more, since the man is his pupil; moreover, he knows that more information is wanted. He must, therefore, be wishing to impart information he is reluctant to write down. This supposition is only tenable on the assumption that he thinks that Mr. X is no good at philosophy. This, then, is what he is implicating.)

This is another case of damning with faint praise.

We can intentionally violate the rule of Relevance by pointedly changing the subject. Grice again:

> At a genteel tea party A says "Mrs. X is an old bag." There is a moment of appalled silence, then B says "The weather has been quite delightful this summer, hasn't it?"

The conversational implication here needs no explanation. We can also violate the demand for brevity and thereby *not* say something that could be said briefly. Here is one final example from Grice:

> Miss X produced a series of sounds which corresponded closely with the score of "Home Sweet Home."

By not saying simply that Miss X *sang* "Home Sweet Home," the speaker indicates, through a conversational implication, that he is not willing to call what she did singing.

---

[4] Grice, "Logic and Conversation," pp. 412 ff. in Appendix B.

DECEPTION

In the examples we have examined thus far, a speaker intentionally violates a conversational rule in order to achieve some special effect, for example, damning with faint praise. It is important in these cases that the listeners *recognize* that a rule is being intentionally broken, for otherwise they may simply be misled. At other times, however, the speaker does intentionally break the rules to mislead his listeners. The speaker may violate Grice's first rule of quality by uttering something he knows to be false with the intention of producing a false belief in his listeners. That's called lying. Notice that lying depends on the general acceptance of the Cooperative Principle. Because people generally assume that people are telling the truth, successful lying is possible.

Flat out lying is not the only way (and often not the most effective way) of intentionally misleading people. We can say something literally true that, at the same time, conversationally implies something false. (This is sometimes called making a *false suggestion*.) If a son tells his parents that *he has had some trouble with the car,* that could be true, but deeply misleading, if, in fact, he had totaled it. It would be misleading because it would violate the rule of strength (or quantity). In saying only that he had some trouble with the car, he conversationally implies that nothing very serious happened. He conversationally implies this because, in the context, he is expected to come clean and reveal *all* that actually happened.

A more complex example of false suggestion arose in a law suit that went all the way to the Supreme Court.

BRONSTON v. UNITED STATES

Supreme Court of the United States, 1973
409 U.S. 352

Mr. Chief Justice Burger delivered the opinion of the Court.

Petitioner's perjury conviction was founded on the answers given by him as a witness at that bankruptcy hearing, and in particular on the following colloquy with a lawyer for a creditor of Bronston Productions:

"Q. Do you have any bank accounts in Swiss banks, Mr. Bronston?
"A. No, sir.
"Q. Have you ever?
"A. The company had an account here for about six months, in Zurich.

"Q. Have you any nominees who have bank accounts in Swiss banks?

"A. No sir.

"Q. Have you ever?

"A. No, sir."

It is undisputed that for a period of nearly five years, between October 1959 and June 1964, petitioner had a personal bank account at the International Credit Bank in Geneva, Switzerland, into which he made deposits and upon which he drew checks totaling more than $180,000. It is likewise undisputed that petitioner's answers were literally truthful. (i) Petitioner did not at the time of questioning have a Swiss bank account. (ii) Bronston Productions, Inc., did have the account in Zurich described by petitioner. (iii) Neither at the time of questioning nor before did petitioner have nominees who had Swiss accounts. The government's prosecution for perjury went forward on the theory that in order to mislead his questioner, petitioner answered the second question with literal truthfulness but unresponsively addressed his answer to the company's assets and not to his own—thereby implying that he had no personal Swiss bank account at the relevant time.

It is hard to read the witness's response to the second question in any other way than as a deliberate attempt to mislead the court, for his response plainly implies that the did not have a personal account in a Swiss bank, when, in fact, he did. But the issue before the court was not whether he intentionally misled the court, but whether in doing so he committed perjury.[5] The lower courts ruled that he had. The Supreme Court reversed this decision, in part for the following reasons:

> It should come as no surprise that a participant in a bankruptcy proceeding may have something to conceal and consciously tried to do so, or that a debtor may be embarrassed at his plight and yield information reluctantly. It is the responsibility of the lawyer to probe; testimonial interrogation, and cross examination in particular, is a probing, prying, pressing form of inquiry. If a witness evades, it is the lawyer's responsibility to recognize the evasion and to bring the witness back to the mark, to flush out the whole truth with the tools of adversary examination.

---

[5] 18 U.S.C. § 1621 provides: "Whoever, having taken an oath before a competent tribunal . . . that he will testify . . . truly, . . . willfully and contrary to such oath states or subscribes any material matter which he does not believe to be true, is guilty of perjury, and shall . . . be fined not more than $2,000 or imprisoned not more than five years, or both. . . ."

In other words, in a courtroom, where the relationship is typically adversarial rather than cooperative, not all the standard conversational rules are in force, or fully in force. In particular, it would be unrealistic to assume that the rule of strength will be consistently honored; therefore it becomes the task of the cross examiner to force the witness to produce all the relevant facts.

SOME OTHER RHETORICAL DEVICES

Conversational implication is so much a part of our everyday use of language that we hardly notice that we are employing it. Consider how *rhetorical questions* work. Normally when we ask a question we are seeking information, but not always. If I ask someone, "Can you hurry up?" I certainly know that he *can* hurry up. The point of the question is to force the person to *admit* that he can hurry up, and that in turn suggests that he should. For this reason a rhetorical question can have the force of an assertion or an order. Again, if I say to someone, "Do you expect me to believe that?" I am indicating the person should answer this question *no,* and thus my question has the force of the assertion, "I *don't* believe that."

It is important to see that the same question can be rhetorical in one context but not in another. If we hear (or think we hear) someone in the basement, I might ask you, "Do you want me to call the police?" Here I am genuinely interested in your opinion, for calling the police might be unnecessary or even dangerous. On the other hand, if I am trying to get someone to move his car from my driveway, these same words will have the force of a rhetorical question. My question "Do you want me to call the police?"" has the expected answer *no* and because of this conversationally implies the threat, "If you don't move your car, I'll call the police"—or maybe, "If you don't want me to call the police, move your car!" Rhetorical questions are used (and often abused) in everyday arguments. They are, as we shall see, often a sign of a weakness in an argument.

With rhetorical questions, we expect our *words* to be taken literally; our words have their standard meanings even though the question itself is not used in the standard (information-seeking) way. At other times, we do not expect our listeners to take even our words at face value. We tend to exaggerate. If someone says, "I was stunned to see her again," we don't suppose that the person was wobbly in the knees and nearly unconscious at the sight of her. Here, "stunned" is taken to mean "very surprised." Similarly, when people claim to be hungry enough to eat a bear, that usually means that they are very hungry. In most cases, it does not dawn on us to take these words at face value, for to do so would be to attribute to the speaker a wildly false belief about his or her powers of ingestion.

Sometimes, then, we do not intend our words to be taken literally, but even beyond this, we sometimes expect our listeners to interpret us as meaning just the *opposite* of what we say. This occurs, for example, with *irony* and *sarcasm*. At a crucial point in a game, the second baseman fires the ball ten feet over the first baseman's head and someone shouts: "Great throw." Literally, it was not a great throw; it was just the opposite of a great throw. How does the listener know enough to interpret it in this way? Sometimes this is indicated by tone of voice. A sarcastic tone of voice usually indicates the person means the opposite of what he or she is saying. But even without sarcasm, the remark, "Great throw," is not likely to be taken literally. The person who says this knows, after all, that it was not a great throw. He is thus knowingly saying something false, and so his utterance violates Grice's first rule of quality, "Do not say what you believe to be false." Furthermore, the person is not trying to lie or mislead anyone, since everyone knows that the remark is false. This forces us to the conclusion, which we draw immediately, that the person does not wish to be taken literally. By saying something outrageously inappropriate, the person draws attention to the true state of affairs, that is, just how bad the throw really was.

Sometimes, though not always, the use of *metaphors* involves saying something which taken nonmetaphorically would be literally false. If someone says that her professor is an old goat, we do not suppose that she is saying her teacher is a four-footed, often smelly, animal of the genus *Capra*. We automatically take such a remark as metaphorical because the alternative, taking it literally, would be to attribute to the person a belief so wildly out of wack with reality as to border on insanity. Taken as a metaphor, the remark indicates that the speaker finds some striking and salient similarities between her professor and old goats.

Usually metaphorical remarks, taken nonmetaphorically, are literally false—but not always. For example, "No man is an island" is literally true. We treat this remark as a metaphor because, taken literally, it is so obviously and boringly true that we cannot imagine why anyone would want to say it. Taken literally, it would make no greater contribution to the conversation than any other irrelevant truth—for example, that no man is a socket wrench. As a metaphor it is an apt, if somewhat overworked, way of indicating that no one is isolated and self-contained.

These remarks on conversational implication underscore important features concerning the way our language works. First, in using language, we typically convey a great deal more information than is contained in what we actually say. Sometimes, in fact, the main point we are trying to communicate is not put into words at all. Beyond this, what we literally do say is often not meant to be taken literally. We speak loosely, we exaggerate, we employ irony and sarcasm, and we use metaphors. Sometimes these departures from literal meaning or literal assertion cause confusion, and that's why they usually should be avoided in rigorous argument, but in many cases they do no harm and lend vividness and force to our language. An understanding of *unexpressed* meaning is crucial for understanding interpersonal relations. For this reason, it is important for understanding literature. It is also, as we shall see, crucial for the understanding of arguments.

EXERCISE 3

People often say things in order to conversationally imply something else. Assuming a natural conversational setting, what might a person intend to conversationally imply with the following remarks? Briefly explain why each of these conversational implications holds, that is, explain the relationship between what the speaker *literally* says and what he or she intends to convey.
- (a) It's getting a little chilly in here.
- (b) The crowd didn't actually throw bottles at him. (Said of a rock singer)
- (c) You can trust him if you want to.
- (d) I got here before he did. (Said at a lunch counter)
- (e) He hasn't been sent to jail yet.
- (f) Do you expect me to believe that?
- (g) There are planes leaving every day for Russia. (Said to a student radical)
- (h) I had some trouble with the car.
- (i) These sweet potatoes are very filling.
- (j) That exam blew me away.
- (k) The West wasn't won with a registered gun.
- (l) A midair collision can ruin your whole day.

EXERCISE 4

Each of the following remarks, if taken quite literally, is either false, or otherwise plainly defective. First, explain why each remark is either false or defective on a literal reading. Second, state what you take to be the conversational implication of each remark. Third, explain the source of this conversational implication by making reference to Grice's conversational rules.

(1) "Love you, love you, eight days a week." Beatles lyric

(2) "An army travels on its stomach." Napoleon

(3) "The way to a man's heart is through his stomach." Traditional saying

(4) "If you have seen one redwood, you've seen them all." Attributed to James Watt

(5) "Ich bin ein Berliner." ("I am a Berliner.") John F. Kennedy, in a speech before the Berlin Wall

(6) "Let them eat cake!" Attributed (apparently falsely) to Marie Antoinette upon hearing that the people were rioting for bread.

(7) "It isn't a car, it's a Volkswagen." Advertisement

(8) "If God made us in His image, we have certainly returned the compliment." Voltaire

(9) "The only thing we have to fear is fear itself." Franklin D. Roosevelt

(10) " 'Beauty is truth, truth beauty,'—that is all
Ye know on earth, and all ye need to know."
John Keats, *Ode on a Grecian Urn*

DISCUSSION QUESTIONS

(1) Refer back to the dialogue quoted in *Bronston v. United States.* Because it is difficult to read the witness's second response as anything but a willful attempt to deceive, why should this case be treated differently from lying? Alternatively, why not drop the demand that witnesses tell the truth, and make it the responsibility of the lawyers to get at the truth itself, rather than just the whole truth, through *probing, prying, pressing inquiry?*

(2) During the 1980 presidential campaign, Jimmy Carter made the following statement in Atlanta, Georgia:

> You have seen in this campaign the stirring of hate and the rebirth of code words like "states rights" . . . racism has no place in this country.

In response, George Bush, the Republican vice-presidential nominee, said that he was "appalled at the ugly, mean little remark Jimmy Carter made last night." Beyond the meaning of the literal statement, what are the obvious conversational implications of Carter's statement? Do they amount, as Bush seems to think, to accusing the two principal Republican candidates of racism?

(3) In the 1984 presidential campaign, George Bush, referring to the Marines killed in the 1984 Beirut bombing, remarked:

> And for somebody to suggest, as our opponents have, that these men have died in shame, they had better not tell the parents of these young Marines.

The next day, Walter Mondale, the Democratic presidential nominee, responded angrily:

> Mr. Bush, we love this country as much as you do. And Mr Bush, we honor the men and women who died for our country and we grieve as much for their families as you do."

He concluded by saying:

> Apologize, and do it today!

What are the obvious implications of Bush's original remark? Given this, did Mondale have good reasons to demand an apology?

In the days that followed, Bush refused to apologize even though he could not produce an instance of either Mondale or Ferraro using the word "shame" with respect to the Marines. He quoted Ferraro as saying that the Marines "died or are missing without a purpose and for a policy that's never been explained." He then went on to say:

> Mr. Mondale and Mrs. Ferraro can argue all they want. But the fact is, accusing young men of dying without a purpose and for no reason is in the lexicon of the American people a shame.

The next day, Bush cited the dictionary in defense of his original statement. He quoted Mondale as saying that with the killing of the Marines "once again we're humiliated in this region." Bush then said:

> Abase in Webster's, as I understand it, is defined as deep shame, and when you look up humiliation, it refers you to abase.

Who do you think got the better of this exchange? Why?

2

The Language of Argument

Using the techniques developed in Chapter 1, this chapter will examine the use of language to formulate arguments and will provide methods for analyzing genuine arguments in their richness and complexity. The first stage in analyzing an argument is the discovery of its basic *structure*. To do this, we will examine the words, phrases, and special constructions that indicate the premises and conclusions of an argument. The second stage is the study of techniques used to *strengthen* an argument. These include guarding premises so that they are less subject to criticism, offering assurances concerning debatable claims, and discounting possible criticisms in advance. Finally, we will examine the role of *evaluative* and *expressive* language in arguments.

In the previous chapter we saw that language is used for a great many purposes beyond stating things that are either true or false. When we issue an order or make a bet, we are not stating anything. Turning now to arguments, we see that they, like orders and bets, are not statements. Although arguments are typically made up of statements, they are not themselves statements. A single example illustrates this:

> Socrates is older than Plato; Plato is older than Aristotle; therefore, Socrates is older than Aristotle.

Taken as a whole, this sentence does not express anything either true or false; instead, it is used to *derive* a conclusion from some premises.

THE BASIC STRUCTURE OF ARGUMENTS

Arguments are not statements, yet they are constructed out of statements. Now let's ask a very simple question: What *words* indicate that an argument is being presented? Suppose we start with a simple list of statements:

> Socrates is mortal.
> All men are mortal.
> Socrates is a man.

This is not an argument, but we can turn it into an argument by using the single word "therefore":

> Socrates is mortal.
> All men are mortal.
> *Therefore,* Socrates is a man.

We now have an argument—in fact, a very bad argument, since the conclusion does not follow from the reasons stated in its behalf, but it is an argument nonetheless. The word "therefore" converts these sentences into an argument by signaling that the statement following it is a *conclusion* and that the statement or statements that come before it are offered as *reasons* in behalf of this conclusion. Here is another way of turning this list into an argument:

> Socrates is mortal,
> *since* all men are mortal
> and Socrates is a man.

This produces a new argument—this time, a good argument, because the conclusion does follow from the premises offered in its behalf. The word "since" operates roughly in an opposite way from "therefore." The word "since" indicates that the statement or statements that follow it are *reasons* and that the statement (if any) that comes before it is the *conclusion*. There is, however, a variation on this: the conclusion is sometimes tacked onto the end of the argument:

> *Since* all men are mortal and Socrates is a man, Socrates is mortal.

"Since" flags reasons; the remaining connected statement is then taken to be the conclusion, whether it appears at the beginning or at the end of the sentence.

Here is a partial list of connecting terms that introduce an argumentative structure into language by marking out reasons for a conclusion:

accordingly	thus	since
for	hence	then
because	so	therefore

We shall call these terms *warranting connectives*, because, in various ways, they each present one or more statements as the *warrant* or *backing* for some other statement.[1]

Sometimes a single sentence will contain more than one of these warranting connectives. Here is an example:

> *Since* all men are mortal, Socrates is mortal, *for* Socrates is a man.

Both the words "since" and "for" signal the appearance of a reason. In this case, the conclusion occurs in the *middle* of the sentence, which drives home the point that a conclusion can appear anywhere in a sentence formulating an argument: at the beginning, in the middle, or at the end. Our ability to locate the conclusion of an argument thus depends on our understanding of warranting connectives.

---

[1] It is important to realize that these words are not always used as warranting connectives, that is, as terms that introduce an argumentative structure. The words "since" and "then" are often used as indicators of time, as in "He's been an American citizen since 1973" and "He ate a hotdog, then a hamburger." The word "for" is often used as a preposition, for example, "John works for IBM." Since some of these terms have a variety of meanings, it is not possible to identify warranting connectives in a mechanical way just by looking at words. It is necessary to examine the *meaning* of words in the context in which they occur.

There are a variety of other ways in which an argumentative structure can be introduced into our language. In the first chapter we saw that argumentative performatives can do this. If someone says "I conclude that . . . ," the words that follow are given the status of a conclusion. More pretentiously, if someone says "I here base my argument on the claim that . . . ," what comes next has the status of premise. In fact, there are a wide variety of phrases available to signal that an argument is being presented. Here is just a small sample:

> from which we see that . . .
> from which it follows that . . .
> from which we may conclude that . . .
> which goes to show that . . .
> which establishes that . . .

Examining actual arguments will show that this list can be extended almost indefinitely.

IF . . . THEN. . . .

If-then sentences contain a common, but special, kind of warranting connective. If-then sentences are called conditional sentences, and though they often occur in arguments, they do not themselves usually present arguments. Consider the following indicative conditional:

> If the Dodgers get better hitting, then they will win the Western Division.

The sentence that occurs between the "if" and the "then" is called the *antecedent* of the conditional; the sentence that occurs after the "then" is called its *consequent*. In using an indicative conditional, we are not asserting the truth of its antecedent, and we are usually not asserting the truth of the consequent, either. Thus the person who makes the above remark is not claiming that the Dodgers will win the Western Division; instead, he is saying that if they get better hitting, they will win. Furthermore, he is not saying that they will get better hitting, for the word "if" cancels this suggestion. So the person who utters this sentence is not committing himself to either of the following claims:

> The Dodgers will get better hitting.
> The Dodgers will win the Western Division.

Because the speaker is not committing himself to either of these claims, he is not presenting an argument; that is, he is not trying to establish the truth of some claim by citing other truths that establish it.

Yet there is obviously some close connection between conditional statements and arguments.[2] For indicative conditionals, at least,[3] the following explanation seems reasonable. Although indicative conditionals do not present arguments, they provide a pattern that can be converted into an argument whenever the antecedent is taken to be true.[4] Thus we often hear people arguing in the following way:

> If international terrorism continues to grow, there will be a worldwide crisis. But international terrorism will certainly continue to grow, so a world crisis is on the way.

The first sentence is an indicative conditional; it makes no positive claims about terrorism or a coming world crisis. The next sentence indicates that the antecedent of this conditional is true and proceeds immediately to the conclusion that the consequent must be true as well. This use of indicative conditionals for formulating arguments is typical, and for this reason we shall call the *if-then* connective a warranting connective.

ARGUMENTS IN STANDARD FORM

Since arguments come in all shapes and forms, it will help to have a standard way of presenting arguments. For centuries, logicians have used a format of the following kind:

$$\begin{array}{l} \text{All men are mortal.} \\ \underline{\text{Socrates is a man.}} \\ \therefore \text{ Socrates is mortal.} \end{array}$$

The *reasons* (or *premises*) are listed above the line; the *conclusion* is listed below the line; and the symbol "∴" is read "therefore." Arguments presented this way are said to be in *standard form*.

The notion of a standard form is useful because it helps us see

---

[2] One way of telling someone not to argue is to say that we do not want to hear any *if*s, *and*s, or *but*s.

[3] Special problems arise with other conditionals, for example, subjunctive conditionals. They will not be discussed in this work.

[4] We also get an argument when the consequent is shown to be *false*. This will be discussed in Chapter 8.

that the same argument can be expressed in different ways. For example, the following two sentences formulate the argument we just now stated in standard form above.

Socrates is mortal, since all men are mortal, and Socrates is a man.

All men are mortal, so Socrates is mortal, since he is a man.

More importantly, by putting arguments into standard form, we perform the most obvious, and in some ways most important, step in the analysis of an argument: *the identification of premises and conclusion.*

EXERCISE 1

Some sentences express arguments, some do not.
  (a) Identify which of the following numbered sentences expresses an argument.
  (b) For each that does,
      (i) circle the warranting connective (or connectives), and
      (ii) restate the argument in standard form.

  (1) Since Chicago is north of Boston, and Boston is north of Charleston, Chicago is north of Charleston.
  (2) Toward evening, clouds formed and the sky grew darker; then the storm broke.
  (3) Texas has a greater area than Topeka, and Topeka has a greater area than the Bronz Zoo, so Texas has a greater area than the Bronx Zoo.
  (4) Both houses of Congress may pass a bill, but the President may still veto it.
  (5) Other airlines will carry more passengers because United Airlines is on strike.
  (6) Since Jesse James left town, taking his gang with him, things have been a lot quieter.
  (7) Witches float because witches are made of wood, and wood floats.

In the arguments we have considered so far, the premises and the conclusions are clearly marked out by independent clauses tied together with warranting connectives. Arguments as they are presented in daily life don't always take this simple form. To see this, consider the following argument:

> Socialism is doomed to failure because it does not provide the incentives needed for a prosperous economy.

The simplest unpacking of this argument yields the following restatement in standard form:

> Socialism does not provide the incentives needed
> for a prosperous economy.
> _____
> ∴ Socialism is doomed to failure.

But if we look at the premise of this argument, we see that it actually contains *two* claims that should be separated into independent premises. The following, then, is a better representation of the argument:

> Incentives are needed for a prosperous economy
> Socialism does not provide such incentives.
> _____
> ∴ Socialism is doomed to failure.

In fact, this argument also depends upon some background principles that have been left unstated (for example, that economies which are not prosperous are doomed to failure), and later[5] we shall examine such unstated (or suppressed) premises in detail. But the first step in analyzing an argument is to identify the premises and conclusions in what a person has actually said. Since people speak and argue in complicated ways, this is not always a simple task.

EXERCISE 2

Put the following argument in standard form:

> Since many newly emerging nations do not have the capital resources necessary for sustained growth, they will continue to need help from industrial nations.

---

[5] In Chapter 6.

VALIDITY, TRUTH, AND SOUNDNESS

To be an argument at all, some statement must be marked out as the conclusion, and other statements must be marked out as the reasons (or premises) for that conclusion. But not all arguments are good arguments, so, having identified an argument, the next task is to *evaluate* it. Evaluating arguments is a complex business, and, in fact, this entire book is aimed primarily at developing procedures for doing so. There are, however, certain fundamental terms used in evaluating arguments that should be introduced from the start. They are *validity*, *truth*, and *soundness*. Here they will be introduced informally; later (in Chapters 7 and 8) they will be examined with more rigor.

Validity. *Validity* is a technical notion, but it closely matches the commonsense idea of a conclusion *following from* its premises. Now to say that a conclusion follows from its premises means that the conclusion must be true if the premises are true. We will take this to be our definition of validity: an argument is valid if and only if the premises cannot all be true and the conclusion false.[6]

Validity is one criterion for a good *deductive* argument, that is, deductive arguments are put forward as meeting this standard. Other arguments—in particular, *inductive* arguments—are not intended to meet this rigorous standard. The criteria for evaluating inductive arguments will be examined in Chapter 9; for now we will concentrate on deductive arguments.

Truth. A second (obvious) criterion for evaluating deductive arguments is that the premises must be *true*. Here it is important not to confuse truth with validity. Because arguments are not assertions, they are, as we have already seen, neither true nor false. *Arguments are either valid or invalid, never either true or false.* The difference between validity and truth becomes obvious when we notice that an argument can be valid even when all the statements it contains are false:

> All fishes have wings.
> Whales are fishes.
> ∴ Whales have wings.

This is a bad argument, bad because both premises are false, but the premises are related to the conclusion in a way that satisfies our defi-

---

[6] Equivalently, we can also say that an argument is valid if and only if it is impossible for all the premises to be true and the conclusion false. Or, to put the definition positively, an argument is valid if the truth of the premises necessitates the truth of the conclusion.

nition of validity: if the premises were true, then the conclusion could not be false. Here is another example of a valid argument with false premises:

All fishes have lungs.
Whales are fishes.

∴ Whales have lungs.

This time, though valid, both premises are false and the conclusion, as it turns out, true.

Although the notions of truth and validity are different, there is one important relationship between them: given our definition of validity, there can be no valid arguments that lead us from true premises to a false conclusion. This should square with your commonsense ideas about reasoning: if you reason correctly, you should not be led from truth into error.

Soundness. It should be clear that an argument can be valid but still unacceptable. A valid argument with false premises will be rejected just because one of its premises is false. We thus make at least *two* demands of an argument that we will accept as proving its conclusion:

(1) The argument must be *valid*.
(2) The premises must be *true*.

When an argument meets both these standards, it is said to be *sound*. If it fails to meet either one, it is said to be *unsound*. Thus an argument is unsound if it is invalid; it is also unsound if at least one of its premises is false.

	Premises True	At Least One False Premise
Valid	Sound	Unsound
Invalid	Unsound	Unsound

The goal of proof is a sound argument, not just a valid argument.[7]

---

[7] In fact, we demand *more* of an argument than just soundness, for circular arguments can be sound. We will examine circular arguments closely in Chapter 4.

You will be asked to evaluate, then construct, arguments using the following statements. Assume that the truth value assignments given to the right of each statement are correct.

(1) All seniors are arrogant. (T)
(2) All seniors are talented. (F)
(3) All arrogant people are immodest. (T)
(4) All seniors are insightful. (F)
(5) All talented people are immodest. (F)
(6) All arrogant people are talented. (F)
(7) All talented people are insightful. (T).
(8) All talented people are ugly. (F)
(9) All seniors are ugly. (F)
(10) All arrogant people are seniors. (F)
(11) All seniors are immodest. (T)

Part 1. Using these somewhat arbitrarily assigned truth values, label each of the following arguments as (a) either valid or invalid and (b) either sound or unsound.

(a) All seniors are arrogant.
All arrogant people are immodest.
∴ All seniors are immodest.

(b) All arrogant people are immodest.
All talented people are insightful.
∴ All seniors are immodest.

(c) All arrogant people are seniors.
All seniors are immodest.
∴ All arrogant people are immodest.

(d) All arrogant people are immodest.
All seniors are immodest.
∴ All seniors are immodest.

Part 2. Using the same set of statements, but not repeating the examples given in Part 1, construct arguments with two premises and a conclusion such that:

(a) The argument is valid, but all the premises are false, and the conclusion is false as well.

(b) The argument is valid, both premises false, and the conclusion true.

(c) The argument is valid, one premise is true, one premise false, and the conclusion is true.

(d) The argument is valid, one premise is true, one false, and the conclusion is false.

ASSURING, GUARDING, AND DISCOUNTING

Although the goal of argument is soundness rather than mere validity, we usually expect even *more* from an argument than soundness. In the first place, an argument can be sound, but trivially uninteresting:

> Nigeria is in Africa.
> ————————————
> ∴ Nigeria is in Africa.

Here the premise is true, and the argument is valid. The argument is valid because (quite trivially) the premise cannot be true without the conclusion (which repeats it) being true as well. Yet the argument is completely worthless as a *proof* that Nigeria is in Africa. Though both valid and sound, the argument is said to be circular.

We will examine circular arguments in detail later on in Chapter 4, but it is obvious why such arguments are useless. If A is trying to prove something to B that B has doubts about, then citing the very matter in question will not do any good. In general, for A to prove something to B, A must marshall facts that B accepts and then show that they justify the claim at issue. In circular arguments, the doubt about the conclusion immediately turns into a doubt about the premise as well. But now A seems presented with a problem: A cannot cite a proposition in its own behalf, for that would be circular reasoning, so A has to cite other propositions. If, however, A cites other propositions as premises leading to A's conclusion, the question naturally arises as to why B should accept *them*. Doesn't A have to present arguments in their behalf as well? Yet if A does that, A will just introduce further premises that are also in need of proof, and so on indefinitely. It now looks as if every argument, to be successful, will have to be infinitely long!

The answer to this ancient problem depends on the fact that the activity of arguing or presenting proofs relies on a shared set of beliefs and a certain amount of trust. When I present reasons, I try to cite these shared beliefs—things that will not *in fact* be challenged. Beyond this, I expect people to believe me when I cite information that only I possess. But there are limits to this, for people do believe things that are false and sometimes lie about what they know to be true. This presents a practical problem: how can I present my reasons in a way that does not produce just another demand for an argument—that is, a demand for more reasons? Here we use three main strategies:

(1) *Assuring:* indicating that we have back-up reasons that we can produce on demand.
(2) *Guarding:* weakening our claims so that they are less subject to attack.
(3) *Discounting:* anticipating criticisms and dismissing them. In these ways we build a defensive perimeter around our premises.

Assuring

When will we want to give assurances about some statement we have made? If we state something that we know everyone believes, assurances are not necessary. For that matter, if everyone believes something, we may not even state it at all; we let others "fill in" this step in the argument. We offer assurances when we think that someone *might* challenge what we say. In giving assurances we sometimes cite authorities:

Doctors agree . . .
Recent studies have shown . . .
It has been established that . . .
I can assure you that . . .
An unimpeachable source close to the White House says . . .

Here we do not actually cite reasons; we merely indicate that they can be produced on demand. In a context of trust, this is often sufficient.

On the other hand, we as critics should view assuring remarks with some suspicion. Following the rule of Quality, we should expect a person to give assurances only when he has a good reason to do so. Yet in point of fact, assuring remarks often mark the *weakest* parts of the argument, not the strongest parts. If someone says "I hardly need argue that . . . ," it is often useful to ask why he has gone to the trouble of saying it. In particular, when we distrust an argument—as we sometimes do—this is precisely the place to look for weakness. You should develop a keen eye for phrases of the following kind:

It's certain that . . .

Everyone agrees that . . .

Of course, no one will deny that . . .

It is just common sense that . . .

There is no question that . . .

If these phrases are used, they are used for some reason. Sometimes the reason is a good one; sometimes, however, it is a bad one. In honest argumentation, they save time and simplify discussion. In a dishonest argument, they are used to paper over cracks.[8]

Guarding

Guarding represents a different strategy for protecting premises from attack. We reduce our claim to something less strong. Thus instead of saying *all,* we say *most.* Instead of saying something straight out, we use a qualifying phrase like "it is almost certain that," "it is very likely that," and so on. Law school professors like the phrase "it is arguable that. . . ." This is wonderfully noncommittal, for it really doesn't indicate how strong the argument is, yet it does get the statement into the argument.

Broadly speaking, there are two ways of guarding what we have said:

(1) Weakening the extent of what has been said: retreating from "all" to "most," from "most" to "some," and so on.

(2) Using probability phrases like "it is likely that," "virtually certain that," and so on.

If we weaken a claim sufficiently, we can make it completely immune to criticism. What can be said against a remark of the following kind: "There is some small chance that perhaps a few politicians are honest on at least some occasions." You would have to have a *very* low opinion of politicians to deny this statement. On the other hand, if we weaken our premises in this way to avoid criticism, we must pay a price. The premise no longer gives strong support to the conclusion. The general strategy is this: We should weaken our premises sufficiently to avoid criticism, but not weaken them so much that they no longer provide strong evidence for the conclusion. Balancing these two factors is one of the most important strategies in making and criticizing arguments.

Just as it was useful to zero in on *assuring* terms, it is useful to keep track of *guarding* terms. Guarding terms are easily corrupted. They

---

[8] This topic will be discussed more fully in Chapter 4.

can be used to insinuate things that cannot be stated explicitly into a conversation. Consider the effect of the following remark: "Perhaps the Secretary of State has not been candid with the Congress." This doesn't actually *say* that the Secretary has been less than candid with the Congress, but it suggests it. Furthermore, it suggests it in a way that is hard to combat. A more subtle device for corrupting guarding terms is to introduce a statement in a guarded form and then go on to speak as if it were not guarded at all. After a while, the word "perhaps" disappears.

> Perhaps the Secretary of State has not been candid with the Congress. Of course, he has a right to his own views and I am sure that he is acting honestly. All the same, this is a democracy where officials, even in the Administration, are accountable to Congress.

Discounting

The general pattern of discounting is to cite a possible criticism in order to reject it or counter it. Notice how different the following statements sound:

> The ring is beautiful, but expensive.
> The ring is expensive, but beautiful.

Both statements express the very same facts—that the ring is beautiful and that the ring is expensive. Yet they operate in different ways. We might use the first as a reason for *not* buying the ring; we can use the second as a reason *for* buying it. The first sentence acknowledges that the ring is beautiful, but overrides this by pointing out that it is expensive. In reverse fashion, the second statement acknowledges that the ring is expensive, but overrides this by pointing out that it is beautiful. The word "but" discounts the statement that comes before it in favor of the statement that follows it.

"Although" is also a discounting connective, but it operates in reverse fashion from the word "but." We can see this using the same example:

> Although the ring is expensive, it is beautiful.
> Although the ring is beautiful, it is expensive.

Here the statement following the word "although" is discounted in favor of the connected statement. A partial list of terms that function as discounting connectives includes the following conjunctions:

although	however
but	nevertheless

<table>
<tr><td>nonetheless</td><td>yet</td></tr>
<tr><td>still</td><td>though</td></tr>
</table>

The clearest cases of discounting occur when we are dealing with facts that point in different directions: that the ring is beautiful is a reason for buying it, that it is expensive is a reason for not buying it. We discount the fact that goes against the position we wish to take. Discounting is, however, often more subtle than this. We sometimes use discounting to block certain conversational implications of what we have said. This comes out in examples of the following kind:

> Jones is an aggressive player, but he is not dirty.
> The situation is difficult, but not hopeless.
> The Democrats have the upper hand in Congress, but only for the time being.
> A truce has been declared, but who knows for how long?

Take just the last example. The claim that a truce has been declared naturally suggests that peace has been restored. The but-clause cancels out this suggestion. The nuances of discounting terms can be very subtle, and a correct analysis is not always easy. All the same, the role of discounting terms is often very important in capturing the force of an argument. These terms anticipate criticisms, control conversational implications, and, in general, point to structures within an argument that are not actually stated.

It is important not to confuse *discounting* a claim with *denying* it. To say that a ring is beautiful but expensive is to acknowledge that it is, after all, beautiful. An assertion of the form "A but B" has three components:

(1) The assertion of A.
(2) The assertion of B.
(3) The indication that the truth of B is more important than the truth of A.

EXERCISE 4

(a) Construct three interesting examples of statements containing assuring terms.
(b) Do the same for guarding terms.
(c) Do the same for discounting terms, indicating which statement is being discounted in favor of the other.

For each of the numbered words or expressions in the following sentences, indicate whether it is a *warranting connective*, an *assuring term*, a *guarding term*, a *discounting term*, or *none of these*.

(1) *Although*[1] no mechanism has been discovered, *most*[2] *researchers in the field agree*[3] that smoking *greatly increases the chances*[4] of heart disease.

(2) *Since*[5] *historically*[6] public debt leads to inflation, *there can be no doubt*[7] that, *despite*[8] recent trends, inflation will return.

(3) *Take it from me,*[9] there hasn't been a decent centerfielder *since*[10] Joe Dimaggio.

(4) *Whatever anyone tells you,*[11] there is *little*[12] to the rumor that Queen Elizabeth will step down *for*[13] her son Prince Charles.

(5) The early deaths of Janis Joplin and Jimmy Hendrix *show*[14] how *really*[15] dangerous drugs are.

(6) I *think*[16] he is out back somewhere.

(7) I *think,*[17] *therefore*[18] I am.

◆ (8) I *think,*[19] therefore I *think*[20] I am.

EVALUATIVE AND EXPRESSIVE LANGUAGE

Although some words in our language are relatively neutral, others carry strong positive or negative connotations. That is, in using many words we are not only describing something, but also *evaluating* it or *expressing some attitude toward* it. Generally speaking, *evaluative* terms, as they are called, apply to lines of conduct. They interconnect to form a rich system of terms that allows us to indicate whether (and to what degree) actions are justified or unjustified. For example, those who hold that South Africa's system of apartheid is morally wrong, hold that there is moral justification for its abolition.

One important feature of evaluative statements is that they make a claim to objectivity. In this way they stand in contrast to utterances that merely *express* personal feelings. If I say that I just love SpaghettiOs, then I am expressing a personal taste, one that I realize others may not share. On the other hand, if I call something *good*, then I am making a claim that goes beyond my personal feelings, one to be defended on shared grounds with others. Thus if a person makes an evaluative claim (a value judgment), we have a right to ask for the reasons that back this evaluative claim. On the other hand, if a person merely expresses his or her personal feelings, then we should ask why this person's feelings should be taken any more seriously than anyone else's.

Slanting

It is important to see that there is nothing intrinsically wrong with using evaluative and expressive language. Sometimes forceful language is justified. At times, however, people use evaluative language without offering any justification for the evaluations they make. At other times they use highly charged expressive language as a *substitute* for argument. When either of these latter things takes place, we are dealing with *slanting*. Slanting involves the improper use of evaluative and expressive language to place something in a good or bad light without adequate justification.

Ethnic and racial slurs are obvious examples of slanted language. To say that someone is a Jew is to comment on his or her ethnic origin: to call someone a kike conveys the same information, but combines it with an expression of contempt. Actually, in this area, connotations are so prevalent that we have to look to scientific language to find more or less neutral language. For example, "white" is a positive term, whereas "whitey" (and "honkey") are negative. "Caucasian" is more or less scientific and neutral. Here we must use the guarding expression "more or less" because all the language in this area is highly charged. For many, "Black" is a positive term, and "nigger" is a term of contempt, but "Negro" is not really neutral in the way, for example, that "Mongolian" is. These tensions in the language reflect deeper tensions in our society.

When we stop to think about it, it is surprising how many words appear in our language that are intended to express contempt. Beyond racial and ethnic slurs, our language contains a vast system of words charged with negative connotations. Our language contains a rich system of obscenities. When we describe something using obscene language, we are usually (though not always) condemning it. There seems to be no end to the ways in which we can describe things in demeaning, degrading, and insulting ways. New forms of insult are constantly invented as the old ones lose their sting.

We should also notice that the connotations of a word vary with context; they depend on who is saying what to whom. An irresponsible conservative will accuse his liberal opponents of being communists, thereby associating them with an organization generally held in contempt in this country. On the other hand, it wouldn't have made sense to *accuse* Lenin of having been a communist. That's not something that Lenin would want to deny—he was proud of it. In the reverse fashion, radicals sometimes call their more conservative opponents "fascists."

Again, it would not have made sense to *accuse* Hitler or Mussolini of being fascists. From their point of view, being a fascist was something good, not bad. Thus, even where the descriptive meaning of a word remains more or less fixed, the positive and negative connotations can vary with context. Calling someone a liberal can count as praise, as an attack from the right, or as an attack from the left, depending on the speaker and the audience.

Finally, positive and negative connotations can be subtle. Consider a word like "clever." Descriptively, it indicates quick mental ability and carries a positive connotation. In contrast, "cunning," which has much the same descriptive content, often carries a negative connotation. It thus makes a difference which one of these words we choose. It also makes a difference where we apply them. You can praise a light opera by calling it clever, but it would surely be taken as a criticism if you called a grand opera clever. This, needless to say, turns upon the rule of Quantity. Grand operas are supposed to be more than clever. When something is supposed to be profound and serious, it is insulting just to call it clever. Prayers, for example, should not be clever.

Sometimes innocuous words can shift connotations. The word "too" is the perfect example of this. This word introduces a negative connotation, sometimes turning a positive quality into a negative one. Compare the following sentences:

John is smart.	John is too smart.
John is honest.	John is too honest.
John is ambitious.	John is too ambitious.
John is nice.	John is too nice.
John is friendly.	John is too friendly.

The word "too" indicates an excess, and thereby contains a criticism. If you look at the items in the second column, you will see that the criticism is sometimes rather brutal—for example, calling someone "too friendly."

Persuasive Definitions

A particularly subtle form of slanting involves the use of a definition to gain an argumentative advantage. Charles L. Stevenson calls such definitions *persuasive definitions*.[9] Here is an example:

---

[9] Charles L. Stevenson, "Persuasive Definitions," *Mind*, XLVII (July, 1938).

Russian Communism is really state capitalism.

Who would say this? Certainly not a capitalist, who thinks capitalism is a *good* thing and communism is *bad*. Nor would Russian Communists say this, because they think that capitalism is *bad* and have no desire to associate their system with it. On the other hand, this is just the kind of statement that a Chinese Communist might use against the Russians. To a Chinese Communist, capitalism is a bad thing; thus calling Russian Communism "state capitalism" applies all the standard attacks against capitalism to the Russians. The pattern looks like this:

Something to be criticized.	Definitional link	Something considered bad.

Here is another example that uses the same pattern:

Admissions quotas in favor of minorities are nothing more than reverse discrimination.

Since discrimination is usually thought to be something bad, a person will have a hard time making a case for minority quotas if he is trapped into accepting "reverse discrimination" as a defining characteristic of a system of minority quotas. Sometimes these definitions are crude and heavy handed, for example:

Abortion is fetal murder.

Since murder is, by definition, a wrongful act of killing, this definition assumes the very point at issue. At other times the argumentative move can be quite subtle, for example:

Abortion is the killing of an unborn person.

At first sight, this definition may seem neutral. It does not contain any obviously charged word like "murder." All the same, it is one of the central issues in the debate over abortion whether a human fetus is already a person. This is a matter to be established by argument, not by definition. In general we have a right to be suspicious of anyone who tries to gain an argumentative advantage through an appeal to definitions. Confronted with a definition in the midst of an argument, we should always ask whether the definition clarifies the issues or merely slants them.

For each of the following sentences, construct two others—one that reverses the emotive force and one that is more or less neutral. The symbol 0 stands for neutral, + for positive emotive force, and − for negative emotive force.

Example: − Professor Conrad is rude.
  + Professor Conrad is uncompromisingly honest in his criticisms.
  0 Professor Conrad often upsets people with his criticisms.

(1) − Martin is a lazy lout.
(2) + Brenda is vivacious.
(3) + John is a natural leader.
(4) + Selby is a methodical worker.
(5) − Marsha is a snob.
(6) + Clara is imaginative.
(7) − Bartlett is a buffoon.
(8) − Wayne is a goody-goody.
(9) − Sidney talks incessantly.
(10) − Dudley is a weenie.
(11) ? Floyd is a hotdog. (Decide whether this is + or −.)
(12) + Martha is liberated.
(13) + Ralph is sensitive.
(14) + Betty is a fierce competitor.
(15) − Psychology is a trendy department.
(16) − This is a Mickey Mouse exercise.

DISCUSSION QUESTIONS

(1) Why can't an invalid argument be sound?
(2) Why are there no valid arguments with true premises and a false conclusion?
(3) Why are there no sound arguments with a false conclusion?

(4) After reading Robin Lakoff's essay "Talking about Women" (Appendix C of this book), test her hypothesis that the language used in talking about women often reveals a sexist bias in our society. To do this, collect a series of articles concerning women and see if they reveal the kind of bias Lakoff describes. Because many writers are now self-consciously trying to avoid the appearance of sexism, blatant examples may be less easily found in recent writing than in articles written a few years ago. One way to bring this matter into sharper focus is to compare the language used about a woman with the language used about a man in a similar context, for example, in a description of the individual's appointment to some high position.

3

The Art of Close Analysis

This chapter will be largely dedicated to a single purpose: the close and careful analysis of a speech drawn from the *Congressional Record,* using the argumentative devices introduced in Chapter 2. The point of this study is to show in detail how these methods of analysis can be applied to an actual argument of some richness and complexity.

AN EXTENDED EXAMPLE

It is now time to apply all of these notions to a genuine argument. Our example will be a debate that occurred in the House of Representatives on the question whether there should be an increase in the allowance given to members of the House for clerical help—the so-called "clerk hire allowance." The argument against the increase presented by Representative Kyl (Republican, Iowa) will be examined in detail. We will put it under an analytic microscope.

The choice of this example may seem odd, for the question of clerk hire allowance is not one of the burning issues of our time. This, in fact, is one reason for choosing it. It will be useful to begin with an example where feelings do not run high in order to learn the habit of objective analysis. Later on we shall examine arguments where almost everyone has strong feelings and try to maintain an objective standpoint even there. The example is a good one for two other reasons: (1) it contains most of the argumentative devices we have listed and, (2) relatively speaking, it is quite a strong argument. This last remark may seem ironic after we seemingly tear the argument quite to shreds, but in comparison to other arguments we shall examine, it stands up quite well.

We can begin by reading through the section of the *Congressional Record*[1] without comment:

Clerk Hire Allowance, House of Representatives

Mr. FRIEDEL. Mr. Speaker, by direction of the Committee on House Administration, I call up the resolution (H. Res. 219) to increase the basic clerk hire allowance of each Member of the House, and for other purposes, and ask for its immediate consideration.

The Clerk read the resolution as follows:

Resolved, That effective April 1, 1961, there shall be paid out of the contingent fund of the House, until otherwise provided by law, such sums as may be necessary to increase the basic clerk hire allowance of each Member and the Resident Commissioner from Puerto Rico by an additional $3,000 per annum, and each such Member and Resident Commissioner shall be entitled to one clerk in addition to those to which he is otherwise entitled by law.

---

[1] *Congressional Record,* Vol. 107, Part 3 (March 15, 1961), pp. 4059–60.

Mr. FRIEDEL. Mr. Speaker, this resolution allows an additional $3,000 per annum for clerk hire and an additional clerk for each Member of the House and the Resident Commissioner from Puerto Rico. Our subcommittee heard the testimony, and we were convinced of the need for this provision to be made. A few Members are paying out of their own pocket for additional clerk hire. This $3,000 is the minimum amount we felt was necessary to help Members pay the expenses of running their offices. Of course, we know that the mail is not as heavy in some of the districts as it is in others, and, of course, if the Member does not use the money, it remains in the contingent fund.

Mr. KYL. Mr. Speaker, will the gentleman yield?

Mr. FRIEDEL. I yield to the gentleman from Iowa [Mr. KYL] for a statement.

Mr. KYL. Mr. Speaker, I oppose this measure. I oppose it first because it is expensive. I further oppose it because it is untimely.

I do not intend to belabor this first contention. We have been presented a budget of about $82 billion. We have had recommended to us a whole series of additional programs or extensions of programs for priming the pump, for depressed areas, for the needy, for unemployed, for river pollution projects, and recreation projects, aid to education, and many more. All are listed as "must" activities. These extensions are not within the budget. Furthermore, if business conditions are as deplorable as the newspapers indicate, the Government's income will not be as high as anticipated. It is not enough to say we are spending so much now, a little more will not hurt. What we spend, we will either have to recover in taxes, or add to the staggering national debt.

The amount of increase does not appear large. I trust, however, there is no one among us who would suggest that the addition of a clerk would not entail allowances for another desk, another typewriter, more materials, and it is not beyond the realm of possibility that the next step would then be a request for additional office space, and ultimately new buildings. Some will say, "All the Members will not use their maximum, so the cost will not be great." And this is true. If the exceptions are sufficient in number to constitute a valid argument, then there is no broad general need for this measure. Furthermore, some Members will use these additional funds to raise salaries. Competition will force all salaries upward in all offices and then on committee staffs, and so on. We may even find ourselves in a position of paying more money for fewer clerks and in a tighter bind on per person workload.

This measure proposes to increase the allowance from $17,500 base clerical allowance to $20,500 base salary allowance. No member of this House can tell us what this means in gross salary. That computation is almost impossible. Such a completely absurd system has developed through the years on salary computations for clerical hire that we have under discussion a mathematical monstrosity. We are usually told that the gross allowed is approximately $35,000. This is inaccurate. In one office the total might be less than $35,000 and in another, in complete compliance with the law and without any conscious padding, the amount may be in excess of $42,000. This is possible because of a weird set of formulae which determine that three clerks at $5,000 cost less than five clerks at $3,000. Five times three might total the same as three times five everywhere else in the world—but not in figuring clerk hire in the House.

This is an application of an absurdity. It is a violation of bookkeeping principles, accounting principles, business principles and a violation of commonsense. Listen to the formula:

First, 20 percent increase of first $1,200; 10 percent additional from $1,200 to $4,600; 5 percent further additional from $4,600 to $7,000.

Second, after applying the increases provided in paragraph 1, add an additional 14 percent or a flat $250 whichever is the greater, but this increase must not exceed 25 percent.

Third, after applying the increases provided in both paragraphs 1 and 2, add an additional increase of 10 percent in lieu of overtime.

Fourth, after applying the increases provided in paragraphs 1, 2, and 3, add an additional increase of $330.

Fifth, after applying the increases provided in paragraphs 1, 2, 3, and 4, add an additional increase of 5 percent.

Sixth, after applying the increases provided in paragraphs 1, 2, 3, 4, and 5, add an additional increase of 10 percent but not more than $800 nor less than $300 a year.

Seventh, after applying the increases provided in paragraphs 1, 2, 3, 4, 5, and 6, add an additional increase of 7½ percent.

Eighth, after applying the increases provided in paragraphs 1, 2, 3, 4, 5, 6, and 7, add an additional increase of 10 percent.

Ninth, after applying the increases provided in paragraphs 1, 2, 3, 4, 5, 6, 7, and 8, add an additional increase of 7½ percent.

The Disbursing Office has a set of tables to figure house salaries for office staffs and for about 900 other employees. It contains 45 sheets with 40 entries per sheet. In the Senate, at least, they have simplified the process some by figuring their base in multiplies of 60, thus eliminating 11 categories. Committee staffers, incidentally, have an $8,880 base in comparison to the House $7,000 base limitation.

Now, Mr. Speaker, I have planned to introduce an amendment or a substitute which would grant additional clerk hire where there is a demonstrable need based on heavier than average population or "election at large" and possible other factors. But after becoming involved in this mathematical maze, I realize the folly of proceeding one step until we have corrected this situation. We can offer all kinds of excuses for avoiding a solution. We cannot offer reasonable arguments that it should not be done or that it cannot be done.

Someone has suggested that the Members of this great body prefer to keep the present program because someone back in the home district might object to the gross figures. I know this is not so. When a Representative is busy on minimum wage, or aid to education, or civil rights, such matters of housekeeping seem too picayune to merit attention. The Member simply checks the table and hires what he can hire under the provisions and then forgets the whole business. But I know the Members also want the people back home to realize that what we do here is open and frank and accurate, and that we set an example in businesslike procedures. The more we can demonstrate responsibility the greater will be the faith in Congress.

May I summarize. It is obvious that some Members need more clerical help because of large population and large land area. I have been working for some time with the best help we can get, on a measure which would take these items into consideration. Those Members who are really in need of assistance should realize that this temporary, hastily conceived proposition we debate today will probably obviate their getting a satisfactory total solution.

First, we should await redistricting of the Nation.

Second, we should consider appropriate allowance for oversize districts considering both population and total geographic area.

Finally, I hope we can develop a sound and sensible formula for computing salaries of office clerks and other statutory employees in the same category.

Before going any further, it will be useful to record your general reactions to this speech. Perhaps you think that on the whole Kyl gives a well-reasoned argument in behalf of his position. Alternatively, you might think that he is making a big fuss over nothing, trying to confuse people with numbers, and just generally being obnoxious. When you are finished examining this argument in detail, you can look back and ask yourself why you formed this original impression and how, if at all, you have changed your mind.

The first step in the close analysis of an argument is to go through the text, labeling the various argumentative devices we have examined. Here some abbreviations will be useful:

warranting connective	W
assuring term	A
guarding term	G
discounting term	D
argumentative performative	AP
evaluative/expressive term	E (+ *or* −)
rhetorical device	R

The last label is a catch-all for the various rhetorical devices discussed in Chapter 1, such as rhetorical questions, irony, metaphor, and so on. There is no label for slanting, because the decision whether or not the use of evaluative or expressive terms amounts to slanting depends on the justification the writer provides for employing them. Often this decision can only be made after the entire argument is examined.

Even this simple process of labeling brings out features of an argument that could pass by unnoticed. It also directs us to ask sharp critical questions. To see this, we can look at each part of the argument in detail.

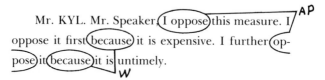

Mr. KYL. Mr. Speaker, I oppose this measure. I oppose it first because it is expensive. I further oppose it because it is untimely.

This is a model of clarity. By the use of a performative utterance in the opening sentence, Kyl makes it clear that he opposes the measure. Then by twice using the warranting connective "because," he gives his two main reasons for opposing it: *it is expensive* and *it is untimely*. We must now see if he makes good each of these claims. This paragraph begins the argument for the claim that the measure is expensive:

> I do not intend to belabor this first contention. We have been presented a budget of about $82 billion. We have had recommended to us a whole series of additional programs or extensions of programs for priming the pump, for depressed areas, for the needy, for unemployed, for river pollution projects, and recreation projects, aid to education, and many more. All are listed as "must" activities. These extensions are not within the budget. Furthermore, if business conditions are as deplorable as the newspapers indicate the Government's income will not be as high as anticipated. It is not enough to say we are spending so much now, a little more will not hurt. What we spend, we will either have to recover in taxes, or add to the staggering national debt.

(a) "I do not intend to belabor this first contention. . . ." This is an example of *assuring*. The obvious conversational implication is that the point is so obvious that little has to be said in its support. Yet there is something strange going on here. Having said that he will *not* belabor the claim that the bill is expensive, Kyl actually goes on to say quite a bit on the subject. It is a good idea to look closely when someone says that he or she is not going to do something, for often just the opposite is happening. For example, saying "I am not suggesting that Smith is dishonest" is one way of suggesting that Smith *is* dishonest. If no such suggestion is being made, why raise the issue at all?

(b) Kyl now proceeds in a rather flat way, stating that the proposed budget comes to $82 billion and that it contains many new programs and extensions of former programs. Since these are matters of public record and nobody is likely to deny them, there is no need for guarding or assuring. Kyl also claims, without qualification, that these extensions are not within the budget. This recital of facts does, however, carry an important conversational implication: Since the budget is already out of balance, any further extensions should be viewed with suspicion.

(c) Putting the word "must" in quotation marks, or saying it in a sarcastic tone of voice, is a common device for denying something. The plain suggestion is that some of these measures are *not* must activities at all. We see the same device in a more dramatic fashion when Mark Anthony ironically repeats that "Brutus is an honorable man." Anyway, Kyl here suggests that some of the items already in the budget are not necessary. He does this, of course, without defending this suggestion.

(d) "If business conditions are as deplorable as the newspapers indicate, the Government's income will not be as high as anticipated." The sentence as a whole is an *indicative conditional* (with the word "then" dropped out). As such, the sentence does not produce an argument, but instead, provides a pattern for an argument. For the moment, let's drop out the phrase "as the newspapers indicate"; we then get:

> If business conditions are deplorable, then the Government's income will not be as high as anticipated.

This seems like a perfectly reasonable conditional claim, and if Kyl could establish that business conditions *are* deplorable, he would have moved his argument along in an important way. Yet, he doesn't say that business conditions are deplorable, instead, he slides in the *guarding* expression "as the newspapers *indicate.*" Thus the premises of his argument come to this:

(1) If business conditions are deplorable, then the Government's income will not be as high as anticipated.
(2) Newspapers indicate that business conditions are deplorable.

Given the highly guarded second premise, no strong conclusion follows.[2]

(e) "It is not enough to say we are spending so much now, a little more will not hurt." The opening phrase is, of course, used to deny what follows it. Kyl is plainly rejecting the argument that we are spending so much now, a little more will not hurt. Yet his argument has a peculiar twist, for who would come right out and make such an argument? If you stop to think for a minute, it should be clear that nobody would want to put it that way. A liberal, for example, would use quite different phrasing. He might say something like this: "Considering the large benefits that will flow from this measure, it is more than worth the small costs." What Kyl has done is to attribute a bad argument to his opponents and then reject it in an indignant tone. This is a common device,[3] and when it is used, it is often useful to ask whether anyone would actually argue or speak in the way suggested. When the answer to this question is no, as it often is, it is also useful to ask what the speaker's opponent would have said instead. This leads to a further question: Has the arguer even addressed himself to the *real* arguments of his opponents?

So far, Kyl has not addressed himself to the first main point of his argument, that the measure is *expensive*. This is not a criticism, because he is really making the preliminary point that the matter of expense is significant. Here he has stated some incontestable facts—for example, that the budget is already out of balance. Beyond this he has indicated, with varying degrees of strength, that the financial situation is grave. It is against this background that the detailed argument concerning the cost of the measure is actually presented in the next paragraph.

> The amount of increase does not appear large.
> A — I trust however, there is no one among us who would   D
> suggest that the addition of a clerk would not entail
> allowances for another desk, another typewriter, more   G
> materials, and it is not beyond the realm of possibil-
> ity that the next step would then be a request for ad-
> ditional office space, and ultimately new buildings.
> R — Some will say, "All the Members will not use their
> maximum, so the cost will not be great." And this is

---

[2] This passage also contains a vague *appeal to authority*, since no specific newspaper is cited. We will discuss appeals to authority in the next chapter.

[3] Another example is that of a professor who spoke to student radicals in the following way: "I can understand that the younger generation wants a free ride—they want to get things without really working for them, but. . . ."

true. (If) the exceptions are sufficient in number to
constitute a valid argument, (then) there is no broad
general need for this measure. Furthermore, some
Members will use these additional funds to raise salaries. Competition will force all salaries upward in all
offices and then on committee staffs, and so on. We
may even find ourselves in a position of paying more
money for fewer clerks and in a tighter bind on per
person workload.

(a) "The amount of increase does not appear large." Words like
"appear" and "seem" are sometimes used for guarding, but we must be
careful not to apply labels in an unthinking way. The above sentence is
the beginning of a *discounting* argument. As soon as you hear this sentence, you can feel that a word like "but" or "however" is about to appear. Sure enough, it does.

(b) "I trust, however, there is no one among us who would suggest that the addition of a clerk would not entail allowances for another
desk, another typewriter, more materials. . . ." This is the beginning
of Kyl's argument that is intended to rebut the argument that the increase in expenses will not be large. Appearances to the contrary, he is
saying, the increase will be large. He then ticks off some additional expenses that are entailed by hiring new clerks. Notice that the whole sentence is covered by the assuring phrase, "I trust . . . that there is no
one among us who would suggest. . . ." This implies that anyone who
would make such a suggestion is merely stupid. But the trouble with
Kyl's argument so far is this: He has pointed out genuine additional
expenses, but they are not, after all, very large. It is important for him
to get some genuinely large sums of money into his argument. This is
the point of his next remark:

(c) "And it is not beyond the realm of possibility, that the next
step would then be a request for additional office space, and ultimately
new buildings." Here, at last, we have some genuinely large sums of
money in the picture, but the difficulty is that the entire claim is totally
guarded by the phrase, "it is not beyond the realm of possibility." There
are very few things that *are* beyond the realm of possibility. Kyl's problem, then, is this: There are certain additional expenses that he can point
to without qualification, but these tend to be small. On the other hand,
when he points out genuinely large expenses, he can only do so in a
guarded way. So we are still waiting for a proof that the expense will
be large. (Parenthetically, it should be pointed out that Kyl's prediction
of new buildings actually came true.)

(d) "Some will say, 'All the Members will not use their maximum, so the cost will not be great.' And this is true. If the exceptions are sufficient in number to constitute a valid argument, then there is no broad general need for this measure." This looks like a "tricky" argument, and for this reason alone it demands close attention. The phrase "some will say" is a standard way of beginning a discounting argument. This *is*, in fact, a discounting argument, but its form is rather subtle. Kyl cites what some will say, and then adds, somewhat surprisingly: "And this is true." To understand what is going on here, we must have a good feel for conversational implication. Kyl imagines someone reasoning in the following way:

> All the Members will not use their maximum.
>
> So the cost will not be great.
>
> Therefore, since the measure will not be expensive, let's adopt it.

Given the same starting pint, Kyl tries to derive just the *opposite* conclusion along the following lines:

> All the Members will not use their maximum.
>
> If very few use their maximums, then the cost will not be great.
>
> But if very few use their maximum, then there is no broad general need for this measure.
>
> Therefore, whether it is expensive or not, we should reject this measure.

In order to get clear about this argument, we can put it into schematic form:

> *Kyl's argument*
> If (1) expensive, then   → Reject
> If (2) inexpensive, then, because that demonstrates no general need,   → Reject
>
> *The opposite argument*
> If (1) inexpensive, then   → Accept
> If (2) expensive, then, because that demonstrates a general need,   → Accept

When the arguments are spread out in this fashion, it should be clear that they have equal strength. Both are no good. The question that must be settled is this: Does a genuine need exist that can be met in an economically sound manner? If there is no need for the measure, then it should be rejected however inexpensive. Again, if there is a need, then some expense is worth paying. The real problem is to balance the need against expense and then to decide on this basis whether the measure as a whole is worth adopting. Kyl's argument is a *sophistry* because it has no tendency to answer the real question at hand. By a sophistry we shall mean a clever but fallacious argument intended to establish a point through trickery. Incidentally, it is one of the marks of a sophistical argument that, though it may baffle, it almost never convinces. I think that very few readers will have found this argument persuasive even if they could not say exactly what is wrong with it. The appearance of a sophistical argument (or even a complex and tangled argument) is a sign that the argument is weak. Remember, where a case is strong, people usually argue in a straightforward way.

(e) "Furthermore, some Members will use these additional funds to raise salaries. Competition will force all salaries upward in all offices and then on committee staffs, and so on." The word "furthermore" signals that further *reasons* are forthcoming. Here Kyl returns to the argument that the measure is more expensive than it might at first sight appear. Notice that he speaks here in an unqualified way; no guarding appears. Yet the critic is bound to ask whether Kyl has any right to make these projections. Beyond this, Kyl here projects a *parade of horrors*. He pictures this measure leading, by gradual steps, to quite disastrous consequences. Here the little phrase "and so on" carries a great burden in the argument. Once more, we must simply ask ourselves whether these projections seem reasonable.

(f) "We may even find ourselves in a position of paying more money for fewer clerks and in a tighter bind on per person workload." Once more, the use of a strong guarding expression takes back most of the force of the argument. Notice that if Kyl could have said straight out that the measure *will* put us in a position of paying more money for fewer clerks and in a tighter bind on per person workload, that would have counted as a very strong objection. You can hardly do better in criticizing a position than showing that it will have just the opposite result from what is intended. In fact, however, Kyl has not established this; he has only said that this is something that we "may even find."

Before we turn to the second half of Kyl's argument, which we shall see in a moment is much stronger, we should point out that our analysis has not been entirely fair. Speaking before the House of Representatives, Kyl is in an *adversary* situation. He is not trying to prove things for all time; rather, he is responding to a position held by others. Part of what he is doing is *raising objections*, and a sensitive evaluation of the argument demands a detailed understanding of the nuances of the debate. But even granting this, it should be remembered that objections themselves must be made for good reasons. The problem so far in Kyl's argument is that the major reasons behind his objections have constantly been guarded in a very strong way.

Turning now to the second part of Kyl's argument—that the measure is untimely—we see that he moves along in a clear and direct way with little guarding.

This measure proposes to increase the allowance from $17,500 base clerical allowance to $20,500 base salary allowance. No member of this House can tell us what this means in gross salary. That computation G — is (almost) impossible. Such (a completely absurd system) has developed through the years on salary computations for clerical hire that we have under discussion a (mathematical monstrosity) We are usually told that the gross allowed is approximately $35,000. This is inaccurate. In one office the total might be less than $35,000 and in another, in complete compliance with the law and without any conscious padding, the amount may be in excess of $42,000. This is possible because of a (weird set of formulae) which determines that three clerks at $5,000 cost less than five clerks at $3,000. (Five times three might total the same as three times five everywhere else in the world—but not in figuring clerk hire in the House.)

This is application of (an absurdity.) It is a violation of bookkeeping principles, accounting principles, business principles and a (violation of commonsense.) Listen to the formula. . . .

E-
E-
E-
R
E-

The main point of the argument is clear enough: Kyl is saying that the present system of clerk salary allowance is utterly confusing, and this matter should be straightened out before *any* other measures in this area are adopted. There is, of course, a great deal of negative evaluation in this passage. Notice the words and phrases that Kyl uses.

completely absurd system
weird set of formulae
a violation of common sense
mathematical monstrosity
an absurdity

There is also a dash of irony in the remark that five times three might total the same as three times five everywhere else in the world, but not in figuring clerk hire in the House. Remember, there is nothing wrong with using negative evaluative and expressive terms if they are deserved. We would only describe the use of such terms as *slanting* if they had been used without adequate justification. Looking at the nine-step formula on page 52, you can decide for yourself whether Kyl is on strong grounds in using this negative language.

> Now, Mr. Speaker, I have planned to introduce an amendment or a substitute which would grant additional clerk hire where there is a demonstrable need based on heavier than average population or "election at large" and possible other factors.

(a) This passage rejects any suggestion that Kyl is unaware that a genuine problem does exist in some districts. It also indicates that he is willing to do something about it.

(b) The phrase "and possible other factors" is not very important, but it seems to be included to anticipate other reasons for clerk hire that should at least be considered.

> D--But after becoming involved in this mathematical
> maze, I realize the folly of proceeding one step until E-
> A
> we have corrected this situation.

(a) Here Kyl clearly states his reason for saying that the measure is untimely. Notice that the reason offered has been well documented and is not hedged in by qualifications.

(b) The phrases "mathematical maze" and "folly" are again negatively evaluative.

> E -
> We can offer all kinds of excuses for avoiding a
> solution. We cannot offer reasonable arguments that
> it should not be done or that it cannot be done.

(a) Notice that the first sentence ridicules the opponents' arguments by calling them *excuses*, a term with negative connotations. The second sentence gives assurances that such a solution can be found.

> Someone has suggested that the Members of this
> great body prefer to keep the present program be-
> cause someone back in the home district might ob-

ject to the gross figures. I know this is not so. When
a Representative is busy on minimum wage, or aid to
education, or civil rights, such matters of housekeeping seem too picayune to merit attention. The Member simply checks the table and hires what he can hire
under the provisions and then forgets the whole

D ——————————————————————————————— **A**
business. (But)(I know) the Members also want the
people back home to realize that what we do here is

E+ ——(open and frank and accurate,)and that we set an example in businesslike procedures. The more we can
demonstrate responsibility the greater will be the faith
in Congress.

(a) Once more the seas of rhetoric run high. Someone (though
not Kyl himself) has suggested that the Members of the House wish to
conceal information. He disavows the very thought that he would make
such a suggestion by the sentence "I know this is not so." All the same,
he has gotten this suggestion into the argument.

(b) Kyl then suggests another reason why the Members of the
House will not be concerned with this measure: it is too *picayune*. The
last two sentences rebut the suggestion that it is too small to merit close
attention. Even on small matters, the more the House is "open and frank
and accurate," the more it will "set an example in businesslike procedures" and thus "demonstrate responsibility" that will increase "the faith
in Congress." This is actually an important part of Kyl's argument, for
presumably his main problem is to get the other Members of the House
to take the matter seriously.

———————————————————————————— **A**
May I summarize. (It is obvious that) some Members need more clerical help(because) of large popu- **W**
lation and large land area.(I have been working for) **A**
(some time with the best help we can get,)on a measure which would take these items into consideration. Those Members who are really in need of
A ——————————————————————————————— **E-**
assistance should(realize) that this(temporary, hastily
conceived)proposition we debate today will(probably) **G**
obviate their getting a satisfactory total solution.

(a) This is a concise summary. Kyl once more assures the House that he is aware that a genuine problem exists. He also indicates that he is working on it.

(b) The phrase "temporary, hastily conceived proposition we debate today" refers back to his arguments concerning untimeliness.

(c) The claim that "it will probably obviate their getting a satisfactory total solution" refers back to the economic argument. Notice, however, that, as before, the economic claim is guarded by the word "probably."

> First, we should await redistricting of the Nation.
>
> Second, we should consider appropriate allowance for oversize districts considering both population and total geographic area.
>
> Finally, I hope we can develop a sound and sensible formula for computing salaries of office clerks and other statutory employees in the same category. — E+

This is straightforward except that a new factor is introduced: we should await redistricting of the nation. This was not mentioned earlier in the argument, and so seems a bit out of place in a summary. Perhaps the point is so obvious that it did not need any argument to support it. On the other hand, it is often useful to keep track of things that are smuggled into the argument at the very end. If redistricting was about to occur in the *near* future, this would give a strong reason for delaying action on the measure. Because the point is potentially so strong, we might wonder why Kyl has made so little of it. Here, perhaps, we are getting too subtle.

EXERCISE 1

The following is a statement made by Ronald Reagan opposing the idea of a mutual freeze on nuclear arms.* Various words and phrases (and one blank) are identified for your comment.

---

*The occasion of this speech was the President's radio address to the nation on April 17, 1982.

REAGAN ON A NUCLEAR FREEZE

Today *I know*[1] there are a great many people who are pointing to the *unimaginable horror*[2] of *nuclear*[3] war. *I welcome that concern.*[4] Those who governed America throughout the nuclear age and we who govern it today have had to recognize that a nuclear war cannot be won and (   )[5] must never be fought. *So*[6] to those who protest against nuclear war I can only say I'm with you. Like my predecessors it is now my responsibility to do my utmost to prevent such a war. No one feels more than I the need for peace . . .[7]

Since[8] the end of World War II there's not been another world conflict. *But*[9] there have been and are wars going on in various other parts of the world. This stretch of 37 years since WW II *has been the result of*[10] our maintaining a balance of power between the United States and the Soviet Union and between the strategic capabilities of either side.

As long as the balance has been maintained, both sides have been given an overwhelming incentive for peace. In the 1970's, the United States altered that balance by, *in effect,*[11] *unilaterally*[12] restraining our own military defenses while the Soviet Union engaged in an unprecedented buildup of both its conventional and nuclear forces. *As a result,*[13] the military balance which permitted us to maintain the peace is now threatened. *If*[14] steps are not taken to modernize our defense, the United States will progressively lose the ability to deter the Soviet Union from employing force or threats of force against us and our allies.

It would be wonderful[15] *if*[16] we could restore our balance with the Soviet Union without increasing our military power. And, *ideally,*[17] it would be a long step in assuring peace *if*[18] we could have significant and verifiable reductions of arms on both sides.

But[19] let's not fool ourselves. The Soviet Union will not come to any conference table bearing gifts. Soviet negotiators will not make unilateral concessions. To achieve parity, we *must*[20] make it plain that we have the will to achieve parity by our own effort.

Many have been attracted to the idea of a nuclear freeze. *Well, that would be fine if we were equal in strategic capability. We're not. We cannot accept an agreement which perpetuates current disparities.*[21]

For each of the numbered expressions, either use the abbreviations listed opposite to label the kind of argumentative move that is made *(if any)*, or answer the specific questions, as follows:

1–4. Write labels.
   5. What logical term could be inserted here?
   6. Write label.
   7. What is the point of this whole opening paragraph?
8–14. Write labels.
  15. What is conversationally implied by the phrase, "It would be wonderful"?
  16. Write label.
  17. What is conversationally implied by using the word "ideally"?
  18. Write label.
  19. What is being discounted here?
  20. What logical term can be inserted here?
  21. Put this closing summary argument in standard form. Then decide whether the conclusion follows validly from the premises.

Use the following abbreviations to label various expressions:

warranting connective	W
assuring term	A
guarding term	G
discounting term	D
argumentative performative	AP
evaluative/expressive (+, −)	E+ *or* E−
slanting (+, −)	S+ *or* S−
none of the above	N

EXERCISE 2

Decide for yourself which are the key argumentative terms in the following brief argument, then subject it to a close analysis. After you have completed your close analysis, state what you take to be its central argument. What criticisms, if any, do you have of the argument?

EXERCISE 3

Provide a close analysis and evaluation of the following defense of fraternities.†

** This ad first appeared in the late 1960s or early 1970s in the *New York Times* and was written by Tiffany's chairman of that period, Walter Hoving.

† This appeared as a letter to the editor in *The New York Times*, June 16, 1985. It begins with a reference to an earlier article on fraternities by Fred M. Hechinger, but knowledge of that article is not necessary for understanding Rev. Stemper's argument.

Fraternities, Where Men May Come to Terms
With Other Men

To the Editor:

"The Fraternities Show Signs of New Strength," Fred M. Hechinger's analysis of the nature of college fraternities (Science Times, May 21) and the reason for their present growth is superficial. Apart from its condescending tone, it misses the point.

College fraternities are growing today because college curriculums are increasingly technical, preprofessional, competitive, and in most instances remote from the principal challenge of finding meaning in life. Their growth is not unrelated to the rapid rise in teen-age suicide: a pervasive sense that no one—certainly no institution—really cares for the nation's youth.

Local college fraternity chapters provide the only segment of the undergraduate's life he controls. Thus, it is one of the few arenas open to creative expression in self-government, same-sex relationships, and forensic abilities apart from some evaluatory scrutiny by thesis-grading, recommendation-writing members of college faculties and administrations.

Within a fraternity, a student can live without looking over his shoulder—if, in fact, this is still possible in our society. If there is occasional violence associated with initiations and reprehensible treatment of women, the cause is much more deeply rooted in the materialism of our culture, which reduces "life" to "career."

In borrowing from older fraternal and classical traditions, modern college fraternities have provided in the 1980's symbolic structures within which men might come to terms with other men. Far from "a return to a macho kind of adolescence tinged with elitist exclusivity," nurturing, compassion and empathy are commonplace in the college fraternity—sometimes for the first and last time in a man's life with other male friends.

Such vulnerabilities come hard for most young men. A collegiate brotherhood provides the same shelter, in social terms, as a room of one's own provides or a first automobile in adolescence. It is a symbol of self.

A disturbing aspect of the article is the equation of college fraternities with antifeminism. Women have taught men in recent years the meaning of solidarity. A genuine tragedy of our times is that men's liberation movements were a casualty of the post-1960's era.

A man—and a male institution—may affirm a feminist critique of society and still seek to enrich male bonding. One could argue that an objective of feminism is that men should get on with other men in more constructive ways. Fraternities and fraternal orders are the only institutions in our society that have this objective as a primary and lasting goal. For this reason alone, cynical superficiality should give way to honest respect.

(Rev.) WILLIAM H. STEMPER JR.
New York, May 24, 1985

The writer is bishop's vicar for corporate affairs of the Episcopal Diocese of New York.

DISCUSSION QUESTIONS

(1) As admitted earlier, the clerk hire debate is not one of today's burning issues. Identify five topics that could easily provide arguments appropriate for close analysis, and then arrange each topic along a continuum from "cool" to "hot." Which topics interest you the most? Why?

(2) If, as some social critics have maintained, the pervasive nature of television has created generation upon generation of intellectually passive automotons, why study close analysis?

(3) Earlier we identified sophistry as a clever but fallacious argument intended to establish a point through trickery. What is the best sophistical argument you have ever encountered? Why is it sophistical?

(4) Television commercials are often arguments in miniature. For example, the commercial that begins "I'm not a doctor but I play one on TV" combines a veiled appeal to authority with guarding—and in only ten words. Recount several recent commercials and identify the argumentative devices at work.

4

Fallacies

In this chapter we shall examine some of the standard ways in which arguments can be defective. Defects in arguments will be considered under three main headings: *fallacies of clarity, fallacies of relevance,* and *fallacies of vacuity.* Fallacies of clarity arise when language is not used precisely enough for the argumentative context. *Vagueness* and *ambiguity,* two common forms of unclarity, will be defined and discussed in detail. Fallacies of relevance arise when a claim is made which, true or not, has no tendency to establish the point at issue. Such irrelevance comes in endless forms, but only two will be discussed in detail: *arguments ad hominem* and *appeals to authority.* Fallacies of vacuity arise when an argument's very form precludes it from establishing the truth of its conclusion. *Circular arguments* and arguments that are said to *beg the question* fall into this category. So do arguments that make themselves immune to criticism by being *self-sealing.*

FALLACIES OF CLARITY

In a good argument, a person states a conclusion clearly and then, with equal clarity, gives reasons for this conclusion. The arguments of every-day life often fall short of this standard. Usually, unclear language is a sign of unclear thought. There are times, however, when people are intentionally unclear—their goal is to confuse others. This is called *obfuscation.*

Before we look at the various ways in which language can be un-clear, a word of caution is needed. There is no such thing as absolute clarity. Whether something is clear or not depends on the context in which it occurs. A botanist does not use the commonsense vocabulary in describing and classifying plants. At the same time, it would be fool-ish for a person to use botanical terms in describing the appearance of his backyard. Thus, as Aristotle said, it is the mark of an educated per-son not to expect more rigor than the subject matter will allow. Because clarity and rigor are context-dependent, it takes judgment and good sense to pitch an argument at the right level.

Vagueness

Perhaps the most common form of unclarity is *vagueness.* It arises in the following way. Many of our concepts admit of *borderline cases.* The standard example is baldness. A person with a full flowing head of hair is not bald. A person without a hair on his head is bald. In between, however, there is a range of cases where we are not prepared to say definitely whether the person is bald or not. Here we say something less definite, such as this person is "going" bald. Notice that our inabil-ity to apply the concept of baldness in this borderline case is not due to ignorance. It will not help, for example, to count the number of hairs on the person's head. Even if we knew the exact number, we would still not be able to say whether the person was bald or not. The same is true of most adjectives that concern properties admitting of degrees—for example, *rich, healthy, tall, wise,* and *ruthless.* We can also encounter bor-derline cases with common nouns. Consider the common noun *game.* Baseball is a game and so is chess, but how about tossing a frisbee? Is that a game? Is Russian roulette a game? Are prize fighting and bull fighting games? As we try to answer these questions, we feel an incli-nation to say Yes and an inclination to say No. This uncertainty shows that these concepts admit of borderline cases.

For the most part this feature of our language—that we use terms without sharply defined limits—causes little difficulty. In fact, this is a useful feature of our language, for suppose we *did* have to count the number of hairs on a person's head before we could say whether he was bald or not. Yet difficulties can arise when borderline cases themselves are at issue. Suppose that a state passes a law forbidding all actions that tend to corrupt the public morals. The law is backed up by stiff fines and imprisonment. There will be many cases that clearly fall under this law and many cases that clearly do not fall under it. But in a very wide range of cases, it will just not be clear whether they fall under this law or not. Here we shall say that the law is *vague;* laws are sometimes called unconstitutional for this very reason. In calling the law vague, we are *criticizing* it. We are not simply noticing the existence of borderline cases, for there will usually be borderline cases no matter how careful we are. *We shall say, then, that a concept is vague, if, in a given context, it leaves open too wide a range of borderline cases for the successful use of that concept in that context.*

To further illustrate this notion of context dependence, consider the expression "light football player." There are, of course, borderline cases between those football players who are light and those who are not light. But on these grounds alone we would not say that the expression is vague. It is a perfectly serviceable expression, and we can indicate borderline cases by saying that "Jones is a bit light for a football player." Suppose, however, that Ohio State and Cal Tech wish to have a game between their light football players. It is obvious that the previous understanding of what counts as being light is too vague for this new context. At Ohio State, anyone under 210 pounds is considered light. At Cal Tech, anyone over 150 pounds is considered heavy. What is needed then is a ruling—for example, anyone under 175 pounds will be considered a lightweight. This is a common situation. A concept that is perfectly okay in one area becomes vague when applied to some other (usually more specialized) area. This vagueness is removed by adopting more precise rules. Vagueness is resolved by definition.

EXERCISE 1

Each of the following sentences contains words or expressions that are potentially vague. Reduce this vagueness by replacing the underlined expression with one that is more precise.
For example:

Harold *has a bad reputation.*
Harold is a known thief.

(1) John *has a nice income.*
(2) Cocaine *is a dangerous drug.*
(3) Marian *is a clever woman.*

(4) Nancy *is a terrific tennis player.*

(5) Mark is *not doing too well.*

(6) Hank's *a big fellow.*

(7) Reagan *won by a landslide.*

(8) Kevin *worked like a dog.*

Heaps and Slippery Slopes

The existence of borderline cases makes possible various styles of fallacious reasoning that have been identified (and used) since ancient times. One such argument was called the argument "from the *heap*," for it was intended to show that there are no heaps. As a variation on this, we will show that no one can become rich. The argument goes

(1) If someone has one cent, he is not rich.
(2) If someone is not rich, then giving him one cent will not make him rich.

∴ No matter how many times you give a person a cent, he will not pass from being not rich to being rich.

Everyone will agree that there is something wrong with this argument, for if we hand over a billion pennies to someone, that person will be worth ten million dollars. If he or she started out with nothing, that would certainly count as passing from being not rich to being rich.

Although there is some disagreement among philosophers about the correct way to analyze this argument, we can see that it turns upon borderline cases in the following way: If we laid down a ruling (maybe for tax purposes) that anyone with a million dollars or more is rich and anyone with less than this is not rich, then the argument would fail. A person with $999,999.99 would pass from not being rich to being rich when given a single penny. But, of course, we do not use the word "rich" with this precision. We know some clear cases of people who are rich and some other clear cases of people who are not rich. In between there is a fuzzy area where we are not prepared to say that people either are or are not rich. In this fuzzy area, a penny one way or the other will make no difference. Once we see the form of the argument from the heap, we see how we might "prove" that nobody is tall, fat, or bald and, finally, that there are no heaps. Wherever we find one thing passing over into its opposite through a gradual series of borderline cases, we can pull the following trick: find some increase that will not be large enough to carry us outside the borderline area, and then use the pattern of argument given above.

But what exactly is wrong with the argument from the heap? As a matter of fact, this is not an easy question to answer and remains a subject of debate. Here is one way of viewing this problem. Consider a case where we would all agree that a person would pass from being fat to being thin by losing at least 100 pounds. Now if this person lost an ounce a day for five years, he or she would have lost at least this much. Of course, there would be no particular day on which this person would pass from being fat to not being fat. Yet losing an ounce a day for five years is *equivalent* to losing more than 100 pounds. So the argument from the heap seems to depend upon the idea that a series of insignificant changes cannot be equivalent to a significant change. Surely this is a strange assumption. Here we might be met with the reply that, for a change to occur, it must occur at some particular time and place. The answer is that this merely shows a misunderstanding of concepts that admit of borderline cases. We can examine this issue more closely by looking at a near cousin to arguments from the heap—so-called "slippery slope" arguments.

Slippery slope arguments exploit borderline cases in a different way than arguments from the heap. Here, instead of getting trapped in the borderline area, we inch our way through it in order to show that there is no real difference between things at opposite ends of a scale. Whereas the argument from the heap could be used to show that nobody is really bald, a slippery slope argument could be trotted out to show that there is no *real difference* between being bald and not being bald.

Slippery slope arguments are no better than arguments from the heap, but, strangely, they are sometimes taken quite seriously. Consider the difference between living and nonliving things:

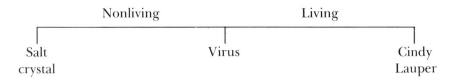

We notice first that a salt crystal is *not* alive. Yet a salt crystal is very similar to other more complex crystals, and these crystals are similar to certain viruses. We might even say that a virus just *is* a highly complex crystalline structure. But a virus is on the borderline between living and nonliving things. A virus does not take nourishment and does not reproduce itself. Instead, a virus invades the reproductive mechanisms of cells and these cells then produce the virus. As viruses become more complex, the differences between them and "higher" life forms become less obvious. Through a whole series of such small transitions, we finally reach a creature who is obviously alive: Cindy Lauper. So far, we have merely described a series of gradual transitions along a *continuum*. We get a slippery slope argument when we draw the following conclusion from these facts: Therefore there is no genuine difference between living and nonliving things since living processes are nothing more than complex nonliving processes.

Slippery slope arguments have been used to deny the difference between sanity and insanity, health and sickness, and amateur and professional athletics. (We can imagine someone saying that a professional athlete is just an athlete who gets paid more than other athletes who are called "amateurs.") All such arguments depend upon the following principles:

(1) We should not draw a distinction between things that are not significantly different.

(2) If A is not significantly different from B and B is not significantly different from C, then A is not significantly different from C.

This first principle is interesting, complicated, and at least *generally* true. We shall examine it more closely in a moment. The second principle is obviously false. A series of insignificant differences can add up to a significant difference. As Senator Everett Dirksen once said, "A billion dollars here and a billion dollars there can add up to some real money."

Those who use slippery slope arguments often use the phrase "it's just a matter of degree." What is usually wrong with this phrase is the emphasis on the word "just," which suggests that differences of degree don't count. The difference between gluttony and starvation is a matter of degree—how much food you consume—but it is not *just* a matter of degree.

Where Do You Draw the Line?

We can now turn to some arguments concerning borderline cases that can be much more important. In the middle of an argument a person can offer a challenge by asking the question, "Where do you draw the line?" This challenge makes sense only when there is a range of intermediate or borderline cases where a line is difficult to draw. But sometimes, even if the line is difficult to draw, this challenge is out of place. If I say that Hank Aaron was a superstar, I am not going to be refuted if I cannot draw a sharp dividing line between athletes who are superstars and those who are not. There are some difficult borderline cases, but Hank Aaron isn't one of them. Nor will we be impressed if someone tells us that the difference between Hank Aaron and the thousands of players who never made it to the major leagues is "just a *matter of degree.*" Of course it is a matter of degree, but the difference in degree is so great that it should be marked by a special word. Arguing that we cannot distinguish things on opposite ends of a scale because we cannot justify any particular dividing point in the middle of the scale is just another variation of the slippery slope argument.

There are, however, occasions when the challenge to draw a line is relevant. For example, most schools and universities have grading systems that draw a fundamental distinction between passing grades and a failing grade. Of course, a person who barely passes a course does not perform very differently from one who barely fails a course, yet they are treated very differently. Students who barely pass a course get credit for it; those who barely fail it do not. This, in turn, can lead to serious consequences in an academic career and even beyond it. It is not unreasonable to ask for a justification of a procedure that treats cases that are so similar in such strikingly different ways. In other words, we are not just being tender-hearted; we are raising an issue of fairness or justice. It seems unfair to treat very similar cases in strikingly different ways, but this occurs any time we draw a sharp line between closely similar cases.

Questions concerning where a line should be drawn often raise problems for law and legislation. For example, the U.S. Supreme Court, in *California* v. *Carney*, had to rule on the following issue. Generally, given reasonable cause, the police do not have to obtain a warrant to search a motor vehicle, for the obvious reason that the vehicle might be driven away while the police go to a judge to obtain one. On the other hand, with few exceptions, the police do need a warrant to search a person's home. In this particular case the vehicle was an "oversized van, fully mobile," parked in a downtown parking lot in San Diego. Looking for marijuana, the San Diego Police searched it without first obtaining a warrant. Because the van was a fully mobile vehicle, it seemed to fall under the first principle, but because it also served as its owner's home, it seemed to fall under the second.

The difficulty, as the Court saw, was that there is a grey area between those things that clearly are motor vehicles and not homes (for example, a motor cycle) and those things that clearly are homes and not motor vehicles (for example, Uncle Tom's Cabin.) Chief Justice Warren Burger wondered about a mobile home in a trailer park hooked up to utility lines with its wheels removed. Justice Sandra Day O'Connor asked whether a tent, because it too is highly mobile, could also be searched without a warrant. As the discussion continued, houseboats (with or without motors or oars), covered wagons, and finally a house being moved from one place to another on a trailer truck came under examination. In the end, our highest court decided that the van in question certainly was a vehicle and could be searched without first obtaining a warrant to do so. As for the other instances it considered, as it often does, the Court deferred action until another case presented itself.[1]

Questions about where to draw the line often have broader implications than the case just examined. In instituting a poverty program, for example, it will be obvious that certain people are in need of aid and others are not. Yet the program itself must have some specific cut-off point. Those just above this point and those just below it will be treated differently even though the differences between them are negligible.

Sometimes we can find practical ways of dealing with problems of this kind. With a poverty program we can use a graduated scale based on need. Those with a greater need will receive more aid, and the aid will decrease as the cut-off point is approached. In this way, there will be only a small difference between those just below the cut-off point who receive minimal aid and those just above it who receive no aid at all. But sometimes this strategy is not available. Consider the death penalty. Most societies have reserved the death penalty for the most serious crimes. But where should we draw the line between crimes punishable by death and crimes not punishable by death? There is no possibility of introducing a sliding scale, since death does not admit of degrees. It seems to be an unavoidable consequence of the death penalty that similar cases will be treated in radically different ways. A defender of the death penalty can argue that it is fair since, once the line is drawn, the public will have fair warning about which crimes are subject to the death penalty. It will then be each person's decision whether to cross this line or not. It remains a matter of debate, however, whether the law can be administered in a way that makes this argument plausible. If the laws themselves are administered in an arbitrary way, arguments of this kind lose their force.

The finality and completeness of death raises a profoundly difficult problem in another area too: the legalization of abortion. There are some people who think that abortion is never justified. There are others who think that it doesn't need any justification at all. Between these extremes, there are many people who believe that abortion is justified in certain circumstances but not in others. There are also those who think that abortion should be allowed for a certain number of months of pregnancy, but not thereafter. People in the middle positions face the problem of deciding where to draw a line, and for this reason they are subject to criticism from both extreme positions. This problem admits of no easy solution. Since every line we draw will seem arbitrary to some extent, and since the issues here are profoundly im-

---

[1] The case was reported by Linda Greenhouse in "Of Tents with Wheels and Houses with Oars," *The New York Times*, May 15, 1985.

portant, the only way a person who holds a middle position can face this problem honestly is to argue that it is better to draw some line—even an arbitrary one—than to draw no line at all.

In an earlier discussion, we saw that, *in general,* we should not draw a sharp distinction between things that are not significantly different. This principle becomes more than a matter of logic when the distinction involves questions of life and death. Yet sometimes we abandon this principle with hardly a thought. There is surely no obvious reason why the voting age should be 18 rather than 17 or 19.[2] The previous voting age of 21 was arbitrary in the same way. But in this area, most people agree that the need to draw a clear line someplace more than outweighs the arbitrariness of drawing it in some particular place. To cite another example, most people agree that it is important to have uniform speed laws for motor vehicles even though it is arbitrary whether the limit is 50, 55, or 60 miles per hour. In other situations, arbitrariness is not so easily accepted. To summarize, the question, "Where do you draw the line?" is sometimes a variation on the slippery slope argument and so is just a quibble, whereas at other times it raises fundamental questions of fairness and justice. We must learn to distinguish the two kinds of cases—dismissing the first and doing the best we can with the second.

EXERCISE 2

For your own amusement, construct examples of an argument from the heap and a slippery slope argument.

EXERCISE 3

More seriously, discuss a case where drawing a sharp line can produce important moral, social, or political problems. The arguments on abortion given in Part Two (pp. 291–316) may serve this purpose.

---

[2] An answer to this is that people should be allowed to vote at 18 since they can, in times of war, be drafted at 18. This is not much of an answer, for it is also arbitrary to draft people at the age of 18.

Ambiguity

The idea of *vagueness* is based upon a common feature of words in our language. Many of them leave open a range of borderline cases. When these borderline cases cause difficulty, we say that the use of such terms is vague. The notion of *ambiguity* is also based upon a common feature of our language. Words often have a number of different meanings. For example, *The New Merriam-Webster Pocket Dictionary* has the following entry under the word "cardinal":

> Cardinal *adj. 1:* of basic importance: Chief, Main, Primary, *2:* of cardinal red color.
> *n. 1:* an ecclesiastical official of the Roman Catholic Church ranking next below the Pope, *2:* a bright red, *3:* any of several American finches of which the male is bright red.

In the plural, "The Cardinals" is the name of various athletic teams that inhabit St. Louis; "cardinal" also describes the numbers used in simple counting.

It is not likely that people would get confused about these very different meanings of the word "cardinal," but we might imagine a priest, a bird watcher, and a baseball fan all hearing the remark: "The cardinals are in town." The priest would prepare for a solemn occasion, the bird watcher would get out his binoculars, and the baseball fan would head for the stadium. If a term is used so that such confusions arise, we say that it is used *ambiguously*.

Examples of ambiguity are perhaps more common in logic texts than in everyday life, for context usually settles which of a variety of meanings is appropriate. Yet sometimes genuine misunderstandings do arise in everyday life. An American and a European discussing "football" may have different games in mind. The European is talking about what *we* call "soccer"; the American is talking about what *they* call "American football." It is characteristic of the ambiguous use of a term that when it comes to light we are likely to say something like, "Oh, you mean *that* kind of cardinal!" or "Oh, you were talking about *American* football!" In a context where the use of a word is ambiguous, we do not know which of *two* meanings to attach to a word. In a context where the use of a word is vague, we cannot attach *any* clear meaning to the use of a word.

So far we have talked about the ambiguity of terms or individual words. But sometimes we do not know what interpretation to give to a phrase or a sentence because its grammar or syntax admits of more than one interpretation. Thus if we talk about *the conquest of the Persians*, we might be referring either to the Persians' conquering someone or to someone's conquering the Persians. Sometimes a sentence admits of a great many possible interpretations. For example, consider the sentence:

> Only sons marry only daughters.

One thing that this might mean is that a person who is a male only child will marry a person who is a female only child. Again, it might mean that sons are the only persons who only marry daughters.[3]

The process of rewriting a sentence so that its meaning becomes clear is called *disambiguating*. One way of disambiguating a sentence is to continue it in a way that forces one interpretation. This is a way of filling out a context. Consider the sentence, "Mary had a little lamb." Notice how the meaning changes completely under the following continuations:

(1) Mary had a little lamb; he followed her to school.
(2) Mary had a little lamb and then a little broccoli.

Just in passing, it is not altogether obvious how we should describe the ambiguity in the sentence "Mary had a little lamb." The most obvious suggestion is that the word "had" is ambiguous, meaning "owned" on the first reading and "ate" on a second reading. Notice, however, that this also forces alternative readings for the expression "a little lamb." Presumably, it was a small whole live lamb that followed Mary to school, whereas it would have been a small piece of cooked lamb that she ate. So if we try to locate the ambiguity in particular words, we must say that not only the word "had" but also the word "lamb" is being used ambiguously. This is a reasonable approach, but another is available. In everyday speech we often leave things out. Thus, instead of saying "Mary had a little *piece of meat derived from a* lamb *to eat,*" we just say "Mary had a little lamb," dropping out the italicized words on the assumption that they will be understood. In most contexts, such deletions cause no misunderstanding. But sometimes deletions are misunderstood, and this can produce ambiguity.

EXERCISE 4

Show that each of the following sentences admits of at least two interpretations by either rewriting the sentence as a whole in two different ways or by expanding the sentence two different ways in order to clarify the context.

---

[3] This example comes from Paul Benacerraf.

Example: Kenneth let us down.

Rewriting: Kenneth lowered us.

Kenneth disappointed us.

Expanding: Kenneth let us down with a rope.

Kenneth let us down just when we needed him.

(1) Reggie Jackson was safe at home.
(2) I don't know what state Meredith is in.
(3) Where did you get bitten?
(4) The President sent her congratulations.
(5) Visiting professors can be boring.
♦ (6) There is some explanation for everything.
(7) Wendy ran the marathon.
♦ (8) The meaning of the term "altering" is changing.

EXERCISE 5

Perform the same exercise on the following newspaper headlines. They actually appeared in print and are collected in a marvelous book entitled *Squad Helps Dog Bite Victim.*[4]

(1) Milk drinkers turn to powder
(2) Anti-busing rider killed by Senate
(3) Gandhi stoned in rally in India
(4) College Graduates Blind Senior Citizen
(5) Jumping bean prices affect the poor
(6) Tuna biting off Washington Coast
(7) Time for Football and Meatball Stew
(8) Police kill man with ax
(9) Squad Helps Dog Bite Victim

EXERCISE 6

Ambiguous headlines often carry unfortunate double meanings. Rewrite each of the following sentences to correct this.[5]

---

[4] Columbia Journalism Review Editors, *Squad Helps Dog Bite Victim & Other Flubs from the Nation's Press* (Garden City, N.Y.: Doubleday, 1980).
[5] These examples also come from *Squad Helps Dog Bite Victim.*

Example: Prostitutes appeal to Pope
Revision: Prostitutes petition Pope

(1) Legalized Outhouses Aired by Legislature
(2) Survivor of Siamese Twins Joins Parents
(3) Judge Permits Club to Continue Sex Bar
(4) Teenage prostitution problem is mounting

Fallacies of Ambiguity

Ambiguity can cause misunderstanding. More often, it produces hilarious or embarrassing side effects, and it is hard to get your arguments taken seriously if your listeners are giggling over an unintended *double entendre*. Ambiguity can also generate bad arguments that are said to involve the *fallacy of equivocation*. An argument is said to commit this fallacy when it relies on using the same term or larger expression in different senses.

An example, attributed to Bertrand Russell, illustrates this fallacy. The following is a perfectly good argument:

(1) The Apostles were followers of Christ.
Paul was an Apostle.

∴   Paul was a follower of Christ.

The following argument, though grammatically similar, is obviously a bad argument:

(2) The Apostles were twelve.
Paul was an Apostle.

∴   Paul was twelve.

At a superficial level, it is natural to read the conclusion as saying that Paul was *twelve years old*. But if we interpret the first premise in the same way, then the argument, though valid, is unsound—because the first premise, on this reading, is false. The Apostles, at the time they were Apostles, were not twelve years old.

There is, however, a better way of reading the argument that reveals a deeper ambiguity. The first premise obviously means that the Apostles were *twelve in number*. Using this interpretation, let's took at the argument again.

(3) The Apostles were twelve in number.
Paul was an Apostle.

∴   Paul was twelve in number.

Having clarified the meaning of the word "twelve," we get an argument which, if anything, is worse, because the conclusion (along with being false) barely makes sense. What went wrong? Both premises are true, so, since the conclusion is false, the argument must be invalid. But why is it invalid? The answer lies in the correct interpretation of the second premise. To say that Paul was an Apostle means that Paul was a member of the Apostles. Taken this way, the argument looks like this:

(4) The Apostles as a group were twelve in number.
     Paul was a member of the group of Apostles.
     _____
∴   Paul was a member of a group that was twelve in number.

This, of course, is a sound argument. We get a fallacy of equivocation when, as in (3), the verb "was" is interpreted in different ways in the premise and the conclusion.

Although usually discussed in traditional logic texts, fallacies of equivocation do not seem to cause serious confusion in the common affairs of life. It is hard to imagine, for example, that anyone would be convinced that Paul was twelve (either in age or in number) by the argument given above. Nonetheless, it is clear how to deal with an argument that may trade on equivocation: *restate the argument with sufficient clarity such that the premises and conclusion can be given only one reasonable interpretation.*

EXERCISE 7

Each of the following arguments trades on an ambiguity. For each, locate the ambiguity by showing that one or more of the statements can be interpreted in different ways.

(1) You passed no one on the road; therefore, you walk faster than no one.

(2) Everything must have a cause; therefore, there must be something that is the cause of everything.

(3) "The only proof capable of being given that an object is visible is that people actually see it. The only proof that a sound is audible is that people hear it; . . . In like manner . . . the sole evidence it is possible to produce that anything is desirable is that people actually desire it." (J. S. Mill in his *Utilitarianism*.)

(4) Six is an odd number of legs for a horse, and odd numbers cannot be divided by two, so six cannot be divided by two.

(5) I have a right to buy lottery tickets. Therefore, when I buy lottery tickets I am doing something right.

(6) If I have only one friend, then I cannot say that I have *any number* of friends. So one is not a number. (From Tim Duggan.)

Definitions

It is sometimes suggested that a great many disputes could be avoided if people simply took the precaution of defining their terms. To some extent this is true, but definitions will not solve all problems, and a mindless insistence upon definitions can turn a serious discussion into a semantic quibble. Furthermore, definitions themselves can be confusing or obfuscating as, for example, when an economist tells us:

I define inflation as too much money chasing too few goods.

Not only is this definition metaphorical and obscure, it also has built into it a theory on the causes of inflation.

Definitions are, of course, important, but to use them correctly, we must realize that they come in various forms and serve various purposes. There are at least five kinds of definition to be distinguished.

(1) *Lexical, or dictionary, definitions:* We consult a dictionary when we are ignorant about the meaning of a word in a particular language. Except for an occasional diagram, a dictionary explains the meaning of a word by using other words that, presumably, the reader already understands. If you do not happen to know what the words "jejune," "ketone," or "Kreis" means, then you can look these words up in an English, a scientific, or a German dictionary respectively. Lexical definitions supply us with information about the standard meaning of words in a particular language.

(2) *Stipulative definitions* are used to assign a meaning to a new (usually technical) term or to assign a new or special meaning to a familiar term. Thus mathematicians introduced the term "googol" to stand for the number expressed by 1 followed by one hundred zeroes. Economists have given the term "money," which in common parlance means currency, that is, something you can put in your pocket, a much wider meaning. For economists money includes both currency and those assets which are readily convertible into currency.

(3) *Precising definitions* are used to resolve vagueness. They are used to draw a sharp (or sharper) boundary around the extension of a term

which, in ordinary usage, has a fuzzy or indeterminate boundary. For example, for most purposes it is not important to decide how big a population center must be in order to count as a city rather than as a town. We can deal with the borderline cases by using such phrases as "very small city" or "quite a large town." On most occasions it will not make much difference which phrase we use. Yet it is not hard to imagine a situation in which it might make a difference whether a center of population is a city or not; as a city, it might be eligible for redevelopment funds that are not available to towns. Here a precising definition—a definition that draws a sharp boundary where none formerly existed—is essential. Precising definitions are like stipulative definitions; they involve a decision. They are not completely arbitrary, however, since they usually conform to the accepted understanding of the meaning of a term. (It would be reasonable to define a city as any population center with more than 50,000 people. It would be unreasonable to define a city as any population center with more than 17 people.)

(4) *Disambiguating definitions* tell us in which sense a word is being used. (When I said that banks were collapsing, I meant the river banks, not the financial institutions.)

(5) Finally, *theoretical definitions* are introduced to give a systematic order to a subject matter. For example, in mathematics, every term must be either a primitive (undefined) term or a term defined by means of these primitive terms. In a similar way, we might try to represent family relationships using only the primitive notions of parent, male, and female. We could then construct definitions of the following kind:

"A is the brother of B."   =   "A and B have the same parents and A is male."

"A is B's grandmother."   =   "A is a parent of a parent of B and A is female."[6]

Things become more complicated when we try to define such notions as "second cousin once removed," yet by extending these definitions from simple to more complicated cases, our system of family relationships can be given a systematic development. This process may even prove useful in comparing our system of family relationships with that of some other society. Formulating definitions of this kind for family relationships is relatively easy, but similar activities in science and mathematics can demand the insight of a genius.

---

[6] Notice that in these definitions an individual word is not defined in isolation; instead, a whole sentence containing the word is replaced by another whole sentence in which the defined word does not appear. Definitions of this kind are called "contextual definitions" because a context containing the word is the unit of definition.

The Role of Definitions

In the middle of discussions people often ask for definitions or even state, usually with an air of triumph, that everything depends upon the way you define your terms. We saw in the opening chapter that definitions are not always needed, and, in most cases, issues do not turn upon the way in which words are defined. Heavy-handed calls for definitions are unfortunate because they often derail honest discussion and can also obscure those cases in which a demand for a definition is in order. When asked for a definition, it is appropriate to reply: "What sort of definition do you want, and why do you want it?" Of course, if you are using a word in a way that departs from customary usage, or using it in some special way of your own, or using a word that is too vague for the given context, or using a word in an ambiguous way, then the request for a definition is perfectly in order. In such cases the demand for a definition represents an important move within the argument rather than a distraction from it.

EXERCISE 8

(a) Find the lexical definitions for the words "jejune" and "clarion."

(b) Give a stipulative definition for the word "klurg." Stipulate a word to stand for the chunks of ice that form under car fenders in winter.

(c) Give precising definitions for the words "book" and "alcoholic beverage." (Supply the context that gives your precising definition a point.)

(d) Give disambiguating definitions for the words "chair" and "pen."

(e) Using the notions of parent(s), male, and female as basic, give definitions of the following family relationships:
  (1) A and B are sisters.   (3) A is B's niece.
  (2) A is B's half brother.   (4) A is B's cousin.

FALLACIES OF RELEVANCE

In a good argument we present statements that are true in order to offer support for some conclusion. One way to mimic arguing without really arguing is to state things that are certainly true, but have no bearing on the truth of the conclusion. Speaking and arguing in this way violates what Grice calls a rule of Relevance. Now we might wonder why irrelevant remarks can have any influence at all. The answer is that we generally assume that a person's remarks are relevant, for this is one of the conditions for smooth and successful conversation. That it is possible to exploit this natural assumption is shown in the following passage from *The Catcher in the Rye*.

> . . . the new elevator boy was sort of on the stupid side. I told him, in this very casual voice, to take me up the Dicksteins' . . .
>
> He had the elevator doors all shut and all, and was all set to take me up, and then he turned around and said, "They ain't in. They're at a party on the fourteenth floor."
>
> "That's all right," I said. "I'm supposed to wait for them. I'm their nephew."
>
> He gave me this sort of stupid, suspicious look. "You better wait in the lobby, fella," he said.
>
> "I'd like to—I really would," I said. "But I have a bad leg. I have to hold it in a certain position. I think I'd better sit down in the chair outside their door."
>
> He didn't know what the hell I was talking about, so all he said was "oh" and took me up. Not bad, boy. It's funny. All you have to do is say something nobody understands and they'll do practically anything you want them to."[7]

It's clear what is going on here. When someone offers something as a reason, it is conversationally implied that there is some connection between it and the thing you are arguing for. In most cases the connection is obvious, and there is no need to spell it out. In other cases the connection is not obvious, but in the spirit of cooperation others are willing to assume that it exists. In the present case, there seems to be no connection between having a bad leg and sitting in one *particular* chair. Why, then, doesn't the elevator operator challenge this statement? Part of the reason is that it is not easy to challenge what people say; among other things, it is not polite. But politeness doesn't seem to hold the elevator operator back; instead, he does not want to appear stupid. The person who offers a reason conversationally implies a connection and we do not like to admit that we fail to see this connection. This combination of generosity and pride leads us to accept all sorts of irrelevant statements as reasons.

The Presidential campaign debates of 1976 also provided some splendid examples of fallacies of irrelevance. Here is one example involving an exchange with Jimmy Carter:

---

[7] J. D. Salinger, *The Catcher in the Rye* (New York: Bantam Book Co., 1964), pp. 157–58.

Question: . . . What should the role of the United States in the world be and in that connection, concerning your limited experience in foreign affairs and the fact that you take some pride in being a Washington outsider, don't you think it would be appropriate to tell the American voters, before the election, the people you would like to have in key positions . . . ?

In response, Carter first indicated that it would be inappropriate to announce his appointments at that time, and then went on to say:

> I've travelled the last twenty-one months among the people of this country. I've talked with them and I've listened. And I've seen it first hand in a very vivid way the deep hurt that's come to this country in the aftermath of Vietnam and Cambodia and Chile and Pakistan and Angola and Watergate, CIA revelations.

Notice that the question itself is not a model of clarity. It falls into three parts: (1) A broad, unfocused question about foreign policy, (2) a reference to Carter's limited experience in foreign affairs, and (3) a direct question about appointments. Carter responds directly to the third item, but he is obviously reacting most strongly to the second aspect of the question because it challenges his qualifications to be President. He speaks of his firsthand knowledge of *the people's concern with* foreign affairs—which is not exactly to the point—and then drifts off into plain irrelevance by referring to Watergate. Hearing this, a visitor from another planet would think that Watergate was a country.

Fallacies of relevance are surprisingly common in everyday life. The best strategy for dealing with them is simply to cross out all irrelevant claims and then see what is left. Sometimes nothing is left. On the other hand, we should not be heavy-handed in making charges of irrelevance. Sometimes the occurrence of irrelevance is innocent; good arguments often contain irrelevant asides. More importantly, relevance is often secured by way of a conversational implication, so we really have to know what is going on in a given context in order to decide whether a remark is relevant or not.

We can illustrate this last point by examining two classical fallacies of irrelevance: the *argument ad hominem* and appeals to authority.

Arguments ad Hominem

Literally, an *argument ad hominem* is an argument directed against the arguer rather than against his argument or against the conclusion of his argument. On the face of it, this seems to involve irrelevance, for the character of the person should have nothing to do with the truth of what he says or the soundness of what he argues. But consider a case in point, as set out on the following page.

A: It is time for the United States to develop more normal relations with Cuba.

B: Yeah, so you can make a bundle importing cigars from those Commies.

B's reply is certainly an ad hominem attack; it is an attack upon the motives of the speaker and not upon what the speaker has said. Yet the remark is not without some relevance—it is not off the wall. In a conversational exchange, we rely on the integrity of the person who is speaking, and when we have reasons to believe that the person's integrity is questionable, we sometimes say so. This is the significance of B's remark. He points to a fact that gives us some reason not to trust A's integrity in a discussion of U.S. relations with Cuba. We will therefore have to draw a distinction between an ad hominem attack and an ad hominem fallacy. In the context of an argument, we sometimes challenge a person's *right* to perform certain speech acts. Sometimes these attacks are justified, sometimes they are not. They must be judged on their own terms. On the other hand, an attack of this kind is sometimes illicitly turned into an attack on the *truth* of what a person says or on the soundness of that person's argument. We then have an instance of

© 1956 by United Feature Syndicate, Inc.

an *ad hominem fallacy*. In general, the truth of a statement or the soundness of an argument does not depend upon who produces them.

This difference is illustrated by the Biblical story of Job. Job is described as a person who "was blameless and upright, one who feared God and turned away from evil." Satan challenges God to allow him to subject Job to the worst calamities to see if Job's faith will remain unchanged. After the most extreme misfortune, Job finally cries out and asks why he should be made to suffer so.

> Then the Lord answered Job out of the whirlwind:
> Who is this that darkens counsel by words without knowledge?
> Gird up your loins like a man.
> I will question you, and you shall declare to me.
> Where were you when I laid the foundations of the earth?
> Tell me, if you have understanding.

God then continues with a long list of matters about which Job is completely ignorant. If we read all this as *an answer* to Job's complaints, then it must seem an ad hominem fallacy, for how can talk about Job's ignorance justify his apparently unmerited suffering? On the other hand, if we interpret God's statements as *an attack* upon Job's right to ask such a question, then they will not be read as answers to it, and no fallacy has been committed. Whether there is a fallacy or not depends on which speech act God performs.

Although there is an important difference between ad hominem attacks and ad hominem fallacies, there is no shortage of the latter. One mark of an ad hominem fallacy is that the personal attack may have nothing to do with the matter at hand. A person's physical appearance, ethnic background, sex, bathing habits, or dress may *sometimes* give us reason to challenge his or her speech acts, but usually they do not. Ad hominem fallacies deal almost exclusively in such matters.

EXERCISE 9

Do the following arguments involve ad hominem fallacies?

(1) Responding to an economist, someone remarks, "If you're so smart, why ain't you rich?"
(2) If members of Congress were eligible for the draft, they would not vote for it.

(3) Rejecting atheism, someone remarks, "There are no atheists in foxholes."

(4) Attacking pro-abortionists, Ronald Reagan said, ". . . I've noticed that everybody that is for abortion has already been born."

Appeals to Authority

Often in the midst of an argument we cite an authority to back up what we say. As we saw in Chapter 2, this is a standard way of offering assurances. In citing an authority, instead of giving reasons for what we say, we indicate that someone (the authority cited) could give them. Although logicians sometimes speak of the *fallacy* of appealing to authorities, we should notice in the first place that there is often nothing wrong with citing authorities or experts to support what we say. An authority is a person or institution with a privileged position concerning certain information. Through training, a doctor is an expert on certain diseases. A person who works in the Department of Agriculture can be an expert on America's soybean production. Someone who grew up in the swamps might be an expert on trapping muskrats. Since some people stand in a better position to know things than others, there is nothing wrong with citing them as authorities. In fact, an appeal to experts and authorities is essential if we are to make up our minds on subjects outside our own range of competence.

At the same time, appeals to authority can be abused, and there are some obvious questions we should ask whenever such an appeal is made. Most obviously, we should always ask *whether the authority cited is, in fact, an authority in the area under discussion.* If an answer to this question is *No,* then we are dealing with a fallacy of *relevance.* For example, being a movie star does not qualify a person to speak on the merits of a particular brand of elbow macaroni. Endorsements by athletes of hair cremes, deodorants, beer, and automobiles are in the same boat. Of course, we have to be careful in making this charge. It is possible that certain athletes make systematic studies of deodorants before giving one deodorant their endorsement. But it is not likely.

Of course, most people realize that athletes, movie stars, and the like are featured in advertisements primarily to attract attention and not because they are experts concerning the products they are promoting. It is more surprising how often non-authorities or the wrong authorities are brought in to judge serious matters. To cite one example, Uri Geller had little difficulty in convincing a group of distinguished British scientists that he possessed psychic powers. In particular, he was able to convince them that he could bend spoons by mental powers alone. In contrast, James Randi, a professional magician, had little difficulty in detecting and unmasking the tricks that bamboozled the scientific observers.[8] The remarkable feature of this case was not that a group of scientists could be fooled by a magician, but rather that these scientists assumed that they had the expertise necessary to decide whether a paranormal phenomenon had taken place or not. After all, the most obvious explanation of Geller's feats was that he had somehow cheated. To test this possibility, what was needed, as it turned out, was not a scientist with impeccable scholarly credentials, but a magician who could do the same tricks himself and therefore knew what to look for.

It is, of course, difficult to decide whether someone is an expert in a field when you yourself are not. There are, however, certain clues that will help you make this decision. If the "expert" spends a great deal of time showing off knowledge that is not relevant to the matter at hand, then you have reason to be suspicious. Furthermore, if the authority claims to have detailed knowledge of things that he or she could not possibly know—for example, about what was said in private conversations that he or she did not hear or, even more strikingly, about the thoughts that were taking place in other people's minds, then you have very little reason to trust whatever else that person has to say. You know, for example, that he or she has no qualms about making things up, that is, about lying. Finally it is often possible to spot-check certain claims in order to make sure that they are correct. It may take one expert to tell another, but it often takes very little more than good common sense and an unwillingness to be fooled to detect a fraud.

Even in those cases where it is clear that the person cited is an expert in the field, we can still ask *whether the question is of the kind that can be settled by an appeal to experts.* It is important to raise this question, because authorities often *disagree,* and since they disagree, some of them must be wrong. In fact, sometimes the very best experts simply get things wrong. For example, in 1932 Albert Einstein, who was surely an expert in the field, declared that "there is not the slightest indication that [nuclear] energy will ever be obtainable. It would mean that the atom would have to be shattered at will." Just a year later, the atom was, in fact, split. Even so, a leading British physicist, Lord Ernest Rutherford, insisted that the splitting of the atom would not lead to the development of nuclear power, saying, "The energy produced by the atom is a very poor kind of thing. Anyone who expects a source of power from the

---

[8] For an entertaining and instructive account of this case, see James Randi's *The Magic of Uri Geller* (New York: Ballantine Books, 1975).

transformation of these atoms is talking moonshine."[9] Given the knowledge available at the time, both Einstein and Rutherford may have been justified in their claims, but their assertions were, after all, more speculations than scientifically justified statements of fact. The lesson to be learned from this is that the very best experts are often fallible, and become more fallible when they go beyond established facts in their discipline to speculate about the future.

Although this may seem obvious, we often forget to ask *whether the authority has been cited correctly*. When a person cites an authority, he or she is making a factual claim that so-and-so holds some particular view. Sometimes the claim is false. Here is an example:

> According to medical authorities, poison ivy is contagious when it is oozing.

This is false, for according to medical authorities, poison ivy is never contagious. Yet many people hold that it is contagious, and they think that they have medical opinion on their side. It is hard to deal with people who cite authorities incorrectly, for we do not carry an almanac or encyclopedia around with us. Yet it is a good idea to spot-check appeals to authority, for, short of lying, people often twist authorities to their own opinions.

It is also worth asking *whether the authority cited can be trusted to tell the truth*. To put this more bluntly, we should ask ourselves whether a particular authority has any good reason to lie or misrepresent facts. Presumably, the officials who know most about Russian food production will be the heads of the various agricultural bureaus. But it would be utterly naive to take their reports at face value. Failures in agricultural production have been a standing embarrassment of the Russian economy, and, as a consequence, there is pressure at every level to put a good face on things. Even if the state officials were inclined to tell the truth, which is a charitable assumption, the information they receive is probably not very accurate.

Experts also lie because it can bring fame and professional advancement. Science, sometimes at the very highest level, has been embarrassed by problems of the falsification and misrepresentation of data. Consider the case of Sir Cyril Burt. Burt's research concerned the inheritance of intelligence. More specifically, he wanted to show that there

---

[9]Both quotations are cited in *The Experts Speak* by Christopher Cerf and Victor Navasky (New York: Panthonn Books, 1984), page 215. This work contains a marvelous collection of false and sometimes just plain stupid things that have been claimed by experts. One notable example is the remark made by the Union General John B. Sedgwick just before being fatally shot in the head by a Confederate marksman: "They couldn't hit an elephant at this dist—" (cited on page 135).

is a significant correlation between the IQs of parents and their children. The difficulty was to find a way to screen out other influences, for example, that of home environment. To overcome this, Burt undertook a systematic study of identical twins who had been separated at birth and raised in different social settings. His study revealed a very high correlation between the IQs of these twins and that gave strong reason to believe that IQ, to some significant extent, depends on heredity rather than environment. Unfortunately, Burt's data, or at least a significantly large portion of it, were cooked—that is, made up.

It is interesting that Burt's bogus research could go unchallenged for so long. It is also interesting how he was finally unmasked. First of all, his results seemed to many to be too good to be true. He claimed to have found more than fifty identical twins who had been separated at birth and raised in contrasting environments. Given the rarity of such creatures, that's a very large number to have found. Secondly, the correlations he claimed to find were extremely high, indeed, much higher than usually found in research in this area. Both of these facts raised suspicions. Stephen Jay Gould describes Burt's final undoing as follows:

> Princeton psychologist Leon Kamin first noted that, while Burt had increased his sample of twins from fewer than twenty to more than fifty in a series of publications, the average correlation between pairs for IQ remained unchanged to the third decimal place—a statistical situation so unlikely that it matches our vernacular definition of impossible. Then, in 1976, Oliver Gillie, medical correspondent of the London *Sunday Times*, elevated the charge from inexcusable carelessness to conscious fakery. Gillie discovered among many other things, that Burt's two "collaborators" . . . the women who supposedly collected and processeed his data, either never existed at all, or at least could not have been in contact with Burt while he wrote the papers bearing their names.[10]

Outright fraud of this kind, especially by someone so highly placed, is, admittedly, uncommon. Yet it does occur, and provides a good reason for being suspicious of authorities, especially when their results have not been given independent confirmation.

One last question we can ask is *why the appeal to authority is being made at all*. To cite an authority is to give assurances and, as we noticed earlier, we usually give assurances to strengthen the weak points in our arguments. It is surprising how often we can see what is wrong with an argument just by noticing where it is backed by appeals to authority. Beyond this, we should be suspicious of arguments that rely on too many

---

[10] Stephen Jay Gould, *The Mismeasure of Man*, (New York: W. W. Norton, 1981), p. 234.

authorities. (We might call this the fallacy of excessive footnotes.) Good arguments tend to stand on their own.

To go back to the beginning, in our complicated and specialized world, reliance on experts and authorities is unavoidable. Yet we can still be critical of appeals to authority by asking these questions:

(1) Is the authority cited in fact an authority in the areas under discussion?
(2) Is this the kind of question that can be settled by expert opinion?
(3) Has the authority been cited correctly?
(4) Can the authority cited be trusted to tell the truth?
(5) Why is an appeal to authority being made at all?

FALLACIES OF VACUITY

Circular Reasoning and Begging the Question

One purpose of arguments is to establish the truth of a claim to someone who doubts it. In a typical situation, A makes a claim, B raises objections to it, then A tries to find additional reasons justifying his or her original statement.

Schematically:

A asserts that p is true.

B raises objections x, y, and z against it.

A then offers additional reasons in order to overcome these objections.

To start with the simplest case, A cannot meet B's challenge simply by *repeating* his or her original assertion. If someone is maintaining that arms races inevitably lead to war, it will not help to offer as a justification for the claim that arms races inevitably lead to war. Here the person would be putting forth as a premise the very point at issue. This is called *circular reasoning*. The argument would look like this:

Arms races inevitably lead to war.

∴ Arms races inevitably lead to war.

The argument is, of course, *valid*, since the premise cannot be true without the conclusion being true as well. If the premise is true, then the argument is *sound* as well. All the same, the argument has no force because any objection to the conclusion is straight off an objection to the premise cited in its behalf.

In fact, people do not usually commit the fallacy of circular reasoning in such a transparent way. Instead of using the conclusion of the argument as a premise in its behalf, they simply use as a premise the conclusion restated in different words. This would happen, for example, if someone argued that abortion is wrong because it is wrong to intentionally kill a human fetus by terminating a pregnancy before it reaches full term. Here the reason simply restates the conclusion in different words because abortion just is the intentional killing of a human fetus through the termination of a pregnancy before its full term.

Closely related to the fallacy of circular reasoning is the subtle fallacy called *begging the question*. In circular reasoning, the conclusion itself or a restatement of the conclusion in different words is used as a premise in the argument. In begging the question, a statement is made that presupposes or depends upon the point at issue. The following argument involves this fallacy.

> It's always wrong to murder human beings.
> Capital punishment involves murdering human beings.
>
> ∴ Capital punishment is wrong.

Here the first premise is definitionally true, since calling something murder implies that it is a *wrongful* killing. The second premise is, however, *question begging*, for in calling capital punishment murder, the point at issue has been assumed, that is, that capital punishment is something wrong.

More subtle than this, opponents of abortion typically refer to the *human fetus* as an *unborn baby* or simply as a *baby*. It may seem a matter of indifference how the fetus is referred to, but this is not true. One of the central points in the debate over abortion is whether the fetus has the status of a person and thus has the rights that a person has. It is generally acknowledged in our society that babies are persons and therefore have the rights of persons. By referring to the fetus as an unborn baby (or simply as a baby), a point that demands argument is taken for granted without argument, and that counts as begging the question.[11] Similarly, if someone argues the pro-choice position simply on the grounds that a woman has a right to control the destiny of her

---

[11] Of course, many opponents of abortion *do* argue for the claim that a human fetus has the moral status of a person and thus do not beg this central question in the debate.

own body, this also begs an important question, because it takes for granted the claim that the fetus is part of a woman's body and not an independent being with rights of its own.[12]

EXERCISE 10

Explain why each of the following arguments involves either circular reasoning or begging the question.

(1) Capitalism is the only correct economic system because without it, free enterprise is impossible.

(2) Gun control laws are wrong because they violate the citizen's right to bear arms.

(3) Intoxicating beverages should be banned because they can make people drunk.

(4) The Bible is the inerrant word of God, because God speaks only the truth, and because repeatedly in the Bible God tells us that the Bible consists of His words.

(5) We have to accept change, because without change there is no progress.

(6) Premarital sex is wrong because premarital sex is fornication, and fornication is a sin.

(7) The drinking age should be lowered to eighteen because eighteen-year-olds are mature enough to drink.

(8) College athletes should be paid to play sports because they are professionals anyway.

Self-Sealers and Vacuity

It is characteristic of certain positions that no evidence can *possibly* refute them. This may seem like a wonderful feature for a position to have. In fact, however, it *usually* makes the position useless. We can start with a silly example. A Perfect Sage claims to be able to predict the future in detail. The Perfect Sage's predictions take the following form:

---

[12] Many defenders of the pro-choice position avoid this fallacy by arguing *explicitly* that the fetus does not have the status of a person or that the rights of the bearer of the fetus override those of the fetus.

Two weeks from today at 4:37 you are going to be doing . . .
exactly what you will be doing.

This prediction cannot possibly be wrong, but, of course, it doesn't tell us anything in particular about the future. Whatever happens, the prediction is going to be true, and this is just what is wrong with it. The prediction is *empty* or *vacuous*.

People do not, of course, go around making predictions of the kind just noticed, but, strange to say, they sometimes hold positions that are empty or vacuous in just the same way. A clairvoyant claims to be able to predict the future, but every time a prediction fails, he says that this just proves that someone set up bad vibrations that interfered with his visions. If the prediction comes true, that shows his clairvoyance; if it does not come true, that proves interference. No matter what happens, then, the clairvoyant cannot be wrong. So his predictions are as empty and vacuous as those of the Perfect Sage.

Positions that are set up in this way so that nothing can possibly refute them we will call *self-sealers*.[13] A self-sealing position is one that is so constructed that no criticism can possibly be brought against it. This shows its vacuity, and it is precisely for this reason that we reject it.

People do not usually hold self-sealing positions in a blatant way—they tend to back into them. A person who holds that the American economy is controlled by an international Jewish conspiracy will point out people of Jewish extraction (or with Jewish names) who occupy important positions in financial institutions. This at least counts as evidence, though not very strong evidence. There are a great many people in these institutions who are not Jews. To counter this claim, the person now argues that many of these other people are secretly Jews or are tools of the Jewish conspiracy. The Jews have allowed some non-Jews to hold important positions in order to conceal their conspiracy. What evidence is there for this? Well, really none, but that only helps to prove how clever the conspiracy is. The position has now become self-sealing, for all evidence cited *against* the existence of the conspiracy will be converted into evidence *for* its cleverness. Unlike our previous examples, which were artificial, reasoning of this kind actually does take place.

Self-sealing arguments are hard to deal with, for people who use them will often shift their ground. A person will begin by holding a significant position that implies that facts are one way rather than another, but under the pressure of criticism he will self-seal it so that no evidence can possibly count against it. That is, he will slide back and forth between two positions—one that is not self-sealed, and so is sig-

---

[13] I owe this phrase to Ted Honderich. I now know that he owes it, directly or indirectly, to Leon Lipson.

nificant, but subject to criticism, and another that is self-sealed, and so is not subject to criticism, but insignificant. The charge that is leveled against a theory that vacillates in this way is that it is either *vacuous* or *false:* vacuous if self-sealing, false if not.

One way of challenging a self-sealing position is to ask what possible fact could prove it wrong. This is a good question to ask, but it can be misunderstood and met with the triumphant reply: "Nothing can prove my position wrong, because it is true." A better way to show the insignificance of a self-sealing theory is to put the question in a different form: If your position has any significance, it should tell us that certain things will occur whereas certain other things will not occur. If it cannot do this, it really tells us nothing at all; so please make some specific predictions and we will see how they come out.

Ideologies and world views tend to be self-sealing. The Marxist ideology has this quality. If a revolution occurs, then this was predicted by one part of the theory; if it does not occur, then that too was predicted by another part of the theory. The position also has another quite special twist. If you fail to see the truth of the Marxist ideology, that just shows that your social consciousness has not been raised. The very fact that you reject the Marxist ideology shows that you are not yet capable of understanding it and that you are in need of re-education. This is perfect self-sealing. Sometimes psychoanalytic theory gets involved in this same kind of self-sealing. People who vigorously disagree with certain psychoanalytic claims can be accused of repressing these facts. If a boy *denies* that he wants to murder his father and sleep with his mother, this itself is taken as evidence of the strength of these desires and of his unwillingness to acknowledge them. If this kind of reasoning gets out of hand, then psychoanalytic theory also becomes self-sealing and empty. Freud was aware of this danger; this was the basis of his remark that sometimes a cigar is just a cigar.

So far, we have seen two ways in which an argument can be self-sealing: (1) it can invent an *ad hoc* or arbitrary way of dismissing every possible criticism. The clairvoyant and the astrologer can always point to interfering conditions without going to the trouble of saying what they are. The anti-Semite can always cite Jewish cleverness to explain away counter-evidence. (2) A theory can counter criticism by attacking its critics. The critic of Marxism is charged with having a decadent bourgeois consciousness which blinds him to the facts of class conflict. The critic's response to psychoanalytic theory is analyzed (and then dismissed) as repression, a reaction formation, or something or other.

Yet another form of self-sealing is this: Words are used in such a way that a position becomes true *by definition.* For example, a person makes the strong claim that all human actions are selfish. This is an interesting remark, but it seems to be false, for it is easy to think of cases where people have acted in self-sacrificing ways. To counter these obvious objections, the argument takes the following turn: When a person acts in a self-sacrificing way, what he *wants* to do is help another, even at his own expense. This is his desire or his motive, and that is what he acts to fulfill. So the action is selfish after all. It should be obvious that this is a self-sealing move, for it will not help to cite any behavior—even self-destructive behavior—as counter-evidence. If a person desires to harm himself, then he acts to fulfill his desire and the act is again selfish.

It is not hard to see what has happened in this case. The arguer has chosen to use the word "selfish" in a new and peculiar way: a person is said to act selfishly if he acts to do what he desires to do. This is not what we usually mean by this word. We say that a person acts selfishly if he is too much concerned with his own interests at the expense of the interests of others. On this standard use of the word "selfish" there are any number of counter-examples to the claim that all human actions are selfish. But these counter-examples do not apply when the word "selfish" is used in a new way, where "acting selfishly" comes close to meaning just "acting." The point is that under this new meaning of "selfish" it becomes empty (or almost empty) to say that all human actions are selfish. We are thus back to a familiar situation: Under one interpretation (the ordinary interpretation), the claim that all human actions are selfish is interesting, and false. Under another interpretation (an extraordinary interpretation), the claim is true but uninteresting. The position gets all its *apparent* interest and plausibility from a rapid two-step back and forth between these positions.

Self-sealing arguments are not easy to handle, for they change their form under pressure. The best strategy is to begin by charging a person who uses such an argument with saying something trivial, vacuous, or boring. If, to meet this charge, he or she says something quite specific and important, then argument can proceed along normal lines. But it is not always easy to get down to brass tacks in this way. This becomes clear if you examine an argument between a Marxist and a non-Marxist, or between individuals with different religious views. Their positions are sealed against objections from each other, and the arguments are almost always at cross purposes.

DISCUSSION QUESTIONS

(1) During the nineteenth century, evidence mounted that apparently showed that the earth has existed for millions, perhaps hundreds of millions, of years. This seemed to contradict the account given in Genesis that holds that the earth was created less than 10,000 years ago. In response to

this challenge, Philip Henry Gosse replied roughly as follows: In creating Adam and Eve, God would endow them
with a navel, and thus it would seem that they had been
born in the normal way and thus also seem that they had existed for a number of years before they were created by
God. Beyond this, their hair, fingernails, bones, and so on
would all show evidence of growth, again giving evidence of
previous existence. The same would be true of the trees that
surrounded them in the Garden of Eden which would have
rings. Furthermore, the sediment in rivers would suggest
that they had flowed for many years in the past. In sum, although the earth was created fairly recently, God would
have created it in a way that would make it appear that it
had existed for many years, perhaps millions of years, in the
past. Thus the actual creation of the earth less than 10,000
years ago is compatible with scientific evidence that suggests
that it is much older than this. Evaluate this line of reasoning.

(2) Defenders of extrasensory perception or ESP sometimes argue in the following way: In order to exhibit their powers,
many psychics must operate in a friendly and supportive atmosphere. When people are critical or suspicious, psychics
sense this, and these "bad vibrations" prevent them from
performing effectively. This is shown by the fact that many
psychics find it difficult to perform under sterile laboratory
conditions. Evaluate this argument.

(3) To what extent, *if at all*, does the following essay involve an
ad hominem fallacy?

Protesters Are "Ugly, Stupid" *

JEFFREY HART

It's an interesting question. Why do so many political protesters tend to be, to
put it mildly, physically ugly?

South Africa has been this spring's protest issue on the college campus.
At Princeton, 800 students demanded that the university withdraw its money
from corporations doing business there. A similar number turned out at Harvard, a much smaller number at Dartmouth, etc.

---

*King Features.

For now, I want to set aside the substance, pro or con, of the investment in South Africa issue.

But it is simply a visual fact that the students and non-students marching in these picket lines with hand-lettered placards are mostly quite unattractive human beings.

First of all, the most casual glance indicates that most of them were not very well endowed by nature to begin with. They are either too fat or too thin, they tend to be strangely proportioned. Often, various features are somehow . . . wrong. They do not stride forth as if they had a valid claim on existence. They shuffle. Some move as if one leg were a couple of inches shorter than the other.

But if nature failed to give most of these people much to work with, they themselves have certainly not improved matters much. Ill-fitting blue jeans seem to be the uniform. Sloppy shirts. Hair looks unkempt, unwashed. They wear a variety of stupid looking shoes. Yuck.

But why is this?

Surely it is not logically excluded that a handsome or beautiful individual might oppose apartheid, hate it, want to do something about it. Why, then, are most of these protesters so . . . unacceptable?

It is possible, at least I here advance the theory, that the real protest of these people shuffling around has nothing much to do with South Africa. Perhaps they are really protesting against what they see when they look in the mirror. Perhaps this is a kind of cosmic protest against the way things, the way they, actually are. Comes the revolution—and, boy, it would take some revolution—they will be attractive human beings.

Their ugliness seems an act of will. Perhaps they think it symbolizes proletarian status, the great unwashed. But, of course, the actual proletariat does not consider itself ugly. The American worker has a collection of Linda Ronstadt records, a motorboat, and a Volvo.

Of course the South Africa protest marchers, most of them, implicitly desire a "socialist" solution there.

Another alternative has not occurred to them. Suppose foreign capital poured into that resource-rich region. Might it not overwhelm the musty 19th Century apartheid system with the economic pressures of modernity, make black workers much too valuable to mistreat? That, at least, is one possibility.

But it has not occurred to these dim types, shuffling along with their tired slogans. They are not only ugly, they are stupid.

5

Other Uses of Arguments

In earlier chapters we have spoken about arguments as if their only function were to prove something or to justify some claim. This chapter will attempt to correct this one-sided view by exploring uses of argument other than justification. Sometimes the primary intention of an argument is not to establish some truth, but to criticize or refute an argument. The patterns of successful *refutations* mirror the criteria for a sound and significant argument, for the point of a refutory argument is to show that one of these criteria has not been met. Another very important use of arguments is to formulate *explanations*. In seeking an explanation, we are not trying to prove that something is true; we are trying to understand why it is true. One way of making sense out of a perplexing fact is to show how it can be derived from understood principles.

REFUTATIONS

To refute an argument is to show that it is no good. Given the nature of the argument, this can be done in two main ways: (1) we can show that the conclusion does not follow from the premises, and (2) we can challenge the truth of at least one of the premises. In the previous chapter we examined a number of ways we can attack an argument in the first way—that is, by claiming that it involves a *fallacy*. Here we can examine some ways that we can challenge the truth of the premises themselves.

Consider the following example. For centuries many people have believed in astrology. They have believed, that is, that their lives are determined to some significant extent by the configuration of the stars at the time of their birth. As evidence for this, astrologers often point out successful predictions that they have made in the past. A beautiful rebuttal to this argument is found in St. Augustine's *Confessions*. St. Augustine was captivated by astrology until his conversion to Christianity. He then abandoned it, he says, for the following reason:

> I turned my attention to the case of twins, who are generally born within a short time of each other. Whatever significance in the natural order the astrologers may attribute to this interval of time, it is

too short to be appreciated by human observation and no allowance can be made for it in the charts which an astrologer has to consult in order to cast a true horoscope. His predictions, then, will not be true, because he would have consulted the same charts for both Esau and Jacob and would have made the same predictions for each of them, whereas it is a fact that the same things did not happen to them both. Therefore, either he would have been wrong in his predictions or, if his forecast was correct, he would not have predicted the same future for each. And yet he would have consulted the same chart in each case. This proves that if he had foretold the truth, it would have been by luck, not by skill.[1]

It may take a few moments to see the full force of this simple argument, but consider what replies astrologers might make. They could argue that the small difference in time between the births does make a difference, but since past horoscopes have not been cast on this basis, they must all be incorrect and their success simply luck. On the other side, if these past horoscopes were correct in ignoring the small time differences, then astrology fails to explain why twins often lead such different lives.

One way for astrologers to avoid St. Augustine's argument would be to make their claim more modest. Instead of saying that our entire lives are *determined* by the configuration of the heavens at our birth, they could hedge their position by saying that this configuration has an important *influence* on our lives. This move takes some of the excitement out of astrology, for in admitting to *other* influences on our lives, the astrologer can no longer make detailed predictions without having knowledge of the natural and social sciences. But the advantage of this hedging move is that it will allow the astrologer to explain away a great many mistaken predictions. Whenever a particular prediction fails, the astrologer can always say that some other influence interfered with the influence of the stars. If the astrologer is willing to make this move no matter how many predictions come out wrong, then the position is *self-sealing* and so empty of content. So astrologers who wish to maintain that the stars have any influence at all on our lives must produce positive statistical evidence to support their claim. The status of such statistical evidence is examined in a recent textbook on astronomy:

> From time to time astrologers have presented statistical "proofs" of astrology, but without exception when they are checked over by competent mathematicians they are found to be baseless.[2]

---

[1] St. Augustine, *Confessions*, R. S. Pine-Coffin, trans. (Harmondsworth, England: Penguin Books, 1961), p. 142.
[2] George O. Abell, *Exploration of the Universe*, 3rd ed. (New York: Holt, Rinehart and Winston, 1975), p. 33.

© 1956 by United Feature Syndicate, Inc.

Counter-Examples

The central move in St. Augustine's attack upon astrologers' defense of their profession is to challenge the key premise of their argument. In particular, he produces what is called a *counter-example* to the claim that the positions of the stars at the time of birth determine the kind of life a person will lead thereafter. By citing the very different lives that twins have led (as well as the very different lives that people born at precisely the same time have led), he offers a counter-example to this claimed connection.

Counter-examples are typically aimed at universal claims. This is true because a *single* contrary instance will show that a universal claim is false. If someone claims that *all* snakes lay eggs, then pointing out that the Black Snake bears its young alive is sufficient to refute this claim. If the person retreats to the somewhat weaker claim that *most* snakes lay eggs, it becomes much harder to refute his claim. A single example of a snake that bears its young alive is not enough; to refute this claim we would have to show that a majority of snakes do not lay eggs. Here, instead of trying to refute his statement, we may ask him to produce his *argument* in behalf of it. We can then attack this argument. Finally, if the person retreats to the very weak claim that at least some snakes lay eggs, then his statement becomes very difficult to refute. Even if it were false (which it is not), to show this we would have to check every fool snake and establish that it does not lay eggs. So, as a rough-and-ready rule, we can say that the stronger a statement is, the more subject it is to refutation; the weaker it is, the less subject it is to refutation.

Citing the fact that black snakes bear their young alive in order to refute the claim that all snakes lay eggs is called presenting a *counter-example*. The pattern of reasoning is perfectly simple: If someone claims that *everything* of a certain kind has a certain feature, we need find only *one* thing of that kind lacking that feature in order to refute the claim. Although the pattern of argument is simple in form, it is not always easy to think of counter-examples. Some people are much better at it than others. Socrates was a genius in this respect. He wandered through the streets of ancient Athens questioning various people—often important political figures—challenging them to explain what they meant by various terms such as *justice, knowledge, courage, friendship,* and *piety.* As narrated by Plato, these exchanges all fall into a standard pattern: Socrates asks for a definition of some important notion; after some skirmishing, a definition is offered; Socrates immediately finds a counter-example to this definition; the definition is then changed or replaced by another; once more Socrates produces a counter-example; and so on. With effortless ease, Socrates seemed able to produce counter-examples to any definition or any principle that others offered. There is no better introduction to the art of giving counter-examples than some specimens of the Socratic method.

In *The Republic,* Socrates is inquiring into the nature of justice. He begins by interrogating Cephalus, an old and distinguished Greek citizen. Cephalus, in discussing the value of wealth, suggests that justice consists in telling the truth and restoring things we have been entrusted with. The dialogue goes as follows:

> *Cephalus:* Now in this, as I believe, lies the chief value of wealth, not for everyone, perhaps, but for the right-thinking man. It can do much to save us from going to that other world in fear of having cheated or deceived anyone even unintentionally or of being in debt to some god for sacrifice or to some man for money. Wealth has many other uses, of course; but, taking one with another, I should regard this as the best use that can be made of it by a man of sense.

> *Socrates:* You put your case admirably, Cephalus. . . . But take this matter of doing right: can we say that it really consists in nothing more nor less than telling the truth and paying back anything we

may have received? Are not these very actions sometimes right and sometimes wrong? Suppose, for example, a friend who had lent us a weapon were to go mad and then ask for it back, surely anyone would say we ought not to return it. It would not be "right" to do so; nor yet to tell the truth without reserve to a madman.

Cephalus: No, it would not.

Socrates: Right conduct, then, cannot be defined as telling the truth and restoring anything we have been trusted with.[3]

Whereas many of Plato's *Dialogues* show Socrates making fools—and also enemies—of people who claim to know things that they do not know, other dialogues have a different quality. They show Socrates and his interlocutors involved in a cooperative activity searching after philosophical understanding. The *Theaetetus* is a dialogue of this kind. Theaetetus was a brilliant young man, gifted in mathematics. In the dialogue he and Socrates try (unsuccessfully) to arrive at a correct definition of *knowledge.* They notice an important difference between knowledge and mere belief: It is possible for someone to *believe* something that is false, but it is not possible for someone to *know* something that is false. This leads Theaetetus to suggest a simple definition of knowledge: Knowledge equals true belief. After all, someone cannot have a true belief concerning something that is false. This proposed definition is refuted in the following exchange.

Socrates: [There is] a whole profession to prove that true belief is not knowledge.

Theaetetus: How so? What profession?

Socrates: The profession of those paragons of intellect known as orators and lawyers. There you have men who use their skill to produce conviction, not by instruction, but by making people believe whatever they want them to believe. You can hardly imagine teachers so clever as to be able, in the short time allowed by the clock, to instruct their hearers thoroughly in the true facts of a case of robbery or other violence which those hearers had not witnessed.

Theaetetus: No, I cannot imagine that; but they can convince them.

Socrates: And by convincing you mean making them believe something.

Theaetetus: Of course.

---

[3] *The Republic of Plato,* Francis M. Cornford, trans. (New York: Oxford University Press, 1941), p. 7.

Socrates: And when a jury is rightly convinced of facts which can be known only by an eye-witness, then, judging by hearsay and accept a true belief, they are judging without knowledge, although, if they find the right verdict, their conviction is correct?

Theaetetus: Certainly.

Socrates: But if true belief and knowledge were the same thing, the best of jurymen could never have a correct belief without knowledge. It now appears that they must be different things.[4]

One thing to notice about both of these counter-examples is that they are *completely decisive.* Cephalus does not stand by his position and argue that it would be right to return the sword to his demented friend, nor does Theaetetus dig in his heels and insist that the ignorant members of the jury do know that the person is innocent provided only that they believe it and it is true. Faced with the counter-examples, they both retreat at once. Why is this? Why not stay with the definition and reject the counter-examples as false? The answer is that for many concepts there is general agreement about their application to particular cases, even if there is no general agreement about a correct definition. To take an extreme example, everyone agrees that Hitler was a dictator (even Hitler), and no one supposes that Thomas Jefferson was a dictator (even his enemies). So any definition of *a dictator* that would lead us to say that Hitler was not a dictator and Thomas Jefferson was a dictator must be wrong. A less extreme example is the notion of negligence—an idea important in the law. We have some perfectly clear cases of negligence: a person amusing himself by setting off skyrockets in the Sistine Chapel, for example. On the other hand, a person who deliberately drives off a road to avoid striking a child is clearly *not* acting negligently. In between these clear cases there are any number of difficult ones that help give lawyers a living. Because of these borderline cases, no perfectly exact definition of negligence is possible. But any definition of negligence that does not square with the clear cases is just plain wrong, and this can be shown by citing one of these clear cases as a counter-example.

Ethics is an area where arguments often turn upon counter-examples. Although various forms of relativity remain fashionable, in our day-to-day life there is a surprisingly wide range of agreement concerning what actions are right and what actions are wrong. That is, whatever theory we might hold, we usually agree about particular cases. We tend not to notice this agreement because disagreement is interesting and exciting, whereas agreement is not. The task of an ethical theory is

---

[4] Plato, *Theaetetus,* Francis M. Cornford, trans., in his *Plato's Theory of Knowledge* (New York: Liberal Arts Press, 1957), p. 141.

to discover those principles which tell us what actions are right and what actions are wrong. One important test of an ethical theory is whether it squares with these clear cases where agreement exists.

Consider the Utilitarian Principle. According to that principle, an action is right if it is the action that will produce the greatest possible total happiness. Admittedly, the idea of happiness is vague and stands in need of explanation. For this discussion, however, we can ignore this complication. At first sight, this principle has much to recommend it. How, we might ask, could it ever be better to act in a way that produces less happiness than would be produced by acting in another way? Furthermore, the world would be a much better place if people uniformly followed this principle. All the same, the Utilitarian Principle is subject to a counter-example that has led most—though not all—philosophers to reject it as the *single* basic principle of ethics. One version of this counter-example goes as follows: It is certainly possible for a society to exist where a small slave population leading a wretched life allows the rest of the population to lead a blissfully happy life. In such a society, any other arrangement would, in fact, lower the total happiness. For example, any attempt to improve the lives of the slaves would be over-balanced by a loss of happiness in the slave-holding class. This may seem like a far-fetched situation, but if it were to occur, the utilitarian would have to approve of this society and argue against any changes in it. To most people this is unacceptable, for it offends our sense of fairness. "Why," we want to ask, "should one segment of society be assigned wretched lives so that others can be happy? How can the society be morally sound when human rights are infringed on in this way?" Considerations of this kind have led *most* philosophers to abandon strict utilitarianism as the single principle of morality. Some philosophers have modified the principle to meet objections; some have supplemented it with other principles; some have simply rejected it in favor of another theory.

Sometimes counter-examples force clarification. Consider the traditional moral precept, "Do unto others as you would have them do unto you." Like utilitarianism, this principle captures an important moral insight, but, if taken quite literally, it is even more subject to counter-examples. Jones, a sado-masochist, enjoys beating other people. When asked whether he would like to be treated in that way, he replies, "Yes." It is obvious that the Golden Rule was not intended to approve of Jones's behavior. The task, then, is to reformulate its principle to avoid this counter-example.

No discussion of counter-examples is complete without a mention of the Morgenbesser Retort. Though the exact story is now shrouded in the mists of time, it has come down to us from the 1950s in the following form. In a lecture, a British philosopher remarked that he knew of many languages where a double negative means an affirmative, but not one language where a double affirmative means a negative. From the back of the room came Morgenbesser's famous retort: "Yeah, Yeah."

EXERCISE 1

Find a counter-example to each of the following claims.

Examples: *Claim:* Three points determine a plane.
Counter-example: Three points on a line do not determine a plane.

Claim: "Sugar" is the only word in which an *s* is pronounced *sh*.
Counter-example: Oh *sure.*

(1) What you don't know can't hurt you.
(2) You can never get enough of a good thing.
(3) You shouldn't ask someone to do something that you are not willing to do yourself.
(4) It is always wrong to tell a lie.
(5) You can't be too careful.
(6) It's all right to treat someone in a given way provided that you do not mind being treated that way yourself.

These two cases are more difficult:

♦ (7) If it is wrong for one person to do something, then it must be wrong for everyone to do it.
♦ (8) Wherever you use the world *nearly,* you could use the word *almost* instead, without affecting that truth or the good sense of what you have said.

EXPLANATIONS

Explanations answer questions about *how* or *why* something happened. We explain how a mongoose got out of his cage by pointing to a hole he dug under the fence. We explain why Smith was acquitted by saying that he got off on a technicality. The purpose of explanations is to make sense out of things. Sometimes simply filling in the details of a story provides an explanation. For example, we can explain how a two-year-old girl foiled a bank robbery by saying that the robber tripped over her while fleeing from the bank. Here we have made sense out of an unusual event by putting it in the context of a plausible *narrative*. It is unusual for a two-year-old girl to foil a bank robbery, but there is nothing unusual about a person tripping over a child when running recklessly at full speed.

Very many of our explanations in everyday life have this narrative form. One standard puzzle specifically calls for this kind of explanation. We are told, for example, of a person who, when alone, always rides an elevator to the eighteenth floor, gets off, and then walks up the remaining five floors to her apartment. We want to know why she behaves in this way. Various lame suggestions are made: she likes to visit people on her way home; she's taking exercise; and so on. None of these explanations makes sense because none accounts for the *invariability* of her behavior. Surely she isn't visiting friends when she comes home at five in the morning, nor is this a reasonable time for taking exercise. Her behavior is completely explained, however, when we are told a single fact: that she is quite short and can reach only up to the button for the eighteenth floor. When she is alone, that is as far as she can take the elevator.

Although the narrative is probably the most common form of explanation in everyday life, we also use *arguments* for giving explanations. We can explain a certain event by deriving it from established principles and accepted facts. This derivation has the form of an argument. Although explanations of this kind do occur in daily life, the clearest examples come from science. A scientist can explain the movements of a complex mechanism by deriving them from the laws of mechanics. A psychologist can explain a person's apparently strange behavior by citing laws governing the unconscious mind. Broadly speaking, the pattern of explanation will employ an argument of the following form.

> Accepted principles or laws.
> A statement of initial conditions.
> ───────────────────────────────
> ∴ A statement of the phenomenon to be explained.

By "initial conditions" we mean those facts in the context which, together with the accepted principles and laws, allow us to derive the result that the event to be explained will occur.

This sounds very abstract, which it is, but one extended example should clarify these ideas. Suppose we put an ice cube into a glass and then fill the glass to the very brim. It will look something like this:

What will happen when the ice cube melts? Will the water overflow? Will it remain at the same level? Will it actually go down? Here we are asking for a *prediction* and it will, of course, make sense to ask a person to *justify* whatever prediction he or she makes.

Stumped by this question, we let the ice cube melt to see what happens. In fact, the water level remains unchanged. We are no longer faced with a problem of prediction, for we can now see what happened: When ice cubes melt (or, anyway, when *this* ice cube melted), the water level stays the same (or, at least, it stayed the same in *this* case). After a few experiments we convince ourselves that this result always occurs. We now have a new question: *Why* does this occur? In short, we want an explanation of this phenomenon. The explanation turns upon the law of buoyancy:

> An object is buoyed up by a force equal to the weight of the water it displaces.

So if we put an object in water, it will continue to sink until it displaces a volume of water whose weight is equal to its own weight. (An object heavier than water will continue to sink, but it will feel lighter under water.) With all this in mind, go back to the original problem. In the following diagram, the shaded area indicates the volume of water displaced by the ice cube.

We know from the law of buoyancy that the weight of the ice cube will be equal to the weight of the volume of water it displaces. But an ice cube is itself simply water in a solid state. It is a quantity of water equal to the quantity of water it displaces. More simply, when it melts, it will exactly fill in the volume of water it displaced, so the water level will remain unchanged.

We can now see how this explanation conforms to the argumentative pattern mentioned above:

	Accepted principles or laws.	(Primarily the law of buoyancy.)
	Initial conditions.	(An ice cube floating in a glass of water filled to the brim.)
∴	Phenomenon to be explained.	(The level of the water remaining unchanged after the ice cube melts.)

There are some things to notice about this explanation. First of all, it is a pretty good explanation. People with only a slight understanding of science can follow it and see why the water level remains unchanged. We should also notice that it is not a *complete* explanation, for certain things are simply taken for granted—for example, that things do not change weight when they pass from a solid to a liquid state. To put the explanation into perfect argumentative form, this assumption and many others would have to be stated explicitly. This is never done in everyday life, and is only rarely done in the most exact sciences.

Here is an example of an explanation that is less technical. Houses in Indonesia sometimes have their electrical outlets in the middle of the wall rather than at floor level. Why? A beginning of an explanation is that flooding is a danger in the Netherlands. Citing this fact does not help much, however, unless one remembers that Indonesia was formerly a Dutch colony. Even remembering this leaves gaps in the explanation. We can understand why the Dutch might put their electrical outlets above floor level in the Netherlands. It is safer in a country where flooding is a danger. Is flooding, then, a similar danger in Indonesia? Apparently not. So why did the Dutch continue this practice in Indonesia? To answer this question we must cite another broad principle: Colonial settlers tend to preserve their home customs, practices, and styles. In this particular case, the Dutch continued to build Dutch-looking houses with the electrical outlets where (for them) they are normally placed—that is, in the middle of the wall rather than at floor level.

Even though this is not a scientific explanation, notice that it shares many features of the scientific explanation examined previously. First we have a curious fact: the location of electrical outlets in some houses in Indonesia. By way of explanation, certain important facts are cited:

Indonesia was a Dutch colony.

Flooding is a danger in the Netherlands.

(And so on.)

These facts are then woven together by certain general principles:

> Where flooding is a danger, it is safer to put electrical outlets above floor level.
>
> Colonial settlers tend to preserve their home customs, practices, and styles even when their practical significance is diminished.
>
> (And so on.)

Taken together, these facts and principles make sense of an anomalous fact—that is, they explain it.[5]

Explanations are satisfactory for *practical* purposes if they remove bewilderment or surprise. An explanation is satisfactory if it tells us *how* or *why* something happened in a way that is relevant to the concerns of a particular context. But how far can explanations go? In explaining why the water level remains the same when the ice cube melts, we cited the law of buoyancy. Now why should that law be true? What explains it? To explain the law of buoyancy, we would have to derive it from other laws that are more general and, perhaps, more intelligible. In fact, this has been done. Archimedes simultaneously proved and explained the Law of Buoyancy by deriving it from the Laws of the Lever.[6] How about the Laws of the Lever? Can they be proved and explained by deriving them from still higher and more comprehensive laws? Perhaps. Yet reasons give out, and sooner or later explanation and justification come to an end. It is the task of science and all rational inquiry to move that boundary further and further back.

EXERCISE 2

Write a brief explanation of one of the following:

(1) Why a lighter-than-air balloon rises.
(2) Why there is an infield fly rule in baseball.
(3) Why there is an international date line.
(4) Why there are more psychoanalysts in New York City than in any other city or, for that matter, in most countries in the world.

---

[5] This example comes from my former teacher Alan Ross Anderson.
[6] This proof, which is a model of elegant scientific reasoning, is given in Chapter 13 of this book.

(5) Why the cost of food tends to be higher in city slums than in wealthy suburbs.

What facts and what general principles are employed in your explanations? (Don't forget those principles that may seem too obvious to mention.)

EXCUSES

Sometimes when we have acted in an improper or particularly stupid way, we are asked to explain our actions or explain ourselves. "Why in the world did you do that?" is a request for an explanation of our behavior. Although such explanations lack the rigor of a scientific explanation, they share some of its features. In explaining our behavior we point to certain facts and general principles that together make sense out of what we have done. Take a simple example:

A: Why did you shove Harold into the gulch?
B: He was about to be shot by an assassin.

Here the response makes sense out of a piece of peculiar behavior by citing a single fact: An assassin was about to shoot Harold. But this explanation also depends upon some general principles that are so obvious that we simply take them for granted. For example, we assume that saving a person's life is, in general, a good thing; that a person in a gulch is less likely to be struck by a bullet than a person standing in plain view; that the amount of harm that might come from falling into a gulch is much less than the harm that would be caused by being struck by a bullet. Against the background of these principles and others, B's remark explains his otherwise inexplicable conduct.

Staying with this same example, we can see that B's remark also *justifies* his conduct. Not only can we make sense out of what he has done, we are also likely to approve of it. Next, notice what happens when we change the example in the following way:

A: Why did you shove Harold into the gulch?
B: I mistakenly thought that he was about to be shot.

B's remark still explains why he acted as he did. That is, we can still understand his behavior. It no longer justifies, or at least fully justifies, his conduct. Here we would say that B is offering an *excuse* for what he did. Broadly speaking, an excuse is an explanation of human behavior intended to put it in the best possible light. It will often happen that the best possible light will involve the admission of some wrongdoing. In the second dialogue, B admits to having made a mistake. In some contexts this might be a serious admission, but in the present context B does better admitting that he was, perhaps, stupid, rather than acknowledging that he shoved poor Harold into the gulch as a simple act of malice.

We evaluate excuses in much the same way that we evaluate other explanations. An excuse will involve statements of fact and these may be either true or false. We can also challenge the background principles employed in the excuse. We will not be impressed by someone who tells us that he ran seven stoplights so that he would not be late for a kickoff. Getting to a kickoff on time does not warrant such obviously dangerous behavior. Finally, as with other explanations, the facts together with the background principles should make sense out of a piece of behavior.

Presented with an excuse, we can ask the following questions:

(1) Broadly speaking, what are the facts?
(2) With what is the person liable to be charged?
(3) What lesser wrong will the person settle for instead?
(4) How does the explanation accomplish this task?

In our example, (1) B shoved Harold into a gulch. (2) On the face of it, this looks like an attempt to injure Harold. (3) B is willing to admit that he made a mistake of fact. (4) Given this admission, his action can be seen as a laudable, if flawed, attempt to save Harold from death or serious injury.

EXERCISE 3

Imagine that you have written a letter home asking for money. In the closing paragraph, you feel called upon to offer some excuse for not writing for two months. Write such an excuse (not just an apology) in a perfectly natural way, and then analyze it, using the questions given above.

EXERCISE 4

In William Shakespeare's *Much Ado About Nothing*, Benedict, after previously denouncing women and marriage in the strongest terms, is trapped into falling in love with Beatrice. In the following passage he attempts to explain his sudden turnabout. Using the four questions given opposite, analyze this passage.

> I may chance have some odd quirks and remnants of wit broken on me because I have railed so long against marriage. But doth not the appetite alter? A man loves the meat in his youth that he cannot endure in his age. Shall gulps and sentences and these paper bullets of the brain awe a man from the career of his humor? No, the world must be peopled. When I said I would die a bachelor, I did not think I should live till I were married.[7]

EXERCISE 5

Find an example of a public official offering an excuse for something he or she has done. Analyze its structure using the four questions on the opposite page.

DISCUSSION QUESTIONS

(1) In general it is wrong to suppose that refuting an argument shows its conclusion to be false. Why?

(2) It is sometimes said that science tells us *how* things happen but does not tell us *why* they happen. In what ways is this contention right, and in what ways is it wrong?

(3) When a claim is made that someone's conduct is *inexcusable,* what precisely is being asserted? How does it differ from calling the conduct simply bad or even very bad?

(4) Taken literally, "Excuse me" is a request. For what?

---

[7] William Shakespeare, *Much Ado About Nothing,* Act III, Sc. 1.

6

The Deep Analysis of Arguments

Arguments in everyday life are rarely spelled out explicitly. Premises, sometimes important premises, are often omitted. Such omissions are tolerable because we are able to convey a great deal of information indirectly by conversational implication. However, in order to give a critical assessment of an argument, it is often necessary to make explicit these unstated parts of the argument and then put them in systematic order. After this is done, we are in a better position to decide on the soundness or unsoundness of the argument in question. This chapter will present methods for *restating* or *reconstructing* arguments so that they may be evaluated both fairly and in a systematic fashion. These methods will then be applied to disputes where *fundamental disagreements* exist.

SUPPRESSED PREMISES

Linguistic Principles

If we think of arguments as pathways between premises and conclusions, it becomes obvious that some of these pathways are more complicated than others. Yet even the simplest arguments reveal hidden
complexities when examined closely. For example, there is no question
that the following argument is valid:

> Harriet is in New York with her son.
> Therefore, Harriet's son is in New York.

If asked why this conclusion follows from the premises, it would be natural to reply that you cannot be someplace with somebody unless that
person is there too. This is not something we spell out, but, nonetheless, it is the principle that takes us from the premise to the conclusion.

One thing to notice about this principle is that it is quite general,
that is, it does not depend on any special features of the people or places
involved. If Benjamin is in St. Louis with his daughter, then Benjamin's
daughter is in St. Louis. Although the references have changed, the
general pattern of the argument has remained the same. Furthermore,
the principle that lies behind this inference will seem obvious to anyone
who *understands the words used to formulate it*. For this reason we shall say
that principles of this kind are basically *linguistic* in character.

If we look at arguments as they occur in everyday life, we will discover that almost all of them turn on unstated linguistic principles. To
cite just one more example, if a wife is taller than her husband, then
there is at least one woman who is taller than at least one man. This
inference relies on the principle that husbands are men and wives are
women. We do not usually state these linguistic principles, for to do so
will often violate the rule of Strength, discussed in Chapter 1. (Try to
imagine a context in which you would come right out and say, "Husbands, you know, are men." Unless you were speaking to someone just
learning the language, this would be a very peculiar remark.) But even
if in most cases it would be peculiar to come right out and state such
linguistic principles, our arguments typically presuppose them. This
observation reveals yet another way in which our daily use of language
moves within a rich, though largely unnoticed, framework of rules.

Commonly Shared Facts

Not only do our arguments often depend on *linguistic* principles
(for example, that husbands are men), but, as noted briefly in Chapter
1, they often depend on unstated facts understood by those involved in

the conversation. Thus, if we are told that Chester Arthur was a President of the United States, we have a right to assume a great many things about him, for example, that at the time he was President, he was a live human being and, more particularly, a native-born citizen of the United States. Appeals to facts of this kind lie behind the following arguments:

> Benjamin Franklin could not have been our second President because he died before the second election was held.
>
> Henry Kissinger cannot become President because he was born in Germany.

The first argument obviously turns on a question of fact: Did Franklin die before the second presidential election was held? (He did.) But the argument also depends on a more general principle that ties the premise and conclusion together, that is, that the dead are not eligible for the presidency. It might, however, have been otherwise. We can imagine a society in which the deceased are elected to public office as an honor (something akin to posthumous induction into the Baseball Hall of Fame). But our national government is not like that, and this is something that most Americans know. Therefore it would be odd to come right out and say that the deceased cannot hold public office. (In most settings this would involve a violation of the rule of Strength.) Even so, this fact plays a central role in the argument.

Traditionally, logicians have called premises that seem too obvious to mention *suppressed premises*. An argument depending upon suppressed premises is called an *enthymeme* or is said to be *enthymematic*. If we look at arguments that occur in daily life, we discover that they are, almost without exception, enthymematic. Therefore, in order to trace out the pathway between premises and conclusion, it is usually necessary to fill in these suppressed premises as connecting links.

The second argument given above is more complicated. Why should being from Germany disqualify someone from being President of the United States? It seems odd that the Founding Fathers should have something against that particular part of the world. The answer is that the argument depends upon a more general suppressed premise:

> Only a native-born American citizen may become President of the United States.

Thus the argument can be unpacked in the following way:

> Kissinger was born in Germany.
>
> Germany has never been part of the United States.
>
> Therefore, Kissinger is not a native-born United States citizen.
>
> Only a native-born United States citizen may become President of the United States.

Therefore, Kissinger cannot become President of the United States.

The argument has been broken down into two steps, and each step contains a suppressed premise. The first step is intended to show that Kissinger is not a native-born United States citizen, and it relies on the unstated premise that Germany has never been part of the United States. This seems straightforward enough, but notice that the argument further depends upon a *linguistic* suppressed premise concerning what we mean by a "native-born United States citizen." The second part of the argument contains the key idea, namely, that only native-born citizens of the United States are eligible for its presidency. It is this provision of the United States Constitution that lies at the heart of the argument. Knowing this provision is, of course, a more special piece of knowledge than knowing that you have to be alive to be President. (The Founding Fathers felt no need to mention this qualification in the Constitution.) For this reason, more people will see the force of the first argument than the second. The second argument assumes an audience with more specialized knowledge.

To summarize what we have seen thus far: It is only in rare cases that the conclusion of an everyday argument follows immediately from its stated premises. Even for most simple arguments, filling in is necessary if justice is to be done to the force of the argument. Logicians call these unstated facts or principles *suppressed premises*. In the first place, linguistic principles are often suppressed because they are known to virtually all speakers of the language. Nonetheless, they often play an important role in connecting the premises to the conclusion. A second kind of suppressed premise concerns facts that, presumably, are acknowledged by those involved in the conversational exchange. Most people educated in the United States know that you must be a native-born United States citizen to be eligible for the presidency; thus when addressing this audience, there is usually no need to mention the fact. When done appropriately, the suppression of linguistic and factual premises can add greatly to the efficiency of language. Indeed, without the judicious suppression of obvious premises, many arguments would become too cumbersome to be effective.

EXERCISE 1

The following arguments depend for their validity on suppressed premises that are either trivial linguistic principles or commonly shared facts. For each of the following arguments, list these linguistic principles or commonly shared facts. Sometimes there is more than one.

Example: All of Carol's siblings are brothers, therefore she has no sisters.

Supressed Premises: A sibling is either a brother or a sister.
A brother is not a sister.

Example: Harold will not play in the Super Bowl because he has a broken leg.

Suppressed Premise: The Super Bowl is a football game. Generally, at least, a person does not play in football games with a broken leg.

(1) Madonna cannot run for President of the United States because she is under thirty-five.

(2) Nixon wasn't President in 1950, because he was still in the Senate.

(3) There's no one named Rupert here; we have only female patients.

(4) Columbus did not discover the New World, because the Vikings explored Newfoundland centuries earlier.

(5) If there were survivors, they would have been found by now (as a way of arguing that there are no survivors).

(6) Lincoln could not have met Washington, because Washington was dead before Lincoln was born.

(7) Philadelphia cannot play Los Angeles in the World Series because they are both in the National League.

(8) Mildred must be more than 43 because she has a daughter who is 36.

(9) He cannot be a grandfather because he never had children.

(10) That's not acid rock; you can understand the lyrics.

Fundamental Principles

We will now turn to a more important kind of suppressed premise, those that involve fundamental principles. These principles can concern morality, religion, politics, and our general views concerning the nature of the world. We often argue *within* a framework of such principles without actually stating them because we assume (sometimes incorrectly!) that others share them as well. When someone argues that the arms race should be ended because it will lead to the annihilation of the human race, he or she will not feel called upon to say explicitly, "And the annihilation of the human race would be a very bad thing." That, after all, is something that most people take for granted.

Though fundamental principles are often obvious and generally accepted, at times it is not clear what principles are being assumed and just how acceptable they really are. In situations of this kind, the best procedure is to lay out everything with as much clarity as possible by using the method of *argumentative reconstruction*. This is done in the following way:

(1) Do a *close analysis* of the passage containing the argument.
(2) List the explicit premises and the conclusion.
(3) Clarify the premises and the conclusion where necessary.
(4) Attempt to fill in a line of reasoning that will take you from the premise to the conclusion.
(5) Assess the argument for soundness, that is, for the truth of the premises and the validity of the argument.[1]

We are already familiar with the first two steps of this procedure from Chapters 2 and 3, which dealt with the language of argument. No further comment is needed here. In the third step of this procedure, we attempt to make the premises and conclusion sufficiently clear for logical analysis. The goal here is not perfect clarity, for there probably is no such thing. It is, however, often necessary to eliminate ambiguity and reduce vagueness before we can give an argument a fair assessment.

The fourth step of the procedure is complicated, indeed, more complicated than our discussion thus far has suggested. In fact, it must be carried out in tandem with the fifth step, assessing the argument for its soundness. If we are trying to give an argument a charitable interpretation, that is, trying to decide for ourselves whether it is acceptable or not, we set as our goal a reconstruction of the argument that shows that it can be filled out with true suppressed premises that validly imply the conclusion. Two problems typically arise when we make this effort:

(1) When we find a set of premises strong enough to support the conclusion, at least one of these premises is false.
(2) When we modify the premises to avoid falsehood, the conclusion no longer follows from them.

The reconstruction of an argument typically involves shifting back and forth between the demand for a valid argument and the demand for true premises. Eventually, we either show the argument to be sound or we abandon the effort, concluding that the argument in question has no sound reconstruction. Now it is possible that *we* were at fault in not

---

[1] With inductive arguments we assess the argument for its *strength*. Inductive arguments are examined in detail in Chapter 9.

finding a reconstruction that showed the argument to be sound. Perhaps we did not show enough ingenuity in searching for a suppressed premise that would do the trick. There is, in fact, no purely formal or mechanical way of dealing with this problem. A person presenting an argument may reasonably leave out steps provided that they can be easily filled in by those to whom the argument is addressed. So in analyzing an argument, we should be charitable, but our charity has limits. After a reasonable search for those suppressed premises that would show the argument to be sound, we should not blame ourselves if we fail to find them; rather, the blame shifts to the person who formulated the argument for not doing so clearly.

EXERCISE 2

The following arguments depend for their validity on suppressed premises that are fundamental principles in the sense just described. For each of the following arguments, state what these underlying principles might be. (Remember, you do not have to accept an argument to detect its underlying principles.) In some cases there may be more than one underlying principle.

Example: You cannot say that Kirk is guilty because he has not even been tried yet.
Underlying Principle: A person is innocent until proven guilty.

(1) If people can vote and be drafted at 18, then they should be allowed to drink at 18.
(2) We have no right to attack left-wing dictatorships if we support right-wing dictatorships.
(3) If high deficits continue, then inflation will return.
(4) If getting good grades is so easy, why don't more people do it (as a way of arguing that getting good grades is *not* so easy)?
(5) It is wrong to punish someone just to make an example of him.
(6) General Snork has no right to rule because he came to power by a military coup.
(7) Morris does not deserve his wealth, because he merely inherited it.

CAPITAL PUNISHMENT

We can examine these methods at work on the difficult question of the constitutionality of capital punishment. It has been argued before the Supreme Court that the death penalty should be declared unconstitutional because it violates the constitutional provision against "cruel and unusual punishments." The explicitly stated argument has the following form:

> The death penalty violates the constitutional prohibition against cruel and unusual punishments.
> Therefore, the death penalty should be ruled unconstitutional.

The argument plainly depends upon two suppressed premises:

> *SP1:* The death penalty involves cruel and unusual punishment.
> *SP2:* Anything that violates a constitutional prohibition should be declared unconstitutional.

So the argument more fully spelled out looks like this:

(1) *SP:* The death penalty involves cruel and unusual punishment.
(2) The Constitution prohibits cruel and unusual punishments.
(3) *SP:* Anything that violates a constitutional prohibition should be declared unconstitutional.
(4) Therefore, the death penalty should be declared unconstitutional.

This reconstruction seems to be a fair representation of the original argument.

We can now turn to an assessment of this argument. First, the argument is *valid*—given the premises, the conclusion does follow—so that we can turn our attention to the *plausibility* of the premises themselves. The second premise is clearly true, for the Constitution does, in fact, prohibit cruel and unusual punishments.[2] It is not clear, however, just what this prohibition amounts to. In particular, does the punishment have to be *both* cruel *and* unusual to be prohibited, or is it sufficient for it to be *either* cruel *or* unusual? For the moment, let us interpret the language as meaning *both* cruel and unusual.

---

[2] The Eighth Amendment reads, "Excessive bail shall not be required, nor excessive fines imposed, nor cruel and unusual punishments inflicted."

The third premise seems uncontroversial. Indeed, it may sound like a truism to say that anything that violates a constitutional provision should be declared unconstitutional. As a matter of fact, this notion was once a controversial matter, for nothing in the Constitution gives the courts the right to declare acts of legislators unconstitutional and hence void. The courts have acquired and consolidated this right in the years since 1789, and it is still sometimes challenged by those who think that it gives the courts too much power. But even if the judiciary's power to declare laws unconstitutional is not itself a constitutionally stated power, it is so much an accepted part of our system that no one would challenge it in a *courtroom* procedure.

Although the third premise has a more complicated backing than most people realize, it is obviously the first premise—"The death penalty involves cruel and unusual punishment"—that forms the heart of the argument. What we would expect, then, is a good argument to be put forward in its behalf.

Consider the following argument intended to establish this claim:

> That taking a person's life is cruel should go without saying. The important issue is whether such a penalty is unusual. That execution is an unusual penalty is seen from examining court records. Whether a person committing a particular crime will be given the death penalty depends on the kind of legal aid he is given, his willingness to enter into plea bargaining, the personality of the judge, the beliefs and attitudes of the jury, and a great many other considerations. In fact, only in a small percentage of the cases in which it might apply is the death penalty actually handed down.

Let us concentrate on the part of this argument intended to show that the death penalty is an unusual punishment. Of course, in civilized nations the death penalty is reserved for a small range of crimes; but the fact that it is not widespread is hardly the point at issue. The point of the argument is that the death penalty is unusual even for those crimes that are punishable by death. Calling such crimes *capital offenses*, we can restate the argument more carefully as follows:

> Only a small percentage of those found guilty of committing a capital offense are given the death sentence.
> Therefore, the death penalty is, in the relevant sense, an unusual punishment.

We can spread the entire argument out before us:

(1) Taking a human life is a cruel act.
(2) The death penalty is therefore cruel.

(3) Only a small percentage of those found guilty of committing capital offenses are given the death penalty.

(4) Therefore, the death penalty is an unusual punishment.

(5) Therefore, the death penalty is both cruel and unusual.

(6) The Constitution prohibits cruel and unusual punishments.

(7) Anything that violates the Constitution should be declared unconstitutional.

(8) Therefore, the death penalty should be declared unconstitutional.

These propositions provide at least the skeleton of an argument with some force; the conclusion does seem to follow from the premises, and the premises themselves seem plausible. It seems, then, that we have devised a charitable reconstruction of the argument, and we can now see how an opponent might respond to it.

One response is particularly probing. It goes like this:

> It is certainly true that only a small percentage of those who commit capital offenses are actually sentenced to death, but this fact does not reflect badly on the law but on its administration. If judges and juries met their obligations, more people who deserve the death penalty would receive it, and the use of it would no longer be unusual. What is needed, then, is judicial reform and not the removal of the death penalty on constitutional grounds.

This response is a probing one because it insists on a distinction between a law and the effects of its application or, more pointedly, its misapplication. To meet this rejoinder, the original argument could be strengthened in the following way:

> A law should not be judged in isolation from the likely effects of implementing it. Given the nature of our system of criminal justice, for the foreseeable future, the death penalty will continue to be applied to only a small percentage of capital offenders. It will therefore remain an unusual punishment and so be unconstitutional.

We can spell this argument out in the following way:

(1) A law should be declared unconstitutional if its likely consequences are contrary to the Constitution.

(2) A law that uses the death penalty as a punishment will have as its likely consequence a penalty that is cruel and unusual.

(3) Cruel and unusual punishments are explicitly forbidden by the Constitution.

(4) Therefore, any law that employs the death penalty should be declared unconstitutional.

Both the first premise and second premise will lead to further debate. Should a law be declared unconstitutional because there is a good chance that it will be abused in ways that infringe on constitutional rights? Of course, a great many laws have this potential, for example, all laws involving police power. However, only an extremist would suggest that we should abolish all police powers because of this risk of unconstitutional abuse. Yet certain police powers have been limited by court ruling because they have this potential for unconstitutional abuse. Strict rules governing the use of evidence gained from wiretaps are one result. So those who argue in favor of the death penalty must show either that there is a good chance that the application of the death penalty can be made more uniform or show that this failure of uniform application is not sufficiently important to be considered constitutionally intolerable.

The supporter of the death penalty can offer a sharper criticism of the second premise of our last argument. It goes like this:

> Those who argue against the constitutionality of the death penalty on the grounds that it is a cruel and unusual punishment use the expression "cruel and unusual" in a way wholly different from that intended by the framers of the Eighth Amendment. By "cruel" they had in mind punishments that involved torture. By "unusual" they did not mean "rare," for in a good society all punishment would be rare. What they were opposed to were bizarre or ghoulish punishments of the kind that often formed part of public spectacles, especially in barbaric times. Modern methods of execution are neither cruel nor unusual in the constitutionally relevant sense of these words. Therefore laws demanding the death penalty cannot be declared unconstitutional on the grounds that they either directly or indirectly involve a punishment that is cruel and unusual.

The core of this counter-argument can be expressed as follows:

(1) In appeals to the Constitution, its words must be taken as they were originally intended.

(2) Modern methods of carrying out a death penalty are neither "cruel" nor "unusual" if these words are interpreted as they were originally intended.

(3) Therefore the death penalty cannot be declared unconstitutional on the grounds that it violates the amendment against cruel and unusual punishments.

The second premise of this argument states a matter of historical fact that might not be altogether easy to verify. The chances are, however, that it comes close to the truth. Given this, the opponent of the death penalty must either attack the first premise or find some other grounds for holding that the death penalty should be declared unconstitutional.

The first premise may seem like a truism, for how can we be guided by a document if everyone is free to give it the meaning he or she chooses? The literal meaning of the document is simply its meaning; everything else is interpretation. Of course, there are times when it is not easy to discover what the literal meaning is. (In the present case, for example, it is not clear whether the Eighth Amendment prohibits punishments that are *either* cruel *or* unusual or only those that are *both* cruel and unusual.) It seems unlikely, however, that those who drafted the Eighth Amendment used either the word "cruel" or the word "unusual" in the ways they are employed in the anti–capital punishment argument.

Does this last concession end the debate in favor of those who reject the anti–capital punishment argument we have been examining? The argument certainly seems to be weakened, but there are those who would take a bold course by simply denying the first premise of the argument used to refute them. *They would deny, that is, that we are bound to read the Constitution in the way intended by its framers.* An argument in favor of this position might look something like this:

> The great bulk of the Constitution was written in an age almost wholly different from our own. To cite just two examples of this: Women were denied fundamental rights of full citizenship, and slavery was a constitutionally accepted feature of national life. The Constitution has remained a live and relevant document just because it has undergone constant reinterpretation. So even if it is true that the expression "cruel and unusual" meant something quite special to those who framed the Eighth Amendment, plainly a humane desire to make punishment more civilized lay behind it. The present reading of this amendment is in the spirit of its original intention and simply makes it applicable to our own times.

The argument has now moved to an entirely new level: one concerning whether the Constitution should be read strictly in accord with the original intentions of those who wrote it or more freely to accommodate modern realities. But we shall not pursue the discussion further into these complex areas; instead, we should consider how we were led into them. Our original argument did not concern the *general* question of whether capital punishment is right or wrong, nor did it simply concern the question of whether capital punishment is unconstitutional. The argument turned on a much more specific point: Does the death penalty violate the Eighth Amendment's prohibition against cruel and unusual punishments? The argument with which we began seemed to be a straightforward proof that it does. Yet, as we explored principles that lay in back of this deceptively simple argument, the issue became broader and more complex. We finally reached a point at which the force of the original argument was seen to depend on what we consider the proper way to interpret the Constitution—strictly or more freely.

EXERCISE 3

The final argument presented in our examination of whether or not the death penalty violates the Constitutional provision against cruel and unusual punishments attempts to show that the Constitution must be read in a free or liberal way that makes it relevant to present society. Filling in suppressed premises where necessary, restate this argument as a sequence of explicit steps. After you have given the argument the *strongest* restatement you can, evaluate it for its soundness.

ABORTION

Another issue that has been the source of profound disagreement among members of our society is whether (or in what circumstances) abortion should be made illegal. A similar question has arisen concerning so-called mercy killing, or euthanasia. Those who oppose both abortion and euthanasia could defend their position by invoking a general principle of the following kind:

It is always wrong to take a human life.

But this principle by itself does not rule out either abortion or euthanasia. To reach these conclusions, we need further premises of the following kind:

A fetus is a human being.
An utterly comatose person is still a human being.

Given these premises, the anti-abortion and the anti-euthanasia arguments will have the following form:

(1) Abortion involves taking the life of a fetus.
(2) A fetus is a human being.
(3) It is always wrong to take the life of a human being.
(4) Therefore, abortion is wrong.

(1) Euthanasia involves taking the life of a person who is ill.

(2) A living person, however ill, is still a human being.

(3) It is always wrong to take the life of a human being.

(4) Therefore, euthanasia is wrong.

Stated this way, we can see why so much of the debate concerning abortion and euthanasia turns on the question of whether a fetus is already a human being and whether a patient suffering from so-called "brain death" continues to be a human being. But the argument so stated is not characteristically used by most people who adopt a strong anti-abortion or anti-euthanasia position. In particular, very few of those who espouse these positions will accept the third premise of each of these arguments. This comes out in the following way. Many of those who oppose abortion or euthanasia are in favor of the death penalty for certain crimes. Therefore, they do not accept the general principle that it is always wrong to take a human life. Similarly, those who support abortion or euthanasia are not simply indifferent to human life, for these very same people often oppose capital punishment. The question, then, that must be put to those on both sides of the debate is this: What principle allows the taking of a human life in some instances but not in others?

Those who are opposed to abortion or euthanasia could reformulate the third premise in these words:

It is always wrong to take the life of an innocent human being.

Here the word "innocent" allows an exception for the death penalty being imposed on those who are guilty of certain crimes. Even stated this way, however, the principle seems to admit of exceptions. If someone's life is threatened by a madman, it is generally thought that the person has the right to use whatever means are necessary against the madman to prevent this. This may include killing him, yet the insane are usually thought to be innocent of their deeds. So the principle must be modified again:

It is always wrong to take the life of an innocent human being except in certain cases of self-defense.[3]

---

[3] It is possible to find difficulties with this principle that will force further modifications or clarifications. Children, for example, are often the innocent victims of bombing raids, yet the raids are often thought to be justified even though they will have this predictable consequence. At this point it is common to modify the principle again by including a reference to intentions: Although the death of a certain number of innocent children is a foreseeable consequence of the bombing raid, it is not what is intended. We cannot, however, pursue this complex line of reasoning here.

We have arrived, then, at a principle that seems to make sense out of a position that is against abortion but in favor of the death penalty. With these modifications included, the argument now looks like this:

(1) Abortion is taking the life of a human fetus.
(2) A human fetus is a living human being.
(3) A human fetus is an innocent human being.
(4) It is always wrong to take the life of an innocent human being except in cases of self-defense.
(5) Therefore, abortion is always wrong.

But, having made the premises more plausible, we confront a new problem: the argument is invalid as it stands, since the qualification "except in cases of self-defense" has been dropped from the conclusion. The proper conclusion of the argument should be:

(5) Abortion is always wrong except in cases of self-defense.

Rewriting the conclusion in this way has an important consequence: the argument no longer leads to a conclusion that abortion is *always* wrong. The qualified conclusion could permit abortion in those cases in which it is needed to defend the life of the bearer of the fetus. It could then be argued that there is no important difference between our right to defend ourselves against an irrational assailant and a non-rational fetus. In both cases we grant the innocence of the party whose life must be taken, but think that the right to life of the victim in one case or the bearer of the fetus in the other overrides this. In fact, this is the position that many people opposed to abortion take: abortion is wrong except in those cases in which it is plainly needed to save the life of the mother. This is a strong anti-abortion position, since it would condone abortion in only a few exceptional cases. It is the view, in fact, of many who consider themselves strongly opposed to abortion.[4]

The contours of the debate between those who are opposed to abortion and those who are in favor of it are now becoming more clear. Those who oppose abortion need not hold an absolute position banning all abortion. They usually admit that in certain exceptional cases abortion is permitted. They then try to give some reasoned ground for admitting these exceptions. Similarly, those who favor abortion rarely suggest that there should be no constraints on its use. They hold in-

---

[4] A stronger, but still not absolute, anti-abortion position is that abortion is permitted when it is needed to save the life of the mother and there is no chance of the fetus surviving in any case.

stead that abortion should be permitted in a much wider range of cases than their opponents admit. It makes more sense, then, to speak about a liberal and a conservative view of abortion rather than simply about a pro-abortion and an anti-abortion position. (There is a tendency for those engaged in this debate to saddle their opponents with as extreme a position as possible. This merely shows that zeal for a cause can corrupt intellectual honesty.)

We can now examine the way that those who adopt the liberal position will attack the conservative argument as it has just been spelled out. The first premise, which simply defines abortion, should not be a subject for controversy. Nor does it seem likely that the third premise will be attacked on the ground that the fetus is not innocent. To the best of my knowledge, no one has argued that abortion can be justified as a punishment of the fetus. (Justification in terms of saving the bearer's life is altogether different from this.)

The second premise will be a center of controversy, for if it is admitted that a fetus is a human being, then moral and legal considerations will apply directly to it, and the burden of proof will shift and force those who maintain the liberal position to show why these legal and moral considerations should be set aside, or at least modified. An argument intended to show that a fetus is not a human being—or perhaps not a human being up to a certain time after conception—must proceed from some idea of what it is to be a human being. Such arguments often proceed along the following lines:

> No moral significance attaches to being a member of one biological species rather than another, for example, *Homo sapiens* (man) rather than *Quercus rubra* (a red oak). We accord human beings special rights because of their capacity to suffer pain and enjoy pleasure, because they can plan their lives and make choices, because they are subject to praise and blame, and so on. A human fetus lacks these qualities.

A person who uses this line of argument may admit that the fetus differs from an acorn because it is *potentially* a creature that will be endowed with special rights, and this potential itself may have moral significance. The point, however, is that the fetus is not yet a person and therefore the problem is no longer viewed as a choice between the rights of two persons, the bearer and the fetus.

At first it may seem that the question whether a fetus is a human being is merely a quibble. In fact, it raises questions that take us to bedrock issues. The liberal position just sketched gives human beings a special moral status in virtue of their capacities (to suffer, choose, assume responsibility, and the like). On this approach, a fetus will have no—or, at best, greatly diminished—human rights. On the other side, a person with a religious orientation might reject this "image of man" completely. Human beings have special moral significance because they have been created by God in His image; they possess an immortal soul; and so on. If these features are attributed to the fetus, then, once more, the fetus has human rights that cannot be set aside except, possibly, in extreme cases.

How does one deal with such bedrock disagreements? The first thing to see is that logic alone will not settle them. Starting from a certain conception of man, it is possible to argue coherently for a liberal view on abortion; starting from another point of view, it is possible to argue coherently for a conservative view on abortion. The important thing to see is that it is possible to *understand* an opposing view, that is, get a genuine feeling for its inner workings, even if you disagree with it completely. Logical analysis may show that particular arguments are unsound or have unnoticed and unwanted implications. This may force clarification and modification. But the most important service that logical analysis can perform is to lay bare the fundamental principles that lie beneath surface disagreements. Analysis will sometimes show that these disagreements are fundamental and perhaps irreconcilable. Dealing with such irreconcilable differences in a humane way is one of the fundamental tasks of a society dedicated to freedom and a wide range of civil liberties.

In examining the conservative position on abortion, it proved useful to ask how commitments on this issue squared with commitments in other areas. It proved particularly interesting to ask how a person could simultaneously be a conservative on abortion and a proponent of the death penalty for certain criminal offenses. We saw that this apparent inconsistency could be overcome by insisting on the innocence of the fetus and the guilt of the capital offender as significant factors. People who take a liberal stand on abortion also adopt positions that may seem inconsistent. For example, it is quite common to find a person with a very liberal approach to abortion who also rejects capital punishment altogether. It will be useful to ask how these apparently anti-life, pro-life positions can be combined.

Once more, the question whether a fetus is already a human being (in the sense of a person) may form an important part of the discussion. The criminal is, after all, a human being. If the fetus is not, then the cases are separated and there is no conflict between always being opposed to taking the life of a criminal and not always being opposed to taking the life of a fetus. This, however, is probably not the whole story or even the most important part of it. Those who adopt a liberal position on abortion often do so on the basis of an argument from *human welfare*. They argue that abortion can sometimes be justified in terms of the welfare of the woman who bears the fetus, or in terms of the welfare of the family it will be born into, or even in terms of the welfare of the child itself if it were to be born into an impoverished situation. On the other side, it is argued that the death penalty does not benefit human welfare. In itself it is a harsh and dehumanizing practice and in its effects does not serve as a useful deterrent. So the cases are distinguished once more: abortion at least sometimes contributes to human welfare, whereas the death penalty does not. This argument, when spelled out, looks like this:

(1) An action that best contributes to human welfare is correct.
(2) Abortion sometimes is the best way of maximizing human welfare.
(3) Therefore, abortion is sometimes correct.

It is then claimed that a similar argument cannot be produced justifying the death penalty because it does not maximize human welfare. It is argued, in particular, that it does not serve as a deterrent to capital offenses.

What are we to say about this argument from human welfare? It seems valid in form, so we can turn to the premises themselves and ask if they are acceptable. The first (and leading) premise of the argument is subject to two immediate criticisms. First of all, it is vague. Probably what a person who uses this kind of argument has in mind by speaking of human welfare is a certain level of material and psychological well-being. More simply, an action is said to be right if it best makes people happy. Of course, this is still vague, but it is clear enough to make the premise a target of the second, more important, criticism. While maximizing human welfare may, in general, be a good thing, it is not the only relevant consideration in deciding how to act. To cite the previous example used against positions of this kind, it might be true that our society would be much more prosperous on the whole if 10 percent of the population were designated slaves who would do all menial work. In this way the general level of prosperity and happiness might be much higher than the level that could be achieved without a slave caste. Yet, even if a society could be made generally happy in this way, most people would reject such a system on grounds that it is unfair to the slave class. For reasons of this kind, most people would modify the first premise of the argument we are now examining in the following way:

(1) An action that best increases human welfare is right, provided that it is fairly applied.

But if the first premise is modified in this way, then the entire argument must be restated to reflect this revision. It will now look like this:

(1) An action that best increases human welfare is right, provided that it is fairly applied.

(2) Abortion is sometimes an action that best increases human welfare.

(3) Therefore, abortion is sometimes right provided that it is fairly applied.

It should be obvious how conservatives on abortion will reply to this argument. They will maintain that abortion always (or almost always) involves unfair application, namely, to the fetus. Once more we have encountered a standard situation: given a strong premise (Premise 1), it is possible to derive a particular conclusion, but this strong premise is subject to criticism and therefore must be modified. When the conclusion is modified, it no longer supports the original conclusion that the person presenting the argument wishes to establish. (A like situation arose in examining the conservative position on abortion on page 132).

The argument does not stop here. A person who holds a liberal position on abortion might reply in a number of ways. Again, the burden of the argument may shift to the question of whether or not a human fetus is a human being and therefore possessed of the right to fair treatment. It might also be argued that sometimes, at least, questions of human welfare are more important than the issue of fair or equal treatment. During war, for example, members of a certain segment of the population are called upon to risk their lives for the good of the whole. Indeed, in many emergencies, fair and equal treatment must be set aside or modified for the sake of preserving the society as a whole.

When the argument is put on this new basis, the question then becomes this: Are there circumstances in which matters of welfare become so urgent that the rights of the fetus (here assuming that the fetus has rights) are overriden? The obvious case in which this might happen is when the life of the bearer of the fetus is plainly threatened. For many conservatives on abortion, this does count as a case in which abortion is permitted. Those who hold to the liberal position will maintain that severe psychological, financial, or personal losses may also take precedence over the life of the fetus. How severe must these losses be? From our previous discussion of slippery slope arguments, we know that we should not expect a sharp line to exist here, and, indeed, people will tend to be spread out in their opinions in a continuum ranging from a belief in complete prohibition to no prohibition. Very few people occupy the end points on this continuum, yet it still leaves room for profound disagreements on fundamental issues.

Weighing Factors

Our discussion has brought us to the following point: disagreements concerning abortion cannot be reduced to a yes-no dispute. Most conservatives on abortion acknowledge that it is permissible in some (though very few) cases. Most liberals on abortion admit that there are some (though not restrictively many) limitations on its use. The way people place themselves on this continuum does not depend on any simple acceptance of one argument over another, but instead on the *weight* they give certain factors. To what extent does a fetus have human rights? The conservative position we examined earlier grants the fetus full (or close to full) human rights. The liberal position usually grants diminished rights to the fetus. (Only rarely does the liberal deny the fetus any rights at all.) In what areas do questions of welfare override certain individual rights? The conservative in this matter usually restricts this to those cases in which the very life of the mother is plainly threatened. As the position on abortion becomes more liberal, the more extensive becomes the range of cases in which the rights of the fetus are set aside in favor of the rights of the bearer of the fetus.

Where a particular person strikes this balance is not only a function of basic moral beliefs, but also a function of different weights assigned to them. Except for those who occupy extreme positions, there is surprising agreement in moral principles between the conservatives concerning abortion and those who are liberal concerning it. In an ideal world, the rights of the fetus and the rights of the bearer of the fetus would never conflict, and the profound and often tragic issue of weighing one moral demand against another would not arise. Logical analysis is not capable of solving such fundamental problems as this, but it can help us understand their underlying structure and in this way help bring honest intelligence to bear upon them.

◆ *EXERCISE 4**

An anti-abortion measure known as the Hyde Amendment has been attached to various appropriation bills over the last few years. It has been stated in a variety of ways, but a version that was held constitutional by the Supreme Court has the following form:

> None of the funds provided for in this paragraph shall be used to perform abortions except where the life of the mother would be endangered if the fetus were carried to term, or except in such medical procedures necessary for the victims of rape or incest, where such rape or incest has been reported promptly to a law enforcement agency or public health service.

---

*Suitable for a term project.

Using the techniques developed in this chapter, construct the strongest possible argument that will give a reasoned basis for both the overall anti-abortion standpoint of the Hyde Amendment and the three exceptions it allows. This will involve presenting arguments in support of the three exceptions that do not, at the same time, undercut the general (anti-abortion) intention of the amendment. You must spell out all of these arguments in detail. After giving the position a fair statement, assess its plausibility.

◆ EXERCISE 5*

Chapter 12 contains four essays concerning the morality of abortion. Using the techniques developed in this chapter, show the fundamental structure of one of these four positions and assess its strength.

DISCUSSION QUESTIONS

(1) Quite often those who hold a strong *right-to-life* position in opposing abortion also favor capital punishment for certain crimes. What underlying principles could a person hold to reconcile this apparent conflict concerning the sanctity of human life?

(2) Quite often those who hold a strong *pro-choice* position in defending abortion are also strongly opposed to capital punishment. What underlying principles could a person hold in order to respect the life of a human criminal but not the life of a human fetus?

(3) What underlying principles could protect human lives with only a few exceptions, yet allow us to take the lives of animals for food, clothing, and entertainment?

---

*Suitable for a term project.

7

The Formal Analysis of Argument: Part One

This chapter will examine some more technical procedures for analyzing arguments. In particular, it will consider the notion of *validity*, for this is the central concept of logic. The first part of the chapter will show how the notion of validity first introduced in Chapter 2 can be developed rigorously in one area, the so-called *Propositional Logic*. This branch of logic deals with those connectives like "and" and "or" that allow us to build up complex propositions from simpler ones. Throughout most of the chapter, the focus will be theoretical rather than immediately practical. It is intended to provide insight into the concept of validity by examining it in an ideal setting. The chapter will close with a discussion of the relationship between the ideal language of symbolic logic and the language we ordinarily speak.

VALIDITY AND FORMAL ANALYSIS OF ARGUMENT

When we carry out an informal analysis of argument, we pay close attention to the key terms used to present the argument and then ask ourselves whether these key terms have been used properly. The procedure is informal because, so far, we have no exact techniques for answering the question: Is such and such a term used correctly? We rely, instead, on logical instincts which, on the whole, are pretty good.

Except in complicated or tricky cases, most people can tell whether one claim follows from another. But if we ask the average intelligent person *why* the one claim follows from the other, he or she will probably have little to say except, perhaps, that it is obvious. That is, it is often easy to see that one claim follows from another, but to explain why turns out to be difficult. This quality of "following from" is called validity, as we saw in Chapter 2. The purpose of this chapter is to get some better idea of this notion—to begin, at least, to understand what we are saying when we assert that one claim follows from another.

The focus of our attention will be the *concept* of validity. We are not, for the time being at least, interested in whether this or that argument is valid—we want to understand validity itself. To this end, the arguments we will examine are so simple that you will not be able to imagine anyone not understanding them at a glance. Who needs logic to deal with arguments of this kind? There is, however, good reason for dealing with simple—*trivially simple*—arguments at the start. The analytic approach to a complex issue is first to break it down into sub-issues, repeating the process until we reach problems simple enough to be solved. After these simpler problems are solved, we can reverse the process and construct solutions to larger and more complex problems. When done correctly, the *result* of such an analytic process may seem dull and obvious—and it often is. The *discovery* of such a process, in contrast, often demands the insight of genius.

THE PROPOSITIONAL CALCULUS

Conjunction

The first system of arguments that we shall examine concerns sentential (or propositional) connectives. Sentential connectives are terms that allow us to combine two or more sentences into a single sentence. For example, given the propositions "John is tall" and "Harry is short," we can use the term "and" to *conjoin* them, forming a single compound proposition "John is tall and Harry is short." Now let us look carefully at this simple word "and" and ask how it functions. "And," in fact, is a curious word, for it doesn't seem to stand for anything, at least in the way in which a proper name ("Churchill") and a common noun ("dog") seem to stand for things. Instead of asking what this word stands for, we can ask a different question: What *truth conditions* govern this connective? That is, under what conditions are propositions containing this connective true? To answer this question, we imagine every possible way in which the component propositions can be true or false. Then for each combination we decide what truth value to assign to the entire proposition. This may sound complicated, but an example will make it clear:

John is tall.	Harry is short.	John is tall and Harry is short.
T	T	T
T	F	F
F	T	F
F	F	F

Here the first two columns cover every possibility for the component propositions to be either true or false. The third column states the truth value of the whole proposition for each combination. Pretty obviously, the conjunction of two propositions is true if both of the component propositions are true; otherwise it is false.

It should also be obvious that our reflections have not depended on the particular sentences we have selected. We could have been talking about dinosaurs instead of people, and we still would have come to the conclusion that the conjunction of two propositions is true if both propositions are true, but false otherwise. In order to reflect the generality of our conclusion, we can drop reference to particular sentences altogether and use *variables* instead. Just as the letters x, y, and z can stand for arbitrary numbers in mathematics, we can let the letters p, q, r, s, . . . stand for arbitrary propositions in logic. We will also use the symbol "&" for "and."

Consider the expression "p & q." Is it true or false? There is obviously no answer to this question. This is not because we do not know what "p" and "q" stand for, for in fact "p" and "q" do not stand for anything at all. Thus "p & q" is not a statement, but a pattern for a whole series of statements. To reflect this, we shall say that "p & q" is a *statement form*. It is a pattern, or form, for a whole series of statements, including "John is tall and Harry is short." To repeat the central idea, we can pass from a statement to a statement form by uniformly replacing statements with statement variables.

Statement	*Statement form*
John is tall and Harry is short.	p & q

When we proceed in the opposite direction by uniformly substituting statements for statement variables, we get what we shall call a *substitution instance* of that statement form.

Statement form	Substitution instance
p & q	Roses are red and violets are blue.

Thus, "John is tall and Harry is short" and "Roses are red and violets are blue" are both substitution instances of the statement form "p & q." These ideas are perfectly simple, but to get clear about them, it is important to notice that "p" can also be a statement form, with "Roses are red and violets are blue" as one of its substitution instances. There is no rule against substituting complex statements for statement variables. Perhaps a bit more surprisingly, our definitions allow "Roses are red and roses are red" to be a substitution instance of "p & q." We get a substitution instance of a statement form by uniformly replacing the same variable by the same statement throughout. We have not said that different variables must be replaced by different statements throughout. Different variables may be replaced by the same statement, but different statements may not be replaced by the same variable. To summarize the discussion thus far:

"Roses are red and violets are blue" is a substitution instance of "p & q."

"Roses are red and violets are blue" is also a substitution instance of "p."

"Roses are red and roses are red" is a substitution instance of "p & q."

"Roses are red and roses are red" is a substitution instance of "p & p."

"Roses are red and violets are blue" is not a substitution instance of "p & p."

"Roses are red" is not a substitution instance of "p & p."[1]

---

[1] One cautionary note. The word "and" is not always used to connect two distinct sentences. Sometimes a sentence has to be rewritten to see that it is equivalent to a sentence that has this form. For example, "John and Amy attended the University of Miami" obviously means the same thing as "John attended the University of Miami and Amy attended the University of Miami." The first way of speaking is shorter, hence more convenient. At other times, the word "and" is not used to connect sentences at all. For example, "Harry and Mike are two tough hombres" does not mean the same thing as "Harry is two tough hombres and Mike is two tough hombres." The original sentence does not express the conjunction of two statements; it expresses a single statement about two people. Sometimes it is not obvious how the word "and" is being used. The sentence "Mary and John are married" can mean that they are *each* married, or that they are married to *each other*. In the first case "and" occurs as a sentential connective; in the second case it does not. Here we are only interested in "and" as it occurs as a sentential connective.

EXERCISE 1

The statement "The night is young and you're so beautiful" is a substitution instance of which of the following statement forms?

(1) p.
(2) p & q.
(3) p & r.
(4) p & p.
(5) p or q.

EXERCISE 2

Find three statement forms of which the following statement is a substitution instance:

> The night is young and you're so beautiful and my flight leaves in thirty minutes.

The expression "p & q" is neither true nor false because it is a *statement form*, not a statement. We get a statement (something that is either true or false) only when we replace these variables by statements. When such a substitution is made, we get a true statement if both substituted statements are true; otherwise, we get a false statement. These reflections are summarized in the following truth-table definition for conjunction, now using variables where previously we used specific statements.

p	q	p & q
T	T	T
T	F	F
F	T	F
F	F	F

Next we can look at an argument involving conjunction. Here is one that is ridiculously simple:

> Harry is short and John is tall.
>
> ∴ Harry is short.

This argument is obviously valid. But why is the argument valid? Why does the conclusion follow from the premise? The answer in this case seems obvious, but we will spell it out in detail as a guide for more difficult cases. Suppose we replace these particular statements by statement forms, using a different variable for each distinct statement throughout the argument. This yields what we shall call an *argument form*, as for example

$$\frac{p \;\&\; q}{\therefore\; p}$$

This is a pattern for endlessly many arguments, each of which is called a substitution instance of this argument form. Every argument that has this general form will also be valid. It really doesn't matter which propositions we put back into this schema; the resulting argument will be valid—so long as we are careful to substitute the same statement for the same variable throughout.

Let us pursue this matter further. If an argument has true premises and a false conclusion, then we know at once that it is invalid. But in saying that an argument is *valid*, we are not only saying that it does not have true premises and a false conclusion; we are saying that the argument *cannot* have a false conclusion when the premises are true. Sometimes this is true because the argument has a structure that rules out the very possibility of true premises and a false conclusion. We can appeal to the notion of an argument form to make sense out of this idea. A somewhat more complicated truth table will make this clear:

		Premise	Conclusion
p	q	$p \;\&\; q$	p
T	T	T	T
T	F	F	T
F	T	F	F
F	F	F	F

The first two columns give all the combinations for the truth values of the statements that we might substitute for p and q. The third column gives the truth value of the premise for each of these combinations and, finally, the fourth column gives the truth value for the conclusion for each combination. (Here, of course, this merely involves repeating the first column. Later on, things will become more complicated and interesting.) If we look at this truth table, we see that no matter how we make substitutions for the variables, we never get a case where the premise is true and the conclusion is false. Here it is important to remember that a valid argument can have false premises, for one proposition can follow from another that is false. Of course, an argument that is sound cannot have a false premise, since a sound argument is defined as a valid argument with true premises.[2]

Let us summarize this discussion. In the case we have examined, validity depends on the form of an argument and not on its particular content. A first principle, then, is this:

> An argument is valid if it is an instance of a valid argument form.

So the argument "Harry is short and John is tall, therefore Harry is short" is valid because it is an instance of the valid argument form "p & q ∴ p." Next we must ask what makes an argument form valid. The answer to this is given in this principle:

> An argument form is valid if it has no substitution instances where the premises are true and the conclusion is false.

We have just seen that the argument form "p & q ∴ p" meets this test. The truth-table analysis showed that. Incidentally, we can use the same truth table to show that the following argument is valid:

John is tall.	p
Harry is short.	q
∴ John is tall and Harry is short.	∴ p & q

The argument on the left is a substitution instance of the argument form on the right, and a glance at the truth table will show that there is no case where all the premises (that is, p and q) are true and where the conclusion (that is, p & q) is false. This pretty well tells the story of the logical properties of the logical connective we call conjunction.

Notice that we have not said that *every* argument that is valid is so in virtue of its form. There may be arguments where the conclusion follows from the premises but where we cannot show that the argument's validity is a matter of logical form. There are, in fact, many arguments that cannot be shown to be valid in terms of their form. Some of these arguments will be examined in the next chapter, where further methods for showing logical form will be developed. Explaining validity by means of logical form has been an ideal of logical theory, but

---

[2] The difference between validity and soundness is explained in Chapter 2.

there are arguments, many of them quite commonplace, where this ideal has yet to be adequately fulfilled. Many arguments in mathematics fall into this category, as does the following very simple argument:

John is taller than Mary.
Mary is taller than Bill.
∴ John is taller than Bill.

At present, however, we shall only consider arguments where the strategy we used for analyzing conjunction continues to work.

Disjunction

Just as we can form a conjunction of two propositions by using the connective "and," we can form a *disjunction* of two propositions by using "or," as in the following compound sentence:

John will win or Harry will win.

Again, it is easy to see that the truth of this whole statement depends on the truth of the component statements. If they are both false, then the statement as a whole is false. If just one of them is true, then the statement as a whole is true. But suppose they are both true, what shall we say then? Sometimes when we say "either–or" we seem to rule out the possibility of both. "You may have chicken or steak" probably means that you cannot have both. Sometimes, however, both are not ruled out— for example, when we say to someone, "If you want to see tall mountains, go to California or Colorado." So one way (in fact, the standard way) to deal with this problem is to say that "or" has two meanings: one *exclusive,* which rules out both, and one *inclusive,* which does not rule out both. We could thus give two truth-table definitions, one for each of these senses of the word "or":

Exclusive			Inclusive		
p	q	p or q	p	q	p or q
T	T	F	T	T	T
T	F	T	T	F	T
F	T	T	F	T	T
F	F	F	F	F	F

For reasons that will become clear in a moment, we will adopt the inclusive sense of the word "or." Where necessary, we will define the exclusive sense using the inclusive sense as a starting point. Logicians symbolize *disjunctions* using the connective "v." The truth table for this connective has the following form:

p	q	$p \vee q$
T	T	T
T	F	T
F	T	T
F	F	F

We shall look at some arguments involving this connective in a moment.

Negation

With conjunction and disjunction, we begin with two propositions and construct a new proposition from them. There is another way in which we can construct a new proposition from another—through *negating* it. Given the proposition "John is clever," we can get a new proposition "John is not clever" simply by inserting the word "not" in the correct place in the sentence. What, exactly, does the word "not" mean? This can be a difficult question to answer, especially if we begin with the assumption that all words stand for things. Does it stand for nothing or, maybe, nothingness? Although some respectable philosophers have sometimes spoken in this way, it is important to see that the word "not" does not stand for anything at all. It has an altogether different function in the language. To see this, think how conjunction and disjunction work. Given two propositions, the word "and" allows us to construct another proposition that is true only when both original propositions are true, and is false otherwise. Turning to disjunction, given two propositions, the word "or" allows us to construct another proposition that is false only when both the original propositions are false, and true otherwise. (Our truth-table definitions reflect these facts.) Using these definitions as a model, how should we define *negation?* A parallel answer is that the negation of a proposition is true just in case the original proposition is false and it is false just in case the original proposition is true. Using the symbol ~ to stand for negation, this gives us the following truth-table definition:

p	$\sim p$
T	F
F	T

How Truth-Functional Connectives Work

We have now defined *conjunction, disjunction,* and *negation.* That, all by itself, is sufficient to complete the branch of modern logic called Propositional Logic. The definitions themselves may seem peculiar. They do not look like the definitions we find in a dictionary. But the form of these definitions is important, for it tells us something interesting about the character of such words as "and," "or," and "not." Two things are worth noting: (1) These expressions are used to construct new propositions from old. (2) The newly constructed proposition is always a *truth function* of the original propositions—that is, the truth value of the new proposition is always determined by the truth value of the original propositions. For this reason they are called *truth-functional connectives.* (Of course, with negation, we start with a *single* proposition.) For example, suppose that A and B are two true propositions and G and H are two false propositions. We can then determine the truth values of more complex propositions built from them using conjunction, disjunction, and negation. Sometimes the correct assignment is obvious at a glance:

$A \& B$	True
$A \& G$	False
$\sim G$	True
$A \vee H$	True
$\sim A \& G$	False

As in mathematics, parentheses can be used to distinguish groupings. Parentheses bring out an important difference between the following two expressions:

$$\sim A \& G \qquad \sim(A \& G)$$

Notice that in one expression the negation symbol applies only to the proposition A, whereas in the other expression it applies to the entire proposition $(A \& G)$. The first expression above is false, then, and the second expression is true.

As expressions become more complex, we reach a point where it is no longer obvious how the truth values of the component propositions determine the truth value of the entire proposition. Here a regular procedure is helpful. The easiest method is to fill in the truth values of the basic propositions and then, step by step, make assignments progressively wider, going from the inside out. For example:

$$\sim((A \vee G) \quad \& \quad \sim(\sim H \& B))$$
$$\sim((T \vee F) \quad \& \quad \sim(\sim F \& T))$$

$$\sim((T \lor F) \quad \& \quad \sim(T \And T))$$
$$\sim(T \quad \& \quad \sim(T))$$
$$\sim(T \quad \& \quad F)$$
$$\sim(F)$$
$$T$$

With very little practice, you can master this technique in dealing with even highly complex examples.

EXERCISE 3

Given that *A*, *B*, and *C* are true propositions and *X*, *Y*, and *Z* are false propositions, determine the truth values of the following complex propositions:

(1) (*A* v *Z*) & B
(2) ~(*Z* v *Z*)
(3) ~~(*A* v *B*)
(4) (*A* v *X*) & (*B* v *Z*)
(5) (*A* & *X*) v (*B* & *Z*)
(6) ~(*A* v (*Z* v *X*))
(7) ~(*A* v ~(*Z* v *X*))
(8) ~*Z* v (*Z* & *A*)
(9) *A* v ((~*B* & *C*) v ~(~*B* v ~(*Z* v *B*)))
(10) *A* & ((~*B* & *C*) v ~(~*B* v ~(*Z* v *B*)))

But what is the point of all this? In everyday life we rarely run into an expression as complicated as the one given in our example. Our purpose here is to sharpen our sensitivity to how truth-functional connectives work, and then to express our insights in clear ways. This is important because the validity of many arguments depends on the logical features of these truth-functional connectives. We can now turn directly to this subject.

Earlier we saw that every argument of the form "*p* & *q* ∴ *p*" will be valid. This is obvious in itself, but we saw that this claim could be justified by an appeal to truth tables. A truth-table analysis shows us that an argument of this form can never have an instance where the premise is true and the conclusion is false. We can now apply this same technique to arguments that are more complex. In the beginning we will take arguments that are still easy to follow without the use of technical help. At the end, we will consider some arguments that most people cannot follow without guidance.

Consider the following argument:

Harry is spending his summer in Florida or California.
Harry is not spending his summer in California or New York.
Therefore, Harry is spending his summer in Florida.

We can use the following abbreviations:

A = Harry is spending his summer in Florida.
B = Harry is spending his summer in California.
C = Harry is spending his summer in New York.

Using these abbreviations, and then substituting the variables p, q, and r, the argument looks like this:

$$A \lor B \qquad\qquad p \lor q$$
$$\sim(B \lor C) \qquad\qquad \sim(q \lor r)$$
$$\therefore A \qquad\qquad\qquad \therefore p$$

The expression on the right gives the argument *form* of the argument presented on the left. To see whether the argument is valid, we ask if the argument form is valid. The procedure is cumbersome, but perfectly mechanical:

			Pr.		Pr.	Cn.
p	q	r	$(p \lor q)$	$(q \lor r)$	$\sim(q \lor r)$	p
T	T	T	T	T	F	T
T	T	F	T	T	F	T
T	F	T	T	T	F	T
T	F	F	T	F	T	T *O.K.*
F	T	T	T	T	F	F
F	T	F	T	T	F	F
F	F	T	F	T	F	F
F	F	F	F	F	T	F

Notice that there is only one combination of truth values where both premises are true, and in that case the conclusion is true as well. So the original argument is valid since it is an instance of a valid argument form, i.e., an argument form with no instances of true premises combined with a false conclusion.

This last truth table may need some explaining. First, why do we get eight rows in this truth table where before we got only four? The answer to this is that we need to test the argument form for *every possible combination of truth values* for the component propositions. With two variables, there are four combinations: (TT), (TF), (FT), and (FF). With three variables, there are eight combinations: (TTT), (TTF), (TFT), (TFF), (FTT), (FTF), (FFT), and (FFF). The general rule is this: If an argument form has *n* variables, the truth table used in its analysis must have 2^n rows. For four variables there will be sixteen rows; for five variables, thirty-two rows; for six variables, sixty-four rows; and so on. You can be sure that you capture all possible combinations of truth values by using the following pattern in constructing the columns of your truth table:

First column	*Second column*	*Third column* . . .
First half T's, second half F's	First quarter T's, second quarter F's	First eighth T's, second eighth F's

A glance at the earlier examples in this chapter will show that we have been using this pattern. Of course, as soon as an argument becomes very complex, these truth tables become very large indeed. But there is no need to worry about this, since we will not consider complex arguments. (Those who do turn to a computer for help.)

The style of the truth table above is also significant. The premises (Pr.) are plainly labeled and so is the conclusion (Cn.). A line is drawn under every row where the premises are all true. (In this case, there is only one such row.) If the conclusion on this line is also true, it is marked "O.K." If every line where the premises are all true is okay, the argument form is valid. Marking all this out may seem rather childish, but it is worth doing. First, it helps guard against mistakes; more importantly, it draws one's attention to the purpose of the procedure being used. Cranking out truth tables without understanding what they are about—or even why they might be helpful—does not enlighten the mind or elevate the spirit.

For the sake of contrast, we can next consider an invalid argument:

> Harry is spending his summer in Florida or California.
> Harry is not spending his summer both in California and New York.
>
> ∴ Harry is spending his summer in Florida.

Using the same abbreviations as earlier for Harry's vacation plans, this becomes:

Argument	Argument form
$A \lor B$	$p \lor q$
~$(B \And C)$	~$(q \And r)$
∴ A	∴ p

Truth-table analysis:

			Pr.		Pr.	Cn.
p	q	r	$(p \lor q)$	$(q \And r)$	~$(q \And r)$	p
T	T	T	T	T	F	T
T	T	F	T	F	T	T
T	F	T	T	F	T	T
T	F	F	T	F	T	T
F	T	T	T	T	F	F
F	T	F	T	F	T	F
F	F	T	F	F	T	F
F	F	F	F	F	T	F

This time, we find four rows where all the premises are true. In three cases the conclusion is true as well, but in one case the conclusion is false. The argument form is thus invalid, since it is possible for it to have a substitution instance where all the premises are true and the conclusion is false. In the present case, this possibility arises in the sixth row of the truth table, where A would be false, B true, and C false.

<hr>

EXERCISE 4

Using the truth-table technique outlined above, test the following argument forms for validity:

(1) $p \lor q$
     p
    ∴ ~q

(2) $\sim(p \lor q)$

$\therefore \sim q$

(3) $\sim(p \And q)$

$\sim q$

$\therefore \sim p$

(4) p

$\sim(p \lor q)$

$\therefore \sim q$

(5) p

$\sim(p \lor q)$

$\therefore r$

(6) $(p \And q) \lor (p \And r)$

$\therefore p \And (q \lor r)$

(7) $(p \lor q) \And (p \lor r)$

$\therefore p \And (q \lor r)$

(8) $p \And q$

$\therefore (p \lor r) \And q$

SOME FURTHER CONNECTIVES

We have developed the logic of propositions using only three basic notions corresponding (perhaps roughly) to the English words "and," "or," and "not." Now let us go back to the question of the two possible senses—exclusive and inclusive—of the word "or." Sometimes "or" seems to rule out the possibility that both options are open; at other times "or" seems to allow this possibility. This is the difference between exclusive and inclusive disjunction, respectively.

Suppose we use the symbol $\underline{\lor}$ to stand for exclusive disjunction. (After this discussion, we will not use it again.) We could then define this new connective in the following way:

$$(p \underline{\lor} q) = \text{(by definition)} ((p \lor q) \And \sim(p \And q))$$

It is not hard to see that the expression on the right side of this definition captures the force of exclusive disjunction. Since we can always define exclusive disjunction when we want it, there is no need to introduce it into our system of basic notions.

Construct a truth-table analysis of the expression on the right side of the preceding definition and compare it with the truth-table definition of exclusive disjunction given on page 146.

Actually, in analyzing arguments we have been defining new logical connectives without much thinking about it. For example, *not both p and q* was symbolized as "$\sim(p \ \& \ q)$." *Neither p nor q* was symbolized as "$\sim(p \ v \ q)$." Let us look more closely at the example "$\sim(p \ v \ q)$." Perhaps we should have symbolized it as "$\sim p \ \& \ \sim q$." As a matter of fact, we could have used this symbolization, because the two expressions amount to the same thing. Again, this may be obvious, but we can prove it by using a truth table in yet another way. Compare the truth-table analysis of these two expressions:

					*		*
p	q	$\sim p$	$\sim q$	$\sim p \ \& \ \sim q$		$(p \ v \ q)$	$\sim(p \ v \ q)$
T	T	F	F	F		T	F
T	F	F	T	F		T	F
F	T	T	F	F		T	F
F	F	T	T	T		F	T

Under "$\sim p \ \& \ \sim q$" we find the column (FFFT), and we find the same sequence under "$\sim(p \ v \ q)$." This shows that for every possible substitution we make, these two expressions will yield statements of the same truth value. We shall say that these statement forms are *truth-functionally equivalent*.

Given the notion of truth-functional equivalence, the possibility of more than one translation can often be solved. If two translations are truth-functionally equivalent, then it does not matter which one we use in testing for validity. Of course, some translations will seem more natural than others. For example, "$p \ v \ q$" is truth-functionally equivalent to

$$\sim((\sim p \ \& \ \sim p) \ \& \ (\sim q \ v \ \sim q))$$

The first expression is obviously more natural than the second, even though they are truth-functionally equivalent.

So far in this chapter we have seen that by using conjunction, disjunction, and negation, it is possible to construct complex statements out of simple statements. A distinctive feature of compound statements constructed in these three ways is that the truth of the compound statement is always a function of the truth of its component propositions. Thus, these three notions allow us to construct truth-functionally compound statements. Some arguments depend for their validity simply upon these truth-functional connectives. When this is so, it is possible to test for validity in a purely mechanical way. This can be done through the use of truth tables. Thus, in this area at least, we are able to give a clear account of validity and to specify exact procedures for testing for validity. Now we shall go on to examine an area where the application of this approach is more problematic. It concerns *conditionals*.

CONDITIONALS

Conditionals often occur in arguments. They have the form, "If ____, then _____." Sometimes conditionals appear in the indicative mood:

If it rains, the crop will be saved.

Sometimes they occur in the subjunctive mood:

If it had rained, the crop would have been saved.

There are also conditional imperatives:

If a fire breaks out, call the fire department first!

There are conditional promises:

If you get into trouble, give me a call and I promise to help you.

Indeed, conditionals get a great deal of use in our language, and they very often appear in arguments. It is important, therefore, to understand them.

Unfortunately, there is no general agreement among experts about the correct way to analyze conditionals. We shall simplify matters by considering only *indicative* conditionals, but even here there is no settled opinion about the correct position to adopt. It may seem surprising that disagreement should exist concerning such a simple and fundamental notion as the if-then construction. Nonetheless, be prepared that this discussion will have none of the settled character of the previous one. First we shall describe the most standard treatment of conditionals; second, we shall consider a number of alternatives to it.

For conjunction, disjunction, and negation, the truth-table methods provided an approach that was at once plausible and effective. An indicative conditional is also compounded out of two simpler propositions, and this suggests that we might be able to offer a truth-table definition for conditionals as well. What should the truth table look like? When we try to answer this question, we get stuck almost at once, for it is unclear how we should fill in the table in three out of four cases.

p	q	If p, then q.
T	T	?
T	F	F
F	T	?
F	F	?

Let us call "p" the *antecedent* of this conditional and "q" its *consequent*. It seems obvious that a conditional cannot be true if the antecedent is true and the consequent false. We record this by putting an F in the second row. But suppose p and q are replaced by two arbitrary true propositions, say, "two plus two equals four" and "Chile is in South America." What shall we say about the conditional:

If two plus two equals four, then Chile is in South America.

The first thing to say is that this is a very strange statement, because the arithmetic remark in the antecedent doesn't seem to have anything to do with the geographical remark in the consequent. So this conditional is odd—indeed, extremely odd—but is it true or false? At this point a reasonable response is bafflement.

Now consider the following argument, which is intended to solve all these problems by giving good reasons for assigning truth values in each row of the truth table. One thing that seems obvious is that if "If p, then q" is true, then it is not the case that "p" is true and "q" is false. That in turn means that "$\sim(p \ \& \sim q)$" must be true. Now let's reason in the opposite direction. Suppose that we know that "$\sim(p \ \& \sim q)$" is true. For this to be true, "$p \ \& \sim q$" must be false. We know that from the truth-table definition of negation. Next let us suppose that "p" is true. Then "$\sim q$" must be false. We know that from the truth-table definition of conjunction. Finally, if "$\sim q$" is false, then "q" itself must be true. This line of reasoning is supposed to show that we can derive "If p, then q" from "Not both p and not q." The first step in the argument was intended to show that we can derive "Not both p and not q" from "If p, then q." But if each of these expressions is derivable from the other, this suggests that they are equivalent. We use this background argument as a justification of the following definition:

If p, then q = (by definition) Not both p and not q.

We can put this into symbols using a horseshoe to symbolize conditionals:

$$p \supset q = \text{(by definition)} \sim(p \ \& \ \sim q)$$

Given this definition, we can now construct the truth table for indicative conditionals. It is simply the truth table for "$\sim(p \ \& \ \sim q)$":

p	q	$\sim(p \ \& \ \sim q)$	$(p \supset q)$	$(\sim p \ \vee \ q)$
T	T	T	T	T
T	F	F	F	F
F	T	T	T	T
F	F	T	T	T

Notice that "$(\sim p \ \vee \ q)$" is also truth-functionally equivalent to the other expressions. We have included "$(\sim p \ \vee \ q)$" because traditionally it has been used to define "$p \supset q$." For reasons that are now obscure, when a conditional is defined in this truth-functional way, it is called a *material conditional*.

Now let us suppose, for the moment, that the notion of a material conditional corresponds exactly with our idea of an indicative conditional. What would follow from this? The answer is that we could treat conditionals in the same way in which we have treated conjunction, disjunction, and negation. A conditional would be just one more kind of truth-functionally compound statement capable of definition by truth tables. Furthermore, arguments that depend on this notion (together with conjunction, disjunction, and negation) could be settled by appeal to truth-table techniques. Let us pause for a moment to examine this.

One of the most common patterns of reasoning is called *modus ponens*. It looks like this:

If p, then q. $p \supset q$
$\underline{\quad p \quad\quad\quad\quad\quad\quad}$ $\underline{\quad p \quad\quad}$
$\therefore q$ $\therefore q$

The truth-table definition of material implication shows at once that this pattern of argument is valid.

Pr.		Pr.	Cn.
p	q	$p \supset q$	q
T	T	T	T
T	F	F	F
F	T	T	T
F	F	T	F

EXERCISE 6

Show that the argument form called *modus tollens* is valid. It looks like this:

$$p \supset q$$
$$\frac{\sim q}{}$$
$$\therefore \sim p$$

These same techniques allow us to show that one of the traditional fallacies is, indeed, a fallacy. It is called the fallacy of denying the antecedent, and it looks like this:

$$p \supset q$$
$$\frac{\sim p}{}$$
$$\therefore \sim q$$

The truth-table analysis showing the invalidity of this argument has the following form:

		Pr.	Pr.	Cn.
p	q	$p \supset q$	$\sim p$	$\sim q$
T	T	T	F	F
T	F	F	F	T
F	T	T	T	F
F	F	T	T	T

EXERCISE 7

A second standard fallacy is called affirming the consequent. It looks like this:

$$p \supset q$$
$$\underline{q}$$
$$\therefore p$$

Using truth-table techniques, show that this argument form is invalid.

We can examine one last argument that has been historically significant. It is called the *hypothetical syllogism* and has the following form:

$$p \supset q$$
$$\underline{q \supset r}$$
$$\therefore p \supset r$$

Since we are dealing with an argument form containing three variables, we must perform the boring task of constructing a truth table with eight rows:

			Pr.	Pr.	Cn.
p	q	r	$p \supset q$	$q \supset r$	$p \supset r$
T	T	T	T	T	T
T	T	F	T	F	F
T	F	T	F	T	T
T	F	F	F	T	F
F	T	T	T	T	T
F	T	F	T	F	T
F	F	T	T	T	T
F	F	F	T	T	T

This is fit work for a computer, not for a human being, but it is important to see that it actually works.

CONDITIONALS **159**

Why is it important to see that these techniques work? Most people, after all, could see that hypothetical syllogisms are correct without going through all this tedious business. We seem only to be piling boredom on top of triviality. This protest deserves an answer. Suppose we ask someone *why* he or she thinks that the conclusion follows from the premises in a hypothetical syllogism. The person might answer that anyone can see that—something, by the way, that is false. Beyond this he or she might say that it all depends upon the meanings of the words, or that it is all a matter of definition. But if we go on to ask *which words* and *what definitions,* most people will fall silent. What we have done is to discover that the validity of some arguments depends on the meanings of such words as "and," "or," "not," and "if-then." We have then gone on to give explicit definitions of these terms—definitions, by the way, that help us to see how these terms function in an argument. Finally, by getting all these *simple* things right, we have produced what is called a *decision procedure* for determining the validity of every argument involving only conjunction, disjunction, negation, and conditionals. Our truth-table techniques give us an automatic procedure for settling questions of validity in this area. In fact, truth-table techniques have practical applications, for example, in computer programming. But the important point here is that through understanding how these techniques work, we can gain a deeper insight into the notion of validity.

EXERCISE 8

Using the truth-table techniques employed above, test the following argument forms for validity. (For your own entertainment, guess about the validity of the argument form before working it out.)

(1) $p \supset q$

$\therefore q \supset p$

(2) $p \supset q$

$\therefore \sim q \supset \sim p$

(3) $(p \lor q) \supset r$

$\therefore p \supset r$

(4) $(p \& q) \supset r$

$\therefore p \supset r$

(5) $p \supset q$

$\quad q \supset r$

$\therefore p \supset (q \& r)$

(6) $(p \vee q)$ & $(p \vee r)$
      $\sim r$
      _____

∴ $\sim q \supset p$

(7) $(p \supset q)$ & $(p \supset \sim r)$
      r & $\sim q$
      _____

∴ $\sim p$

(8) $p \supset q$
      $q \supset r$
      _____

∴ $\sim r \supset \sim p$

(9) $p \supset (q \supset r)$
      _____

∴ $(p$ & $q) \supset r$

(10) $p \supset (q \supset r)$
      $p \supset q$
      _____

∴ r

LOGICAL LANGUAGE AND EVERYDAY LANGUAGE

Early in this chapter we started out by talking about such common words as "and" and "or," and then slipped over to talking about *conjunction* and *disjunction*. The transition was a bit sneaky, but intentional. To understand what is going on here, we can ask how closely these logical notions we have defined match their everyday counterparts. We will start with conjunction, and then come back to the more difficult question of conditionals. At first sight, the match seems to be very bad indeed.

In everyday discourse, we do not go about conjoining random bits of information. We do not say, for example, that two plus two equals four and Chile is in South America. We already know why we do not say such things, for unless the context is quite extraordinary, this is bound to violate the rule of Relevance. But if we are interested in validity, the rule of Relevance—together with all other pragmatic rules—is simply beside the point.

The formal notion of conjunction is also insensitive to another important feature of our everyday discourse: context. It reduces all conjunctions to their bare truth-functional content. We have already seen that the following remarks have a very different force in the context of an argument:

The ring is beautiful, but expensive.

The ring is expensive, but beautiful.

These two remarks will mean opposite things in the context of an actual argument, but from a purely formal point of view they are equivalent. We can translate the first sentence as "*B & E*" and the second as "*E & B*." Their truth-functional equivalence is too obvious to need proof.

It might seem that if formal analysis cannot distinguish an "and" from a "but," then it can hardly be of any use at all. This is not true. A formal analysis of an argument will tell us just one thing: whether the argument is valid or not. If we expect the analysis to tell us more than this, we will be disappointed. It is important to remember two things: (1) we expect arguments to be valid; (2) usually we expect much more than this from an argument. To elaborate upon the second point, we usually expect an argument to be sound as well as valid—we expect the premises to be true. Beyond this, we expect the argument to be informative, intelligible, convincing, and so forth. Validity, then, is an important aspect of an argument and formal analysis helps us to evaluate it. But validity is not the only aspect of an argument that concerns us; in many contexts it is not even our chief concern.

We can now look at our analysis of conditionals, for here we find some striking departures between the logician's analysis and everyday use. The following arguments are all valid:

(1) p (2) $\sim p$
$$\therefore q \supset p \qquad \therefore p \supset q$$
(3) $p \ \& \sim p$ (4) q
$$\therefore q \qquad\qquad \therefore p \ v \sim p$$

We can see that these arguments are all valid by checking them with the following truth table:

p	q	$\sim p$	$\sim q$	$q \supset p$	$p \supset q$	$p \ \& \sim p$	$p \ v \sim p$
T	T	F	F	T	T	F	T
T	F	F	T	T	F	F	T
F	T	T	F	F	T	F	T
F	F	T	T	T	T	F	T

Yet, though valid, all these argument forms seem odd—so odd that they have actually been called *paradoxical*. The first argument form seems to say this: If a proposition is true, then it is implied by any proposition whatsoever. Here is an example of an argument that satisfies this argument form and is therefore valid:

Lincoln was President.
If air is hard, Lincoln was President.

This is a *very* peculiar argument to call valid. First we want to know what air has to do with Lincoln's having been President. Beyond this, how can his having been President depend upon the falsehood that air is hard? We can give these questions even more force by noticing that even the following argument is valid:

> Lincoln was President.
> If Lincoln was not President, then Lincoln was President.

This is an instance of the valid argument form: "$p \therefore \sim p \supset p$."

The other three argument forms are also paradoxical. They seem to say the following things: (2) A false proposition implies anything whatsoever. (3) Anything whatsoever follows from a contradiction. "p & $\sim p$" is the statement form for a *contradiction,* or what people sometimes call a self-contradiction. Look at the truth table and you will see that it is false for all possible truth value combinations. (4) A tautology may be validly inferred from any proposition whatsoever. (Logicians call "p v $\sim p$" the statement form for a *tautology.* Just the reverse of a contradiction, a tautology is true no matter what truth values are assigned to its constituent parts.)

At this point, nonphilosophers become impatient, whereas philosophers become worried. We started out with principles that seemed to be both obvious and simple. Now, quite suddenly, we are being overwhelmed with a whole series of peculiar results. What in the world has happened, and what should be done about it? Philosophers remain divided in the answers they give to these questions. The responses fall into two main categories: (1) Simply give up the idea that conditionals can be defined truth-functionally and search for a different and better analysis of conditionals that avoids the difficulties involved in truth-functional analysis. (2) Take the difficult line and argue that there is nothing wrong with calling the above argument forms valid.

The first approach is highly technical and cannot be pursued in detail in this book. The general idea is this: Instead of identifying "If p, then q" with "Not both p and not q," identify it with "Not *possibly* both p and not q." This provides a stronger notion of a conditional and avoids some—though not all—of the suspicious arguments noticed above. This theory is given a systematic development by offering a logical analysis of the notion of *possibility.* This branch of logic is called *modal logic,* and has shown remarkable development in recent years.

Paul Grice, whose theories played a prominent part in Chapter 1, has taken the second line. He acknowledges—as anyone must—that the four argument forms above are decidedly odd. He denies, however, that this oddness has anything to do with *validity.* Validity (that is, *formal* validity) concerns one thing and one thing only: An argument is valid if it is an instance of an argument form that never takes us from true premises to a false conclusion. The above arguments are valid by this definition of validity. Of course, arguments can be defective in all sorts of other ways. Look at the third and fourth arguments. Since "q" can be replaced by any proposition (true or false), the rule of Relevance will often be violated. It is worth pointing out violations of the rule of Relevance, but, according to Grice, this has nothing to do with validity. Now if we look at the first two arguments we see that they can also lead to arguments that contain a violation of the rule of Relevance. They also invite violations of the rule of Quantity. A conditional will be true just in case the consequent is true. Given this, it doesn't matter whether the antecedent is true or false. Again, a conditional is true just in case the antecedent is false—and it doesn't matter, given this, whether the consequent is true or false. Yet it can be very misleading to *use* a conditional on the basis of these logical features. For example, it would be very misleading for a museum guard to say, "If you give me five dollars, then I will let you into the exhibition," when, in fact, he will let you in in any case. For Grice, this is misleading since it violates the rule of Quantity. Yet, strictly speaking, it is not false. Strictly speaking, it is true.

The Grice line is attractive, for, among other things, it allows us to accept the truth-functional account of conditionals with all its simplicity. Yet sometimes it is difficult to swallow. Consider the following remark:

> If God exists, then there is evil in the world.

If Grice's analysis is correct, even the most pious will have to admit that this conditional is true provided only that he is willing to admit that there is evil in the world. Yet this conditional plainly suggests that God's existence has something to do with the evil in the world, and the pious will wish to deny this suggestion. Grice would agree: The conditional plainly suggests that there is some connection between God's existence and the evil in the world—presumably, that is the point of connecting them in a conditional. All the same, this is something that is suggested, not asserted, and once more we come to the conclusion that this conditional is misleading—and therefore in need of criticism and correction—but still, strictly speaking, true.

Philosophers and logicians have had various responses to Grice's position. No consensus has emerged on this issue. The author of this book finds it on the whole convincing and we shall adopt it in this book. This will have two advantages: (1) This appeal to pragmatics fits in well with our previous discussions, and (2) it provides a way of keeping the logic simple and within the range of a beginning student. Other philosophers and logicians continue to work toward a definition superior to the truth-table definition for indicative conditionals.

Other Conditionals in Ordinary Language

So far we have considered only one form in which conditionals appear in everyday language: the indicative conditional "If p, then q." But, as we have noted, conditionals come in a variety of forms and some of them demand subtle treatment.

We can first consider the contrast between constructions using "if" and those using "only if":

(1) I'll clean the barn if Hazel will help me.

(2) I'll clean the barn only if Hazel will help me.

Adopting the following abbreviations:

B = I'll clean the barn
H = Hazel will help me

the first sentence is translated as follows:

(1) $H \supset B$

Notice that in the prose version of (1), the antecedent and consequent appear in reverse order. "q if p" means the same thing as "If p, then q."

How shall we translate the second sentence? Here we should move slowly and first notice what seems incontestable: If Hazel does not help me, then I will not clean the barn. This is translated in the following way:

(2) $\sim H \supset \sim B$

And that is equivalent[3] to:

(2) $B \supset H$

A more difficult question arises when we ask whether an implication runs the other way. When I say that I will clean the barn only if Hazel will help me, am I committing myself to cleaning the barn if she does help me? There is a strong temptation to answer the question "yes" and then give a fuller translation of (2) in the following way:

(2) $(B \supset H) \, \& \, (H \supset B)$

---

[3] If this equivalence is not obvious, it can be quickly established by using a truth table.

Logicians call such two-way implications *biconditionals,* and we shall discuss them in a moment. But adding this second conjunct is almost surely a mistake, for we can think of parallel cases where we would not be tempted to include it. A government regulation might read as follows:

A person is eligible for retirement only if he or she is past 65.

From this it does not follow that anyone past 65 is eligible for retirement, for there may be other requirements as well.

Why were we tempted to use a biconditional in translating sentences containing the connective "only if"? Why, that is, are we tempted to think that the statement "I'll clean the barn only if Hazel will help me" implies "If Hazel helps me, then I will clean the barn"? The answer turns upon the notion of conversational implication first met in Chapter 1. If I am *not* going to clean the barn, whether Hazel helps me or not, then it will be misleading—a violation of the rule of Quantity— to say that I will clean the barn only if Hazel helps me. For this reason, in many contexts, the use of a sentence of the form "*p* only if *q*" will conversationally imply a commitment "*p* if and only if *q*."

We can next look at sentences of the form "*p* if and only if *q*"— so-called biconditionals. If I say that I will clean the barn if and only if Hazel will help me, then I am saying that I will clean it if she helps and I will not clean it if she does not help. Translated, this becomes:

$(H \supset B) \& (\sim H \supset \sim B)$

This is equivalent to:

$(H \supset B) \& (B \supset H)$

We thus have an implication going both ways—the characteristic form of a biconditional. In fact, constructions containing the expression "if and only if" do not often appear in everyday speech. They appear almost exclusively in technical or legal writing. In ordinary conversation, we capture the force of a biconditional by saying something like this:

I will clean the barn, but only if Hazel helps me.

The decision whether to translate a remark of everyday conversation into a conditional or a biconditional is often subtle and difficult. We have already noticed that the use of sentences of the form "*p* only if *q*" will often conversationally imply a commitment to the biconditional "*p* if and only if *q*." In the same way, the *use* of the conditional "*p* if *q*" will also carry this same implication. If I plan to clean the barn whether Hazel helps me or not, it will certainly be misleading—again, a violation of the rule of Quantity—to say that I will clean the barn *if* Hazel helps me.

So far, then, we have the following results:

(1) "*q* if *p*" translates "($p \supset q$)." However, the use of "*q* if *p*" often has the conversational force of a biconditional.
(2) "*q* only if *p*" translates "($q \supset p$)." However, the use of "*q* only if *p*" often has the conversational force of a biconditional.
(3) "*q* if and only if *p*" translates "($p \supset q$) & ($q \supset p$)." The biconditional, "*q* if and only if *p*," is more often conversationally implied than explicitly stated in everyday discourse.

We can close this discussion by considering one further, rather difficult, case. What is the force of saying "*p unless q*"? Is this a biconditional, or just a conditional? If it is just a conditional, which way does the implication go? There is a strong temptation to treat this as a biconditional, but the following example shows this to be wrong:

Reagan will not win re-election unless he carries the Northeast.

This sentence clearly indicates that Reagan will not win re-election if he does not carry the Northeast. Using abbreviations:

N = Reagan will carry the Northeast.
W = Reagan will win reelection.
$\sim N \supset \sim W$

The original statement does not imply—even conversationally—that he will win re-election if he does carry the Northeast. The expression "$\sim p$ unless *q*" means the same thing as the expression "*p* only if *q*," and they both translate:

$(p \supset q)$

SUMMARY

In this chapter we have tried to get a clear conception of the notion of validity in one particular area. We have studied the logic of truth-functionally compound statements. These are arguments that depend for their validity on the logical properties of *conjunction, disjunction, negation,* and *material implication.* We have offered truth-table definitions of these notions and laid down a truth-table method for testing the validity of arguments that turn upon these connectives. Although we have not shown this, we have, in fact, developed a method for testing the validity of *all* arguments whose validity depends upon the character of these truth-functional connectives.

Translate each of the following sentences into symbolic notation, using the suggested symbols as abbreviations.

(1) The Reds will win only if the Dodgers collapse. (*R, D*)

(2) The Steelers will win if their defense holds up. (*S, D*)

(3) If it rains or snows, the game will be called off. (*R, S, O*)

(4) Unless there is a panic, stock prices will continue to rise. (*P, R*)

(5) If the house comes up for sale and if I have money in hand, I will bid on it. (*S, M, B*)

(6) You can be a success if only you try. (*S, T*)

(7) You will get a good bargain provided you get there early. (*B, E*)

(8) You cannot lead a happy life without friends. (Let *H* = "You can lead a happy life," and let *F* = "You have friends.")

Translate each of the following arguments into symbolic notation. Then (a) test the argument for validity using truth-table techniques and (b) comment on any violations of conversational rules.

Example: Harold is clever, so if Harold isn't clever, then Anna isn't clever either. (*H, A*)

H	p
$\sim H \supset \sim A$	$\sim p \supset \sim q$

(a) Pr.   Cn.

p	q	$\sim p$	$\sim q$	$\sim p \supset \sim q$
T	T	F	F	T
T	F	F	T	T
F	T	T	F	F
F	F	T	T	T

(b) The argument violates the rule of Relevance.

(1) Jones is brave, so Jones is brave or Jones is brave. (*J*)

(2) The Democrats will run either Jones or Borg. If Borg runs they will lose the South and if Jones runs they will lose the North. So the Democrats will lose either the North or South. (*J, B, S, N*)

(3) Although Brown will pitch, the Rams will lose. If the Rams lose, their manager will get fired, so their manager will get fired. (*B, L, F*)

(4) America will win the Olympics unless Russia does and Russia will win the Olympics unless East Germany does, so America will win the Olympics unless East Germany does. (*A, R, E*)

(5) If you dial 0, you will get the operator, so if you dial 0 and do not get the operator, then there is something wrong with the telephone. (*D, O, W*)

(6) The Republicans will carry either New Mexico or Arizona, but since they will carry Arizona they will not carry New Mexico. (*A, N*)

(7) John will play only if the situation is hopeless, but the situation will be hopeless, so John will play. (*P, H*)

(8) (a) Reagan will win the election whether he wins Idaho or not, therefore Reagan will win the election. (*R, I*)
(b) Reagan will win the election, therefore Reagan will win the election whether he wins Idaho or not. (*R, I*)
(c) Reagan will win the election, therefore Reagan will win the election whether he wins a majority or not. (*R, M*)

(9) If you flip the switch then the light will go on, but if the light goes on, then the generator is working; so if you flip the switch, then the generator is working. (*F, L, G*)
(This example is due to Charles L. Stevenson.)

◆ *EXERCISE 11* *

Decide whether each of the following claims is true or false, and then defend your answer:

(1) An argument that is a substitution instance of a valid argument form is always valid.

---

*For chapter review.

(2) An argument that is a substitution instance of an invalid argument form is always invalid.

(3) An invalid argument is always a substitution instance of an invalid argument form.

DISCUSSION QUESTIONS

(1) If "not-p unless q" is translated as "$p \supset q$," then "p unless q" should be translated as "p v q." Why?

(2) Is a valid argument always a substitution instance of a valid argument form?

(3) Whatever its conclusion, an argument with inconsistent premises will always be valid. First of all, why is this true? Second, why doesn't this allow us to prove anything we please?

(4) As we have seen in Chapter 4, arguments are sometimes criticized for being circular. Are such arguments valid or invalid? Are they ever sound? In answering this question pay close attention to the exact definitions of validity and soundness.

8

The Formal Analysis of Argument: Part Two

In Chapter 7 we saw how validity can depend on the external connections between propositions. By examining in detail the theory of *immediate inference* and the theory of the *categorical syllogism*, this chapter will demonstrate how validity can depend on the internal structure of propositions. Our interest in these two aspects of logic is mostly theoretical. Understanding the theory of the syllogism deepens our understanding of validity even if this theory is, in most cases, difficult to apply directly to complex arguments in daily life.

Armed with the techniques developed in Chapter 7, we can look at the following argument:

All squares are rectangles.
All rectangles have parallel sides.

∴ All squares have parallel sides.

At a glance it is obvious that the conclusion follows from the premises—it is a valid argument. Furthermore, if it is valid, it may be valid in virtue of its *form*. In order to show the form of this argument, we might try something of the following kind:

$$p \supset q$$
$$q \supset r$$
$$\therefore p \supset r$$

BUT THIS IS A MISTAKE, and a bad mistake. We have used the letters "p," "q," and "r" as *propositional variables*—they stand for arbitrary propositions. But the proposition "All squares are rectangles" is not itself composed of two propositions.

In fact, if we attempt to translate the above argument into the language of the propositional calculus, we get the following result:

$$p$$
$$q$$
$$\therefore r$$

This, of course, is not a valid argument form. But if we look back at the original argument we see that it is obviously valid. This shows that the Propositional Logic—however adequate it is in its own areas—is not capable of explaining the validity of *all* valid arguments. To broaden our understanding of the notion of validity, we will examine a branch of logic developed in ancient times, *the theory of the syllogism*.

CATEGORICAL PROPOSITIONS

In the argument above, the first premise asserts some kind of relationship between squares and rectangles; the second premise asserts some kind of relationship between rectangles and things with parallel sides; finally *in virtue of this*, the conclusion asserts a relationship between squares and things having parallel sides. Our task, now, is to understand these relationships as clearly as possible so that we can discover the *basis* for the validity of this argument. Again we shall adopt the strategy of starting from very simple cases and using the insights gained there for dealing with more complicated cases.

A natural way to represent the relationships expressed by the propositions in an argument is through diagrams. Suppose we draw one circle standing for all things that are squares and another circle standing for all things that are rectangles. The claim that all squares are rectangles may be represented by placing the circle representing squares completely inside the circle representing rectangles.

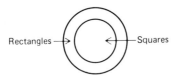

Another way of representing this relationship is to begin with overlapping circles.

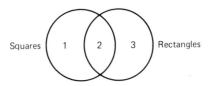

We then shade out the portions of the circles that represent nothing. Since all squares are rectangles, there is nothing that is a square that is not a rectangle—that is, there is nothing in region 1. So our diagram looks like this:

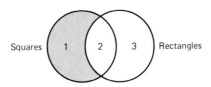

Either method of representation seems plausible. We shall, however, use the system of overlapping circles because in the long run they actually work better. They are called Venn diagrams.

Having examined *one* relationship that can exist between two classes, it is natural to wonder what other relationships might exist. Going to the opposite extreme from our first example, two classes may have *nothing* in common. The proposition "No triangles are squares" expresses such a relationship. We diagram this by indicating that there is nothing in common between squares and triangles.

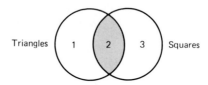

In these first two extreme cases we have indicated that one class is either completely included in another ("All squares are rectangles") or completely excluded from another ("No triangles are squares"). Sometimes, however, we make the weaker remark that two classes have at least *some* things in common. We say, for example, that "some aliens are spies." How shall we indicate this on the following diagram?

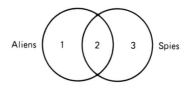

In this case, we do not want to cross out any whole region. We do not want to cross out region 1 because we are not saying that *all* aliens are spies. Plainly, we do not want to cross out region 2, for we are actually saying that some persons are both aliens and spies. Finally, we do not want to cross out region 3, for we are not saying that all spies are aliens. Saying that some aliens are spies does not rule out the possibility that some spies are homegrown.

It is plain, then, that we need some new device to represent claims that two classes have at least *some* members in common. We shall do this in the following way:

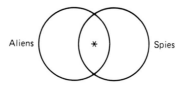

Here the asterisk indicates that there is at least one person who is both an alien and a spy. Notice, by the way, that we are departing a bit from an everyday way of speaking. "Some" is usually taken to mean *more than*

one; here we let it mean *at least one.* In fact, this makes things simpler and will really cause no trouble.

Given this new method of diagramming class relationships, we can immediately think of other possibilities. The following diagram indicates that there is someone who is an alien but not a spy. In more natural language, it represents the claim that *some aliens are not spies.*

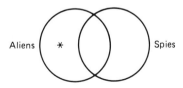

Next we can indicate that there is someone who is a spy but not an alien. More simply, we are representing the claim that *some spies are not aliens.*

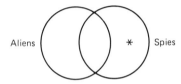

Finally, we can indicate that there is someone who is neither a spy nor an alien:

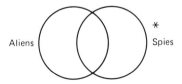

DOMAIN OF DISCOURSE

The last example raises a special problem. When we try to think of something that is neither a spy nor an alien, we naturally think of a *person*—say, Nancy Reagan. But how about Mt. Whitney and the number seven? Neither of these things is either a spy or an alien. Yet it seems odd to say that Mt. Whitney is neither a spy nor an alien. How could it be either of these things? Talk about spies and aliens typically concerns people. We can put it this way: Talking about spies and aliens normally *presupposes* that we are considering only persons. To reflect the notion of limiting our discussion to a certain kind of thing, we will make our diagrams a bit more elaborate. We will enclose the intersecting circles with a box that indicates the *domain of discourse* (DD). Some examples will make this clear:

1. All squares are rectangles (domain of discourse: plane figures):

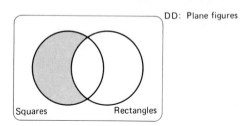

2. Some aliens are not spies (domain of discourse: people):

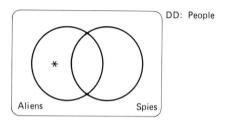

Deciding upon a domain of discourse is somewhat arbitrary. It depends on good sense and present interests. In the first example, we might have taken *four-sided figures* as the domain of discourse, and perhaps in the second example *people in the United States* might have done perfectly well. Actually, we will be quite casual about specifying a domain of discourse, and will only do so when it serves some useful purpose.

THE FOUR BASIC PROPOSITIONS

It is easy to see that two classes can be related in a great many different ways. Nonetheless, it is possible to examine all these relationships in terms of four basic propositions:

A: All *A* is *B*.   E: No *A* is *B*.
I: Some *A* is *B*.   O: Some *A* is not *B*.

The diagram for each of these propositions (see the top of the opposite page) is instructive. These basic propositions, together with their labels and diagrams, should be memorized because they will be used constantly.

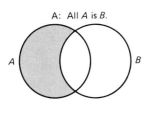

A: All A is B.

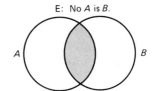

E: No A is B.

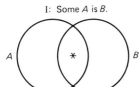

I: Some A is B.

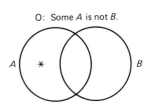

O: Some A is not B.

Using just the four basic propositions, indicate what information is given in each of the following diagrams:

Example:

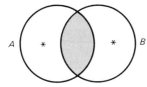

No A is B.
Some A is not B.
Some B is not A.
No B is A.

1.

2.

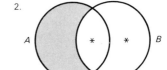

3.

4.

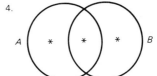

5.

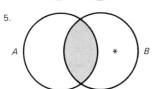

6.

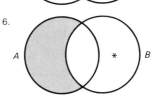

EXISTENTIAL IMPORT

We must now turn to a difficult problem that logicians have not fully settled. Usually when we make a statement it is obvious that we are *talking about* certain things. If someone claims that all whales are mammals, he is then talking about whales and saying that they are mammals. That is, in making this statement about whales, he *seems to be taking for granted the existence of whales.* He is not exactly saying that there are whales, yet his remark commits him to the existence of whales. To mark this commitment, we can put an asterisk (*) into our diagram for the *A* proposition:

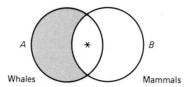

We now see at once that if *all whales are mammals,* than *at least some whales are mammals.* This is not a very exciting inference, but one that strikes us as valid. We can now see why this inference is valid by noticing that the diagram for the A proposition given above already contains the information contained in the I proposition given below:

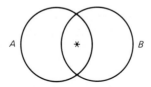

In the same way, we can see why the proposition "No aliens are spies" implies the proposition "Some aliens are not spies." In saying that no aliens are spies, we seem to be committing ourselves to the existence of aliens and saying of them that none of them are spies. If we reflect this commitment in the diagram for the E proposition, as follows,

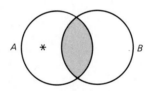

we see at once that it implies the O proposition which, as we know, is represented in the following way:

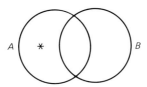

So far, then, everything seems simple enough. We can understand the relationships between the A and I as well as the E and O propositions simply by marking the commitment to existence in the A and E propositions. The difficulty is that we sometimes seem to use both the A and E propositions without any such existential commitment. If I say that all elves are small, I am not committing myself to the existence of elves; I am speaking about fictitious or mythical creatures. There are problems concerned with fictitious things, but they will not concern us here. A more difficult problem arises with a remark of the following kind: "All trespassers will be fined." In saying this, I am not committing myself to the existence of trespassers; I am only saying, "*If* there are trespassers, *then* they will be fined." Given this one example of an A proposition that carries no commitment concerning things referred to in the subject term, it is easy to think of many others.

Once more, then, we must make a decision. (Remember that we had to make decisions concerning the truth-table definitions of both disjunction and implication.) Classical logic was developed on the assumption that both the A and E propositions carry existential import.[1] Modern logic makes the opposite decision, treating the claim that all men are mortal as equivalent to the claim that if someone is a man, then he is mortal. This way of speaking carries no commitment to the existence of men. If we want to indicate the existence of men, then we must say so explicitly. The difference is shown in the following diagrams:

---

[1] More generally, the classical approach seems to restrict its domains of discourse to existing things, or, speaking in modern terms, we might think of it as developing a logic of *non-empty* sets. If we pursue this notion, then the *predicate* term, along with the *subject* term, will carry existential import. We would then have to represent the E and the O propositions in the following ways:

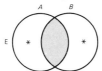 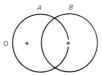

We will not pursue this matter, however, because the theory of valid inferences will be developed primarily on the modern approach.

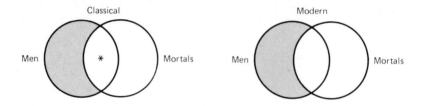

Classical   Modern

Men   *   Mortals   Men   Mortals

An important consequence of this difference is that in the classical approach the A proposition implies the I proposition, whereas in the modern approach it does not.

Which approach shall we adopt? In the long run, the modern approach has proved a more powerful method. All the same, there is something beautiful about the classical approach and it is worth exploring in its own right. Our decision, then, is this: We will adopt the modern approach and *not* assign existential import to the A and E propositions. At the same time, we can develop the classical approach simply by adding an indication of existential commitment where it is needed. In this way we can examine both the modern and the classical approach to this area of logic.

THE CLASSIFICATION OF THE BASIC PROPOSITIONS

Traditionally, these basic propositions have been classified under the following distinctions:

Quality: Affirmative/Negative
Quantity: Universal/Particular

Quality

The A and I propositions are affirmative propositions, and the E and O propositions are negative propositions. The intuitive difference between an affirmative proposition and a negative proposition seems obvious: In an affirmative proposition we *affirm* something; in a negative proposition we *deny* or *negate* something. Yet is is not always easy to apply this distinction to particular cases. Is the following proposition affirmative or negative?

John is absent.

If you decide that it is negative because absent just means "not here," then how do you classify this proposition?

John is not absent.

It seems odd to call a proposition affirmative when it has the transparent form of a denial.

Fortunately, in the present context, we do not have to worry about such questions. We shall classify propositions in terms of their form and not in terms of the meaning of the subject and predicate words. Thus the same thought can be expressed in propositions of different forms. For example:

All clergy are noncombatants.
No clergy are combatants.

Although these propositions express the same thought, the first is an A proposition, the second is an E proposition. For evident reasons, then, we call the E and the O propositions negative, and the A and the I propositions affirmative.

Quantity

The A and E propositions are *universal* propositions, and the I and O propositions are *particular* propositions. The distinction between universal and particular propositions turns on the character of the subject term in the proposition. In a universal proposition we speak about *all* of the members of the subject class; in a *particular* proposition we speak about *some* of them. So the A proposition is said to be universal and the I and O propositions are said to be particular. It does not take much thought to see that the E proposition is universal. If I say that no *A* is *B*, I am plainly speaking of *all* the things that are *A* and saying that none of them is *B*. We can summarize this nomenclature in the following table:

		Quality	
		Affirmative	Negatve
Quantity	Universal	A	E
	Particular	I	O

THE SQUARE OF OPPOSITION

We can now examine some logical relationships that obtain between these four basic propositions. The first system of relationships form what has been called the *square of opposition*. The approach here is classical, with existential commitment indicated for the A and E propositions.

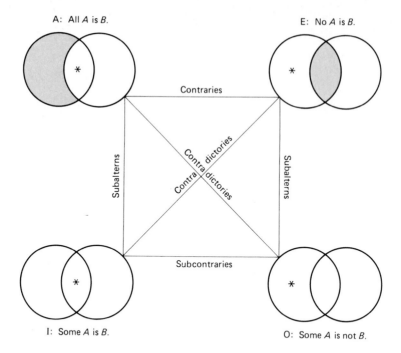

A: All *A* is *B*.
E: No *A* is *B*.

Contraries

Subalterns

Contradictories

Contradictories

Subalterns

Subcontraries

I: Some *A* is *B*.
O: Some *A* is not *B*.

This diagram shows the relationship that each proposition has to the other three. All of these relationships have specific names which are explained below.

Contraries

Two propositions are said to be *contraries* of one another if they are so related that

(1) They cannot both be true.
(2) They can, however, both be false.

On the classical interpretation (but not the modern interpretation), the A and E propositions at the top of the square of oppositions are contraries of one another.

In common life, the relationship between the A and the E propositions is captured by the notion that one thing is the *complete opposite* of another. The complete opposite of "Everyone is here" is "No one is here." Clearly, such complete opposites cannot both be true at once. If we look at the diagrams for the A and E propositions, we see this at once. The middle region of the A proposition diagram shows the existence of something that is both *A* and *B*, whereas the middle region of the E proposition diagram is shaded out, showing that nothing is both

A and B. It should also be clear that both the A and E propositions may be false. Suppose that there is some A that is B and also some *A* that is not *B:*

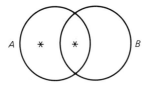

Going from left to right, the first asterisk shows that "All *A* is *B*" is false; the second asterisk shows that "No *A* is *B*" is false.

Contradictories

Two propositions are said to be *contradictories* of each other (or to *contradict* each other) when they are so related that

(1) They cannot both be true.
(2) They cannot both be false.

More simply, contradictory pairs of propositions always have *opposite* truth values. On both the classical and the modern interpretation the A and O propositions are contradictories of one another and so are the E and I propositions.

Once more these relationships are reflected in the diagrams we have drawn for these propositions. Here we will only examine the A and O propositions.

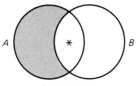

A: All *A* is *B*.

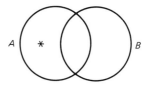

O: Some *A* is not *B*.

It is easy to see that these two propositions cannot both be true, for the second diagram has an asterisk in a region that is shaded out in the first diagram. But why must at least one of these propositions be true? Actually, it is rather easy to explain this in the *modern* approach, where there is no existential commitment for the A and E propositions. The explanation in the classical approach is more complicated.

In the modern approach we can represent the denial of a proposition by a simple procedure. The only information given in our diagram is represented either by *shading out* some region, thereby indicating that nothing exists in it, or by *putting an asterisk* in a region, thereby indicating that something does exist in it. We are given no indication about unmarked regions. To represent the denial of a proposition, we simply reverse the information in the diagram. That is, where there is an asterisk, we put in shading; where there is shading, we put in an asterisk. Everything else is left unchanged. Thus in the modern approach, we can see at once that the A and O propositions are denials of one another so that they must always take opposite truth values.

A: All A is B.

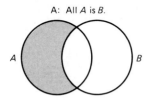

O: Some A is not B.

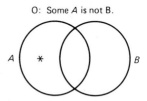

The situation in the classical interpretation is much less tidy. The basic idea in the classical approach is that in asserting that all *A* is *B*, we are committing ourselves to the existence of things that are *A*. We reflect this commitment by putting an asterisk in the middle region of the diagram for the A proposition. But now the interpretation of the denial of this proposition is no longer a straightforward business of reversing information. The following is *not* what we want:

A: All A is B.

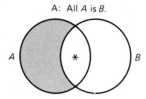

E: No A is B.

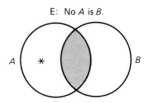

Here we have wound up with the wrong result, for we want the O proposition to be the contradiction of the A proposition and not the E proposition. The result we do want is this:

A: All A is B.

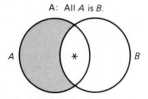

O: Some A is not B.

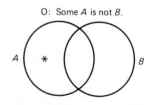

To get the right result, we shall make the following ruling: Even in the classical approach we shall ignore existential import, except in those cases where a particular inference depends on it. In those cases, *we shall plug in the existential import only after all other logical maneuvers have been made.* So we are back to our simple modern diagram:

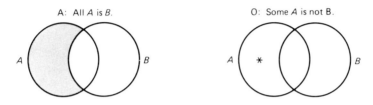

A: All A is B.

O: Some A is not B.

There is no need here to further decorate this diagram with indications of existential import, since nothing turns on it.

Subcontraries

Propositions are *subcontraries* of one another when the following is the case:

(1) Both can be true.
(2) Both, however, cannot be false.

On the classical approach (but not the modern approach), the I and O propositions are subcontraries. To see how this works out, compare the diagrams for the I and O propositions.

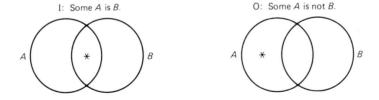

I: Some A is B.

O: Some A is not B.

Consider just the left-hand side of this diagram:

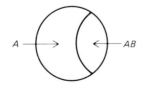

We know that in the classical approach, a presuppositional asterisk must go into this diagram somewhere. But if the asterisk goes into the overlapping region *AB*, then the I proposition is true; if the asterisk goes into the nonoverlapping region of *A*, then the O proposition is true. So at least one of them is true. Finally, nothing rules out the possibility that there might be an asterisk in each region. In that case both the I and the O propositions would be true, and the situation would look like this:

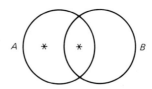

Subalternation

Subalternation is the relationship that holds down the sides of the classical square of opposition. Quite simply, the A proposition implies the I proposition and the E proposition implies the O proposition. Again, this relationship depends on the existential commitment found in the classical approach, and does not hold in the modern approach. We can use our diagrams for testing these implications in the following way: First diagram the premise, and then diagram the conclusion. If the inference from premise to conclusion is valid, then the information contained in the diagram for the conclusion must already be contained in the information given in the diagram for the premise. The validity for subalternation is illustrated by the following diagrams:

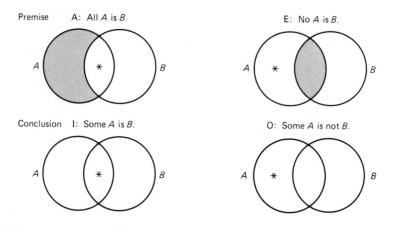

Another way of describing this test is as follows: Draw both the diagram for the premise and the conclusion, and then try to add the information contained in the diagram for the conclusion to the diagram for the premise. If the argument is valid, that information is already present in the diagram for the premise and no addition to it is needed.

We can summarize the information given by the classical square of opposition using two charts. We shall ask two questions. First, for each proposition, what consequences follow from the assumption that it is true?

		A	E	I	O
	A	T	F	T	F
Assumed true	E	F	T	F	T
	I	?	F	T	?
	O	F	?	?	T

Secondly, for each proposition, what consequences follow from the assumption that it is false?

		A	E	I	O
	A	F	?	?	T
Assumed false	E	?	F	T	?
	I	F	T	F	T
	O	T	F	T	F

CONVERSATIONAL IMPLICATION AND THE SQUARE OF OPPOSITION

As we have examined the classical treatment of the square of opposition, we have seen that at almost every turn the argument depended on the notion of existential commitment. The one exception was the relationship of contradictories, but in all other cases we have to make this commitment explicit in order to show that the relationships hold. We might say that the classical approach depends upon making *explicit* what is *implicit* in the use of these basic propositions.

We can now look at a different approach that is familiar to us from earlier discussions. Instead of saying that the A proposition *implies* the existence of things that are A, we can say that the *use* of an A proposition *normally conversationally implies that the person believes that there are things that are A*. We have to speak in this qualified way because there are times when the use of an A proposition has no such conversational implication. Remember the example of someone saying, "All trespassers will be fined." This does not conversationally imply that the person who says it believes that there will be trespassers. (Having announced this, he may now believe just the opposite.) Reflections of this kind lead to a different way of treating the square of opposition. We can take the logically simple approach of dropping the assumption that the A and E propo-

sitions carry existential import. We then get the result that *only* the
relationships of contradictories continue to hold. All the other relationships now fail.

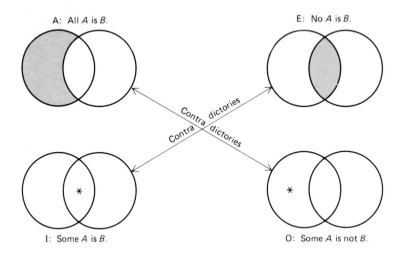

This is all that is left of the traditional square of opposition in the modern approach.

We can, however, reflect more of the traditional relationships by
adding to this square the conversational implications that arise in standard contexts:

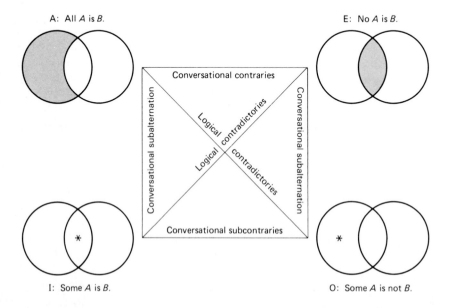

Here only the relationship of contradictories is a logical one; all the other relationships depend on conversational implication and thus are labeled as conversational relationships.

Will it make much difference whether we adopt the classical or the modern approach to the propositions that form the square of opposition? For some purposes it will hardly make any difference at all. In the practical affairs of life it usually does not make any difference whether something is logically implied *by what is said* or conversationally implied *by the saying of it*. In fact, it is only relatively recently that philosophers have become aware of this difference in something like a clear-headed way. Yet from the point of view of logical theory, the distinction is crucial. When we mix up logical implications and conversational implications, our logic first of all becomes very complicated. This comes out, for example, in trying to explain contradictories on the classical square of opposition.

Beyond leading to complications, mixing up logical and conversational implication can actually lead to inconsistency. This can be illustrated by noticing another way that conversational rules apply to the use of the propositions on the square of opposition. The use of these propositions is governed by Grice's rule of Quantity—that is, where justified, we are expected to use the stronger A or E propositions rather than the weaker I or O propositions. Thus when we use either the I or O propositions, we conversationally imply that we are not in a position to use the stronger A or E propositions. A simple example will show how this works: Filled with greed, a person takes every last piece of candy from a box. When asked if he has taken the candy, he replies, "I took some of the candy." Now, strictly speaking, this is true. The person did take some of the candy. Yet his remark plainly suggests that he took *only* some of it. Here the violation of the conversational rule is so extreme that it is tempting to call the person's reply an outright lie. In general, then, the use of an I proposition by a speaker contextually implies that the speaker does not believe the A proposition to be true; sometimes it implies, even more strongly, that he knows the A proposition to be false. We get this stronger implication when the speaker is in a position to know whether the A proposition is true or not. For example, the person who takes all the candy is obviously in a position to know what he has done. It is for this reason that his remark conversationally implies the *denial* of the assertion that he took all of the candy.

Now the very same relationship holds between the weak O proposition and the strong E proposition. The use of an O proposition by a speaker conversationally implies that the speaker does not believe the E proposition, and sometimes, even more strongly, that he knows it not to be true. This leads to a result that squares with our commonsense understanding of language: When someone says, "Some are . . ." this conversationally implies "Some are not . . ."; conversely, when some-

one says, "Some are not . . ." this conversationally implies "Some are
. . . ." In general, then, the use of one subaltern conversationally
implies that the use of the other subaltern is also okay.[2]

We are now in a position to see how mixing up conversational rules
with logical rules can lead to lunacy. Consider the following line of reasoning.

(1) All aliens are spies.
∴ (2) Some aliens are spies.
∴ (3) Some aliens are not spies.

∴ (4) If all aliens are spies, some aliens are not spies.

In this strange argument, we wind up with a proposition implying its
own denial, a result we expect to get *only* when we start out from a self-
contradictory proposition. It is not hard to see what has gone wrong
here. The step from (1) to (2) is a logical implication in the classical approach, and a conversational implication in the modern approach. On
the other hand, the step from (2) to (3) must be a conversational implication in either approach. In the conclusion both steps are treated as
logical implications, and disaster results.

EXERCISE 2

Give a similar explanation of the fallacies in the following lines of reasoning:

(1) If you have an obligation to do something, then you are permitted to do it.
If you are permitted to do something, then you are permitted
not to do it.

∴ If you have an obligation to do something, then you are permitted not to do it.

The next line of reasoning is not as serious.

---

[2] Remember that conversational rules, unlike logical rules, hold only in general, for one
conversational rule can be affected and overridden by another.

(2) If something is good, then it is not bad.
   If something is not bad, then it is not so good.
   —————————————————————————————
   ∴ If something is good, then it is not so good.

This last example shows that mixing up logical implications with conversational implications can lead to unwanted results. This, however, does not settle the issue between the classical and the modern approach to the existential import of these basic propositions. A logician is free to argue that existential import is logically implied—not merely conversationally implied—by the A and E propositions. He can then develop his theory accordingly. There is nothing incoherent about such an approach. This text adopts the modern approach for three reasons:

(1) It yields a simpler logical system.
(2) It is part of a much wider system that has proved extraordinarily successful.
(3) It fits in well with the general approach of distinguishing logical implications from conversational implications.

THE THEORY OF IMMEDIATE INFERENCE

The theory of immediate inference concerns arguments with the following features:

(1) They have a single premise. (That is why the inference is called immediate.)
(2) They involve only the four basic propositions.

Of course, there are all sorts of other arguments involving just one premise, but those involving the four basic propositions have been singled out for special attention. These inferences deserve special attention because they occur quite often in everyday reasoning.

We already know about one immediate inference: subalternation. In the classical theory, but not in the modern theory, we can always derive an I proposition from an A proposition, and we can always derive an O proposition from an E proposition. Here we shall consider three standard patterns of immediate inference: conversion, obversion, and contraposition. We will adopt the modern approach, but we will notice where the classical approach differs from it.

Conversion

Conversion is the simplest immediate inference we shall consider. We convert a proposition simply by reversing the subject term and the predicate term. By the subject term, we simply mean the term that occurs in the grammatical subject; by the predicate term, we mean the term that occurs in the grammatical predicate. In the proposition "All spies are aliens," "spies" is the subject term and "aliens" is the predicate term. In this case identifying the predicate term is straightforward, since the grammatical predicate is a noun—a predicate nominative. Often, however, we have to change the grammatical predicate from an adjective to a noun phrase in order to get a noun that refers to a class of things. Though it is a bit artificial, we can always use this device. "All spies are dangerous" becomes "All spies are dangerous things." Here "spies" is the subject term and "dangerous things" is the predicate term. The reason we must make this change is that when we convert a proposition, we need a noun phrase to go into the place of the grammatical subject. In English we cannot say "All dangerous are spies," but we can say "All dangerous things are spies."

We want to know when this operation of conversion is legitimate. That is, we want to know when conversion yields a *valid* immediate inference. To answer this question we can examine the four basic propositions to see what happens when conversion is attempted. Two cases are obvious at first sight. Both the I and the E propositions validly convert. From the I proposition, "Some *S* is *P*," we may validly infer "Some *P* is *S*."

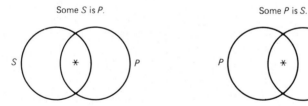

From the E proposition, "No *S* is *P*," we may validly infer "No *P* is *S*."

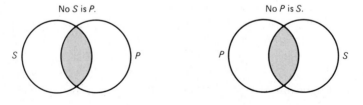

Notice that in both of these cases, the converse has exactly the same diagram as the original proposition. This shows that the E and I propositions not only *imply* their converses, but are *logically equivalent* to them; the implication runs both ways.[3]

It should be obvious that the O proposition cannot, in general, be converted validly. From "Some *S* is not *P*," we may not, in general, infer "Some *P* is not *S*."[4]

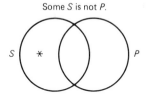
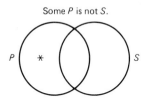

Finally, we can see that the A proposition does not validly convert, either. From "All *S* is *P*," we may not, in general, infer "All *P* is *S*."

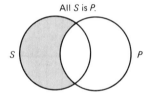
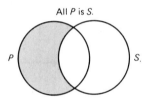

Everything that we have said so far is true in both the modern and the classical approach. To see this, we need only add the symbols indicating existential commitment to the above diagrams and then notice that the reasoning remains unchanged. But there is one important difference between the classical and the modern approach. Given the existential commitment in the classical approach, we may infer from *All S is P* that *Some P is S*. That inference does not hold in the modern approach:

---

[3] Fictitious entities raise a curious problem for conversion of the E proposition on *both* the classical and the modern approach. The converse of *No animals are unicorns* is *No unicorns are animals*, yet many people would consider the first proposition true, but the second proposition false. The example is due to Ted Drange.

[4] There are some strange cases—logicians call them degenerate cases—where inferences of this pattern are valid. For example, from *Some men are not men*, we may validly infer that *Some men are not men*. Here, by making the subject term and predicate term the same, we trivialize conversion. Keeping cases of this kind in mind, we must say that in general, but not always, the conversion of an O proposition does not yield a valid inference. In contrast, the set of valid inferences holds in all cases, including degenerate cases.

Classical: All *S* is *P*. Some *P* is *S*.

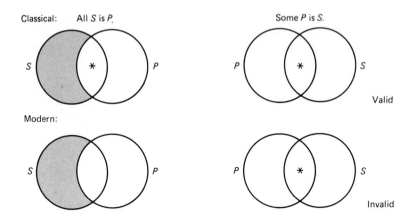

The classical conversion of an A proposition into an I proposition is called *conversion by limitation* since the original universal claim is limited to a particular claim. The following table summarizes these relationships:

Proposition	Conversion	Status
A: All *S* is *P*.	Some *P* is *S*.	Implication by limitation—classical theory only
E: No *S* is *P*.	No *P* is *S*.	Logically equivalent
I: Some *S* is *P*.	Some *P* is *S*.	Logically equivalent
O: Some *S* is not *P*.	Some *P* is not *S*.	Does not hold

Obversion

Before we can deal with *obversion,* we must define the notion of a *complementary class*. The idea is simple enough. Given any class C, its complementary class is just all of those things that are not in C. One standard way of referring to a complementary class is to use the prefix "non." Here are some examples:

Class	Complementary class
Republicans	Non-Republicans
Voters	Nonvoters
Combatants	Noncombatants

If we look at the class of non-Republicans, we see that it is a mixed bag, for as we have defined the notion it includes everything that is not a Republican. This includes coyotes, subatomic particles, prime numbers, the top ten record hits, and the British royal family. Of course, in everyday life we certainly do not wish to include all these things in our notion of a non-Republican. When we speak about non-Republicans, the context will usually make it clear that we are referring to politicians, voters, or party members. We can capture this idea by using a notion introduced earlier: that of a *domain of discourse*. We might say that the domain of discourse here includes all those who are members of American political parties. A non-Republican is someone in this domain of discourse who is not a Republican. We can represent this using the following diagram:

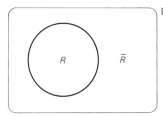

DD: Members of American political parties

A bar over a letter indicates a complementary class. In this case $\overline{R}$ means the class of non-Republicans. As indicated earlier, sometimes it is useful to specify the domain of discourse, sometimes it is not. In this book we will worry about the domain of discourse only when it serves some useful purpose.

We can now define the immediate inference called *obversion*. To pass from a basic proposition to its obverse:

(1) We reverse the *quality* of the proposition, from affirmative to negative or negative to affirmative as the case may be.

(2) We replace the predicate term by its complementary term.

Starting with "All men are mortal," this two-step process works as follows:

All men are mortal.
(1) Reversing the quality yields: No men are mortal.
(2) Replacing the predicate term by its complement yields: No men are nonmortal.

This final proposition is the obverse of "All men are mortal."

We now want to know when this operation of obversion is legitimate—that is, we want to know when obversion yields a valid immediate inference. The answer to this is that a proposition is always *logically equivalent* to its obverse in both the classical and the modern interpretation. To show this, we can run through the four propositions. Since all these equivalences hold between a proposition and its *obverse*, there is no need to draw a diagram twice. The reader should, however, check to see whether the diagram is accurate for both propositions.

A: "All S is P" is logically equivalent to "No S is non-P."

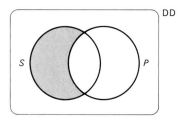

In this diagram, the class of things that are non-P includes all those things in the domain of discourse that are not in P. We can see that there is nothing in the class of things that are S that is also in the complementary class of P, because all the things in S are in the class P. This may sound a bit complicated, but with a very little thought the validity of inferences through obversion becomes quite obvious.

E: "No S is P" is logically equivalent to "All S is non-P."

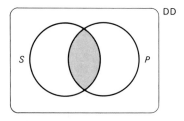

I: "Some S is P" is logically equivalent to "Some S is not non-P."

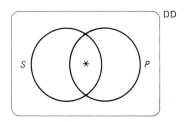

O: From "Some S is not P," we may validly infer that "Some S is non-P."

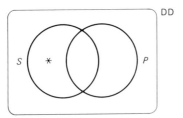

DD

It is important to see that the final inference is a genuine inference and not a mere repetition. "Some S is not P" is an O proposition, whereas "Some S is non-P" is an I proposition. That is, the first proposition formulates a negative proposition—it indicates that there is at least one thing that is not in a certain class. The second proposition is an affirmative proposition, for it indicates that something is in a given class—in this case, a complementary class.

Contraposition

Contraposition is the final relationship we shall examine. We get the contrapositive of a proposition by the following two-step process:

(1) We convert the proposition.
(2) We replace both terms by their complementary terms.

For example, starting with "All men are mortal," this two-step process works as follows:

> All men are mortal.
> (1) Converted, this proposition becomes:
> All mortal (things) are men.
> (2) Replacing each term by its complementary term we get:
> All nonmortal (things) are non-men.

This final proposition is the contrapositive of "All men are mortal."

Following our previous pattern, we must now ask when the contrapositive can be validly inferred from a given proposition. Here the situation is pretty much the reverse of what we discovered for conversion:

> A: "All S is P" is logically equivalent to "All non-P is non-S."

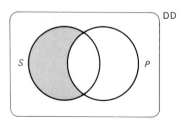

E: From "No S is P" we may not, in general, infer "No non-P is non-S."

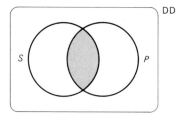 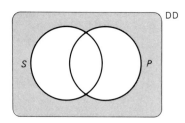

But in the classical approach, though not in the modern approach, *contraposition by limitation* does hold, that is, from "No S is P" we may infer "Some non-P is not non-S."[5]

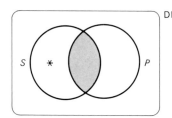 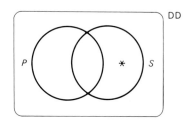

I: From "Some S is P," we may not, in general, infer "Some non-P is non-S."

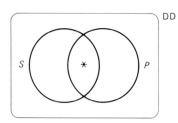 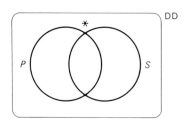

---

[5] At first sight this proposition may seem hard to understand, but with a little thought it actually makes sense.

O: "Some S is not P" is logically equivalent to "Some non-P is not non-S."

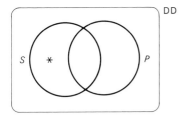
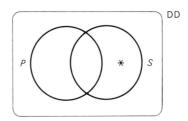

The following table summarizes all these equivalence relationships. The two items in parentheses are not equivalent but are only implied, and they hold only in the classical interpretation.

Proposition	Obversion	Conversion	Contraposition
A: All S is P.	No S is non-P.	(Some P is S.)	All non-P is non-S
E: No S is P.	All S is non-P.	No P is S.	(Some non-P is not non-S.)
I: Some S is P.	Some S is not non-P.	Some P is S.	XXXXXXX
O: Some S is not P.	Some S is non-P	XXXXXXX	Some non-P is not non-S.

If we compare some of the propositions we have been studying with remarks that we make in everyday life, some of them, at least, will seem very artificial. It is hard to imagine a case where we would actually say "Some nonspies are not nonaliens." It would certainly be easier to say "Some nonspies are aliens," which is its equivalent through *obversion*. We can then *convert* this: "Some aliens are nonspies." This is still somewhat unnatural, so by using obversion again we get the natural remark, "Some aliens are not spies." Actually, we could have gotten this result immediately through applying *contraposition* to the original remark. (This shows that the contrapositive of a proposition is the obverse of the converse of the obverse of that proposition—something you need not commit to memory!)

In fact, we do *sometimes* find ourselves in contexts where we use some of these complicated sentences. Discussing the voting patterns of nonresidents, we might find ourselves saying that some nonresidents are not nonvoters. Given the context, this remark loses much of its oddness. Usually, however, we choose simple, clear formulations; the ability to do this depends on an implicit understanding of the logical relationships within this system of propositions. Here we are trying to bring this implicit understanding to the surface so that we can understand it better. That is, we are trying to give clear rules for inferences that we make routinely in everyday life.

EXERCISE 3

For each of the following propositions, decide by using appropriate diagrams which of the above immediate inferences hold. For example:

All ministers are noncombatants.

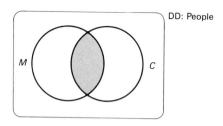

Obverse: No ministers are combatants.

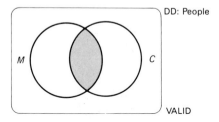

Converse: All noncombatants are ministers.

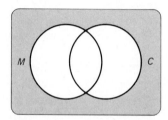

Contrapositive: All non-noncombatants are nonministers. Or more simply: All combatants are nonministers.

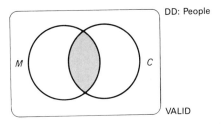

DD: People

M   *C*

VALID

(1) Some dudes are not cowards.

(2) All nonresidents are taxpayers.

(3) Some nonaligned nations are wealthy (nations).

(4) No daughters are sons.

(5) No nonnegotiable stocks are safe (stocks).

(6) All that glitters is not gold.

(7) Some people cannot be bought.

(8) There is no such thing as a bad boy.

EXERCISE 4

Put the following sentences into plain, respectable English. Indicate the immediate inference or immediate inferences you have used to do so. (Be careful!)

(1) No noncombatant is a minister.

(2) Some nonresident is not a non-nonvoter.

(3) Not all snakes are not dangerous (things).

(4) No all-the-time losers are non-nonpersons.

THE THEORY OF THE SYLLOGISM

In an immediate inference, we draw a conclusion directly from a single proposition. The traditional theory of immediate inference explores such inferences as they arise for the basic A E I O propositions. The square of opposition answers the following question: Given the truth or falsity of one of these basic propositions, what, if anything, may we infer concerning the truth or falsity of the remaining basic propositions? We have now extended the theory of immediate inference to include the *conversion* of terms and the construction of *complementary* classes.

The next step in developing the traditional theory concerning these basic propositions is to consider arguments containing two premises rather than just one. An important group of such arguments is called categorical syllogisms. The basic idea behind these arguments is commonsensical. Suppose I wish to prove that "All S is P"—whatever S or P might be. A proof should present some *link* or *connection* between S and P. This link can be some other term we shall label M. In a syllogism we establish a relationship between the terms S and P through some middle term M.

We can now define a categorical syllogism more carefully.

(1) A categorical syllogism is constructed from the basic A, E, I, and O propositions.
(2) Given that the conclusion will contain two terms S and P, we can place the following restrictions on the premises:
  (i) There are only two premises.
  (ii) One premise contains the term S. (This is called the minor premise.)
  (iii) One premise contains the term P. (This is called the major premise.)
  (iv) Each premise contains the middle term M.

Traditionally, the major premise is stated first, the minor premise second. Here are some examples of syllogisms.

All rectangles have four sides. (Major premise)
All squares are rectangles. (Minor premise)

∴ All squares have four sides. (Conclusion)

Subject term = Squares
Predicate term = Being four-sided
Middle term = Rectangles

Schematically, the argument looks like this:

All M is P.
All S is M.

∴ All S is P.

Here is a syllogism containing a negative premise.

No ellipses have sides.
All circles are ellipses.

∴ No circles have sides.

Schematically:

$$\text{No } M \text{ is } P.$$
$$\underline{\text{All } S \text{ is } M.}$$
$$\therefore \text{ No } S \text{ is } P.$$

Finally, here is an example of a syllogism containing a particular proposition.

All squares have equal sides.
Some squares are rectangles.

∴ Some rectangles have equal sides.

Schematically:

$$\text{All } M \text{ is } P.$$
$$\underline{\text{Some } M \text{ is } S.}$$
$$\therefore \text{ Some } S \text{ is } P.$$

VALID AND INVALID SYLLOGISMS

The examples given so far have all been of valid syllogisms—it should be obvious in each case that the conclusion does follow from the premise. It is possible to construct an argument that meets the definition of a categorical syllogism but is still invalid. A glaringly invalid argument will make this clear.

Some figures are circles.
Some figures are squares.

∴ All squares are circles.

This is a dreadful argument, but still it is a categorical syllogism. It is an *invalid* categorical syllogism.

Because some categorical syllogims are valid whereas others are invalid, it will be important to have some systematic method for evaluating them. This subject has been explored for more than two thousand years, and a variety of analytical techniques has been developed. We shall use Venn diagrams.

VENN DIAGRAMS FOR SYLLOGISMS

In the previous section we used Venn diagrams to test the validity of immediate inferences. In a categorical syllogism, three terms appear; thus we are dealing with three classes. To reflect this, we will use diagrams of the following kind:

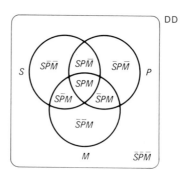

DD

The diagram has eight different compartments:

$$
\begin{array}{ccc}
S & P & \overline{M} \\
S & P & M \\
S & \overline{P} & \overline{M} \\
\overline{S} & \overline{P} & M \\
\overline{S} & P & M \\
\overline{S} & P & \overline{M} \\
\overline{S} & \overline{P} & M \\
\overline{S} & \overline{P} & \overline{M}
\end{array}
$$

Notice that if something is not an S or a P or an M, it falls completely outside the system of overlapping circles. In every other case, a thing is assigned to some compartment within the system of overlapping circles.

To test the validity of a syllogism using Venn diagrams, we first fill in the diagram to reflect the content of the premises. If the argument is valid, then the conclusion will already be contained in the diagram. To see this, consider the diagrams for examples already considered:

> All rectangles are four-sided.
> All squares are rectangles.
> ―――――――――――――――――――――――
> ∴ All squares are four-sided.

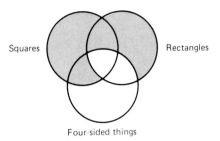

Notice that all the things that are squares are corralled into the region of things that are four-sided. So the argument is valid.

> No ellipses have sides.
> All circles are ellipses.
> ∴ No circles have sides.

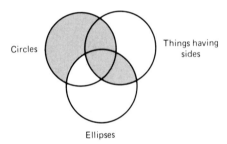

We diagram the conclusion "No circles have sides" as follows:

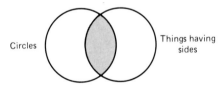

That information is already contained in the Venn diagram for the premises.

> All squares have equal sides.
> Some squares are rectangles.
> ∴ Some rectangles have equal sides.

It is a good strategy to diagram a universal proposition before we diagram a particular proposition. The diagram for the above argument looks like this:

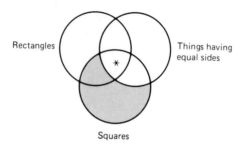

The conclusion—that there is something that is a rectangle that is equal-sided—appears in the diagram for the premises.

EXISTENTIAL IMPORT

In the discussion of immediate inferences, we raised the question whether the universal propositions—the A and the E propositions—carried existential import. That is, when we assert that "All S is P" or that "No S is P," are we committing ourselves to the existence of Ss and Ps? The ruling for traditional logic was that these propositions *do* carry existential import. The same ruling holds for the traditional theory of the syllogism. So far we have continued to employ the modern approach that does not assign existential import to the A and E propositions.

We can begin our study of this matter with an example that has had a curious history:

> All rectangles are four-sided.
> All squares are rectangles.
> _____
> ∴ *Some* squares are four-sided.

The argument is peculiar because the conclusion is weaker than it needs to be. We could, after all, conclude that *all* squares are four-sided. The argument thus violates the conversational rule of Quantity; perhaps for this reason, this syllogism was often not included in traditional lists of valid syllogisms. Yet the argument is valid on the traditional interpretation of existential import and our diagram should show this.

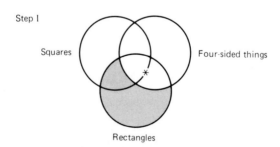

Notice that the asterisk is placed on the line dividing regions SPM and $\overline{SP}M$ since we are not in a position to put it into one region rather than the other. We now draw in the second premise:

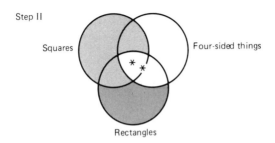

Step II

Squares

Four-sided things

Rectangles

As expected, the conclusion that some squares are four-sided is already diagrammed, so the argument is valid—provided that we commit ourselves to the existential import of A propositions.

Because classical logicians tended to ignore the previous argument, their writings did not bring out the importance of existential import in evaluating it. There is, however, an argument that did appear on the classical lists that makes clear the demand for existential commitment. These are syllogisms of the following kind:

All M is P
All M is S.

∴ Some S is P.

This is diagrammed as follows:

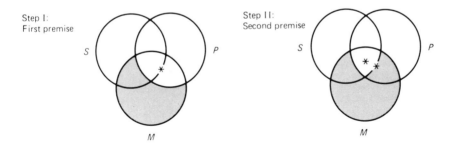

Step I:
First premise

S   P

M

Step II:
Second premise

S   P

M

Again we see that the conclusion follows, but only if we diagram the universal propositions to indicate existential import. This, then, is an argument that was declared valid in the traditional approach, but invalid in the modern approach.

So far we have looked only at valid arguments. Here are some patterns for invalid arguments. The conclusion is diagrammed at the right. It is evident that this diagram is not already contained in the diagram for the premises. The arrows show differences in informational content.

All *M* is *P*.
All *M* is *S*.
_____
∴ All *S* is *P*.   All *S* is *P*.

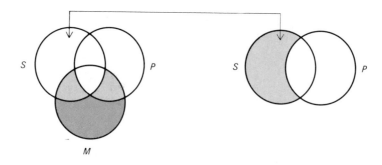

Some *M* is *P*.
Some *S* is *M*.
_____
∴ Some *S* is *P*.   Some *S* is *P*.

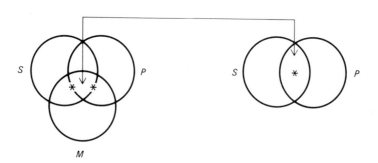

Examine this diagram closely. Notice that in saying "Some *M* is *P*," we had to put the asterisk *on* the line dividing *S* and *P*, since we were not given information saying whether anything falls into *S* or not. For the same reason we had to put the asterisk *on* the line dividing *S* and *P* when diagramming "Some *M* is *S*." The upshot was that we did not indicate that anything exists in the region of overlap between *S* and *P*. But this is what the conclusion demands, so the argument is invalid.

No *M* is *P*.
No *S* is *M*.
───────────
∴ No *S* is *P*.   No *S* is *P*.

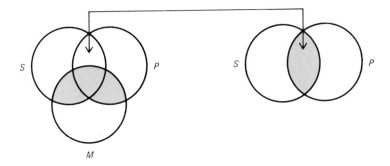

Again we see that this argument is invalid.

The method of Venn diagrams is adequate for deciding the formal validity or invalidity of all possible syllogisms. Furthermore, the use of Venn diagrams makes it easy to distinguish between syllogisms that are classically valid and those that are valid on the modern interpretation of existential import. To get the classical theory, we simply include the presuppositions of existential import in our diagrams; in the modern approach we do not do this.

EXERCISE 5

Adopting the modern approach, test the following syllogisms for validity by using Venn diagrams.

(1) All *M* is *P*.
     All *M* is *S*.
     ─────────
     ∴ All *S* is *P*.

(2) No *M* is *P*.
     Some *S* is *M*.
     ─────────────
     ∴ Some *S* is not *P*.

(3) No *P* is *M*.
     Some *S* is not *M*.
     ─────────────────
     ∴ Some *S* is not *P*.

(4) All *M* is *P*.
     Some *S* is not *M*.
     ─────────────────
     ∴ Some *S* is not *P*.

(5)	Some P is M	(8)	All P is M.
	Some S is not M.		All S is M.
	$\therefore$ Some S is not P.		$\therefore$ All S is P.

(6)	All M is P.	(9)	No S is M.
	No S is M.		Some M is P.
	$\therefore$ No S is P.		$\therefore$ Some S is P.

(7)	All P is M.	(10)	No P is M.
	No S is M.		Some S is M.
	$\therefore$ No S is P.		$\therefore$ Some S is not P.

PROBLEMS IN APPLYING THE THEORY OF THE SYLLOGISM

After students have mastered the techniques for evaluating syllogisms, they naturally turn to arguments that arise in daily life and attempt to use these newly acquired skills. They are usually disappointed with the results. The formal theory of the syllogism seems to bear little relationship to everyday arguments, and there doesn't seem to be any easy way to bridge the gap.

This gap between formal theory and its application occurs for a number of reasons. First, as we saw in Chapter 1, our everyday discourse leaves much unstated. Many things are conversationally implied rather than explicitly asserted. Moreover, we do not feel called on to say many things that are matters of common agreement. Before we can apply the theory of the syllogism to everyday arguments, these things that are simply understood must be *made explicit.* This is often illuminating and sometimes boring, but it usually involves a great deal of work. Second, the theory of the syllogism applies to statements only in a highly stylized form. Before we apply the theory of the syllogism to an argument, we must cast its premises and conclusion into the basic A, E, I, and O forms. This is not always easy either. Finally, there are arguments that the theory of the syllogism is not adequate to evaluate. We saw earlier in this chapter that propositional logic is not adequate to evaluate arguments whose validity depends upon the *internal* structure of propositions. For this reason, we went beyond propositional logic to study the theory of immediate inference and the theory of the syllogism, which do explore this internal structure of propositions. Although this is still a matter of some dispute, most logicians agree that developments beyond the theory of immediate inference and the theory of the syllogism are needed for the analysis of many, quite ordinary, arguments. Here is one example:

George is taller than Harry by a head.

∴ George is taller than Harry.

It is hard to imagine an argument that is more obviously valid, yet its validity cannot be shown by the classical theory of immediate inference or syllogism. (In fact, the correct analysis of this argument is still a matter of debate.)

Why study the theory of the syllogism at all, if it is hard to apply in some circumstances and perhaps impossible to apply in others? The answer to this question was given at the beginning of Chapter 7: The study of formal logic is important because it deepens our insight into the central notion of logic, *validity*. Furthermore, the argument forms we have studied do underlie much of our everyday reasoning, but so much else is going on in a normal conversational setting that this dimension is hardly evident. By examining arguments in idealized forms, we can study their validity in isolation from all the other factors at work in a rich conversational setting.

There is a difference, then, between the techniques developed in Chapters 1 to 6 and the techniques developed in these last two chapters. The first six chapters presented methods of *informal* analysis that may be applied directly to the rich and complex arguments that arise in everyday life. These methods of analysis are not wholly rigorous, but they do provide practical guides for the analysis and evaluation of actual arguments. These two chapters concerning formal logic have the opposite tendency. In comparison with the first six chapters, the level of rigor is very high, but the range of application is correspondingly smaller. In general, the more rigor and precision you insist upon, the less you can talk about.

A SYSTEM OF RULES FOR EVALUATING SYLLOGISMS

The method of Venn diagrams that we have used in this chapter is probably the most natural technique for analyzing syllogisms, because the relationship between overlapping figures is a clear analogy for the relationship between classes. Another method for evaluating syllogisms employs a system of rules. While this system has less intuitive appeal than Venn diagrams, it is easier to apply. The procedure is to lay down a set of rules such that any syllogism that satisfies all of the rules is valid and any syllogism that fails to satisfy any one of them is invalid. A concise summary of one such system is presented here.

Distribution

The central idea for one system of rules is that of the *distribution* or *extension* of a term. The basic idea is that a term is used distributively in a proposition if it is used to refer to the whole of a class or to all of the members in it. We shall first simply state the distributional properties for each of the basic A, E, I, and O propositions and then try to make sense out of this notion.

Proposition	Subject	Predicate
A	Distributed	Undistributed
E	Distributed	Distributed
I	Undistributed	Undistributed
O	Undistributed	Distributed

The two universal propositions A and E have distributed subject terms. In the I and the O propositions we speak about *some* S, therefore the subject term is undistributed for these propositions.

The reasoning runs smoothly for the subject term, but the predicate term is not so easy to deal with. Notice that there is no word like "some" or "all" governing the predicate term.

The reasoning concerning the predicate term usually proceeds along the following lines: Suppose we assert that no squares are circles.

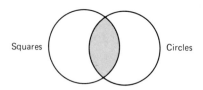

For this to be true, there can be no square that is identical with *any* circle. The appearance of the word "any" shows that the predicate term is distributed in the E proposition. Consider next the O proposition. Some *S* is not *P*. For this to be true, there must be some *S* that is not identical with *any P*. Again, the appearance of the word "any" shows that the predicate term is distributed. Our test for the distribution of terms is then to compare the basic A E I O proposition with a counterpart statement involving identity as follows:

A: All S is P.   For *any* S there is *some* P that is identical with it.
E: No S is P.   For *any* S there is not *any* P that is identical with it.
I: Some S is   For *some* S there is *some* P that is identical with it.
    P.
O: Some S is   For *some* S there is not *any* P that is identical with it.
    not P.

This comparison gives the pattern for the distribution of terms noticed earlier.

Quality

Along with the notion of distribution, the system of rules we are discussing here also uses the idea of the *quality* of a proposition—whether it is affirmative or negative. The following rules are adequate for testing the validity of categorical syllogisms.

Quality:

(1) Nothing follows from two negative premises.
(2) If one premise is negative, then the conclusion must be negative as well.
(2′) If the conclusion is negative, then one premise must be negative.[6]

Distribution:

(3) The middle term must be distributed at least once.
(4) The subject term may not be distributed in the conclusion if it is not distributed in the premises.
(5) The predicate term may not be distributed in the conclusion if it is not distributed in the premises.

The fallacies that result from violating these rules are called by the following names:

---

[6] Rule 2′ is not needed in the modern interpretation of existential import, because any syllogism that violates it will also violate a rule of distribution. It is, however, needed in the classical interpretation, which lacks Rule 6.

Quality:

(1) The Fallacy of Two Negative Premises
(2) The Fallacy of Drawing an Affirmative Conclusion from an Argument with a Negative Premise.
(2') The Fallacy of Drawing a Negative Conclusion from an Argument with two Affirmative Premises

Distribution:

(3) The Fallacy of the Undistributed Middle
(4) The Fallacy of the Illicitly Distributed Subject
(5) The Fallacy of the Illicitly Distributed Predicate

Quantity

The rules of distribution and quality are adequate for the analysis of syllogisms in the classical interpretation. The modern interpretation requires a further rule of *quantity*.

Quantity:

(6) A particular conclusion cannot be derived from two universal premises.

Corresponding to this there is, in the modern approach, a fallacy:

(6) The Fallacy of Deriving a Particular Conclusion from Universal Premises

The following devices facilitate the application of these rules. Mark the propositions in the syllogism " + " or " − " to indicate quality. Circle all terms that are distributed, leaving all undistributed terms uncircled. This makes it easy to see if the first five rules of the syllogism have been satisfied, and so whether the syllogism is valid or invalid in the classical approach. No special devices are needed to check the additional sixth rule needed in the modern approach.

The following examples illustrate these methods:

(1) + All $\widehat{M}$ is P
     + All $\widehat{S}$ is M Valid
   ∴ + All $\widehat{S}$ is P

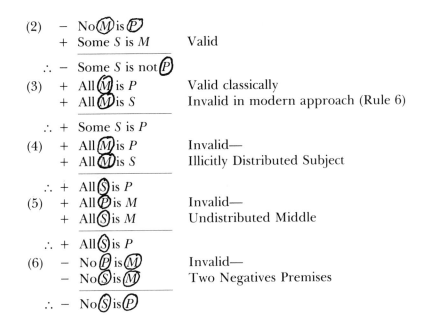

(2) − No $\widehat{M}$ is $\widehat{P}$
    + Some S is M Valid

∴ − Some S is not $\widehat{P}$

(3) + All $\widehat{M}$ is P Valid classically
    + All $\widehat{M}$ is S Invalid in modern approach (Rule 6)

∴ + Some S is P

(4) + All $\widehat{M}$ is P Invalid—
    + All $\widehat{M}$ is S Illicitly Distributed Subject

∴ + All $\widehat{S}$ is P

(5) + All $\widehat{P}$ is M Invalid—
    + All $\widehat{S}$ is M Undistributed Middle

∴ + All $\widehat{S}$ is P

(6) − No $\widehat{P}$ is $\widehat{M}$ Invalid—
    − No $\widehat{S}$ is $\widehat{M}$ Two Negatives Premises

∴ − No $\widehat{S}$ is $\widehat{P}$

EXERCISE 6

Using the system of rules we have developed, test the syllogisms given in Exercise 5 for validity. Where a fallacy occurs, give the name of that fallacy.

◆ EXERCISE 7

To a person familiar with computer programming, this system of rules immediately suggests that a program can be written for the evaluation of syllogisms. In fact, such a program can be written and is only moderately difficult. The first problem is to find some method for encoding all possible syllogisms. After this, the notions of distribution and quality must be given mathematical analogues. In writing such a program, there is a good chance that the programmer will discover on his or her own large portions of Medieval logic.

DISCUSSION QUESTIONS

(1) What are the chief differences between the logical procedures developed in this chapter and those developed in the previous chapter?

(2) If we evaluate arguments as they occur in everyday life by using the exact standards developed in these last two chapters, we discover that our everyday arguments rarely satisfy these standards, at least *explicitly*. Does this show that most of our ordinary arguments are illogical? What else might it show?

9

Inductive Reasoning

This chapter begins by explaining the difference between *deductive* and *inductive* arguments. The difference depends on the relationship between the premises and conclusion of each type of argument. With a valid deductive argument, if the premises are true, then the conclusion *must* be true as well. This is not true for inductive arguments even when they place the conclusion beyond reasonable doubt.

Two kinds of inductive reasoning are examined in detail. First, the chapter describes *inductive generalizations,* where a statistical claim is made about a *population* on the basis of features of a *sample* of that population. The standard fallacies that can arise with such generalization are examined in detail.

Second, the chapter examines *causal generalizations* and suggests ways they can be tested by using a simplified version of *Mill's methods* of *agreement, difference,* and *concomitant variation.*

Since Chapter 2 we have been concerned almost exclusively with *deductive* arguments, but many arguments (perhaps most arguments) encountered in daily life are not intended to be deductive. In particular, many arguments are said to be *inductive* in character. In this chapter we shall examine some of the chief forms that inductive arguments take.

The distinction between *deductive* arguments and *inductive* arguments can be drawn in a variety of ways, but the fundamental difference concerns the relationship between the premises and the conclusion for each type of argument. As we know, in a valid deductive argument, if the premises are true, then it is impossible for the conclusion to be false. For example, the following is a valid deductive argument:

All ravens are black.

∴ If there is a raven on top of Pike's Peak, then it is black.

Since the premise lays down a universal principle governing all ravens, if it's true, then it *must* be true of all ravens (if any) on top of Pike's Peak.

This same relationship between premises and conclusion does not hold for inductive arguments. The following is an example of an inductive argument:

All ravens we have observed have been black.

∴ If there is a raven on top of Pike's Peak, then it is black.

Here we have drawn an inductive inference from the characteristics of ravens we have observed (the sample) to the characteristics of a raven we have not observed. Pretty obviously, the premise of this argument could be true, yet the conclusion could still turn out to be false. The raven on top of Pike's Peak may be an albino.

Because of the strong relationship between the premises and conclusion of a valid deductive argument, it is sometimes said that the premises of valid deductive arguments (if true) provide conclusive support for their conclusions, whereas true premises in inductive arguments provide only partial support for their conclusions. This is obviously correct. Because the premises of a valid deductive argument (if true) necessitate the truth of the conclusion, they supply conclusive support for the conclusion. The same cannot be said for inductive arguments. But it would be altogether misleading to infer from this that inductive arguments are inherently inferior to deductive arguments in supplying a justification or ground for a conclusion. In the first place, inductive arguments often place matters beyond doubt. It is possible that the next pot of water will not boil at any temperature, however high, but this is not something we worry about—we do not take precautions against it.

Second, and more importantly, deductive arguments often enjoy no advantages over their inductive counterparts. We can see this by examining the two arguments just given:

Deductive	Inductive
All ravens are black.	All ravens so far observed have been black.
∴ If there is a raven on top of Pike's Peak, it will be black.	∴ If there is a raven on top of Pike's Peak, it will be black.

Of course, it is true for the deductive argument, and not true for the inductive argument, that if the premise is true, then the conclusion must be true, and this may seem to give an advantage to the deductive argument over the inductive argument. But before we can decide how much support a deductive argument gives its conclusion, we must ask if its premises are, after all, true. That is not something we can just take for granted. Now if we examine the premises of these two arguments, we see that it is easier to establish the truth of the premise of the inductive argument than it is to establish the truth of the premises of the deductive argument. If we have observed carefully and kept good records, then we might be fully confident that all *observed* ravens have been black. On the other hand, how can we show that *all* ravens (observed and unobserved—past, present, and future) are black? The most obvious way, though there may be other ways, would be to observe ravens to see if they are black or not. But this, of course, involves producing an inductive argument (called an inductive generalization) for the premise of the deductive argument. Here our confidence in the truth of the premise of the deductive argument should be no greater than our confidence in the strength of the inference in the inductive generalization. In this case—and it is not unusual—the deductive argument provides no stronger grounds in support of its conclusion than does its inductive counterpart, because any reservations we might have about the *strength* of the inductive inference will be paralleled by doubts concerning the *truth* of the premise of the deductive argument.

Because of these considerations, we will not follow those who draw a distinction between deductive and inductive arguments in terms of the degree of support that they give their conclusions. Instead, we shall draw the distinction in terms of the claimed relationship between premises and conclusion. In arguing deductively, we claim to establish the truth of one proposition by deriving it necessarily from other truths. We can therefore be criticized if the premises we present are not true or if the conclusion does not follow necessarily from them. In arguing inductively, we put forward something as evidence in support of some further claim. Again we can be criticized if these supporting claims are not true, but we cannot be criticized just because the premises do not guarantee truth of the conclusion. When we use an inductive argument, we are not claiming that the premises guarantee the truth of the conclusion; therefore it is inappropriate to criticize an inductive argument for failing to do so.

In passing, we will also avoid the common mistake of saying that deductive arguments always move from the general to the particular, whereas inductive arguments always move from the particular to the general. In fact, both sorts of arguments can move in either way. There are inductive arguments intended to establish particular matters of fact and there are deductive arguments that involve generalizations from particulars.

For example, scientists are currently debating whether or not the extinction of the dinosaurs was caused by the impact of an asteroid. Their discussions are models of inductive reasoning because they are assembling empirical evidence to confirm or disconfirm this hypothesis. Yet they are not trying to establish a generalization or a scientific law; instead they are trying to determine whether a *particular* event occurred some 60 million years ago. Inductive reasoning concerning particular matters of fact occurs constantly in everyday life as well, for example, when we check to see if someone using a computer is messing up our television reception. Deductive arguments from the particular to the general tend to be trivial, hence boring, but they do exist. Here's one: Benjamin Franklin was the first postmaster general; therefore, anyone identical with Benjamin Franklin was the first postmaster general.

Of course, many inductive arguments do move from particular premises to a general conclusion, and many deductive arguments move from the general to the particular. Again, however, this is not the *definitive* difference between these two kinds of arguments, and to suppose that it is can lead to serious misunderstandings. To repeat, the difference between inductive and deductive arguments consists in the claimed relationship between the premises and the conclusion.

Because inductive arguments involve different commitments than deductive arguments, it is a mistake to judge them by the same standards. What, then, are the standards appropriate for assessing inductive arguments? This question can be answered at various levels. At an informal level, we can lay down some general rules—or rules of thumb—that will allow us to avoid many of the more common errors of inductive reasoning. In complicated situations, however, our commonsense principles are often inadequate and can, in fact, let us down. When common sense gets out of its depth, we must turn to the procedures of mathematical statistics for help. Here we shall concern ourselves almost exclusively with informal procedures for the evaluation of inductive arguments, but we shall also examine cases where they are inadequate.

EXERCISE 1

Label each of the following arguments as deductive or inductive:

(1) The sun is coming out, so the rain should stop soon.

(2) It's going to rain tomorrow, so it is either going to rain or going to be clear tomorrow.

(3) Diet cola doesn't keep me awake at night; I drink it all the time without any problems.

(4) No one in Paris seems to understand me, so either my French is rotten or Parisians are unfriendly.

(5) If Harold is innocent, he would not go into hiding; but he is in hiding, so he is not innocent.

(6) The house is a mess, so Jeff must be home from college.

(7) No woman has ever been elected President of the United States; therefore, no woman will ever be elected President of the United States.

(8) There is no even number smaller than two, so one is not an even number.

INDUCTIVE GENERALIZATIONS

Inductive generalizations are a common (perhaps the most common) form of inductive reasoning. Here we cite characteristics of a sample of a population in order to support a claim about the character of the population as a whole. Opinion polls work this way. Suppose a candidate wants to know how popular she is with voters. Since it would be practically impossible to survey all voters, she takes a sample of voting opinion and then infers that the opinions of those sampled indicate the overall opinion of voters. Thus, if 60 percent of the voters sampled say that they will vote for her, she concludes that she will get more or less 60 percent of the vote in the actual election. As we shall see later on, inferences of this kind often go wrong, even when made by experts, but the general pattern of this reasoning is quite clear: statistical features of a sample are used to make statistical claims about the population as a whole.

How do we assess such inferences? To begin to answer this question, we can consider a simple example of an inductive generalization. On various occasions Harold has tried to use Canadian quarters in American telephones and found that they have not worked. From this he draws the conclusion that Canadian quarters do not work in American telephones. Harold's inductive reasoning looks like this:

> In the past, when I have tried to use Canadian quarters in American telephones, they have not worked.

∴ Canadian quarters do not work in American telephones.

The force of the conclusion is that Canadian quarters never work in American telephones.

In evaluating this argument, what questions should we ask? As we proceed through the first half of this chapter, we will loosely frame some questions that can be applied to all inductive generalizations, and when we are through we should be able to restate those questions with greater accuracy. To start with, then, one question we should ask of any argument is about its premises.

(1) Should We Accept the Premises?

Perhaps Harold has a bad memory, or has kept bad records, or is a poor observer. For some obscure reason, he may even be lying. It is important to ask this question explicitly, because fairly often the premises, when challenged, will not stand up to scrutiny.

If we decide that the premises are acceptable, we can then shift our attention to the relationship between the premises and the conclusion and ask how much support the premises give to the conclusion. One commonsense question is this: "Just how many times has Harold tried to use Canadian quarters in American telephones?" If the answer comes back "Three or four times," then our confidence in his argument should drop to almost nothing. So for inductive generalizations, it is always appropriate to ask about the size of the sample.

(2) Is the Sample Large Enough to Avoid Bias?

One reason that we should be suspicious of small samples is that they can be affected by runs of luck. Suppose Harold flips a Canadian quarter four times and it comes up heads each time. From this, he can hardly conclude that Canadian quarters always come up heads when flipped. He could not even reasonably conclude that *this* Canadian quarter would always come up heads when flipped. The reason for this is obvious enough: if you spend a lot of time flipping coins, runs of four heads in a row are not all that unlikely (the odds are actually 1 in 16), and therefore samples of this size can easily be distorted by chance. On the other hand, if Harold flipped the coin 20 times and it continued to come up heads, he would have strong grounds for saying that this coin, at least, will always come up heads. In fact, he would have very strong grounds for thinking that he has a two-headed coin. Because an overly small sample can lead to erroneous conclusions, we can say that it is unfair or biased, simply on a statistical level.

How many is enough? On the assumption, for the moment, that our sampling has been fair in all other respects, how many samples do we need to provide the basis for a strong inductive argument? This is not always an easy question to answer, and sometimes answering it demands subtle mathematical techniques. Suppose your company is selling 100 million computer chips to the Department of Defense, and you have guaranteed that no more than 0.2 percent of them will be defective. It would be prohibitively expensive to test all the chips, and testing only a dozen would hardly be enough to reasonably guarantee that the total shipment of chips met the required specifications. Because testing chips is expensive, you want to test as few as possible, but because meeting the specifications is crucial, you want to test enough to guarantee that you have done so. Answering questions of this kind demands sophisticated statistical techniques beyond the scope of this text.

Sometimes, then, it is difficult to decide how many samples are needed to give reasonable support to inductive generalizations, yet many times it is obvious, without going into technical details, that the sample is too small. Drawing an inductive conclusion from a sample that is too small can lead to the fallacy of hasty generalization, and it is surprising how common this fallacy is. We see a person two or three times and find him cheerful, and we immediately leap to the conclusion that he is a cheerful person. That is, from a few instances of cheerful behavior, we draw a general conclusion about his personality. When we meet him later and find him sad, morose, or grouchy, we then conclude that he has changed—thus swapping one *hasty generalization* for another.

This tendency toward hasty generalization was discussed more than two hundred years ago by the philosopher David Hume, who saw that we have a strong tendency to "follow general rules which we rashly form to ourselves, and which are the source of what we properly call prejudice." This tendency toward hasty generalization has been the subject of extensive psychological investigation. In an article titled "Belief in The Law of Small Numbers," cognitive psychologists Amos Tversky and Daniel Kahneman put the matter this way:

We submit that people view a sample randomly drawn from a population as highly representative, that is, similar to the population in all essential characteristics. Consequently, they expect any two samples drawn from a particular population to be more similar to one another and to the population than sampling theory predicts, at least for small samples.[1]

To return to a previous example, we make our judgments of someone's personality on the basis of a very small sample of his or her behavior and expect this person to behave in similar ways in the future when we encounter further samples of behavior. We are surprised, sometimes indignant, when the future behavior does not match our expectations.

By making our samples sufficiently large, we can guard against distortions due to "runs of luck," but even very large samples can give us a poor basis for an inductive generalization. Suppose that Harold has tried hundreds of times to use a Canadian quarter in an American telephone and it has never worked. This will increase our confidence in his inductive generalization, but size of sample alone is not a sufficient ground for a strong inductive argument. Suppose that Harold has tried the same coin in hundreds of different telephones, or tried a hundred different Canadian coins in the same telephone. In the first case, there might be something wrong with this particular coin; in the second case, there might be something wrong with this particular telephone. In neither case would he have good grounds for making the general claim that no Canadian quarters work in any American telephones. This leads us to the third question we should ask of any inductive generalization.

(3) Is the Sample Biased in Other Ways?

When the sample, however large, is not representative of the population, then again it is said to be unfair or biased. Here we can speak of the fallacy of a *biased sampling*. One of the most famous examples of biased sampling was committed by a magazine named the *Literary Digest*. Before the presidential election of 1936, this magazine sent ten million questionnaires asking which candidate the recipient would vote for: Franklin Roosevelt or Alf Landon. They received two and a half million returns, and on the basis of the results confidently predicted that Landon would win by a landslide: 56 percent for Landon to only 44 percent for Roosevelt. When the election results came in, Roosevelt won

---

[1]Amos Tversky and Daniel Kahneman, "Belief in the Law of Small Numbers," *Psychological Bulletin,* Vol. 76, No. 2 (1971), p. 105.

by even a larger landslide in the opposite direction: 62 percent for Roosevelt to a mere 38 percent for Landon. What went wrong? The sample was certainly large enough; in fact, by contemporary standards it was much larger than needed. It was the way the sample was selected, not its size, that caused the problem: the sample was randomly drawn from names in telephone books and from club membership lists. Now in 1936 there were only 11 million telephones in the United States and many of the poor—especially the rural poor—did not have telephones. During the Great Depression there were more than nine million unemployed in America; they were almost all poor and thus under-represented in the magazine's sample. Finally, a very large percentage of this under-represented group voted for Roosevelt, the Democratic candidate. As a result of this bias in their sampling, along with some others as well, the *Literary Digest* underestimated Roosevelt's percentage of the vote by a whopping *18 percent.*

Looking back, it may be hard to believe that intelligent observers could have done such a ridiculously bad job of sampling opinion, but the story repeats itself, though rarely on the grand scale of the Literary Digest fiasco. In 1948, for example, the Gallup Poll, which had correctly predicted Roosevelt's victory in 1936, predicted, along with other major polls, a clear victory for Dewey over Truman. Confidence was so high in this prediction that the *Chicago Tribune* published a banner headline declaring Dewey won the election. What went wrong this time? The answer here is more subtle. Gallup (and others) went to great pains to make sure that their sample was representative of the voting population. Thus their interviewers were told to poll a certain number of people from particular social groups: rural poor, suburban middle class, urban middle class, ethnic minorities, and so on, so that the proportions of those interviewed matched, as closely possible, the proportions of those likely to vote. (The *Literary Digest* went bankrupt after its misprediction, so the pollsters were taking no chances.) Yet somehow bias crept into the sampling; the question was, how? One speculation was that a significantly large percentage of those sampled didn't tell the truth when they were interviewed; another was that a large number of people changed their minds at the last minute. So maybe the data collected were not very reliable. The explanation generally accepted was more subtle. Although Gallup's workers were told to interview specific numbers of people from particular classes (so many from the suburbs, for example), they were not instructed to choose people randomly from within each group. Without seriously thinking about it, they tended to go to "nicer" neighborhoods and interviewed "nicer" people. Because of this, they biased the sample in the direction of their own (largely) middle class preferences and, as a result, under-represented constituencies that would give Truman his unexpected victory.

SOURCES OF BIAS

Because professionals using modern statistical analysis can make bad inductive generalizations through biased sampling, it is not surprising that our informal inductive generalizations are often inaccurate. It will be useful, then, to look at some of the main sources of bias in sampling. We have already examined two sources of bias: biases due to small samples and biases due to limited personal experience. Here are some other sources of bias.

Prejudice and Stereotypes

People who are prejudiced will find very little good and a great deal bad in those they despise, no matter how these people actually behave. In fact, most people are a mixture of good and bad qualities, and by ignoring the former and dwelling on the latter, it is easy enough for the prejudiced person to confirm his negative opinions. Similarly, stereotypes, which can be either positive or negative, often persist in the face of overwhelming counterevidence. Speaking of the beliefs common in Britain in his own day, David Hume remarked:

> An Irishman cannot have wit, and a Frenchman cannot have solidity; for which reason, though the conversation of the former in any instance be very agreeable, and of the latter very judicious, we have entertain'd such a prejudice against them, that they must be dunces and fops in spite of sense and reason.[2]

Informal Judgmental Heuristics

In daily life, we have to make a great many decisions, some of them important, most of them not. Furthermore, because we have to make a great many decisions, they often have to be made quickly without pausing to weigh evidence carefully. To deal with this overload of decisions, we commonly employ what cognitive psychologists call judgmental heuristics. Technically, a heuristic is a device that provides a general strategy for solving a problem or coming to a decision. (For example, a good heuristic for solving geometry problems is to start with the conclusion you are trying to reach and then work backwards.) Recent research in cognitive psychology has shown, first, that human beings rely very heavily on heuristics and, second, that we often put too much reliance on them. The result is that our inductive inferences often go badly wrong, and that sometimes our thinking gets utterly mixed up. In this regard, two

---

[2]David Hume, *A Treatise of Human Nature*, 2nd ed. (London: Oxford University Press, 1978), pp. 146–47.

heuristics are particularly interesting: the *representative heuristic* and the *availability heuristic*.

The Representative Heuristic. A simple example illustrates how errors can arise from the representative heuristic. You are randomly dealt five-card hands from a standard deck. Which of the following two hands is more likely to come up?

(1)	(2)
Three of Clubs	Ace of Spades
Seven of Diamonds	Ace of Hearts
Nine of Diamonds	Ace of Clubs
Queen of Hearts	Ace of Diamonds
King of Spades	King of Spades

A surprisingly large number of people will automatically say that the second hand is much less likely than the first. Actually, if you think about it for a bit, it should be obvious that any two specific hands have the same likelihood of being dealt. Here people get confused because the first hand is an ordinary hand, the kind that comes up all the time, a representative hand, whereas the second hand is extraordinary and unrepresentative. Here our reliance on representativeness blinds us to a simple and obvious point about probabilities.

A later set of experiments carried out by Tversky and Kahneman yielded an even more remarkable result.[3] Students were given the following description of a fictitious person named Linda:

> Linda is 31 years old, single, outspoken and very bright. She majored in philosophy. As a student, she was deeply concerned with issues of discrimination and social justice, and also participated in anti-nuclear demonstrations.

The students were then asked to rank the following statements with respect to the probability that they were also true of Linda:

> Linda is a teacher in elementary school.
>
> Linda works in a bookstore and takes Yoga classes.
>
> Linda is active in the feminist movement.
>
> Linda is a psychiatric social worker.
>
> Linda is a member of the League of Women Voters.

---

[3]Amos Tversky and Daniel Kahneman, "Extensional Versus Intuitive Reasoning: The Conjunction Fallacy in Probability Judgment," *Psychological Review*, Vol. 90, No. 4 (October 1983), p. 297.

Linda is a bank teller.

Linda is an insurance salesperson.

Linda is a bank teller and is active in the feminist movement.

Not surprisingly, the students thought that it was most likely that Linda was a feminist, and least likely that she was a bank teller. What was surprising was that 89 percent of the subjects in one experiment thought that it was more likely that Linda was both a bank teller and a feminist than that she was simply a bank teller. Now, if you think about that for a moment, you will see that it cannot be right: the probability that two things are true can never be higher than the probability that just one of them is true. Presumably what happens here is something like this: unreflectively, people think that the claim that Linda is both a bank teller and a feminist at least says something plausible about her whereas the simple claim that she is a bank teller isn't plausible at all. But that is just bad reasoning, and here reliance on the representative heuristic doesn't merely give us an inaccurate estimate of a probability, it actually leads us into a logical blunder.

The Availability Heuristic.   Because sampling and taking surveys is expensive, we often do it imaginatively—in our heads. If you ask a baseball fan which team has the better batting average, Detroit or San Diego, he might just remember, he might go look it up, or he might think about each team and try to decide which one has the most good batters. The latter, needless to say, would be a risky business, but many baseball fans have remarkable knowledge of the batting averages of top hitters. Even with this knowledge, however, it is easy to go wrong. The players that naturally come to mind are the stars on each team: they are more available to our memory, and we are likely to make our judgment on the basis of them alone. Yet such a sample can easily be biased because *all* the batters contribute to the team average, not just the stars. (The fact that the weak batters on one team are much better than the weak batters on the other can swing the balance.)

Another experiment by Tversky and Kahneman shows how the influence of the availability heuristic (like the influence of the representative heuristic) can lead to incoherent results. Subjects were asked the following question:

> In four pages of a novel (about 2,000 words), how many words would you expect to find that have the form _____ing (seven-letter words that end with "ing")?

> Indicate your best estimate by circling one of the values below:

> 0   1–2   3–4   5–7   8–10   11–15   16+

A second version of the question requested estimates for words of the form _____n_. The median estimates were 13.4 for *ing* words . . . and 4.7 for _n_ words.[4]

The result is again logically incoherent; there must be *at least* as many *ing* words in the text as _n_ words, since every *ing* word is also an _n_ word. Why didn't people think about this? The answer is that we rely on the availability heuristic and it is easy to think of *ing* words: all sorts of verbs with *ing* endings pop into our minds at once. There is nothing similarly memorable about seven-letter words ending with _n_. Thus relying on what naturally pops into our heads will often produce biased samples that will lead us to draw false, even incoherent, conclusions.

The point of examining these two judgmental heuristics and noting the logical errors that they produce is *not* to suggest that we should cease relying on them. First, there is a good chance that this would not be psychologically possible, because the use of such heuristics seems to be built into our psychological makeup. Second, over a wide range of standard cases, these heuristics give *quick* and largely *accurate* estimates. Difficulties typically arise in using these heuristics when the situation is *nonstandard*, that is, when the situation is complex or out of the normal run of things. This suggests another question we should routinely ask about inductive generalizations:

(4) Is the Situation Sufficiently Standard to Allow the Use of Informal Judgmental Heuristics?

Because this is a mouthful, we might ask, when appropriate, "Is this really the sort of thing that people can figure out in their heads?" When the answer to that question is no, as it often is, then we should turn to the formal procedures of statistical analysis for our answers.

Summary

We should now be able to summarize and restate our questions with more accuracy. Confronted with inductive generalizations, there are five questions that we should routinely ask:

(1) Are the premises acceptable?

(2) Is the sample likely to be biased because it is too small?

---

[4]"Extensional Versus Intuitive Reasoning," p. 295.

(3) Is the sample likely to be biased because it relies on one or more person's vivid but limited experience?

(4) Is the sample likely to be biased because the sampling was affected by prejudice and stereotypes?

(5) Is the sample likely to be biased because it relies on informal heuristics in complex situations where they often prove unreliable?

EXERCISE 2

Ann Landers caused a stir when she announced the results of a mail poll that asked her women readers to respond to the following question:

> Would you be content to be held and treated tenderly, and forget about "the act"?

Her readers were instructed to answer YES or NO and indicate whether they were over (or under) 40 years of age.

The result was that 72 percent of the respondents answered yes and of those who answered yes, 40 percent indicated that they were under 40 years old.

What are we to make of these results? Ann Landers expressed surprise that so many of those who answered yes came from the under-40 group. But for her, "the greatest revelation" was "what the poll says about men as lovers. Clearly, there is trouble in paradise." (*Ask Ann Landers*, January 14 & 15, 1985)

The poll, of course, did not employ scientific methods of sampling (nor did Ann Landers claim that it did), so it is important to look for sources of bias before drawing any conclusions from this poll. Discuss at least three possible sources of bias that could make the Landers sample unrepresentative of the opinions of the population of adult women in America.

CAUSAL GENERALIZATIONS

We often wonder why certain things have happened; why, for example, our car has gone dead in the middle of rush-hour traffic just after its 20,000-mile checkup. We think that there must be some reason for this happening—cars just don't stop for no reason at all—and reasons of this kind we commonly call *causes*. We could just as well have asked, "What caused the car to stop?" The answer might be that it has run out of gas. If you find, in fact, that it *has* run out of gas, then that will be the end of the matter; you will have discovered (or at least *think* you have discovered) why this particular car has stopped running. But even if your thinking is about a particular car on a particular occasion, your reasoning rests on certain *generalizations*; in particular, you are confident that *your* car stopped running when it ran out of gas because you believe that *all* cars stop running when they run out of gas. You probably did not think about this, but your causal reasoning in this particular case appealed to a commonly accepted *causal generalization*: cars won't go without gas. And what holds in this case, holds quite generally: when we offer a causal explanation of a particular event, we appeal, though not always explicitly, to causal generalizations.

A second important reason that we are interested in causal judgments is that we use them to *predict* the consequences of particular actions or events. A race car driver might wonder, for example, what would happen if he added just a bit of nitroglycerine to his fuel mixture: would it give him better acceleration, blow him up, do very little, or what? In fact, the driver may not be in a position to answer this question straight off, but his thinking will be guided by the causal generalization that igniting nitroglycerine can cause a dangerous explosion.

So a similar pattern arises for both causal explanation and causal prediction. These inferences contain two essential elements:

(1) The facts in the particular case. (For example, the car has stopped and the gas gauge says empty, or I have just put a pint of nitroglycerine in the gas tank of my Maserati and I am about to turn the ignition key).

(2) Certain causal generalizations. (For example, that cars do not run without gasoline or that nitroglycerine explodes when ignited).

The key idea, though this will turn out to be more complicated than these simple examples suggest, is that in drawing a causal inference we bring particular facts under causal generalizations. What, then, are *causal generalizations;* where do they come from; and how are they established? We can take these questions up one at a time.

In daily life, to say that one thing caused something else to happen amounts to saying that the first thing made the second happen, or that the second thing happened *because* the first thing happened. In fact, our language contains a great many ways of indicating the presence of a causal relation. Such words as "produced" and "determined" are obvious examples, but a great many other verbs are implicitly causal. For example, to say that Myra broke Stephen's heart is a way of saying that

Myra caused Stephen's heart to be broken. In a similar way, a great many transitive verbs of action (verbs like "build," "divert," and "suppress") are also implicitly causal because they indicate that something (the agent) has brought something about.

It is not difficult to point out commonsense examples of causes, but it is more difficult to explain this notion with clarity. The law uses the so-called *but-for* test for causality. If you want to know whether a person is causally responsible for some event, you ask the following question: "Is it true that *but for* that person's action, the event would not have occurred?" For example, if we want to know whether a person's drunkenness was the cause of an accident, then we ask whether the accident would have occurred even if the person had not been drunk. If the answer to this is yes (perhaps the person was parked in a drunken stupor in his own driveway), then (normally, at least) we will not say that this drunkenness was the cause of the accident.

Surprisingly, the but-for test usually gives reasonable answers concerning whether or not one event is the cause of another. This is surprising because the but-for test merely picks out a *necessary* condition for an event to occur and, typically, there are a great many necessary conditions that we would not call causes.[5] For example, if Alvin punches Mark, giving him a black eye, then, but for Alvin's punching, Mark would not have had a black eye, so we say that Alvin caused it. That sounds right. At the same time, if Mark had ducked, he would not have been struck, and he would not have gotten a black eye. But for his not ducking, Mark would not have gotten a black eye, so he is responsible for his black eye. That sounds wrong. Things get worse the more we think about it. An arsonist, who admittedly threw a fire bomb into a house, can correctly point out that but for the presence of oxygen, the building would not have burned. For that matter, but for the fact that someone built the house, it would not be there in the first place to be burned down. Using the but-for test, there seems to be no end to the places where we can locate the cause of an event.

With all these difficulties, why does the but-for test work at all? Part of the answer is that in daily life we draw a distinction between causes and *standing conditions* (or *background conditions*). Seeing pieces of a vase scattered on the floor, someone asks, "Why is that vase broken?" The answer comes back: "Vases are fragile," or "The vase hit the floor hard," or "The law of gravity was working this afternoon." Of course, all of these are true and but for them the vase may not have

---

[5] The *but-for* test also fails, or seems to fail, for exotic cases where the effect is *overdetermined.* A house might catch fire and then burn down because simultaneously there is a short circuit in the wall and it is struck by lightning. Here it is natural to say that the two events together caused the short circuit, yet it is not true that, but for the occurrence of these two events, the house would not have burned down. If only one of them had occurred, the house would have burned down anyway.

broken, yet we do not want them cited as causes. The original question, "Why is the vase broken?" had this force: Given the background facts we all know, what particular fact or facts account for the vase being broken? Saying that you knocked it over while practicing kung fu would provide just the kind of causal explanation asked for.

Secondly, what we normally call a cause will depend in part on our particular *interests and concerns*. To go back to a previous example, if we are interested in who is morally to blame (or who is morally responsible) for Mark's black eye, then we will probably say that it was Alvin's striking him that caused Mark's black eye. Here the striking (not the failure to duck) is the morally relevant event. But if we change the context to a boxing match, and suppose that Alvin hit Mark with what is called a sucker punch, then Mark might be held responsible for his black eye because he *should* have ducked. We can get a wholly different causal account if we change the context in a more radical way. Suppose that Mark has a horrendous black eye from what, after all, was only a slight tap to the side of the head. Here we are looking for a *medical* explanation and the answer may point out something peculiar about the capillaries in the skin around Mark's eyes.

But even if our causal judgments are affected by the context in which they are used, there seems to be one common feature that runs through all contexts that we can call *regularity* or *uniformity*. When we say that one thing, A, is the cause of another thing, B, we are at least committing ourselves to the claim that, in contexts like the one we are in, an event like A is always followed by an event like B. That is, the occurrence of an event like A in a context like the present one is *sufficient* to bring about B. Perhaps we are asserting more than this, but these commitments can serve as a guide to the standard methods for evaluating causal arguments.

MILL'S METHODS

John Stuart Mill (1806–1873) was a champion of the new empirical and inductive methods of science. He believed that these methods could be extended indefinitely to all fields of human knowledge with resulting benefits to mankind. To further this cause, he introduced a set of procedures for evaluating causal arguments. They came to be known as Mill's Methods. Here we shall examine a modified and simplified version of these methods.

(1) The Method of Agreement

We can begin with an example. Suppose that, to everyone's acute embarrassment, a group of seventh graders show up at school on a Monday with head lice. Everyone, of course, would be anxious to know where they picked them up (and that's a causal question). To begin with, the investigation will be guided by certain ordinary assumptions. First, we know that lice do not appear spontaneously, say, out of shampoo. Second, we know that lice do not often just come flying in through windows; they are generally spread through contact. Finally, to begin with, we can assume that there is a *common* source for this infestation.

Given these background assumptions, it is natural to ask each student what he or she was doing for the last three or four days. We can let the letters A, B, C, . . . Z, stand for their activities *antecedent* to the event to be explained. Suppose the results come out as follows:

Antecedent Activities	Occurrence or Non-Occurrence of the Event to be Explained
A C D E	Brian (yes)
B D E J	Scott (yes)
A D F G	Jennifer (yes)
C D E J	Hope (yes)
A B C D	Brandon (yes)
B C D E	Heather (yes)

It doesn't take long to discover that D is the only antecedent activity that all of the students have in common. Let's suppose that D stands for going to a dance party at Heather's house.

Although this is the only feature that all the students have in common, it would be unreasonable to leap to the conclusion that their unpleasant condition is the result of attending a party at Heather's house. First of all, the explanation does not make obvious sense, for, in general, people do not get lice from attending parties. Second, it may simply be a *coincidence* that those with lice also attended Heather's party. To deal with this possibility, we can use another of Mill's methods.

(2) The Method of Difference

We now have a hypothesis: the infestation was somehow related to attending Heather's party. What we want to test now is whether this common factor really makes a difference. To do this, we look for *closely related cases* where the effect to be explained is *absent;* we then look to see if the proposed factor is absent as well. We want to know whether the presence or absence of the cause makes a difference, and that's why Mill called this the Method of Difference. A simple illustration will show how it works. Suppose Brian, Barry, and Bert are good friends. They do a lot together, yet Brian somehow picked up lice while Barry and Bert did not. The obvious question to ask is, of course, whether Barry and Bert also went to Heather's party. If the answer is no, then our explanatory hypothesis receives even stronger confirmation. Schematically:

Antecedent Activities	Occurrence or Non-Occurrence of the Event to be Explained
A C D E	Brian (yes)
A C F E	Barry (no)
A C G E	Bert (no)

(3) The Joint Method of Agreement and Difference

Using the methods of Agreement and Difference, we have reason to believe that the phenomenon to be explained is somehow connected with attending Heather's party, but we are not yet in a position to assign a *cause* for this phenomenon. There are two reasons for this: (1) our correlation really does not *make sense* out of the phenomenon, and (2) the hypothesis stands in need of further testing. To start with the first point, there is no general correlation between attending parties and contracting lice, and for this reason the correlation doesn't seem to make much sense. Furthermore, because the correlation we have hit upon is not explanatory, it seems reasonable to check this correlation more carefully. Ideally, we would like to find a *perfect* correlation between the phenomena under consideration. Ideally, our hypothesis will be fully confirmed if every seventh grader who contracted lice went to Heather's party and, furthermore, every seventh grader who went to Heather's party contracted lice. Testing for this perfect correlation is the essence of Mill's Joint Method of Agreement and Difference.

Continuing our investigation, suppose we discover that some others who attended the party (Karen, Terry, and Bret) did contract lice, and that further strengthens the correlation, but we also discover that some (including Beth and Joshua) did not. We have thus found *disconfirming* evidence for our hypothesis.

So our further investigations have weakened the evidence in favor of our hypothesis that attending Heather's party explains the phenomenon in question. But the correlation is still so strong that it suggests that attending Heather's party might have had *something* to do with the phenomenon in question. So using Mill's Joint Method of Agreement and Difference, we can ask whether there is any further feature that distinguishes those who attended Heather's party and contracted lice from those who attended her party and did not. In interviewing our second group of students, we also uncover other antecedent activities. Suppose that our new data look like this:

Antecedent Activities	Occurrence or Non-Occurrence of the Event to be Explained
D M N O	Karen (yes)
D M O R	Beth (no)
D N O R	Terry (yes)
D M N R	Bret (yes)
D M R O	Joshua (no)

If we examine the chart, we see that they they all went to the dance party (that's D) and there are a number of other factors that many of them have in common (that's what makes the cases similar). There is, however, only one factor, that is always present when the phenomenon is present, and always absent when it is absent; that's factor N, which indicates that each of these students bought costumes for the party from a sleazy second-hand clothing store.

To end this example, let us suppose that our further investigation establishes a *perfect correlation* between those infected with lice and those buying clothes at this particular store. When we go back to interview our first group of students (Brian, Scott, and the others), we find that prior to the party they all bought clothing at the store too, something we failed to establish in our first collection of data. Will this settle the issue? Probably. Still, we have not achieved absolute certainty, because further investigation could upset this perfect correlation. Problems could also arise in a different way. Suppose that the city health officials inspected the store and found it a model of cleanliness. That would upset our explanatory hypothesis by suggesting that the correlation, however perfect, might just be accidental. That brings us to an important maxim: *A correlation, no matter how perfect, need not be a causal correlation.*

To illustrate this last point, suppose that our investigation turned up the following remarkable fact: those who were Bruce Springsteen fans were infested, those who weren't, weren't. Now whatever one thinks of Bruce Springsteen, it isn't reasonable to suppose that liking him can give you head lice. It simply doesn't make sense. On the other side, suppose that the city health officials did discover that the store was infested; that would pretty well settle the matter. Of course, there is still a *chance* that further investigation could overturn this explanation, but, given this evidence, most people would consider the case solved. First, they have a perfect correlation, which is usually hard to come by. But this perfect correlation does not distinguish this explanation from the weird Bruce Springsteen correlation which, as it turned out, was perfect as well. Second, the explanation seems adequate because it makes sense: that is, it squares with our understanding of how things work. Critters can be carried by clothing, but not by a rock singer's voice. Our causal generalizations lean on each other for support.

This example suggests two questions we should always ask concerning a causal explanation:

(1) How strong are the correlations it is based on?
(2) Is the correlation genuinely explanatory?

Mill's methods (there is one more to come) provide a system for answering the first question. In deciding whether a correlation is genuinely explanatory or merely accidental, we must rely on our general knowledge of the way the world runs. If a well-supported correlation fits in with this background knowledge, we will accept it; if it doesn't, we will write it off as a fluke.

This last remark isn't quite right. If a correlation is strongly supported over a wide range of circumstances, and if the research is carried out with great care, we may accept a correlation as causal (rather than merely accidental) even if we have no idea what the underlying causal mechanism might be. Something approaching this occurred in the early research concerning the relationship between smoking and the incidence of lung cancer and heart disease. The correlation was strikingly high, but no one knew exactly *how* smoking could cause lung cancer or heart disease. For this reason, some people, notably representatives of the tobacco industry, argued that no causal connection had been established, only a correlation that could be accidental. This might have turned out to be correct, but, with further research, the correlation became so well established that it became reasonable to assume that there must be some underlying causal mechanism linking smoking with heart disease and lung cancer—even if it hadn't been discovered yet. This was further supported by the fact that increased smoking led to increased incidence of both lung cancer and heart disease. This takes us to the last of Mill's methods that we shall examine.

(4) The Method of Concomitant Variation

It will help to introduce this method with an example. In recent years a controversy has raged over the impact of acid rain on the environment of the northeastern United States and Canada. Part of the controversy involves the proper interpretation of the data that have been collected. The controversy has arisen for the following reason: the atmosphere always contains a certain amount of acid, much of it from natural sources. It is also known that an excess of acid in the environment can have severe effects both on plants and animals. Lakes are particularly vulnerable to the effects of acid rain. Finally, it is also acknowledged that industries, mostly in the Middle West, discharge large quantities of sulphur dioxide (SO_2) into the air and this increases the acidity of water in the atmosphere. The question, and here the controversy begins, is whether the contribution of acid from these industries is the cause of the environmental damage downwind from them.

How can we settle such a question? The methods we have examined thus far—the methods of agreement, disagreement, and the joint method involving both—provide no immediate help, for they depend on the fact that both the phenomenon to be explained and the proposed phenomenon offered as an explanation sometimes occur and sometimes do not. The first three methods exploit this fact in looking for a *unique* correlation. In this case, however, this does not happen, for there is always a certain amount of acid in the atmosphere, and so it is not possible to check what happens when acid is absent. Similarly, environmental damage, which is the phenomenon to be explained, is so widespread in our modern industrial society that it is also hard to find cases where it does not occur.

So, if there is always acid in the atmosphere, and environmental damage always exists at least to some extent, how can we determine whether the SO_2 released into the atmosphere is *significantly* responsible for the environmental damage in the affected areas? Here we use Mill's *method of concomitant variation.* We ask whether the amount of environmental damage varies directly in proportion to the amount of SO_2 released into the environment. If environmental damage increases with the amount of SO_2 released into the environment and drops when the amount of SO_2 is lowered, then it seems reasonable to suppose that the level of SO_2 in the atmosphere is *positively correlated* with environmental damage. We would have good reason to believe that lowering SO_2 emissions would lower the level of environmental damage, at least to some extent.

Arguments relying on the method of concomitant variation are difficult to evaluate, especially when there is no generally accepted background theory that makes sense of the concomitant variation. Some such variations are well understood. For example, everyone knows that the faster you drive, the more gasoline you consume. (Gasoline consumption varies *inversely* with speed.) Why? There is a good theory here: it takes more energy to drive at a high speed than at a low speed, and this energy is derived from the gasoline consumed in the car's engine. Other correlations are less well understood. There seems to be a correlation between the cholesterol level in the blood and the chances of heart attack. First of all, the correlation here is not nearly as good as the gasoline consumption–speed correlation, for many people with high cholesterol levels do not suffer heart attacks, and many people with low cholesterol levels do. Furthermore, no generally accepted background theory has been found that explains the positive correlation that does seem to exist.

This reference to background theory is important, because two sets of phenomena can be correlated to a very high degree, even with no causal relationship between them. A favorite example that appears in many statistics text is the discovered positive correlation in boys between foot size and quality of handwriting. It is hard to imagine causal correlation holding in either direction. Having big feet should not make you write better and, just as obviously, writing well should not give you big feet. The correct explanation is that both foot size and handwriting ability are positively correlated with age. Here a noncausal correlation between two phenomena (foot size and handwriting ability) is explained by a third common correlation (maturation) that *is* causal.

At times, it is possible to get causal correlations *backwards*. For example, a few years ago, sports statisticians discovered a *negative* correlation between forward passes thrown and winning. That is, the more forward passes that a team threw, the less chance it had of winning. This suggests that passing is not a good strategy, since the more you do it, the more likely you are to lose. Closer examination showed, however, that the causal relationship, in fact, went in the other direction. Toward the end of a game, losing teams tend to throw a great many passes in an effort to catch up. In other words, teams throw a lot of passes because they are losing, rather than the other way around.

Finally, some correlations seem inexplicable. For example, a strong positive correlation holds between the birthrate in Holland and the number of storks nesting in chimneys. There is, of course, a background theory that would explain this—storks bring babies—but that theory is not favored by modern science. For the lack of any better background theory, the phenomenon just seems weird.

So, given a strong correlation between phenomena of types A and B, four possibilities exist:

(1) A is the cause of B.
(2) B is the cause of A.
(3) Some third thing is the cause of both.
(4) The correlation is simply accidental.

Before we accept any one of these possibilities, we must have good reasons for preferring it over the other three.

EXERCISE 3

In each of the following examples a strong correlation, either negative or positive, holds between two sets of phenomena A and B. Try to decide if A is the cause of B, B is the cause of A, both are caused by some third factor C, or the correlation is simply accidental. Explain your choice.

(1) At one time there was a strong negative correlation between the number of mules in a state (A) and the salaries paid to professors at the state university (B). In other words, the more mules, the lower professorial salaries.[6]

(2) It has been claimed that there is a strong positive correlation between those students who take sex education courses (A) and those who contract venereal disease (B).

(3) *"LOCKED DOORS NO BAR TO CRIME, STUDY SAYS*

"Washington (UPI)—Rural Americans with locked doors, watchdogs or guns may face as much risk of burglary as neighbors who leave doors unlocked, a federally financed study says.

"The study, financed in part by a three-year $170,000 grant from the Law Enforcement Assistance Administration, was based on a survey of nearly 900 families in rural Ohio.

"Sixty percent of the rural residents surveyed regularly locked doors [A], but were burglarized more often than residents who left doors unlocked [B]."[7]

(4) There is a high positive correlation between the number of fire engines in a particular borough in New York City (A) and the number of fires that occur there (B).[8]

(5) For a particular United States President, there is a negative correlation between the number of hairs on his head (A) and the population of China (B).

DISCUSSION QUESTIONS

(1) In Exercise 1 of Chapter 3, President Reagan relies on an inductive argument to the effect that World War III has been avoided because of the balance of power between the West and East. What evidence does he offer in support of this conclusion? How strong is his argument? What further evidence might be used to either strengthen the argument or show it to be inadequate?

---

[6] From Gregory A. Kimble, *How to Use (and Misuse) Statistics* (Englewood Cliffs, N.J.: Prentice-Hall, 1978).

[7] "Locked Doors No Bar to Crime, Study Says," *Santa Barbara* [California] *Newspress,* Wednesday, Feb. 16, 1977.

[8] Also from *How to Use (and Misuse) Statistics.*

(2) Now that it seems beyond doubt that smoking is dangerous to people's health, a new debate has arisen concerning the possible health hazards of smoke on nonsmokers. Collect statements pro and con on this issue and evaluate the strength of the inductive arguments on each side.

♦ (3) Although, both in science and in daily life, we rely heavily on the methods of inductive reasoning, a number of perplexing problems exist concerning the legitimacy of this kind of reasoning. The most famous problem concerning induction was formulated by the eighteenth century philosopher David Hume, first in his *Treatise of Human Nature* and then later in his *Enquiry Concerning Human Understanding*. A simplified version of Hume's skeptical argument goes as follows: Our inductive generalizations seem to rest on the assumption that *unobserved* cases will follow the patterns that we discover in *observed* cases. That is, our inductive generalizations seem to presuppose that nature operates uniformly: the way things are observed to behave here and now are accurate indicators of how things behave anywhere and at any time. But by what right can we assume that nature is uniform? Because this claim itself asserts a matter of fact, it could only be established by inductive reasoning. But because all inductive reasoning presupposes the principle that nature is uniform, any inductive justification of this principle would seem to be circular. It seems then, that we have no ultimate justification for our inductive reasoning at all. Is this a good or bad argument?

♦ (4) In mathematics, proofs are sometimes employed using the method of *mathematical induction*. If you are familiar with these procedures, decide whether these proofs are inductive or deductive in character.

10

Taking Chances

This chapter offers an elementary discussion of reasoning about choices when outcomes are uncertain. It shows how the related notions of *probability, expected payoff,* and *relative value* bear on choices of this kind. The chapter concludes with an examination of two common mistakes in reasoning about probabilities, committing the so-called gambler's fallacy, and failing to understand the phenomenon of regression to the mean.

THE LANGUAGE OF UNCERTAINTY

In everyday life we often have to decide things without full information. Psychologists call this *decision making under uncertainty;* we can also call it *taking chances.* We have various ways of expressing our uncertainty. Looking out the window we might say that there is a fifty-fifty chance of rain. More vividly, someone might have remarked that Mondale had as much chance of beating Reagan in the presidential election as a pound of butter in Hell. In each case, the speaker is indicating the relative strength of his or her belief in the occurrence or non-occurrence of some event. To say that there is a fifty-fifty chance that it will rain indicates that we are indifferent in the strength of our belief that it will rain rather than not rain; that is, we don't believe one more strongly than the other. Each event strikes us as being equally likely. The metaphor in the second statement indicates that the person who uttered it believed that the probability of Mondale's beating Reagan was nonexistent.

Our common language provides various ways of expressing probabilities. The guarding terms discussed in Chapter 2 provide examples of informal ways of expressing probability commitments. Thus I can say that it is very likely that Edward Kennedy will seek the Democratic Presidential nomination without saying precisely how likely it is. We can make our probability claims more precise by using numbers. Sometimes we use percentages; for example, the weather bureau might say that there is a 75 percent chance of snow tomorrow. This can naturally be changed to a fraction: the probability is 3/4 that it will snow tomorrow. Finally, this fraction can be changed into a decimal expression: there is a .75 probability that it will snow tomorrow.

The probability scale has two endpoints: the absolute certainty that the event will occur and the absolute certainty that it will not occur. Because you cannot do better than absolute certainty, a probability can neither rise above 100 percent nor drop below 0 percent (neither above 1, nor below 0). (This should sound pretty obvious, but it is possible to become confused when combining percentages and fractions, as when Yogi Berra was supposed to have said that success is one-third talent and 75 percent hard work.) Of course, what we normally call *probability claims* usually fall between these two endpoints. For this reason it sounds somewhat peculiar to say that there is a 100 percent chance of rain and just plain weird to say the chance of rain is 1 out of 1. Even so, these peculiar ways of speaking cause no procedural difficulties and rarely come up in practice.

ESTABLISHING PROBABILITY CLAIMS

When people make probability claims, we have a right to ask why they assign the probability they do. If someone says that there is only one chance in a million that a meltdown will occur in an atomic power plant before the end of the century, we have a right to ask where the ratio 1 in 1 million came from; why that rather than 19 in 85? Broadly speaking, there are two ways of establishing a probability assignment: through *classical a priori* procedures or through *statistical analysis.*

A simple example will bring out the differences between these two approaches. We might wonder, for example, about the chances of drawing an ace from a standard deck of 52 cards. Before we can answer this question, we have to assume that each of the 52 cards has an equal chance of being selected. Given this, an obvious a priori line of reasoning runs as follows: there are 4 aces in a 52-card deck, so the probability of selecting one randomly is 4 in 52. (That reduces to 1 chance in 13.) Here the set of favorable outcomes is a subset of the total number of equally likely (equi-likely) outcomes, and to compute the probability that the favorable outcome will occur, we merely put the number of favorable outcomes over the total number of possible outcomes. This fraction gives us the probability that the event will occur on a random draw.

Favorable equi-likely outcomes/Total equi-likely outcomes $= 4/52 = 1/13$

Notice that in coming to our conclusion that there is 1 chance in 13 of randomly drawing an ace from a 52-card deck, we simply used mathematical reasoning. This illustrates the a priori approach to probabilities. It is called the a priori approach because we arrive at the result simply by reasoning about the circumstances. We could, however, have taken a different approach to establishing the probability of drawing an ace from a 52-card deck: we could make a great many draws from the deck (replacing the cards each time) and then keep track of the results. Using this statistical approach we would discover that an ace tends to come up roughly 1/13 of the time. The statistical approach differs from the a priori approach in two ways: (1) it appeals to ratios of actual occurrences, and (2) it yields only approximate results because there can always be chance deviations from the expected outcome. Having distinguished between them, we can now look at the a priori and the statistical approaches to probability in turn.

A Priori Probability

In calculating the probability of drawing an ace from a fifty-two card deck, we took the ratio of favorable equi-likely outcomes to total equi-likely outcomes. Generally, then, the a priori probability of a hypothesis h, symbolized "Pr(h)," is expressed as follows:

$$Pr(h) = \text{Favorable ELOs/Total ELOs}$$

where "ELO" means "equi-likely outcome." We can illustrate this principle with a slightly more complicated example. What is the probability of throwing an eight on the cast of two dice? Here are all the equi-likely ways in which two dice can turn up on a single cast:

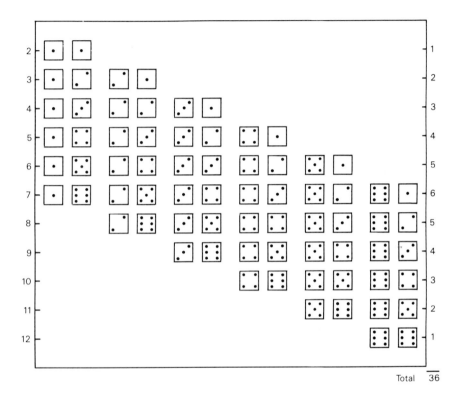

Total 36

As indicated, five of the 36 possible outcomes produce an eight, so the probability of throwing an eight is 5/36.

EXERCISE 1

When you throw two dice:

(1) Which is more likely, throwing a five or an eight?
(2) What is the probability of throwing either a five or an eight?
(3) Which is more likely, to throw a five or an eight, or a two or a seven?

Statistical Analysis

Although a priori methods of probability apply naturally to computing probabilities for games of chance, there are times when its use is inappropriate. For example, the Eastern Division of the American Baseball League has six teams; theoretically, any one of the teams might win. Yet no one supposes that these outcomes are equi-likely; that is, no one supposes that each team has 1 chance in 6 of winning the pennant. Why? Past performance suggests that some teams have a much better chance of winning than others. For example, during the years 1971 through 1973, Baltimore won the division twice and came in third once, winning an average of 59 percent of its games per season. During the same period, Cleveland came in last twice and next to last once, winning an average of 42 percent of its games per season. From this, it seems reasonable to conclude that in 1974 Baltimore had a much better chance of winning the divisional title than did Cleveland.

The principle that lies behind this kind of reasoning is that patterns or regularities that have held in the past with a certain frequency will continue to hold in the future with roughly the same frequency. Here a probability is assigned on the basis of the relative frequency of favorable outcomes (games won) to the total number of outcomes (games played).

Of course, this procedure must be used with great caution, especially where unforeseeable events can make a large difference. For example, over this same 1971–73 period, Detroit came in second, first, and third, winning 55 percent of its games. This suggests that it had a very good chance to win the title in 1974; certainly Detroit should have done better than Cleveland. In fact, in 1974 Detroit plummeted to last place, and Cleveland clawed its way up to fourth! At times, past performance can be completely out of whack with what actually happens. In the years 1962 through 1968 the New York Mets came in last 5 times and next to last twice, winning a measly 35 percent of their games. Then in 1969 they came in first in the Eastern Division, winning almost 62 percent of their games. They then went on to win the National League playoffs and then the World Series from the powerful Baltimore Orioles. Even looking back, with all the advantages of hindsight, it is still hard to see how the Mets pulled it off. At the time people called it a miracle or were reduced to saying such things as, "Well, you never know."

The New York Mets example illustrates, in a dramatic way, the chanciness (the fallibility) of using past regularities to predict the future. An underlying assumption of this kind of reasoning is that in similar circumstances events will occur with about the same frequency. But the expression "similar circumstances" marks an area of difficulty. We are often not in a position to know if past circumstances will continue to hold in the future. (If two star pitchers decide to leave baseball to become Buddhist monks, that may make a tremendous difference, but who would have guessed it?) Similarly, we are often unable to decide how much difference a change in circumstances will make. (Will hiring Billy Martin turn a bad team into a contender? That's hard to say.) Anyway, this suggests that there are some obvious questions we should ask before relying on the frequency of past occurrences in assigning probabilities to the occurrences of past events:

(1) How good are the statistics themselves?
(2) Have any significant circumstances changed?
(3) Do we even know which circumstances matter?

EXERCISE 2

(1) The following is a good piece of statistical reasoning:
> Kenya has never won a gold medal in the Winter Olympics; therefore, it is very unlikely that it will win a gold medal in the next Winter Olympics.

On the other hand, the following is an instance of bad statistical reasoning:
> For the last two Summer Olympics, the host countries (the U.S.S.R. and then the U.S.A.) have won the greatest number of medals in track and field; therefore, in the next Summer Olympics, the host country (Korea) will win the greatest number of medals in track and field.

Explain why the first statistical argument is strong and the second weak.

(2) Explain what's statistically wrong (and perhaps right) with the following argument:
> Most accidents occur within 25 miles of home, so it is less important to wear safety belts 30 miles from home.

To summarize, there are two ways in which we can assign a probability to the occurrence of an event: (1) If it is possible to specify the number of equi-likely outcomes and further specify the number of equi-likely favorable outcomes, then the probability that the event will occur is the ratio of equi-likely favorable outcomes to the total number of equi-likely outcomes. This is the a priori method of computing probabilities and it applies particularly well in computing probabilities in games of chance. However, it rarely has direct application to problems that occur in daily life, for, in general, they cannot be analyzed in terms of ratios between total equi-likely favorable outcomes and total equi-likely outcomes. (2) In those cases where a priori methods do not apply, we attempt to estimate the probability of an event occurring by looking to the past and comparing the ratio of actual favorable outcomes to the total number of actual outcomes. This is called the statistical approach to probability.

SOME LAWS OF PROBABILITY

Suppose that you have determined the probability that an event will occur. What effect should this have on your conduct? This is a complicated question, and one that can be touched on only lightly in this text. There are, however, some simple rules of probability that are worth knowing.

By convention, events are assigned probabilities between 0 and 1 (inclusive). Now an event is either going to occur or not occur; that, at least, is certain (that is, it has a probability of 1). From this it is easy to see how to calculate the probability that the event will not occur given the probability that it will occur: we simply subtract the probability that it will occur from 1. This is our first rule:

Rule 1. The probability that an event will not occur is 1 minus the probability that it will occur. Symbolically

$$\Pr(\text{not } h) = 1 - \Pr(h)$$

For example, the probability of drawing an ace from a standard deck is 1 in 13, so the probability of *not* drawing an ace is 12 in 13. (This makes sense because there are 48 out of 52 ways of not drawing an ace, and this reduces to 12 chances in 13.)

Rule 2. Given two independent events, the probability of their both occurring is the product of their individual probabilities. Symbolically (where h_1 and h_2 are independent)

$$\Pr(h_1 \text{ \& } h_2) = \Pr(h_1) \times \Pr(h_2)$$

Here the word "independent" needs explanation. Suppose you draw a card from the deck, then put it back (shuffle) and draw again. In this case the first draw does not affect the second draw, so it is independent of it. What is the probability of drawing two aces in a row using this system? Using Rule 2, we see that the answer is $1/13 \times 1/13$ or 1 chance in 169. The situation is different if we do not replace the card after the first draw. Here, again, the chances of getting an ace on the first draw are 1 in 13, but if an ace is drawn (and not returned to the pack) then there is one less ace in the deck, so the chances of drawing the second ace are reduced to 3 chances in 51. Thus the probability of drawing two consecutive aces (without returning the first draw to the deck) are $4/52 \times 3/51$ or 1 in 221, which is considerably lower than 1 in 169.

We can generalize Rule 2 beyond two events. However many events we might consider, provided that they are independent of each other, the probability of all of them occurring is the product of each one of them occurring. For example, the chances of flipping a coin and having it come up heads is 1 chance in 2. What are the chances of flipping a coin eight times and having it come up heads every time? The answer is:

$$1/2 \times 1/2 \times 1/2 \times 1/2 \times 1/2 \times 1/2 \times 1/2 \times 1/2$$

which equals 1 chance in 256.

Our next rule allows us to answer questions of the following kind: What are the chances of either an eight or a two coming up on a single throw of the dice? Going back to the chart on page 245, we saw that we could answer this question by counting the number of ways that a two can come up (which is 1) and adding this to the number of ways that an eight can come up (which is 5) and conclude that the chances of one or the other of them coming up is 6 chances in 36 or 1/6. The principle involved in this calculation can be stated as follows:

Rule 3. The probability that at least one of two mutually exclusive events will occur is the sum of the probabilities that each of them will occur. Symbolically (where h_1 and h_2 are mutually exclusive)

$$\Pr(h_1 \text{ or } h_2) = \Pr(h_1) + \Pr(h_2)$$

To say that events are mutually exclusive just means that they can't both occur. You cannot, for example, get both a two and an eight on a single cast of the dice. You might, however, throw neither one of them.

Before stating Rule 4, we can think about a particular example: What is the probability of tossing at least one heads in eight tosses of a coin? Here it is tempting to reason in the following way. There is a 50 percent chance of getting a heads on the first toss and a 50 percent chance of getting a heads on the second toss, so after two tosses it is already certain that we will toss at least one head, and, thus, after eight tosses there should be a 400 percent chance. In other words, you just can't miss. There are two good reasons for thinking that this argument is fishy. First, probability can never exceed 100 percent and, secondly, there must be some chance, however small, that we could toss a coin eight times and not have it come up heads.

The best way to look at this question is to restate it so that the first two rules can be used. Instead of asking what the probability is that a head will come up at least once, we can ask what the probability is that it will *not* come up at least once. Now to say that heads will not come up even once is equivalent to saying that tails will come up eight times in a row. Now by Rule 2 we know how to compute that probability: it's just 1/2 multiplied by itself eight times, and that, as we saw, is 1/256. Finally, by Rule 1 we know that the probability that this will not happen (that heads will come up at least once) is $1 - 1/256$. In other words, the probability of tossing heads at least once in eight tosses is 255/256. That comes pretty close to a certainty, but not quite. We can generalize these results as follows:

> **Rule 4.** The probability that an event will occur at least once in a series of independent trials is simply 1 minus the probability that it will *not* occur in that number of trials. Symbolically (where n is the number of independent trials)

> The probability that h will occur at least once in n trials $= 1 - \text{Pr}(\text{not } h)_n$

Strictly speaking, Rule 4 is unnecessary since it can be derived from Rules 1 and 2, but it is important to know about because it blocks a common misunderstanding about probabilities. *People often think that they have sure things when they do not.*

EXERCISE 3

Compute the probability of making the following draws from a standard 52-card deck:

(1) Drawing either a seven or a five on a single draw.
(2) Drawing neither a seven nor a five on a single draw.
(3) Drawing a seven and then, without returning the first card to the deck, drawing a five on the next draw.
(4) Same as (3), but the first card is returned to the deck and the deck is shuffled after the first draw.
(5) Drawing at least one spade in a series of four consecutive draws, where the card drawn is not returned to the deck.

(6) Same as (5), but the card is returned to the deck after each
     draw and the deck is reshuffled.

EXPECTED PAYOFF

It is obvious that having some sense of probable outcomes is important
for running our lives. If we hear that there is a 95 percent chance of
rain, this usually provides good enough reason for calling off a picnic.
But the exact relationship between probabilities and decisions is complex and often misunderstood. The best way to illustrate these misunderstandings is through looking at gambling situations where the
numbers are fixed and clear.

A $1 bet in the New York State Lottery might make you as much
as $16 million. That sounds good; why not take a shot at $16 million
for only a buck? Of course, there isn't much chance of winning the lottery, and that sounds bad. Why throw a dollar away on nothing? So we
are torn in two directions. What we want to know is just how good the
bet is. Is it, for example, better or worse than the New Jersey State Lottery? To answer questions of this kind, we need to introduce the notion
of *expected payoff*.[1]

The idea of expected payoff takes into account the two features
that determine whether a bet is good or not: the probability of winning
and the amount you get if you do win. The idea is simple enough: the
expected payoff of a bet equals the amount you can win multiplied by
the probability of winning. So, if there is 1 chance in 20 million of winning the New York State Lottery, and you will win $16 million if you
do, then the expected payoff of your one dollar bet is

$$(1/20,000,000) \times \$16,000,000 = \$.80$$

That is, your expected payoff on your one dollar bet is eighty cents.
What does this mean? One way of looking at it is as follows: if you could
somehow buy up all of the lottery tickets and thus insure that you would
win, your $20 million investment would net you $16 million, or 80 cents
on the dollar—certainly a bad investment. Another way of looking at
the situation is as follows: if you invested a great deal of money in the
New York State Lottery over many years, you could expect to win eventually but, in the long run, your payoff would average out to eighty cents
on the dollar. One last way of looking at the situation is this: you go

---

[1] This is often called *expected value*. Here we have adopted the expression expected *payoff*
to make it clear that we are concerned only with the monetary features of a bet.

down to your local drugstore and buy a lottery ticket for $1 and then cash it in for 80 cents. Although almost no one looks at the matter in this way, in effect, that is what you are doing in the long run when you buy lottery tickets.

We are now in a position to draw a distinction between a favorable expected payoff and an unfavorable expected payoff. The expected payoff is favorable when it is greater than the bet itself. (If the chances of winning $16 million on a $1 bet are 1 in 10 million, then the expected payoff for a $1 bet is $1.60.) If the expected payoff of the bet is less than the bet, then the expected payoff is unfavorable. If the expected payoff of the bet is equal to the bet, then the bet is neutral—financially a waste of time.

EXERCISE 4

Compute the probability and the expected value for the following bets. Each time you bet $1 that a certain card or cards will be drawn from a standard 52-card deck. If you win, then you get back the sum indicated.

> Example: Draw a seven of spades. Payoff: $26.
> Probability: 1/52. Expected value: $1/52 \times \$26 = \$.50$.

(1) Draw a seven of spades or a seven of clubs. Payoff: $26.
(2) On consecutive draws, draw a seven of spades and then a seven of clubs. Payoff: $2,000.
(3) On two consecutive draws, do not draw a seven. Payoff: $1.17.
(4) Same as in (3), but the card is returned to the deck and the deck is shuffled after the draw. Payoff: $1.17.

RELATIVE VALUE

Given the fact that lotteries usually have extremely unfavorable expected payoffs, why do millions of people invest billions of dollars in them each year? Part of the answer is that some people are stupid, superstitious, or both. People will sometimes reason, "Sombody has to win, why not me?" They can also convince themselves that their lucky day has come. But that is not the whole story, for most people who put down money on lottery tickets realize that the bet is a bad bet, but think that it is worth doing anyway. People fantasize about what they will do with the money if they win, and that's fun. Furthermore, if the bet is only $1, and the person making the bet is not desparately poor, losing isn't going to hurt much. Even if the expected payoff is only $.40 on a $1 lottery ticket, the expected loss of $.60 might be considered a reasonable price for the fun of thinking about winning.

When we examine the effects that success or failure will have on a particular person relative to his or her needs, resources, and so on, we are then examining what we shall call the *relative value* of a choice. Considerations of this kind often force us to make adjustments in weighing the significance of costs and payoffs. Starting with costs, above we saw that it might not hurt a person much to lose $1 on a lottery ticket. Of course, this person will not have the dollar to spend on something else, and that's a loss, but it may be overriden by other pyschological (and sometimes actual) gains. But suppose that someone took all of his or her resources (emptied the bank account or sold the house) and put them all down on lottery tickets. This would not alter the expected payoff per individual ticket (it would still be about $.40 on the dollar), but the total effect of losing may now become catastrophic. Here losses hurt and are not compensated for by the fun of contemplating winning or the reasonable chance of winning. Compulsive gambling of this kind is sometimes sufficiently irrational to count as a form of mental illness.

Another factor that *typically* affects the relative value of a bet is the *diminishing marginal value* of a payoff as it gets larger. Diminishing marginal value is illustrated by the following example. Suppose I offer to pay a debt by buying you a hamburger. Provided that the debt matches the cost of a hamburger and you feel like having one, you might go along with this. But suppose that I offer to pay off a debt ten times larger by buying you ten hamburgers? The chances are that you will reject the offer, for even though ten hamburgers *cost* ten times as much as one hamburger, they are not *worth* ten times as much to you. At some point you will get stuffed and not want any more. The notion of marginal value applies to money as well. If you are broke, then ten dollars means a lot to you. You might be willing to work hard to get it. If you are wealthy, ten dollars more or less makes very little difference; losing ten dollars might only be an annoyance.

Usually, though not quite always, marginal value diminishes with quantity. Again, an additional dollar is worth less to a millionaire than a dollar to a starving man. Because of this phenomenon of diminishing marginal value, betting on lotteries is even a worse bet than most people suppose. A lottery with a payoff of $16 million sounds attractive, but it doesn't seem to be 16 times more attractive than a payoff of $1 million. So even if the expected payoff of your $1 bet in a lottery is only $.40, the actual value to you is really something less than this, and so the bet is worse even than it seemed at first.

In general, then, when payoffs are large, the relative value of the payoff to someone is reduced because of the effects of diminishing marginal value. But the situation is rather complicated. When people buy lottery tickets to perk up their fantasy lives, a standard fantasy is that of making a killing that will completely change their lives. Perhaps this is the reason that people are attracted to lotteries with large payoffs even when better bets (that is, bets with a better expected payoff) are available with smaller pots. That is, given the following choice, most people, who gamble at all, will go for the first bet rather than the second—even though the second bet has a better expected payoff than the first ($.55 rather than $.50):

Price of Ticket	Chance of Winning	Payoff
$1.00	1/2,000,000	$1,000,000
$1.00	1/2	$2.10

It is possible to think of even more exotic cases where considerations of relative value override simple considerations of expected payoff. Suppose a witch told you that she would turn you into a toad if you did not give her $16 million by tomorrow. You believe her, because you know for a fact that she has turned others into toads. Well, you have $100 to your name that you can invest in tickets for the New York State Lottery. The expected payoff of your $100 bet is $40, again, pretty awful. But now consider the relative value of $100 to you if you are turned into a toad. Toads have no use for money, so to you, as toad, the value of the hundred dollars would drop to nothing. Thus, unless some other more attractive alternatives are available, it would be reasonable to buy these lottery tickets despite the unfavorable expected payoff of the bet.

EXERCISE 5

(1) Though the situation is somewhat farfetched, suppose that you are going to the drugstore to buy medicine for a friend who will die without it. You have only $10—exactly what the medicine costs. Outside the drugstore a young man is playing *three-card monte,* a simple game where the dealer shows you three cards, turns them over, shifts them briefly from hand to hand, and then lays them out, face down, on the top of a box. You are supposed to identify a particular card

(usually the ace of spades) and if you do, you are paid even money. You yourself are a magician and know the sleight-of-hand trick that fools most people and you are sure that you can guess the card right 9 times out of 10. First, what is the expected payoff of a bet of $10? In this context, would it be reasonable to make this bet? Why?

(2) In the witch example, considerations of relative value made a bet reasonable even when the expected payoff of the bet was unfavorable. In the three-card monte example, the reverse happened; a bet is unreasonable even though the expected payoff is favorable. Think of an example of your own illustrating one of these possibilities.

THE GAMBLER'S FALLACY

In assessing probabilities, a little knowledge can be a dangerous thing. Ordinary people often refer to something called the Law of Averages. "In the long run," they say, "things will even out (or average out)." Interpreted one way, this amounts to what mathematicians call the Law of Large Numbers, and it is perfectly correct. For example, when flipping a coin, we expect it to come up heads half the time, so with ten flips, it should come up heads five times. But if we actually check this out, we discover that the number of times it comes out heads in ten flips varies significantly from this predicted value: sometimes coming up heads more than five times, sometimes coming up less. What the Law of Large Numbers tell us is that the actual percentage of heads will tend to come closer to the theoretically predicted percentage of heads the more trials we make. If you flipped a coin a million times, it would be very surprising if the percentage of heads were more than 1 percent away from the predicted 50 percent.

When interpreted as the Law of Large Numbers, the so-called Law of Averages contains an important truth, but it is often interpreted in a way that involves a fundamental fallacy. People sometimes reason in the following way: If they have had a run of bad luck, they should increase their bets because they are due for a run of good luck to even things out. Gambling systems are sometimes based on this fallacious idea. People keep track of the numbers that come up on a roulette wheel trying to discover a number that has not come up for a long time. They then pile their money on that number on the assumption that it is due.

To see that this is a fallacy, we can go back to flipping coins again. Toss a coin until it comes up three heads in a row. (This will take less time than you might imagine.) What is the probability that it will come up heads a fourth time? Put crudely, some people think that the probability of it coming up heads again must be very small because a string of tails is needed to even things out. Less crudely, but just as mistakenly, someone might use Rule 2 and argue that the chances of a coin coming up four times in a row equal $1/2 \times 1/2 \times 1/2 \times 1/2$, or 1 chance in 16, so the chance of it coming up heads again after three occurrences of heads is also 1 in 16. But that's just wrong. Our assumption is that the chances of getting heads on any given toss is 1/2. This is true whatever happened on the preceding tosses. So the probability from the start of tossing heads four times in a row is 1 in 16, but the probability tossing another heads after tossing it heads three times in a row is just 1/2.

REGRESSION TO THE MEAN

The notion of *regression to the mean* is somewhat subtle, but an illustration should help make this notion clear. In a famous example, Israeli fighter plane instructors claimed to notice the following phenomenon: When cadet pilots were praised for their good flying, they tended to do worse the next time up, whereas those cadets who were criticized for poor flying tended to do better. The explanation seemed obvious: the good flyers who were praised got cocky and overconfident and thus didn't fly as well, while the bad flyers who were criticized knuckled down and did better. It seemed, then, that bad flying should be criticized, but good flying should not be praised.

Now it is possible that the explanation and the moral drawn from it are correct. Another possibility is that the observed phenomenon has nothing to do with praise and blame but is simply the result of statistical variation. The statistical explanation runs as follows: in early flight training performance can vary from flight to flight. Sometimes the student pilot does well; sometimes not. Given this variation, some of those who did well on one flight may not do as well on the second; and, of course, the reverse will also be true: as a matter of chance, some who flew badly one time will fly well the next. In other words, it is nothing more than a statistical fact that some who did well and were praised will do worse on their next flight, and some who did badly and were criticized will do better. It could well be that the praise and criticism had nothing to do with these results.

Most people don't know about the phenomenon of regression to the mean, and when they hear about it, they are often not impressed. Here is a simple experiment that illustrates its significance. Suppose that you decide that coming up heads is good for a coin, whereas coming up tails is bad. You now take a jug with one hundred pennies in it and spill them out on the table. You now "praise" the coins that came up heads by putting a red dot of paint on them. You "criticize" coins that came up tails by putting a blue dot of paint on them. You put the coins back in the jug, shake them up, and pour them back on the table. When you examine the coins you find that they fall into four (roughly equal) groups.

(1) Heads with red dots on them.
(2) Tails with blue dots on them.
(3) Heads with no dots on them.
(4) Tails with no dots on them.

In the first group, we have coins that were "praised" without making them worse. In the second group we have coins that were "criticized" without making them better. But the last two groups are more interesting. If a coin shows heads with no dot, it must have a blue dot on its other side; that is, it is a coin that was previously criticized for being tails. Furthermore, if a coin shows tails with no dot, it must have a red dot on the other side; that is, it must have been previously praised for coming up heads. In other words, roughly half of the coins exhibit the phenomenon attributed to the Israeli cadet pilots: they either got worse after praise or got better after blame. On the assumption that little dots of paint would not significantly affect the way a coin will come up, it is obvious that the so-called praise and blame had nothing to do with the matter: the distribution into these four groups can be explained on statistical grounds alone.

There is a moral to be drawn from this: *When trying to understand a phenomenon, we should always ask if it can be explained simply on statistical grounds.* To use commonsense language, we should always entertain the possibility that the phenomenon is just a matter of luck—good or bad. More carefully, we should always entertain the possibility that regression to the mean is a significant component in accounting for some phenomenon. For example, people who do exceptionally well on their first logic exam tend to do less well on their second, and conversely, those who do exceptionally poorly on the first exam tend to do better on the second. One natural explanation is that those who did well got swelled heads and those who did badly finally got down to work. This is like the explanation of the performances by the Isreali fighter pilots, and *in part* it may be correct, but because there is always a certain element of luck in how well a person does on an exam, it may also be due, *in part*, to regression to the mean.

Illustrate the phenomenon of regression to the mean by having, say, ten people take two successive simple true-false exams—answering all the questions by flipping a coin.

MORE ON STATISTICAL SIGNIFICANCE

What are the chances of tossing a fair coin and having it come up heads 19 times in a row? The answer is ($\frac{1}{2}$) multiplied by itself 19 times, which equals 1 chance in 524,288. Now those chances are so remote that you might think it could never really happen. You'd be wrong. Of course, if you sat there flipping a single coin, you might spend a very long time before you hit a sequence of 19 consecutive heads, but there is a way of getting this result (with some help from friends) in a single afternoon. First of all, you start out with $5,242.88 worth of pennies and put them in a large truck. (Actually, the truck would not be all that large.) Dump the coins out and then pick up all the coins that came up heads. Put them back in the truck and repeat the procedure. Do that over and over again, always returning those that came up heads to the truck, and, with tolerably good luck, on the nineteenth dump of the coins you will get at least one coin that comes up heads again. Any such coin will have come up heads 19 times in a row.[2]

What's the point of this example? Specifically, it is intended to show that we often attribute abilities or the lack of abilities to people when, in fact, their performances may be statistically insignificant. When people invest with stock brokers, they tend to shift when they lose money. When they hit upon a broker who earns them money, they stay put and praise this broker's abilities. In fact, some financial advisers seem to be better than others—they have a long history of sound financial advice—but the financial community is, in many ways, like the truckload of pennies we have just examined. There are a great many brokers giving all sorts of different advice and, by chance alone, some of them are bound to give good advice. Furthermore, some of them are bound to have runs of success, just as some of the pennies dumped from the truck will have

---

[2] According to my colleague J. Laurie Snell, starting with 524,288 pennies gives you a 63.2 percent chance of having at least one of the pennies come up heads 19 times in a row. If this seems too risky, you could get more pennies and find more friends to help you with the experiment.

long strings of coming up heads. Thus, in some cases, what appears to be brilliance in predicting stock prices may be nothing more than a run of statistically expected good luck.

SOME PUZZLES CONCERNING PROBABILITY

We will conclude the chapter with several puzzles that will draw on your understanding of many of the concepts we have just discussed.

(1) You are presented with two bags, one containing two ham sandwiches and the other containing a ham sandwich and a cheese sandwich. You reach in one bag and draw out a ham sandwich. What is the probability that the other sandwich in the bag is also a ham sandwich?

(2) You are presented with three bags: two contain a chicken fat sandwich and one contains a cheese sandwich. You are asked to guess which bag contains the cheese sandwich. You do so, and the bag you have selected is set aside. (You obviously have one chance in three of guessing correctly.) From the two remaining bags, one containing a chicken fat sandwich is then removed. You are now given the opportunity to switch your selection to the remaining bag. Will such a switch increase, decrease, or leave unaffected your chances of correctly selecting the bag with the cheese sandwich in it?

(3) Fogelin's Palace in Border, Nevada, offers the following unusual bet. If you win, then you make 50 percent profit on your bet; if you lose, you take a 40 percent loss. That is, if you bet $1 and win, you get back $1.50; if you bet $1 and lose, you get back $.60. The chances of winning are fifty/fifty. This sounds like a marvelous opportunity, but there is one hitch: in order to play, you must let your bet ride with its winnings, or losses, for four plays. For example, starting with $100, a four bet sequence might look like this:

	Win	Win	Lose	Win
Total	$150	$225	$135	$202.50

At the end of this sequence, you can pick up $202.50, and thus make a $102.50 profit.

Now it seems that Fogelin's Palace is a good place to gamble, but consider the following argument on the other side. Because the chances of winning are fifty/fifty, you will, on the average, win half the time. But notice what happens in such a case:

	Win	Lose	Lose	Win
Total	$150	$90	$54	$81

So, even though you have won half the time, you have come out $19 behind.

Surprisingly, it doesn't matter what order the wins and losses come in; if two are wins and two are losses, you come out behind. (You can check this.) So, because you are only going to win roughly half the time, and when you win half the time you actually lose money, it now seems to be a bad idea to gamble at Fogelin's Palace. What should you do, gamble at Fogelin's Palace or not?

Answers to these puzzles appear in Appendix D at the end of this book.

DISCUSSION QUESTION

The idea discussed earlier—that in making decisions under uncertainty we should consider the prospective gains and losses together with relevant probabilities—was clearly stated in the *Port-Royal Logic*, a very influential work on logic published by the French writers Arnauld and Nicole in 1662. Speaking of the majority of mankind, these writers tell us that they

> fall into an illusion which is more deceptive in proportion as it appears to them to be reasonable; it is, that they regard only the greatness or importance of the advantage which they hope for, or of the disadvantage which they fear, without considering at all the probability which there is of that advantageous or disadvantageous event befalling.
>
> Thus, when they apprehend any great evil, as the loss of their livelihood or their fortune, they think it the part of prudence to neglect no precaution for preserving these; and if it is some great good, as the gain of a hundred thousand crowns, they think that they act wisely in seeking to obtain it, if the hazard is a small amount, however little likelihood there may be of a success.

To correct this defect in reasoning, these authors suggest that

> it is necessary to consider not only the good and evil in themselves, but also the probability of their happening and not happening.

This is sound advice, for it will prevent us from taking excessive precautions against large evils that are hardly likely to occur and from squandering money, for example in lotteries, seeking enormous gains that we have only a minute chance of obtaining.

These authors conclude their discussion with a striking remark concerning the reverse situation that obtains concerning *salvation.*

> It belongs to infinite things alone, as eternity and salvation, that they cannot be equalled by any temporal advantage; and thus we ought never to place them in the balance with any of the things of the world. This is why the smallest degree of facility for the attainment of salvation is of higher value than all the blessings of the world put together; and why the slightest peril of being lost is more serious than all temporal evils, considered simply as evils.[3]

The authors conclude that we ought to spend all of our efforts, however great, in an attempt to attain salvation.

This is obviously an argument concerning what we have called *expected payoff* and *relative value.* State it clearly and evaluate it.

---

[3] These passages come from the final chapter of *The Port-Royal Logic,* generally thought to be by Arnauld and Nicole, translated by Thomas Spencer Baynes (Edinburgh: Sutherland and Knox, 1851), pp. 365 ff.

Fields of Argumentation

11

Legal Reasoning

Broadly speaking, a decision in a law case depends upon two matters: (1) a question of *law* and (2) a question of *fact*. For example, a *criminal law* exists prohibiting a certain kind of behavior and assigns a punishment to those who violate it. A person is accused of violating this law, so a trial is held to decide whether *in fact* he has done so. The judge instructs the jury on the law bearing on the case. If the jury then decides that the accused has violated the law, they find him guilty and the judge hands down the punishment stated in the statute. Or, in a civil suit, one party sues another, say, for breach of contract. Because states have laws governing contracts, once more a trial is held to decide whether *in fact* a breach of contract (as defined by these statutes) has occurred. If a breach of contract is found, then the judge awards damages as the law specifies.

Actually many cases fall into this simple pattern, but in order for a case to be settled in this almost mechanical fashion, both the law and the facts must be clear. Often they are not. Starting from the side of the law, statutes and regulations are often vague. For example, a law may insist that people show "reasonable care" not to harm the person or property of another. Needless to say, there is no sharp line between conduct that shows reasonable care and conduct that does not. To cite another example, antitrust laws prohibit "combinations in the restraint of trade"—a notion that may be widely interpreted. The situation becomes more complicated when we take into account the *common law* tradition of English and American law. A particular decision must be made in the context of past decisions and, as far as possible, be consistent with them. The most obvious difficulty with this is that the past decisions may not be consistent with each other. There can also be conflicts between statutes and the common law, between interpretations of statutes, between different statutes, between jurisdictions. We can add to this the complication that a given case may "fall between the cracks." Human beings have a remarkable ability to produce weird cases that would tax even the wisdom of Solomon.

Turning now to facts, they must be established through testimony, and this testimony can also contain conflicts. In a criminal procedure, the prosecution must establish its case beyond a "reasonable doubt" (another inherently vague expression). In a civil case the situation is different. Although the procedural rules can be very complicated, the general idea is this. The case is won by the party who shows that the *preponderance* of evidence favors his or her side of the case. Although this is a bit too simple, it is sometimes said that if the scales tip ever so slightly in favor of A rather than B, then A wins the case. The complicated rules that govern civil procedures are intended to guarantee that each party has a fair chance to show that the preponderance of evidence falls on his or her side of the case.

Together, the vagueness and conflicts within the *law* and the indeterminacy of *facts* often make it impossible to settle legal disputes in a mechanical way. Of course, vagueness and conflict are not special to the law, and it often happens that available facts are not conclusive. But outside the law, we can often just let matters ride—we can postpone a decision until further facts are established, or even declare that the issues are too vague to admit of any decision. This is rarely an option in a legal case. If A sues B, then either A or B must win. Throwing the case out of court amounts to ruling in favor of the defendant. A decision must be made, and usually in a relatively short period of time. Many legal decisions must be made in a context of vague and perhaps conflicting laws, mixed precedents, and incomplete information—all under the pressure of time.

ANALOGY IN LEGAL REASONING

With all this in mind, we can see why, as Edward Levy has remarked, legal reasoning is *analogical*.[1] By this he does not mean that every argument that takes place in a court of law is analogical, for many of the arguments—perhaps most—are guided by commonsense standards. But given the indeterminacies we have noticed, a legal situation may look like this:

Laws and precedents   Laws and precedents
favorable to A.   favorable to B.
                    Fact
                  situation

The attorney for A will try to establish and then stress those facts that bring the case under laws and precedents favorable to his client's side of the case. B's attorney will, of course, proceed in the opposite direction. It is important to see that this debate can take place even when there is *no* disagreement concerning facts. By stressing certain similarities and playing down others, each attorney will try to move the case under those laws and precedents that favor his client's side of the case. Exchanges will often have the following form:

A: Your honor, may I remind the court that in cases of this kind it has always held . . .

B: Your honor, the case before us is of an entirely different sort from those just cited . . .

---

[1] Edward Levi, *An Introduction to Legal Reasoning* (Chicago: University of Chicago Press, 1963). There is no better introduction to the study of legal reasoning than this fine little book.

The pattern of argument here is analogical because the whole point is to get the court to agree that the particular case is *more like* one line of cases than another.

The analogical aspect of legal reasoning is illustrated by the following classic case from the law of contracts: Peevyhouse v. Garland Coal and Mining Co. The case came before the Supreme Court of Oklahoma in 1962. The facts, as summarized by Justice Jackson, are as follows:

Peevyhouse v. Garland Coal & Mining Co.*

JACKSON, J. In the trial court, plaintiffs Willie and Lucille Peevyhouse sued the defendant, Garland Coal and Mining Company, for damages for breach of contract. Judgment was for plaintiffs in an amount considerably less than was sued for. Plaintiffs appeal and defendant cross-appeals.

In the briefs on appeal, the parties present their argument and contentions under several propositions; however, they all stem from the basic question of whether the trial court properly instructed the jury on the measure of damages.

Briefly stated, the facts are as follows: plaintiffs owned a farm containing coal deposits, and in November, 1954, leased the premises to defendant for a period of five years for coal mining purposes. A "strip-mining" operation was contemplated in which the coal would be taken from pits on the surface of the ground, instead of from underground mine shafts. In addition to the usual covenants found in a coal mining lease, defendant specifically agreed to perform certain restorative and remedial work at the end of the lease period. It is unnecessary to set out the details of the work to be done, other than to say that it would involve the moving of many thousands of cubic yards of dirt, at a cost estimated by expert witnesses at about $29,000.00. However, plaintiffs sued for only $25,000.00.

During the trial, it was stipulated that all covenants, and agreements in the lease contract had been fully carried out by both parties, except the remedial work mentioned above; defendant conceded that this work had not been done.

---

*Supreme Court of Oklahoma, 1962. Modified and Rehearing Denied, 1963. 382 P.2d 109. Cert. denied, 1963, 375 U.S. 906, 84 S.Ct. 196, 11 L.Ed.2d 145.

Plaintiffs introduced expert testimony as to the amount and nature of the work to be done, and its estimated cost. Over plaintiffs' objections, defendant thereafter introduced expert testimony as to the "diminution in value" of plaintiffs' farm resulting from the failure of defendant to render performance as agreed in the contract—that is, the difference between the present value of the farm, and what its value would have been if defendant had done what it agreed to do.

At the conclusion of the trial, the court instructed the jury that it must return a verdict for plaintiffs, and left the amount of damages for jury determination. On the measure of damages, the court instructed the jury that it might consider the cost of performance of the work defendant agreed to do, "together with all of the evidence offered on behalf of either party".

It thus appears that the jury was at liberty to consider the "diminution in value" of plaintiffs' farm as well as the cost of "repair work" in determining the amount of damage.

It returned a verdict for plaintiffs for $5000.00—only a fraction of the "cost of performance", *but more than the total value of the farm even after the remedial work is done.*

On appeal, the issue is sharply drawn. Plaintiffs contend that the true measure of damages in this case is what it will cost plaintiffs to obtain performance of the work that was not done because of defendant's default. Defendant argues that the measure of damages is the cost of performance "limited, however, to the total difference in the market value before and after the work was performed".[2]

Part of this case raises no special problems. Garland conceded that it did not fulfill the terms of the contract it had entered into; therefore, there was no question that Garland had breached the contract, and the Court so ruled. The point at issue concerned the correct *measure of damages* to apply. More specifically, having breached the contract, how much does Garland owe the Peevyhouses?

The rough and ready rule for breach of contract is that the person who breaches the contract should put the other party to contract in the position he or she would have been in if the contract had not been breached. This can be done in a variety of ways.[3] The most straightforward way is to demand *specific performance*. If someone has contracted to do something and hasn't, then the court can simply say "Do it!" The Peevyhouses could have asked for specific performance, but since they didn't, that remedy did not come up in this case.

---

[2] It was estimated that restoring the land would increase the value of the property by only $300.

[3] We will not examine all of them here.

Although demanding specific performance is the most obvious way to remedy a breach of contract, it has its shortcomings. Sometimes it is not possible. If a student organization contracts with a rock group to play at its Winter Carnival and the rock group does not show up, then there is no way that the Court can make them *have* shown up. It's too late. Specific performance also can have the disadvantage of getting the court involved in overseeing the completion of the contract. In Peevyhouse, we can imagine the difficulties the Court might have encountered if it had to decide whether or not Garland had done precisely what the contract said it should do in restoring the land.

The most common alternative to requiring specific performance is *to award damages*. Going back to the rough and ready rule, if the person has not done what he or she said she would do in the contract, then the person breached against should receive what the performance is worth. That sounds fair, but brings us to the heart of this case. The Peevyhouses were promised something that would *cost* $29,000, so that, it seems, is what they should receive as damages. On the other hand, the *value* of their land would only be increased by $300 after the restoration was completed and, that, so Garland argued, is the amount of damages they deserve. So the cost test yields one result ($29,000) and the value test yields another ($300). Which is correct?

In fact, there is no straightforward way of settling this question. It all depends on which analogies (comparisons) are taken most seriously. Here is an argument in behalf of the Peevyhouses: since they could have gotten *specific performance* if they had asked for it, they then have a right to damages equivalent to the cost of specific performance. On the other side, the contract between Garland and Peevyhouse concerned coal mining; that was its central concern, and the Peevyhouses profited from this relationship. But if the relationship was primarily financial, then damages should be measured in purely financial terms. Now the actual financial loss to the Peevyhouses was the $300 drop in the value of their land, and that's what they should get. Thus to give prominence to the failure of Garland to do what it said it would do, the lawyer for the Peevyhouses cited cases of breaches in construction contracts where the cost test applies, and the Peevyhouses would get $29,000. Against this, the lawyers for Garland cited cases where the breach of contract involved a lack of full payment, and then $300 in damages seems correct, because that is the sole *financial* loss that the Peevyhouses have suffered. It does not, however, seem possible to decide definitively which of these comparisons is more just. The difficulty of the case is shown by the fact that the Oklahoma Supreme Court divided on the issue and ruled, by a five-to-four split decision, in favor of Garland, awarding the Peevyhouses only $300 in damages. All the courts below had ruled in favor of the Peevyhouses.

THE QUESTION OF CONSTITUTIONALITY

The most fundamental questions in our legal system concern the *con-stitutionality* of laws. It is not the role of the courts to *enact* laws, but the courts have the power to strike down laws if they conflict with provisions in the U.S. Constitution. The Supreme Court of the United States is the final arbiter on questions of constitutionality.

It is easy to imagine clear cases of laws that violate constitutional provisions. If the state of Rhode Island began printing its own money, that would plainly violate the constitutional provision that reserves this right to the Federal Government. But, typically, those constitutional questions that are brought before the courts are not clear cut. On one side stand the constitutional provision and its implications; on the other side there is a statute, again with its implications. The language on both sides is often very general, sometimes unclear, and thus stands in need of *interpretation*. Needless to say, interpretations can often conflict and become the source of controversy.

Consider the Fourteenth Amendment as a case in point: Among other things, it provides that

> No State shall make or enforce any law which shall abridge the privileges or immunities of citizens of the United States; nor shall any State deprive any person of life, liberty, or property, without due process of law, nor deny to any person within its jurisdiction the equal protection of the laws.

We shall concentrate on the so-called *equal protection* clause in this passage. First of all, it is very general. Whatever it means, it cannot mean that laws cannot treat people unequally. Criminal laws treat those who commit crimes quite differently from those who do not. What the clause seems to be getting at is that like cases should be treated in like ways. Put negatively, the clause prohibits *un*equal treatment on arbitrary grounds. This, however, is still both general and vague, for we need principles that determine what sorts of likenesses matter and what kinds of differences are arbitrary.

Going back to the historical context in which the Fourteenth Amendment was adopted, we know that it was intended to prohibit unequal treatment on the basis of "race, color, or previous condition of servitude."[4] More specifically, it was one of those constitutional provisions intended to give full citizenship to the newly emancipated slaves. Protection of the newly freed slaves was the primary purpose of these

---

[4] This phrase actually occurs in the companion Fifteenth Amendment concerning voting rights.

provisions, but the language is more general, giving like protection to all citizens of the United States.

Twenty-eight years after the adoption of the Fourteenth Amendment, the Supreme Court heard the case of Plessy v. Ferguson and ruled that a statute in Louisiana enforcing segregation of the races in public transportation did *not* violate the equal protection clause of the Fourteenth Amendment. In rapid succession a whole series of segregation laws were passed by southern and some border states. They were subsequently upheld by the Courts on the *Plessy* doctrine that *separation of the races on equal terms* (the so-called *separate but equal* doctrine) did not violate the equal protection clause of Fourteenth Amendment. The result was the introduction of the system of racial segregation throughout all of the South and many of the border states.

There are some historical considerations that will help place the decision in *Plessy v. Ferguson* in context. After the Fourteenth Amendment was adopted, various cases arose concerning the application of the equal protection clause outside of the area of racial discrimination.[5] Here the courts decided that it was not its business to examine the details of legislation to make sure that the laws were as equitable as possible. The task of making laws, they held, falls to legislatures, and the courts gave legislatures wide latitude in formulating these laws. Flagrant violations of the equal protection clause could lead to the decision that the law was unconstitutional, but if the unequal treatment of individuals seemed *reasonably* justified by the ends to be achieved, then it would not be held to violate the equal protection clause of the Fourteenth Amendment. This became known as the *rational relation* test for applying the equal protection clause, and it was under this interpretation that the decision in *Plessy v. Ferguson* was made.

A second factor in the interpretation of the equal protection clause was the so-called *state action* doctrine. The equal protection clause literally says that no *state* shall deny any person within its jurisdiction the equal protection of the laws. In a series of cases this was interpreted to mean that only positive actions of the state fell under the equal protection clause. Thus when thugs broke up a black political rally, with the police standing by doing nothing to protect them, the Court ruled that this was not a violation of the equal protection clause because the state itself had not participated in the action.[6]

The state could not appeal to the state action doctrine in *Plessy* because here, plainly, the state had *acted* in passing a law segregating public transportation. Even so, the state action doctrine had an important indirect effect on this decision. The state action doctrine, together with the rational relation test, had severely limited the range of appli-

---

[5] These are the so-called *Slaughter House Cases*.
[6] See *United States v. Cruikshank*.

cation of the equal protection clause. Thus the decision in *Plessy* was made under an interpretation of the equal protection clause that had led to the rejection of a great many appeals to it and the acceptance of very few.

Plessy v. Ferguson*

Mr. Justice Brown delivered the opinion of the Court.

This case turns upon the constitutionality of an act of the general assembly of the state of Louisiana, passed in 1890, providing for separate railway carriages for the white and colored races.

The 1st section of the statute enacts "that all railway companies carrying passengers in their coaches in this state shall provide equal but separate accommodations for the white and colored races, by providing two or more passenger coaches for each passenger train, or by dividing the passenger coaches by a partition so as to secure separate accommodations: *Provided,* That this section shall not be construed to apply to street railroads. No person or persons shall be permitted to occupy seats in coaches other than the ones assigned to them, on account of the race they belong to."

By the 2d section it was enacted "that the officers of such passenger trains shall have power and are hereby required to assign each passenger to the coach or compartment used for the race to which such passenger belongs; any passenger insisting on going into a coach or compartment to which by race he does not belong, shall be liable to a fine of $25 or in lieu thereof to imprisonment for a period of not more than twenty days in the parish prison, and any officer of any railroad insisting on assigning a passenger to a coach or compartment other than the one set aside for the race to which said passenger belongs, shall be liable to a fine of $24, or in lieu thereof to imprisonment for a period of not more than twenty days in the parish prison; and should any passenger refuse to occupy the coach or compartment to which he or she is assigned by the officer of such railway, said officer shall have power to refuse to carry such passenger on his train, and for such refusal neither he nor the railway company which he represents shall be liable for damages in any of the courts of this state.". . .

The information filed in the criminal district court charged in substance that Plessy, being a passenger between two stations within the state of Louisiana, was assigned by officers of the company to the coach used for the race to

---

*163 U.S. 537 1896.

which he belonged, but he insisted upon going into a coach used by the race to which he did not belong. Neither in the information nor plea was his particular race or color averred.

The petition for the writ of prohibition averred that petitioner was seven eighths Caucasian and one eighth African blood; that the mixture of colored blood was not discernible in him, and that he was entitled to very right, privilege, and immunity secured to citizens of the United States of the white race; and that, upon such theory, he took possession of a vacant seat in a coach where passengers of the white race were accommodated, and was ordered by the conductor to vacate said coach and take a seat in another assigned to persons of the colored race, and having refused to comply with such demand he was forcibly ejected with the aid of a police officer, and imprisoned in the parish jail to answer a charge of having violated the above act.

The constitutionality of this act is attacked upon the ground that it conflicts both with the 13th Amendment of the Constitution, abolishing slavery, and the 14th Amendment, which prohibits certain restrictive legislation on the part of the states.

1. That it does not conflict with the 13th Amendment, which abolished slavery and involuntary servitude, except as a punishment for crime, is too clear for argument. . . .

. . . Indeed, we do not understand that the 13th Amendment is strenuously relied upon by the plaintiff in error in this connection.

2. By the 14th Amendment, all persons born or naturalized in the United States, and subject to the jurisdiction thereof, are made citizens of the United States and of the state wherein they reside; and the states are forbidden from making or enforcing any law which shall abridge the privileges or immunities of citizens of the United States, or shall deprive any person within their jurisdiction the equal protection of the laws. . . .

The object of the amendment was undoubtedly to enforce the absolute equality of the two races before the law, but in the nature of things it could not have been intended to abolish distinctions based upon color, or to enforce social, as distinguished from political, equality, or a commingling of the two races upon terms unsatisfactory to either. Laws permitting, and even requiring their separation in places where they are liable to be brought into contact do not necessarily imply the inferiority of either race to the other, and have been generally, if not universally, recognized as within the competency of the state legislatures in the exercise of their police power. The most common instance of this is connected with the establishment of separate schools for white and colored children, which have been held to be a valid exercise of the legislative power even by courts of states where the political rights of the colored race have been longest and most earnestly enforced. . . .

[Justice Brown next reviews a whole series of cases where statutes similar to the one in question have been upheld as constitutional.]

It is . . . suggested by the learned counsel for the plaintiff in error that the same argument that will justify the state legislature in requiring railways to provide separate accommodations for the two races will also authorize them to require separate cars to be provided for people whose hair is of a certain color, or who are aliens, or who belong to certain nationalities, or to enact laws requiring colored people to walk upon one side of the street, and white people upon the other, or requiring white men's houses to be painted white, and colored men's black, or their vehicles or business signs to be of different colors, upon the theory that one side of the street is as good as the other, or that a house or vehicle of one color is as good as one of another color. The reply to all this is that every exercise of the police power must be reasonable, and extend only to such laws as are enacted in good faith for the promotion of the public good, and not for the annoyance or oppression of a particular class. Thus in *Yick Wo* v. *Hopkins* it was held by this court that a municipal ordinance of the city of San Francisco to regulate the carrying on of public laundries within the limits of the municipality violated the provisions of the Constitution of the United States if it conferred upon the municipal authorities arbitrary power, at their own will, and without regard to discretion, in the legal sense of the term, to give or withhold consent as to persons or places, without regard to the competency of the persons applying, or the propriety of the places selected for the carrying on of the business. It was held to be a covert attempt on the part of the municipality to make an arbitrary and unjust discrimination against the Chinese race. While this was the case of a municipal ordinance a like principle has been held to apply to acts of a state legislature passed in the exercise of the police power.

So far, then, as a conflict with the 14th Amendment is concerned, the case reduces itself to the question whether the statute of Louisiana is a reasonable regulation, and with respect to this there must necessarily be a large discretion on the part of the legislature. In determining the question of reasonableness it is at liberty to act with reference to the established usages, customs, and traditions of the people, and with a view to the promotion of their comfort, and the preservation of the public peace and good order. Gauged by this standard, we cannot say that a law which authorizes or even requires the separation of the two races in public conveyances is unreasonable or more obnoxious to the 14th Amendment than the acts of Congress requiring separate schools for colored children in the District of Columbia, the constitutionality of which does not seem to have been questioned, or the corresponding acts of state legislatures.

We consider the underlying fallacy of the plaintiff's argument to consist in the assumption that the enforced separation of the two races stamps the colored race with a badge of inferiority. If this be so, it is not by reason of anything found in the act, but solely because the colored race chooses to put that construction upon it. The argument necessarily assumes that if, as has been more than once the case, and is not unlikely to be so again, the colored race should become the dominant power in the state legislature, and should enact a law in precisely similar terms, it would thereby relegate the white race to an inferior position. We imagine that the white race, at least, would not acquiesce in this assumption. The argument also assumes that social prejudices may be overcome by legislation, and that equal rights cannot be secured to the negro except by an enforced commingling of the two races. We cannot accept this proposition. If the two races are to meet on terms of social equality, it must be the result of natural affinity, a mutual appreciation of each other's merits and a voluntary consent of individuals. As was said by the court of appeals of New York in *People* v. *Gallagher*, "this end can neither be accomplished nor promoted by laws which conflict with the general sentiment of the community upon whom they are designed to operate. When the government, therefore, has secured to each of its citizens equal rights before the law and equal opportunities for improvement and progress, it has accomplished the end for which it is organized and performed all of the functions respecting social advantages with which it is endowed." Legislation is powerless to eradicate racial instincts or to abolish distinctions based upon physical differences, and the attempt to do so can only result in accentuating the difficulties of the present situation. If the civil and political rights of both races be equal, one cannot be inferior to the other civilly or politically. If one race be inferior to the other socially, the Constitution of the United States cannot put them upon the same plane. . . .

The judgment of the Court below is therefore affirmed.

Plessy v. Ferguson was decided in 1896 and was the law of the land until it was overturned by *Brown v. Board of Education* (hereafter *Brown I*) in 1954. Part of background for this decision was a reinterpretation of the *equal protection* clause of the Fourteenth Amendment that gave it more force in dealing with civil rights. The Court continued to use the very weak *rational relation* test when dealing with most cases involving appeals to equal protection. Through a series of cases, two important exceptions to this method of interpretation came into existence. The first involved what were called *fundamental rights;* the second involved so-called *suspect classifications.* Fundamental rights concern such things as the right to vote or the right to procreate. A classification is *suspect* if it concerns race, religion, national origin, and so on. Under the new interpretation of the equal protection clause, states still could pass laws restricting fundamental rights and mentioning a suspect classification, but when they did so, a heavy burden of proof fell upon them to show that the legislation will (1) serve a *compelling* and *legitimate* state interest and (2) that it will do so in the *least intrusive* way possible. In the language of the courts, any law that restricted a fundamental right or made reference to a suspect classification *triggered strict scrutiny.*

It should be clear that the *rational relation* test is easy to meet, whereas the test of *strict scrutiny* is very nearly impossible to satisfy. It is not hard to show that a piece of legislation has some chance of doing at least some good—that's the rational relation test. It is very difficult to show that a piece of legislation is compelling, that is, of overwhelming importance; and it is even more difficult to show that the stated goal cannot be better achieved by any other less intrusive means.

Although the decision itself does address the issue directly, *Brown I* was decided under the strict scrutiny interpretation of the equal protection clause. The upshot of this was that the Court no longer showed great deference to the states, as it did in *Plessy*, and, instead, the burden shifted to the states to justify its system of segregation, in particular in an area that involved what the Court declared to be the *fundamental right* to an equal public education.

Brown v. Board of Education*

Mr. Chief Justice Warren delivered the opinion of the Court.

These cases come to us from the States of Kansas, South Carolina, Virginia, and Delaware. They are premised on different facts and different local conditions, but a common legal question justifies their consideration together in this consolidated opinion.

In each of the cases, minors of the Negro race, through their legal representatives, seek the aid of the courts in obtaining admission to the public schools of their community on a nonsegregated basis. In each instance, they had been denied admission to schools attended by white children under laws requiring or permitting segregation according to race. This segregation was alleged to deprive the plaintiffs of the equal protection of the laws under the Fourteenth Amendment. In each of the cases other than the Delaware case, a three-judge federal district court denied relief to the plaintiffs on the so-called "separate but equal" doctrine announced by this Court in *Plessy* v. *Ferguson*. Under that doctrine, equality of treatment is accorded when the races are provided substantially equal facilities, even though these facilities be separate. In the Delaware case, the Supreme Court of Delaware adhered to that doctrine, but ordered that the plaintiffs be admitted to the white schools because of their superiority to the Negro schools.

The plaintiffs contend that segregated public schools are not "equal" and cannot be made "equal," and that hence they are deprived of the equal protection of the laws. Because of the obvious importance of the question presented, the Court took jurisdiction. Argument was heard in the 1952 Term, and reargument was heard this Term on certain questions propounded by the Court.

Reargument was largely devoted to the circumstances surrounding the adoption of the Fourteenth Amendment in 1868. It covered exhaustively con-

---

*347 U.S. 483 1954.

sideration of the Amendment in Congress, ratification by the states, then existing practices in racial segregation, and the views of proponents and opponents
of the Amendment. This discussion and our own investigation convince us that,
although these sources cast some light, it is not enough to resolve the problem
with which we are faced. At best, they are inconclusive. The most avid proponents of the post-War Amendments undoubtedly intended them to remove all
legal distinctions among "all persons born or naturalized in the United States."
Their opponents, just as certainly, were antagonistic to both the letter and the
spirit of the Amendments and wished them to have the most limited effect. What
others in Congress and the state legislatures had in mind cannot be determined
with any degree of certainty.

An additional reason for the inconclusive nature of the Amendment's
history, with respect to segregated schools, is the status of public education at
that time. In the South, the movement toward free common schools, supported
by general taxation, had not yet taken hold. Education of white children was
largely in the hands of private groups. Education of Negroes was almost non-
existent, and practically all of the race were illiterate. In fact, any education of
Negroes was forbidden by law in some states. Today, in contrast, many Negroes have achieved outstanding success in the arts and sciences as well as in
the business and professional world. It is true that public school education at
the time of the Amendment had advanced further in the North, but the effect
of the Amendment on Northern States was generally ignored in the congressional debates. Even in the North, the conditions of public education did not
approximate those existing today. The curriculum was usually rudimentary;
ungraded schools were common in rural areas; the school term was but three
months a year in many states; and compulsory school attendance was virtually
unknown. As a consequence, it is not surprising that there should be so little in
the history of the Fourteenth Amendment relating to its intended effect on public
education.

In the first cases in this Court construing the Fourteenth Amendment,
decided shortly after its adoption, the Court interpreted it as proscribing all
state-imposed discriminations against the Negro race. The doctrine of "separate but equal" did not make its appearance in this Court until 1896 in the case
of *Plessy* v. *Ferguson* involving not education but transportation. American courts
have since labored with the doctrine for over half a century. In this Court, there
have been six cases involving the "separate but equal" doctrine in the field of
public education. In *Cumming* v. *County Board of Education* and *Gong Lum* v. *Rice*
the validity of the doctrine itself was not challenged. In more recent cases, all
on the graduate school level, inequality was found in that specific benefits en-
joyed by white students were denied to Negro students of the same educational
qualifications. In none of these cases was it necessary to re-examine the doctrine to grant relief to the Negro plaintiff. And in *Sweatt* v. *Painter* the Court
expressly reserved decision on the question whether *Plessy* v. *Ferguson* should
be held inapplicable to public education.

In the instant cases, that question is directly presented. Here, unlike *Sweatt*
v. *Painter*, there are findings below that the Negro and white schools involved

have been equalized, or are being equalized, with respect to buildings, curricula, qualifications and salaries of teachers, and other "tangible" factors. Our decision, therefore, cannot turn on merely a comparison of these tangible factors in the Negro and white schools involved in each of the cases. We must look instead to the effect of segregation itself on public education.

In approaching this problem, we cannot turn the clock back to 1868 when the Amendment was adopted, or even to 1896 when *Plessy* v. *Ferguson* was written. We must consider public education in the light of its full development and its present place in American life throughout the Nation. Only in this way can it be determined if segregation in public schools deprives these plaintiffs of the equal protection of the laws.

Today, education is perhaps the most important function of state and local governments. Compulsory school attendance laws and the great expenditures for education both demonstrate our recognition of the importance of education to our democratic society. It is required in the performance of our most basic public responsibilities, even service in the armed forces. It is the very foundation of good citizenship. Today it is a principal instrument in awakening the child to cultural values, in preparing him for later professional training, and in helping him to adjust normally to his environment. In these days, it is doubtful that any child may reasonably be expected to succeed in life if he is denied the opportunity of an education. Such an opportunity, where the state has undertaken to provide it, is a right which must be made available to all on equal terms.

We come then to the question presented: Does segregation of children in public schools solely on the basis of race, even though the physical facilities and other "tangible" factors may be equal, deprive the children of the minority group of equal educational opportunities? We believe that it does.

In *Sweatt* v. *Painter* in finding that a segregated law school for Negroes could not provide them equal educational opportunities, this Court relied in large part on "those qualities which are incapable of objective measurement but which make for greatness in a law school." In *McLaurin* v. *Oklahoma State Regents* the Court, in requiring that a Negro admitted to a white graduate school be treated like all other students, again resorted to intangible considerations: ". . . his ability to study, to engage in discussions and exchange views with other students, and, in general, to learn his profession." Such considerations apply with added force to children in grade and high schools. To separate them from others of similar age and qualifications solely because of their race generates a feeling of inferiority as to their status in the community that may affect their hearts and minds in a way unlikely ever to be undone. The effect of this separation on their educational opportunities was well stated by a finding in the Kansas case by a court which nevertheless felt compelled to rule against the Negro plaintiffs:

"Segregation of white and colored children in public schools has a detrimental effect upon the colored children. The impact is greater when it has the sanction of the law; for the policy of separating the races is usually interpreted as denoting the inferiority of the negro group. A sense of inferiority affects the motivation of a child to learn. Segregation with the sanction of law, therefore, has a tendency to [retard] the education and mental development of negro children and to deprive them of some of the benefits they would receive in a racial[ly] integrated school system."

Whatever may have been the extent of psychological knowledge at the time of *Plessy* v. *Ferguson,* this finding is amply supported by modern authority. Any language in *Plessy* v. *Ferguson* contrary to this finding is rejected.

We conclude that in the field of public education the doctrine of "separate but equal" has no place. Separate educational facilities are inherently unequal. Therefore, we hold that the plaintiffs and others similarly situated for whom the actions have been brought are, by reason of the segregation complained of, deprived of the equal protection of the laws guaranteed by the Fourteenth Amendment. . . .

Regents of the University of California v. *Bakke* (hereafter referred to as *Bakke*), raised the issue of so-called *reverse discrimination.*[7] The case itself is extraordinarily complex, but the basic facts, as described by the Court, are as follows:

Regents of the University of California v. Bakke—U.S.— (1978)*

[The Medical School of the University of California at Davis (hereinafter Davis) had two admissions programs for the entering class of 100 students—the regular admissions program and the special admissions program. Under the regular procedure, candidates whose overall undergraduate grade point averages fell below 2.5 on a scale of 4.0 were summarily rejected. About one out of six applicants was then given an interview, following which he was rated on a scale

---

[7] Notice that the phrase "reverse discrimination" is already question-begging in the sense discussed in Chapter 4. It has to be shown by argument—and not just assumed—that explicit affirmative action quotas amount to discrimination.
*438 U.S. 268 1978.

of 1 to 100 by each of the committee members (five in 1973 and six in 1974), his rating being based on the interviewers' summaries, his overall grade point average, his science courses grade point average, and his Medical College Admissions Test (MCAT) scores, letters of recommendation, extracurricular activities, and other biographical data, all of which resulted in a total "benchmark score." The full admissions committee then made offers of admission on the basis of their review of the applicant's file and his score, considering and acting upon applications as they were received. The committee chairman was responsible for placing names on the waiting list and had discretion to include persons with "special skills." A separate committee, a majority of whom were members of minority groups, operated the special admissions program. The 1973 and 1974 application forms, respectively, asked candidates whether they wished to be considered as "economically and/or educationally disadvantaged" applicants and members of a "minority group" (blacks, Chicanos, Asians, American Indians). If an applicant of a minority group was found to be "disadvantaged," he would be rated in a manner similar to the one employed by the general admissions committee. Special candidates, however, did not have to meet the 2.5 grade point cut-off and were not ranked against candidates in the general admissions process. About one-fifth of the special applicants were invited for interviews in 1973 and 1974, following which they were given benchmark scores, and the top choices were then given to the general admissions committee, which could reject special candidates for failure to meet course requirements or other specific deficiencies. The special committee continued to recommend candidates until 16 special admission selections had been made. During a four-year period 63 minority students were admitted to Davis under the special program and 44 under the general program. No disadvantaged whites were admitted under the special program, though many applied.

Respondent, a white male, applied to Davis in 1973 and 1974, in both years being considered only under the general admissions program. Though he had a 468 out of 500 score in 1973, he was rejected since no general applicants with scores less than 470 were being accepted after respondent's application, which was filed late in the year, had been processed and completed. At that time four special admission slots were still unfilled. In 1974 respondent applied early, and though he had a total score of 549 out of 600, he was again rejected. In neither year was his name placed on the discretionary waiting list. In both years special applicants were admitted with significantly lower scores than respondent's. After his second rejection, respondent filed this action in state court for mandatory injunctive and declaratory relief to compel his admission to Davis, alleging that the special admissions program operated to exclude him on the basis of his race in violation of the Equal Protection Clause of the Fourteenth Amendment, a provision of the California Constitution, and §601 of Title VI of the Civil Rights Act of 1964, which provides, inter alia, that no person shall on the ground of race or color be excluded from participating in any program receiving federal financial assistance. Petitioner cross-claimed for a declaration that its special admissions program was lawful. The trial court found that the special program operated as a racial quota, because minority applicants in that program were rated only against one another, and 16 places in the class of 100 were reserved for them. Declaring that petitioner could not take race into account in making admissions decisions, the program was held to violate the Federal and State Constitutions and Title VI. Respondent's admission was not ordered, however, for lack of proof that he would have been admitted but for the special program.

The California Supreme Court, applying a strict-scrutiny standard, concluded that the special admissions program was not the least intrusive means of achieving the goals of the admittedly compelling state interests of integrating the medical profession and increasing the number of doctors willing to serve minority patients. Without passing on the state constitutional or federal statutory grounds the court held that petitioner's special admissions program violated the Equal Protection Clause. Since petitioner could not satisfy its burden of demonstrating that respondent, absent the special program, would not have been admitted, the court ordered his admission to Davis.]

To sort things out, you should know that the Supreme Court was asked to rule on the following four issues:

(1) Did the Davis affirmative action program violate the federal and California constitutions? Most importantly, did it violate the Fourteenth Amendment guarantee that "no state shall . . . deny to any person within its jurisdiction the equal protection of the laws"?

(2) Does any reference to race violate these constitutional guarantees?

(3) Did the Davis affirmative action program violate the provisions of Title VI of the Civil Rights Act of 1964, which provides, "No person in the United States shall, on the ground of race, color, or national origin, be excluded from participation in, be denied the benefits of, or be subjected to discrimination under any program or activity receiving Federal financial assistance"?

(4) Should Davis be required to admit Bakke into its Medical School?

The decision of the U.S. Supreme Court was so complicated that it takes a scorecard to follow it. On the first issue, only Justice Powell argued that the Davis program was unconstitutional. Four others (Brennan, Marshall, Blackmun and White) dissented. The remaining four (Stevens, Burger, Stewart, and Rehnquist) chose not to address this constitutional issue. Since a majority did not join Powell in his decision, the Court did *not* declare the Davis program unconstitutional. With respect to the second question, Powell argued against the position that *any* reference to race is unconstitutional. Here he was joined by Brennan, Marshall, Blackmun, and White. With respect to the last two questions, Powell argued that the Davis system did indeed violate Title VI of the Civil Rights Act and he further held that Bakke should be admitted to the Davis medical school. This time he was joined by Burger, Stevens, Stewart, and Rehnquist in favoring Bakke's appeal.

U.S. Supreme Court

(1) Constitutionality of the Davis plan	No decision
(2) Constitutionality of any racial considerations	Allowed (Powell + Brennan, Marshall, Blackmun, and White)
(3) Legality of the Davis plan	Illegal (Powell + Burger, Stewart, Stevens, and Rehnquist)
(4) Admission of Bakke	Admit (Powell + Burger, Stewart, Stevens, and Rehnquist)

Powell wrote a strong opinion arguing that explicit racial quotas do violate the equal protection clause of the fourteenth amendment. Here, in the spirit of *Brown I* and the civil rights cases that followed it, he argued that racial classifications trigger strict scrutiny and that Davis did not meet the high standards imposed by this test. In their opposing opinions, Brennan and Marshall argued for a less exacting (sometimes called *middle level*) test for the constitutionality of racial classification. On this new interpretation of the equal protection clause, reference to race would be constitutionally permissible, provided that (1) the legislation had a benign intent, (2) it served a substantial state interest, and (3) it did not stigmatize those who do not fall within the preferred classification.

What follows is a much shortened and highly edited presentation of the Bakke decision. Virtually all citations have been dropped, and the selections focus almost exclusively on the central and yet to be resolved question of the *constitutionality* of explicit affirmative action quotas. The summary table on the following page should help the reader follow this complex and divided decision.

INTERPRETATIONS OF EQUAL PROTECTION

	Segregation	Antidiscrimination	Affirmative Action
State Action	Only explicit acts of the state are subject to the 14th.	States may in no way aid discrimination and have a positive duty to protect their citizens against it.	The same as antidiscrimination.
Separation and Equality	Separation as such does not imply inequality.	Separation is inherently unequal.	The same as antidiscrimination.
Level of Scrutiny	Single-tier: *Rational relation* test (with deference to state legislatures, especially concerning police powers).	Two-tier: (1) *Rational relation* test except with: (2) *fundamental rights* and *suspect classifications*. These trigger *strict scrutiny* and demand that a *compelling* state interest be served in the *least intrusive* way possible.	Three-tier: (1) and (2) except (3) when dealing with programs that benefit *historically disadvantaged minorities* without *stigmatizing* others. Here *an important* state interest must be served that cannot be met by *significantly less intrusive* means.
Bearers of Rights	Individuals	Individuals	Individuals and groups
Found in	*Plessy v. Ferguson* (majority opinion)	*Brown 1* (court opinion) *Bakke* (Powell opinion)	*Bakke* (Brennan opinion)

Excerpts from Justice Powell's Opinion

. . . The guarantees of the Fourteenth Amendment extend to persons. Its language is explicit: "No state shall . . . deny to any person within its jurisdiction the equal protection of the laws." It is settled beyond question that the "rights created by the first section of the Fourteenth Amendment are, by its terms, guaranteed to the individual. They are personal rights." The guarantee of equal protection cannot mean one thing when applied to one individual and something else when applied to a person of another color. If both are not accorded the same protection, then it is not equal. . . .

". . . [A]ll legal restrictions which curtail the rights of a single racial group are immediately suspect. That is not to say that all such restrictions are unconstitutional. It is to say that courts must subject them to the most rigid scrutiny."

The Court has never questioned the validity of those pronouncements. Racial and ethnic distinctions of any sort are inherently suspect and thus call for the most exacting judicial examination. . . .

Petitioner urges us to adopt for the first time a more restrictive view of the Equal Protection Clause and hold that discrimination against members of the white "majority" cannot be suspect if its purpose can be characterized as "benign." The clock of our liberties, however, cannot be turned back to 1868. It is far too late to argue that the guarantee of equal protection to *all* persons permits the recognition of special wards entitled to a degree of protection greater than that accorded others. "The Fourteenth Amendment is not directed solely against discrimination due to a 'two-class theory'—that is, based upon differences between 'white' and Negro." . . .

If it is the individual who is entitled to judicial protection against classifications based upon his racial or ethnic background because such distinctions impinge upon personal rights, rather than the individual only because of his membership in a particular group, then constitutional standards may be applied consistently. Political judgments regarding the necessity for the particular classification may be weighed in the constitutional balance, but the standard of justification will remain constant. This is as it should be, since those political judgments are the product of rough compromise struck by contending groups within the democratic process. When they touch upon an individual's race or ethnic background, he is entitled to a judicial determination that the burden he is asked to bear on that basis is precisely tailored to serve a compelling governmental interest. The Constitution guarantees that right to every person regardless of his background. . . .

Petitioner contends that on several occasions this Court has approved preferential classifications without applying the most exacting scrutiny. Most of the cases upon which petitioner relies are drawn from three areas: school desegregation, employment discrimination, and sex discrimination. Each of the cases cited presented a situation materially different from the facts of this case. . . . The courts of appeals have fashioned various types of racial preferences as remedies for constitutional or statutory violations resulting in identified, race-based injuries to individuals held entitled to the preference. . . . Such preferences also have been upheld where a legislative or administrative body charged with the responsibility made determinations of past discrimination by the industries affected, and fashioned remedies deemed appropriate to rectify the discrimination. . . . But we have never approved preferential classifications in the absence of proven constitutional or statutory violations. . . .

We have held that in "order to justify the use of a suspect classification, a State must show that its purpose or interest is both constitutionally permissible and substantial, and that its use of the classification is 'necessary . . . to the accomplishment' of its purpose or the safeguarding of its interest." The special admissions program purports to serve the purposes of: (i) "reducing the historic deficit of traditionally disfavored minorities in medical schools and the medical profession," (ii) countering the effects of societal discrimination; (iii) increasing the number of physicians who will practice in communities currently underserved; and (iv) obtaining the educational benefits that flow from an ethnically diverse student body. It is necessary to decide which, if any, of these purposes is substantial enough to support the use of a suspect classification. . . .

If petitioner's purpose is to assure within its student body some specified percentage of a particular group merely because of its race or ethnic origin, such a preferential purpose must be rejected not as insubstantial but as facially invalid. Preferring members of any one group for no reason other than race or ethnic origin is discrimination for its own sake. This the Constitution forbids. . . .

Petitioner identifies, as another purpose of its program, improving the delivery of health care services to communities currently underserved. It may be assumed that in some situations a State's interest in facilitating the health care of its citizens is sufficiently compelling to support the use of a suspect classification. But there is virtually no evidence in the record indicating that petitioner's special admissions program is either needed or geared to promote that goal. The court below addressed this failure of proof: "The University concedes it cannot assure that minority doctors who entered under the program, all of whom express an 'interest' in participating in a disadvantaged community, will actually do so. . . .

[Thus the petitioner] simply has not carried its burden of demonstrating that it must prefer members of particular ethnic groups over all other individuals in order to promote better health care delivery to deprived citizens. Indeed, petitioner has not shown that its preferential classification is likely to have any significant effect on the problem. . . .

The fourth goal asserted by petitioner is the attainment of a diverse student body. This clearly is a constitutionally permissible goal for an institution of higher education. Academic freedom, though not a specifically enumerated constitutional right, long has been viewed as a special concern of the First Amendment. The freedom of a university to make its own judgments as to education includes the selection of its student body. . . .

Thus, in arguing that its universities must be accorded the right to select those students who will contribute the most to the "robust exchange of ideas," petitioner invokes a countervailing constitutional interest, that of the First Amendment. In this light, petitioner must be viewed as seeking to achieve a goal that is of paramount importance in the fulfillment of its mission. . . .

Ethnic diversity, however, is only one element in a range of factors a university properly may consider in attaining the goal of a heterogeneous student body. Although a university must have a wide discretion in making the sensitive judgments as to who should be admitted, constitutional limitations protecting individual rights may not be disregarded. . . .

In summary, it is evident that the Davis special admission program involves the use of an explicit racial classification never before countenanced by this Court. It tells applicants who are not Negro, Asian, or "Chicano" that they are totally excluded for a specific percentage of the seats in an entering class. No matter how strong their qualifications, quantitative and extracurricular, including their own potential for contribution to educational diversity, they are never afforded the chance to compete with applicants from the preferred groups for the special admission seats. At the same time, the preferred applicants have the opportunity to compete for every seat in the class.

The fatal flaw in petitioner's preferential program is its disregard of individual rights as guaranteed by the Fourteenth Amendment. Such rights are not absolute. But when a State's distribution of benefits or imposition or burdens hinges on the color of a person's skin or ancestry, that individual is entitled to a demonstration that the challenged classification is necessary to promote a substantial state interest. Petitioner has failed to carry this burden. For this reason, that portion of the California court's judgment holding petitioner's special admissions program invalid under the Fourteenth Amendment must be affirmed.

Excerpts from Justice Brennan's Opinion

The assertion of human equality is closely associated with the proposition that differences in color or creed, birth or status, are neither significant nor relevant to the way in which persons should be treated. Nonetheless, the position that such factors must be "[c]onstitutionally an irrelevance," summed up by the shorthand phrase "[o]ur Constitution is color-blind," has never been adopted by this Court as the proper meaning of the Equal Protection Clause. Indeed, we have expressly rejected this proposition on a number of occasions.

Our cases have always implied that an "overriding statutory purpose" could be found that would justify racial classifications. More recently, this Court unanimously reversed the Georgia Supreme Court which had held that a desegregation plan voluntarily adopted by a local school board, which assigned students on the basis of race, was per se invalid because it was not colorblind.

And in *North Carolina State Board of Ed.* v. *Swann,* we held, again unanimously, that a statute mandating colorblind school assignment plans could not stand "against the background of segregation," since such a limit on remedies would "render illusory the promise of *Brown.*"

We conclude, therefore, that racial classifications are not per se invalid under the Fourteenth Amendment. Accordingly, we turn to the problem of articulating what our role should be in reviewing state action that expressly classifies by race. . . .

Respondent argues that racial classifications are always suspect and, consequently, that this Court should weigh the importance of the objectives served by Davis' special admissions program to see if they are compelling. In addition, he asserts that this Court must inquire whether, in its judgment, there are alternatives to racial classifications which would suit Davis' purposes. Petitioner, on the other hand, states that our proper role is simply to accept petitioner's determination that the racial classifications used by its program are reasonably related to what it tells us are its benign purposes. We reject petitioner's view, but, because our prior cases are in many respects inapposite to that before us now, we find it necessary to define with precision the meaning of that inexact term, "strict scrutiny." . . .

[The] fact that this case does not fit neatly into our prior analytic framework for race cases does not mean that it should be analyzed by applying the very loose rational-basis standard of review that is the very least that is always applied in equal protection cases. " '[T]he mere recitation of a benign, compensatory purpose is not an automatic shield which protects against any inquiry into the actual purposes underlying a statutory scheme.' " Instead, a number of considerations—developed in gender discrimination cases but which carry even more force when applied to racial classifications—lead us to conclude that racial classifications designed to further remedial purposes " 'must serve important governmental objectives and must be substantially related to achievement of those objectives.' "

First, race, like, "gender-based classifications too often [has] been inexcusably utilized to stereotype and stigmatize politically powerless segments of society." While a carefully tailored statute designed to remedy past discrimination could avoid these vices, we nonetheless have recognized that the line between honest and thoughtful appraisal of the effects of past discrimination and paternalistic stereotyping is not so clear and that a statute based on the latter is patently capable of stigmatizing all women with a badge of inferiority. State programs designed ostensibly to ameliorate the effects of past racial discrimination obviously create the same hazard of stigma, since they may promote racial separatism and reinforce the views of those who believe that members of racial minorities are inherently incapable of succeeding on their own.

Second, race, like gender and illegitimacy, is an immutable characteristic which its possessors are powerless to escape or set aside. While a classification is not per se invalid because it divides classes on the basis of an immutable characteristic, it is nevertheless true that such divisions are contrary to our deep belief that "legal burdens should bear some relationship to individual responsibility or wrongdoing," and that advancement sanctioned, sponsored, or approved by the State should ideally be based on individual merit or achievement, or at the least on factors within the control of an individual. . . .

In sum, because of the significant risk that racial classifications established for ostensibly benign purposes can be misused, causing effects not unlike those created by invidious classifications, it is inappropriate to inquire only whether there is any conceivable basis that might sustain such a classification. Instead, to justify such a classification an important and articulated purpose for its use must be shown. In addition, any statute must be stricken that stigmatizes any group or that singles out those least well represented in the political process to bear the brunt of a benign program. Thus our review under the Fourteenth Amendment should be strict—not " 'strict' in theory and fatal in fact," because it is stigma that causes fatality—but strict and searching nonetheless. . . .

Certainly, on the basis of the undisputed factual submissions before this Court, Davis had a sound basis for believing that the problem of underrepresentation of minorities was substantial and chronic and that the problem was attributable to handicaps imposed on minority applicants by past and present racial discrimination. Until at least 1973, the practice of medicine in this country was, in fact, if not in law, largely the prerogative of whites. In 1950, for example, while Negroes comprised 10% of the total population, Negro physicians constituted only 2.2% of the total number of physicians. The overwhelming majority of these, moreover, were educated in two predominantly Negro medical schools, Howard and Meharry. By 1970, the gap between the proportion of Negroes in medicine and their proportion in the population had widened: The number of Negroes employed in medicine remained frozen at 2.2% while the Negro population had increased to 11.1%. The number of Negro admittees to predominantly white medical schools, moreover, had declined in absolute numbers during the years 1955 to 1964.

Moreover, Davis had a very good reason to believe that the national pattern of underrepresentation of minorities in medicine would be perpetuated if it retained a single admissions standard. For example, the entering classes in 1968 and 1969, the years in which such a standard was used, included only one Chicano and two Negroes out of 100 admittees. Nor is there any relief from this pattern of underrepresentation in the statistics for the regular admissions program in later years.

Davis clearly could conclude that the serious and persistent underrepresentation of minorities in medicine depicted by these statistics is the result of handicaps under which minority applicants labor as a consequence of a background of deliberate, purposeful discrimination against minorities in education and in society generally, as well as in the medical profession. . . .

Green v. County School Board gave explicit recognition to the fact that the habit of discrimination and the cultural tradition of race prejudice cultivated by centuries of legal slavery and segregation were not immediately dissipated when *Brown I* announced the constitutional principle that equal educational opportunity and participation in all aspects of American life could not be denied on the basis of race. Rather, massive official and private resistance prevented, and to a lesser extent still prevents, attainment of equal opportunity in education at all levels and in the professions. The generation of minority students applying to Davis Medical School since it opened in 1968—most of whom were born before or about the time *Brown I* was decided—clearly have been victims of this discrimination. Judicial decrees recognizing discrimination in public education in California testify to the fact of widespread discrimination suffered by California-born minority applicants; many minority group members living in California, moreover, were born and reared in school districts in southern States segregated by law. Since separation of school children by race "generates a feeling of inferiority as to their status in the community that may affect their hearts and minds in a way unlikely ever to be undone," the conclusion is inescapable that applicants to medical school must be few indeed who endured the effects of de jure segregation, the resistance to *Brown I*, or the equally debilitating pervasive private discrimination fostered by our long history of official discrimination, and yet come to the starting line with an education equal to whites. . . .

The second prong of our test—whether the Davis program stigmatizes any discrete group or individual and whether race is reasonably used in light of the program's objectives—is clearly satisfied by the Davis program.

It is not even claimed that Davis' program in any way operates to stigmatize or single out any discrete and insular, or even any identifiable, nonminority group. Nor will harm comparable to that imposed upon racial minorities by exclusion or separation on grounds of race be the likely result of the program. It does not, for example, establish an exclusive preserve for minority students apart from and exclusive of whites. Rather, its purpose is to overcome the effects of segregation by bringing the races together. True, whites are excluded from participation in the special admissions program, but this fact only operates to reduce the number of whites to be admitted in the regular admissions program in order to permit admission of a reasonable percentage—less than their proportion of the California population—of otherwise underrepresented qualified minority applicants.

Nor was Bakke in any sense stamped as inferior by the Medical School's rejection of him. . . . Unlike discrimination against racial minorities, the use of racial preferences for remedial purposes does not inflict a pervasive injury upon individual whites in the sense that wherever they go or whatever they do there is a significant likelihood that they will be treated as second-class citizens because of their color. This distinction does not mean that the exclusion of a white resulting from the preferential use of race is not sufficiently serious to require justification; but it does mean that the injury inflicted by such a policy is not distinguishable from disadvantages caused by a wide range of government actions, none of which has ever been thought impermissible for that reason alone.

In addition, there is simply no evidence that the Davis program discriminates intentionally or unintentionally against any minority group which it purports to benefit. The program does not establish a quota in the invidious sense of a ceiling on the number of minority applicants to be admitted. Nor can the program reasonably be regarded as stigmatizing the program's beneficiaries or their race as inferior. The Davis program does not simply advance less qualified applicants; rather, it compensates applicants, whom it is uncontested are fully qualified to study medicine, for educational disadvantage which it was reasonable to conclude was a product of state-fostered discrimination. Once admitted, these students must satisfy the same degree requirements as regularly admitted students; they are taught by the same faculty in the same classes; and their performance is evaluated by the same standards by which regularly admitted students are judged. Under these circumstances, their performance and degrees must be regarded equally with the regularly admitted students with whom they compete for standing. Since minority graduates cannot justifiably be regarded as less well qualified than nonminority graduates by virtue of the special admissions program, there is no reasonable basis to conclude that minority graduates at schools using such programs would be stigmatized as inferior by the existence of such programs.

BURDEN OF PROOF

A remarkable feature of the line of cases from *Plessy* through *Bakke* is the extent to which the interpretation of the equal protection clause turns on the matter of *burden of proof*. Under the rational relation test that governed *Plessy*, the state bears a very light burden when it is asked to show that its actions do not conflict with the equal protection clause. The strict scrutiny test that governed *Brown I* changes this by placing a very heavy burden of proof on the state to justify any use of suspect classifications or any interference with fundamental rights.[8] The middle level test advocated by Marshall and Brennan is an effort to relax the strict scrutiny test and thus permit legislation that explicitly tries to aid those who have been disadvantaged by past discrimination.

It may seem peculiar that an important legal decision can turn on such a technical and procedural matter as burden of proof. But the question of burden of proof often plays a decisive role in a legal decision, so it is worth knowing something about it.

The two basic questions concerning burden of proof are (1) *who* bears this burden and (2) how *heavy* is the burden. In our system of

---

[8] The burden is so heavy that it has been said to be strict in theory but fatal in fact. This isn't quite right, however, since the Supreme Court has ruled that certain actions have met this test, for example, the internment of American citizens of Japanese descent during World War II. See *Korematsu* v. *United States*, 323 U.S. 214 (1944).

criminal justice, the rules governing burden of proof are fairly straight-forward. The state has the burden of establishing the guilt of the accused. The defendant has no obligation to establish his or her innocence. This is what is meant by saying the defendant is innocent until proven guilty. The burden of proof is also very heavy on the state in criminal procedures, for it must show *beyond reasonable doubt* that the accused is guilty. If it seems only more likely than not that the accused has committed a crime, then the jury should vote for acquittal.

Turning to civil law, there is no simple way of explaining burden of proof. Very roughly, the plaintiff (the one who brings the suit) has an initial burden to establish a *prima facie* case in behalf of his or her complaint. The burden then shifts to the respondent (the one against whom the suit is being brought) to answer these claims. The burden of proof may then shift back and forth depending on the nature of the procedure. Provided that both sides have met their legally required burdens of proof, the case is then decided on the basis of the *preponderance of evidence;* that is, the judge or jury simply decides which party has made the stronger case.

Burden of proof is primarily a legal notion, but is sometimes used, often very loosely, outside the law. The notion of burden of proof is needed within the law because law cases are adversarial and the court has to come to a decision. Imagine a judge saying, "This case is too tough for me; I'm not going to rule on it." Outside the law, people have a very general burden to have good reasons for what they say. That's the second part of Grice's rule of Quality. More specifically, people have a burden to justify accusations that they make or statements that they put forward that run counter to common opinion.

The important thing to see is that you cannot establish the truth of something through an appeal to burden of proof. The following argument is perfectly weird:

> I say that there is life in other parts of the universe. It's up to you to prove me wrong.

Of course, no one can prove that there *isn't* life elsewhere in the universe, but this has no tendency to show that there *is.* Attempts to prove the truth of something through appeals to burden of proof are another example of a *fallacy of relevance.*

♦ DISCUSSION QUESTION

Although Justice Powell argued in *Bakke* that explicit affirmative action quotas are unconstitutional, he rejected the idea that any reference to race would automatically make an admissions procedure unconstitutional. He held that educational institutions have a legitimate right (protected by the First Amendment) to seek ethnic diversity in their student bodies. The central part of his argument is given below. Evaluate it.

In such an admissions program, race or ethnic background may be deemed a "plus" in a particular applicant's file, yet it does not insulate the individual from comparison with all other candidates for the available seats. The file of a particular black applicant may be examined for his potential contribution to diversity without the factor of race being decisive when compared, for example, with that of an applicant identified as an Italian-American if the latter is thought to exhibit qualities more likely to promote beneficial educational pluralism. Such qualities could include exceptional personal talents, unique work or service experience, leadership potential, maturity, demonstrated compassion, a history of overcoming disadvantage, ability to communicate with the poor, or other qualifications deemed important. In short, an admissions program operated in this way is flexible enough to consider all pertinent elements of diversity in light of the particular qualifications of each applicant, and to place them on the same footing for consideration, although not necessarily according them the same weight. Indeed, the weight attributed to a particular quality may vary from year to year depending upon the "mix" both of the student body and the applicants for the incoming class.

This kind of program treats each applicant as an individual in the admissions process. The applicant who loses out on the last available seat to another candidate receiving a "plus" on the basis of ethnic background will not have been foreclosed from all consideration for that seat simply because he was not the right color or had the wrong surname. It would mean only that his combined qualifications, which may have included similar nonobjective factors, did not outweigh those of the other applicant. His qualifications would have been weighed fairly and competitively, and he would have no basis to complain of unequal treatment under the Fourteenth Amendment.

It has been suggested that an admissions program which considers race only as one factor is simply a subtle and more sophisticated—but no less effective—means of according racial preference than the Davis program. A facial intent to discriminate, however, is evident in petitioner's preference program and not denied in this case. No such facial infirmity exists in an admissions program where race or ethnic background is simply one element—to be weighed fairly against other elements—in the selection process. "A boundary line," as Mr. Justice Frankfurter remarked in another connection, "is none the worse for being narrow." And a Court would not assume that a university, professing to employ a facially nondiscriminatory admissions policy, would operate it as a cover for the functional equivalent of a quota system. In short, good faith would be presumed in the absence of a showing to the contrary in the manner permitted by our cases.

12

A Moral Debate

Legal reasoning is possible because there is a shared framework of laws, precedents, procedures, and so on; it is interesting and complex because conflicts (and, hence, disagreements) can arise within this framework. A parallel situation exists for moral reasoning except that the potential for disagreement seems even greater. People in our society accept a great many moral principles as a matter of course. If a policy has no other consequence but to produce widespread misery, it is rejected out of hand. We share a conception of justice that includes, among other things, equality of opportunity and equality before the law. Most people have a conception of human dignity: a human being is not merely a thing to be used and disposed of for personal advantage. To the extent that views of this kind are widely shared and generally acknowledged, a moral community exists and moral discussion, including moral *disagreement,* is possible.

The idea that moral disagreement presupposes a system of shared moral principles may seem paradoxical, but it is not. Our moral disagreements typically arise when there is a *conflict* between moral principles, and people are inclined to resolve this conflict in different ways. If a person cannot see the moral difference between eating a carrot and eating his brother-in-law, we will not be able to get on a sufficient footing with him even to disagree. (This does not mean, of course, that cannibalism is always wrong, but even cannibals recognize that human beings are not just a different food.) The most serious and perplexing disagreements take place when people agree on principles such as welfare, justice, and human dignity, and yet, by weighing these principles differently or seeing the situation in a different light, they arrive at opposing conclusions. It is a disagreement of this kind that we shall examine in this chapter.

It is important to see that we are not here concerned with *ethical theory.* An ethical theory is an attempt to establish the fundamental principle (or principles) by which actions are judged morally right or wrong. A great many such theories have been developed in the history of philosophy. Each has shed some light into the character of our moral thought, but none has received general acceptance. One such theory, ethical skepticism, holds, in effect, that there are no rational procedures for settling ethical disputes. Perhaps ethical skepticism is true, but until it is shown to be true, it would be foolish to abandon our serious concern with ethical issues. In any case, there is no reason to postpone discussion of special moral problems until agreement arises concerning the correct ethical theory. No one thinks that our courts should go into recess until the basic problems in jurisprudence have been resolved.

THE QUESTION OF ABORTION

The selections given below concern the moral and, to a lesser extent, the legal issues raised by abortion. In her essay, "A Defense of Abortion," Judith Jarvis Thompson defends an extensive (though not absolute) right to abortion. In the selection that follows, Baruch Brody attacks the central analogical argument in Thompson's essay. The two remaining essays, the first by President Ronald Reagan, the second by Barbara Ehrenreich, represent very nearly the opposite ends of the spectrum of opinion on this issue.

All these arguments illustrate the analogical character of moral reasoning in a striking way. In fact, it is useful to list the comparisons that are made in each essay. The essays also show that the way in which an issue is raised will have important influence on an argument. Starting out with the rights of a pregnant woman, Thompson and Ehrenreich ask when these should be set aside in favor of the rights of the fetus. Reasoning from this perspective, they are able to find analogical arguments that support an extensive right to abortion. In contrast, Reagan and Brody take the rights of the fetus as the starting point and then produce analogical arguments of their own that support the fetus's right to life. The outcome of this reasoning is that the fetus has extensive rights to life and, therefore, the right to abortion must be limited.

A Defense of Abortion* [1]

JUDITH JARVIS THOMSON

Most opposition to abortion relies on the premise that the fetus is a human being, a person, from the moment of conception. The premise is argued for, but, as I think, not well. Take, for example, the most common argument. We are asked to notice that the development of a human being from conception through birth into childhood is continuous; then it is said that to draw a line, to choose a point in this development and say "before this point the thing is not a person, after this point it is a person" is to make an arbitrary choice, a choice for which in the nature of things no good reason can be given. It is concluded that the fetus is, or anyway that we had better say it is, a person from the moment of conception. But this conclusion does not follow. Similar things might be said about the development of an acorn into an oak tree, and it does not follow that acorns are oak trees, or that we had better say they are. Arguments of this form are sometimes called "slippery slope arguments"—the phrase is perhaps self-explanatory—and it is dismaying that opponents of abortion rely on them so heavily and uncritically.

I am inclined to agree, however, that the prospects for "drawing a line" in the development of the fetus look dim. I am inclined to think also that we shall probably have to agree that the fetus has already become a human person well before birth. Indeed, it comes as a surprise when one first learns how early

*Philosophy and Public Affairs, Vol. 1, No. 1 (Fall 1971), pp. 47–66.
[1] I am very much indebted to James Thomson for discussion, criticism, and many helpful suggestions.

in its life it begins to acquire human characteristics. By the tenth week, for example, it already has a face, arms and legs, fingers and toes; it has internal organs, and brain activity is detectable.[2] On the other hand, I think that the premise is false, that the fetus is not a person from the moment of conception. A newly fertilized ovum, a newly implanted clump of cells, is no more a person than an acorn is an oak tree. But I shall not discuss any of this. For it seems to me to be of great interest to ask what happens if, for the sake of argument, we allow the premise. How, precisely, are we supposed to get from there to the conclusion that abortion is morally impermissible? Opponents of abortion commonly spend most of their time establishing that the fetus is a person, and hardly any time explaining the step from there to the impermissibility of abortion. Perhaps they think the step too simple and obvious to require much comment. Or perhaps instead they are simply being economical in argument. Many of those who defend abortion rely on the premise that the fetus is not a person, but only a bit of tissue that will become a person at birth; and why pay out more arguments than you have to? Whatever the explanation, I suggest that the step they take is neither easy nor obvious, that it calls for closer examination than it is commonly given, and that when we do give it this closer examination we shall feel inclined to reject it.

I propose, then, that we grant that the fetus is a person from the moment of conception. How does the argument go from here? Something like this, I take it. Every person has a right to life. So the fetus has a right to life. No doubt the mother has a right to decide what shall happen in and to her body; everyone would grant that. But surely a person's right to life is stronger and more stringent than the mother's right to decide what happens in and to her body, and so outweighs it. So the fetus may not be killed; an abortion may not be performed.

It sounds plausible. But now let me ask you to imagine this. You wake up in the morning and find yourself back to back in bed with an unconscious violinist. A famous unconscious violinist. He has been found to have a fatal kidney ailment, and the Society of Music Lovers has canvassed all the available medical records and found that you alone have the right blood type to help. They have therefore kidnapped you, and last night the violinist's circulatory system was plugged into yours, so that your kidneys can be used to extract poisons from his blood as well as your own. The director of the hospital now tells you, "Look, we're sorry the Society of Music Lovers did this to you—we would never have permitted it if we had known. But still, they did it, and the violinist now is plugged into you. To unplug you would be to kill him. But never mind, it's only for nine months. By then he will have recovered from his ailment, and can safely

---

[2] Daniel Callahan, *Abortion: Law, Choice and Morality* (New York, 1970), p. 373. This book gives a fascinating survey of the available information on abortion. The Jewish tradition is surveyed in David M. Feldman, *Birth Control in Jewish Law* (New York, 1968), Part 5, the Catholic tradition in John T. Noonan, Jr,. "An Almost Absolute Value in History," in *The Morality of Abortion*, ed. John T. Noonan, Jr. (Cambridge, Mass., 1970).

be unplugged from you." Is it morally incumbent on you to accede to this situation? No doubt it would be very nice of you if you did, a great kindness. But do you *have* to accede to it? What if it were not nine months, but nine years? Or longer still? What if the director of the hospital says, "Tough luck, I agree, but you've now got to stay in bed, with the violinist plugged into you, for the rest of your life. Because remember this. All persons have a right to life, and violinists are persons. Granted you have a right to decide what happens in and to your body, but a person's right to life outweighs your right to decide what happens in and to your body. So you cannot ever be unplugged from him." I imagine you would regard this as outrageous, which suggests that something really is wrong with that plausible-sounding argument I mentioned a moment ago.

In this case, of course, you were kidnapped; you didn't volunteer for the operation that plugged the violinist into your kidneys. Can those who oppose abortion on the ground I mentioned make an exception for a pregnancy due to rape? Certainly. They can say that persons have a right to life only if they didn't come into existence because of rape; or they can say that all persons have a right to life, but that some have less of a right to life than others, in particular, that those who came into existence because of rape have less. But these statements have a rather unpleasant sound. Surely the question of whether you have a right to life at all, or how much of it you have, shouldn't turn on the question of whether or not you are the product of a rape. And in fact the people who oppose abortion on the ground I mentioned do not make this distinction, and hence do not make an exception in the case of rape.

Nor do they make an exception for a case in which the mother had to spend the nine months of her pregnancy in bed. They would agree that would be a great pity, and hard on the mother; but all the same all persons have a right to life, the fetus is a person, and so on. I suspect, in fact, that they would not make an exception for a case in which, miraculously enough, the pregnancy went on for nine years or even the rest of the mother's life.

Some won't even make an exception for a case in which continuation of the pregnancy is likely to shorten the mother's life; they regard abortion as impermissible even to save the mother's life. Such cases are nowadays very rare, and many opponents of abortion do not accept this extreme view. All the same, it is a good place to begin: a number of points of interest come out in respect to it.

1. Let us call the view that abortion is impermissible even to save the mother's life "the extreme view." I want to suggest first that it does not issue from the argument I mentioned earlier without the addition of some fairly powerful premises. Suppose a woman has become pregnant, and now learns that she has a cardiac condition such that she will die if she carries the baby to term. What may be done for her? The fetus, being a person, has a right to life, but as the mother is a person too, so has she a right to life. Presumably they have an equal right to life. How is it supposed to come out that an abortion

may not be performed? If mother and child have an equal right to life, shouldn't we perhaps flip a coin? Or should we add to the mother's right to life her right to decide what happens in and to her body which everybody seems to be ready to grant—the sum of her rights now outweighing the fetus' right to life?

The most familiar argument here is the following. We are told that performing the abortion would be directly killing[3] the child, whereas doing nothing would not be killing the mother, but only letting her die. Moreover, in killing the child, one would be killing an innocent person, for the child has committed no crime, and is not aiming at his mother's death. And then there are a variety of ways in which this might be continued. (1) But as directly killing an innocent person is always and absolutely impermissible, an abortion may not be performed. Or, (2) as directly killing an innocent person is murder, and murder is always and absolutely impermissible, an abortion may not be performed.[4] Or, (3) as one's duty to refrain from directly killing an innocent person is more stringent than one's duty to keep a person from dying, an abortion may not be performed. Or, (4) if one's only options are directly killing an innocent person or letting a person die, one must prefer letting the person die, and thus an abortion may not be performed.[5]

Some people seem to have thought that these are not further premises which must be added if the conclusion is to be reached; but that they follow from the very fact that an innocent person has a right to life.[6] But this seems to me to be a mistake, and perhaps the simplest way to show this is to bring out that while we must certainly grant that innocent persons have a right to life, the theses in (1) through (4) are all false. Take (2), for example. If directly kill-

---

[3] The term "direct" in the arguments I refer to is a technical one. Roughly what is meant by "direct killing" is either killing as an end by itself, or killing as a means to some end, for example, the end of saving someone else's life. See note 6, below, for an example of its use.

[4] Cf. *Encyclical Letter of Pope Pius XI on Christian Marriage*, St. Paul Editions (Boston, n.d.), p. 32: "however much we may pity the mother whose health and even life is gravely imperiled in the performance of the duty allotted to her by nature, nevertheless what could ever be a sufficient reason for excusing in any way the direct murder of the innocent? This is precisely what we are dealing with here." Noonan (*The Morality of Abortion*, p. 43) reads this as follows: "What cause can ever avail to excuse in any way the direct killing of the innocent? For it is a question of that."

[5] The thesis in (4) is in an interesting way weaker than those in (1), (2), and (3): they rule out abortion even in cases in which both mother *and* child will die if the abortion is not performed. By contrast, one who held the view expressed in (4) could consistently say that one needn't prefer letting two persons die to killing one.

[6] Cf. the following passage from Pius XII, *Address to the Italian Catholic Society of Midwives:* "The baby in the maternal breast has the right to life immediately from God—Hence there is no man, no human authority, no science, no medical, eugenic, social, economic or moral 'indication' which can establish or grant a valid juridical ground for a direct deliberate disposition of an innocent human life, that is a disposition which looks to its destruction either as an end or as a means in another end perhaps in itself not illicit. The baby, still not born, is a man in the same degree and for the same reason as the mother" (quoted in Noonan, *The Morality of Abortion*, p. 45).

ing an innocent person is murder, and thus is impermissible, then the mother's directly killing the innocent person inside her is murder, and thus is impermissible. But it cannot seriously be thought to be murder if the mother performs an abortion on herself to save her life. It cannot seriously be said that she *must* refrain, that she *must* sit passively by and wait for her death. Let us look again at the case of you and the violinist. There you are, in bed with the violinist, and the director of the hospital says to you, "It's all most distressing, and I deeply sympathize, but you see this is putting an additional strain on your kidneys, and you'll be dead within the month. But you *have* to stay where you are all the same. Because unplugging you would be directly killing an innocent violinist, and that's murder, and that's impermissible." If anything in the world is true, it is that you do not commit murder, you do not do what is impermissible, if you reach around to your back and unplug yourself from that violinist to save your life.

The main focus of attention in writings on abortion has been on what a third party may or may not do in answer to a request from a woman for an abortion. This is in a way understandable. Things being as they are, there isn't much a woman can safely do to abort herself. So the question asked is what a third party may do, and what the mother may do, if it is mentioned at all, is deduced, almost as an afterthought, from what it is concluded that third parties may do. But it seems to me that to treat the matter in this way is to refuse to grant to the mother that very status of person which is so firmly insisted on for the fetus. For we cannot simply read off what a person may do from what a third party may do. Suppose you find yourself trapped in a tiny house with a growing child. I mean a very tiny house, and a rapidly growing child—you are already up against the wall of the house and in a few minutes you'll be crushed to death. The child on the other hand won't be crushed to death; if nothing is done to stop him from growing he'll be hurt, but in the end he'll simply burst open the house and walk out a free man. Now I could well understand it if a bystander were to say, "There's nothing we can do for you. We cannot choose between your life and his, we cannot be the ones to decide who is to live, we cannot intervene." But it cannot be concluded that you too can do nothing, that you cannot attack it to save your life. However innocent the child may be, you do not have to wait passively while it crushes you to death. Perhaps a pregnant woman is vaguely felt to have the status of house, to which we don't allow the right of self-defense. But if the woman houses the child, it should be remembered that she is a person who houses it.

I should perhaps stop to say explicitly that I am not claiming that people have a right to do anything whatever to save their lives. I think, rather, that there are drastic limits to the right of self-defense. If someone threatens you with death unless you torture someone else to death, I think you have not the right, even to save your life to do so. But the case under consideration here is very different. In our case there are only two people involved, one whose life is threatened, and one who threatens it. Both are innocent: the one who is threatened is not threatened because of any fault, the one who threatens does not threaten because of any fault. For this reason we may feel that we by-standers cannot intervene. But the person threatened can.

In sum, a woman surely can defend her life against the threat to it posed by the unborn child, even if doing so involves its death. And this shows not merely that the theses in (1) through (4) are false; it shows also that the extreme view of abortion is false, and so we need not canvas any other possible ways of arriving at it from the argument I mentioned at the outset.

2. The extreme view could of course be weakened to say that while abortion is permissible to save the mother's life, it may not be performed by a third party, but only by the mother itself. But this cannot be right either. For what we have to keep in mind is that the mother and the unborn child are not like two tenants in a small house which has, by an unfortunate mistake, been rented to both: the mother *owns* the house. The fact that she does adds to the offensiveness of deducing that the mother can do nothing from the supposition that third parties can do nothing. But it does more than this: it casts a bright light on the supposition that third parties can do nothing. Certainly it lets us see that a third party who says "I cannot choose between you" is fooling himself if he thinks this is impartiality. If Jones has found and fastened on a certain coat, which he needs to keep him from freezing, but which Smith also needs to keep him from freezing, then it is not impartiality that says "I cannot choose between you" when Smith owns the coat. Women have said again and again "This body is *my* body!" and they have reason to feel angry, reason to feel that it has been like shouting into the wind. Smith, after all, is hardly likely to bless us if we say to him, "Of course it's your coat; anybody would grant that it is. But no one may choose between you and Jones who is to have it."

We should really ask what it is that says "no one may choose" in the face of the fact that the body that houses the child is the mother's body. It may be simply a failure to appreciate this fact. But it may be something more interesting, namely the sense that one has a right to refuse to lay hands on people, even where it would be just and fair to do so, even where justice seems to require that somebody do so. Thus justice might call for somebody to get Smith's coat back from Jones, and yet you have a right to refuse to be the one to lay hands on Jones, a right to refuse to do physical violence to him. This, I think, must be granted. But then what should be said is not "no one may choose," but only "*I* cannot choose," and indeed not even this, but "*I* will not *act*," leaving it open that somebody else can or should, and in particular that anyone in a position of authority, with the job of securing people's rights, both can and should. So this is no difficulty. I have not been arguing that any given third party must accede to the mother's request that he perform an abortion to save her life, but only that he may.

I suppose that in some views of human life the mother's body is only on loan to her, the loan not being one which gives her any prior claim to it. One who held this view might well think it impartiality to say "I cannot choose." But I shall simply ignore this possibility. My own view is that if a human being has any just, prior claim to anything at all, he has a just, prior claim to his own body. And perhaps this needn't be argued for here anyway, since, as I mentioned, the arguments against abortion we are looking at do grant that the woman has a right to decide what happens in and to her body.

But although they do grant it, I have tried to show that they do not take seriously what is done in granting it. I suggest the same thing will reappear even more clearly when we turn away from cases in which the mother's life is at stake, and attend, as I propose we now do, to the vastly more common cases in which a woman wants an abortion for some less weighty reason than preserving her own life.

3. Where the mother's life is not at stake, the argument I mentioned at the outset seems to have a much stronger pull. "Everyone has a right to life, so the unborn person has a right to life." And isn't the child's right to life weightier than anything other than the mother's own right to life, which she might put forward as ground for an abortion?

This argument treats the right to life as if it were unproblematic. It is not, and this seems to me to be precisely the source of the mistake.

For we should now, at long last, ask what it comes to, to have a right to life. In some views having a right to life includes having a right to be given at least the bare minimum one needs for continued life. But suppose that what in fact *is* the bare minimum a man needs for continued life is something he has no right at all to be given? If I am sick unto death, and the only thing that will save my life is the touch of Henry Fonda's cool hand on my fevered brow, then all the same, I have no right to be given the touch of Henry Fonda's cool hand on my fevered brow. It would be frightfully nice of him to fly in from the West Coast to provide it. It would be less nice, though no doubt well meant, if my friends flew out to the West Coast and carried Henry Fonda back with them. But I have no right at all against anybody that he should do this for me. Or again, to return to the story I told earlier, the fact that for continued life that violinist needs the continued use of your kidneys does not establish that he has a right to be given the continued use of your kidneys. He certainly has no right against you that *you* should give him continued use of your kidneys. For nobody has any right to use your kidneys unless you give him such a right; and nobody has the right against you that you shall give him this right—if you do allow him to go on using your kidneys, this is a kindness on your part, and not something he can claim from you as his due. Nor has he any right against anybody else that *they* should give him continued use of your kidneys. Certainly he had no right against the Society of Music Lovers that they should plug him into you in the first place. And if you now start to unplug yourself, having learned that you will otherwise have to spend nine years in bed with him, there is nobody in the world who must try to prevent you, in order to see to it that he is given something he has a right to be given.

Some people are rather stricter about the right to life. In their view, it does not include the right to be given anything, but amounts to, and only to, the right not to be killed by anybody. But here a related difficulty arises. If everybody is to refrain from killing that violinist then everybody must refrain from doing a great many different sorts of things. Everybody must refrain from slitting his throat, everybody must refrain from shooting him—and everybody must refrain from unplugging you from him. But does he have a right against everybody that they shall refrain from unplugging you from him? To refrain from doing this is to allow him to continue to use your kidneys. It could be argued that he has a right against us that *we* should allow him to continue to use your kidneys. That is, while he had no right against us that we should give him the use of your kidneys, it might be argued that he anyway has a right against us that we shall not now intervene and deprive him of the use of your kidneys. I shall come back to third-party interventions later. But certainly the violinist has no right against you that *you* shall allow him to continue to use your kidneys. As I said, if you do allow him to use them, it is a kindness on your part, and not something you owe him.

The difficulty I point to here is not peculiar to the right to life. It reappears in connection with all the other natural rights; and it is something which an adequate account of rights must deal with. For present purposes it is enough just to draw attention to it. But I would stress that I am not arguing that people do not have a right to life—quite to the contrary, it seems to me that the primary control we must place on the acceptability of an account of rights is that it should turn out in that account to be a truth that all persons have a right to life. I am arguing only that having a right to life does not guarantee having either a right to be given the use of or a right to be allowed continued use of another person's body—even if one needs it for life itself. So the right to life will not serve the opponents of abortion in the very simple and clear way in which they seem to have thought it would.

4. There is another way to bring out the difficulty. In the most ordinary sort of case, to deprive someone of what he has a right to is to treat him unjustly. Suppose a boy and his small brother are jointly given a box of chocolates for Christmas. If the older boy takes the box and refuses to give his brother any of the chocolates, he is unjust to him, for the brother has been given a right to half of them. But suppose that, having learned that otherwise it means nine years in bed with that violinist, you unplug yourself from him. You surely are not being unjust to him, for you gave him no right to use your kidneys, and no one else can have given him any such right. But we have to notice that in unplugging yourself, you are killing him; and violinists, like everybody else, have a right to life, and thus in the view we were considering just now, the right not to be killed. So here you do what he supposedly has a right you shall not do, but you do not act unjustly to him in doing it.

The emendation which may be made at this point is this: the right to life consists not in the right not to be killed, but rather in the right not to be killed unjustly. This runs a risk of circularity, but never mind: it would enable us to square the fact that the violinist has a right to life with the fact that you do not act unjustly toward him in unplugging yourself, thereby killing him. For if you do not kill him unjustly, you do not violate his right to life, and so it is no wonder you do him no injustice.

But if this emendation is accepted, the gap in the argument against abortion stares us plainly in the face: it is by no means enough to show that the fetus is a person, and to remind us that all persons have a right to life—we need to be shown also that killing the fetus violates its right to life, i.e., that abortion is unjust killing. And is it?

I suppose we may take it as a datum that in a case of pregnancy due to rape the mother has not given the unborn person a right to the use of her body for food and shelter. Indeed, in what pregnancy could it be supposed that the mother has given the unborn person such a right? It is not as if there were unborn persons drifting about the world, to whom a woman who wants a child says, "I invite you in."

But it might be argued that there are other ways one can have acquired a right to the use of another person's body than by having been invited to use it by that person. Suppose a woman voluntarily indulges in intercourse, knowing of the chance it will issue in pregnancy, and then she does become pregnant; is she not in part responsible for the presence, in fact the very existence, of the unborn person inside her? No doubt she did not invite it in. But doesn't her partial responsibility for its being there itself give it a right to the use of her body?[7] If so, then her aborting it would be more like the boy's taking away the chocolates, and less like your unplugging yourself from the violinist—doing so would be depriving it of what it does have a right to, and thus would be doing it an injustice.

And then, too, it might be asked whether or not she can kill it even to save her own life: If she voluntarily called it into existence, how can she now kill it, even in self-defense?

The first thing to be said about this is that it is something new. Opponents of abortion have been so concerned to make out the independence of the fetus, in order to establish that it has a right to life, just as the mother does, that they have tended to overlook the possible support they might gain from making out that the fetus is *dependent* on the mother, in order to establish that she has a special kind of responsibility for it, a responsibility that gives it rights against her which are not possessed by any independent person—such as an ailing violinist who is a stranger to her.

On the other hand, this argument would give the unborn person a right to its mother's body only if her pregnancy resulted from a voluntary act, undertaken in full knowledge of the chance a pregnancy might result from it. It would leave out entirely the unborn person whose existence is due to rape. Pending the availability of some further argument, then, we would be left with the conclusion that unborn persons whose existence is due to rape have no right to the use of their mothers' bodies, and thus that aborting them is not depriving them of anything they have a right to and hence is not unjust killing.

---

[7] The need for a discussion of this argument was brought home to me by members of the Society for Ethical and Legal Philosophy, to whom this paper was originally presented.

And we should also notice that it is not at all plain that this argument really does go even as far as it purports to. For there are cases and cases, and the details make a difference. If the room is stuffy, and I therefore open a window to air it, and a burglar climbs in, it would be absurd to say, "Ah, now he can stay, she's given him a right to the use of her house—for she is partially responsible for his presence there, having voluntarily done what enabled him to get in, in full knowledge that there are such things as burglars, and that burglars burgle." It would be still more absurd to say this if I had had bars installed outside my windows, precisely to prevent burglars from getting in, and a burglar got in only because of a defect in the bars. It remains equally absurd if we imagine it is not a burglar who climbs in, but an innocent person who blunders or falls in. Again, suppose it were like this: people-seeds drift about in the air like pollen, and if you open your windows, one may drift in and take root in your carpets or upholstery. You don't want children, so you fix up your windows with fine mesh screens, the very best you can buy. As can happen, however, and on very, very rare occasions does happen, one of the screens is defective; and a seed drifts in and takes root. Does the person-plant who now develops have a right to the use of your house? Surely not—despite the fact that you voluntarily opened your windows, you knowingly kept carpets and upholstered furniture, and you knew that screens were sometimes defective. Someone may argue that you are responsible for its rooting, that it does have a right to your house, because after all you *could* have lived out your life with bare floors and furniture, or with sealed windows and doors. But this won't do—for by the same token anyone can avoid a pregnancy due to rape by having a hysterectomy, or anyway by never leaving home without a (reliable!) army.

It seems to be that the argument we are looking at can establish at most that there are *some* cases in which the unborn person has a right to the use of its mother's body, and therefore *some* cases in which abortion is unjust killing. There is room for much discussion and argument as to precisely which, if any. But I think we should side-step this issue and leave it open, for at any rate the argument certainly does not establish that all abortion is unjust killing.

5. There is room for yet another argument here, however. We surely must all grant that there may be cases in which it would be morally indecent to detach a person from your body at the cost of his life. Suppose you learn that what the violinist needs is not nine years of your life, but only one hour: all you need do to save his life is to spend one hour in that bed with him. Suppose also that letting him use your kidneys for that one hour would not affect your health in the slightest. Admittedly you were kidnapped. Admittedly you did not give anyone permission to plug him into you. Nevertheless it seems to me plain you *ought* to allow him to use your kidneys for that hour—it would be indecent to refuse.

Again, suppose pregnancy lasted only an hour, and constituted no threat to life or health. And suppose that a woman becomes pregnant as a result of rape. Admittedly she did not voluntarily do anything to bring about the existence of a child. Admittedly she did nothing at all which would give the unborn person a right to the use of her body. All the same it might well be said, as in the newly emended violinist story, that she *ought* to allow it to remain for that hour—that it would be indecent in her to refuse.

Now some people are inclined to use the term "right" in such a way that it follows from the fact that you ought to allow a person to use your body for the hour he needs, that he has a right to use your body for the hour he needs, even though he has not been given that right by any person or act. They may say that it follows also that if you refuse, you act unjustly toward him. This use of the term is perhaps so common that it cannot be called wrong; nevertheless it seems to me to be an unfortunate loosening of what we would do better to keep a tight rein on. Suppose that box of chocolates I mentioned earlier had not been given to both boys jointly, but was given only to the older boy. There he sits, stolidly eating his way through the box, his small brother watching enviously. Here we are likely to say "You ought not to be so mean. You ought to give your brother some of those chocolates." My own view is that it just does not follow from the truth of this that the brother has any right to any of the chocolates. If the boy refuses to give his brother any, he is greedy, stingy, callous—but not unjust. I suppose that the people I have in mind will say it does follow that the brother has a right to some of the chocolates, and thus that the boy does act unjustly if he refuses to give his brother any. But the effect of saying this is to obscure what we should keep distinct, namely the difference between the boy's refusal in this case and the boy's refusal in the earlier case, in which the box was given to both boys jointly, and in which the small brother thus had what was from any point of view clear title to half.

A further objection to so using the term "right" that from the fact that A ought to do a thing for B, it follows that B has a right against A that A do it for him, is that it is going to make the question of whether or not a man has a right to a thing turn on how easy it is to provide him with it; and this seems not merely unfortunate, but morally unacceptable. Take the case of Henry Fonda again. I said earlier that I had no right to the touch of his cool hand on my fevered brow, even though I needed it to save my life. I said it would be frightfully nice of him to fly in from the West Coast to provide me with it, but that I had no right against him that he should do so. But suppose he isn't on the West Coast. Suppose he has only to walk across the room, place a hand briefly on my brow—and lo, my life is saved. Then surely he ought to do it, it would be indecent to refuse. Is it to be said "Ah, well, it follows that in this case she has a right to the touch of his hand on her brow, and so it would be an injustice in him to refuse"? So that I have a right to it when it is easy for him to provide it, though no right when it's hard? It's rather a shocking idea that anyone's rights should fade away and disappear as it gets harder and harder to accord them to him.

So my own view is that even though you ought to let the violinist use your kidneys for the one hour he needs, we should not conclude that he has a right to do so—we should say that if you refuse, you are, like the boy who owns all the chocolates and will give none away, self-centered and callous, indecent in fact, but not unjust. And similarly, that even supposing a case in which a woman pregnant due to rape ought to allow the unborn person to use her body for the hour he needs, we should not conclude that he has a right to do so; we should conclude that she is self-centered, callous, indecent, but not unjust, if she refuses. The complaints are no less grave; they are just different. However, there is no need to insist on this point. If anyone does wish to deduce "he has a right" from "you ought," then all the same he must surely grant that there are cases in which it is not morally required of you that you allow that violinist to use your kidneys, and in which he does not have a right to use them, and in which you do not do him an injustice if you refuse. And so also for mother and unborn child. Except in such cases as the unborn person has a right to demand it—and we were leaving open the possibility that there may be such cases—nobody is morally *required* to make large sacrifices, of health, of all other interests and concerns, of all other duties and commitments, for nine years, or even for nine months, in order to keep another person alive.

6. We have in fact to distinguish between two kinds of Samaritan: the Good Samaritan and what we might call the Minimally Decent Samaritan. The story of the Good Samaritan, you will remember, goes like this:

> A certain man went down from Jerusalem to Jericho, and fell among thieves, which stripped him of his raiment, and wounded him, and departed, leaving him half dead.
>
> And by chance there came down a certain priest that way; and when he saw him, he passed by on the other side.
>
> And likewise a Levite, when he was at the place, came and looked on him, and passed by on the other side.
>
> But a certain Samaritan, as he journeyed, came where he was and when he saw him he had compassion on him.
>
> And went to him, and bound up his wounds, pouring in oil and wine, and set him on his own beast, and brought him to an inn, and took care of him.
>
> And on the morrow, when he departed, he took out two pence, and gave them to the host, and said unto him, "Take care of him: and whatsoever thou spendest more, when I come again, I will repay thee."
>
> (Luke 10:30–35)

The Good Samaritan went out of his way, at some cost to himself, to help one in need of it. We are not told what the options were, that is, whether or not the priest and the Levite could have helped by doing less than the Good Samaritan did, but assuming they could have, then the fact they did nothing at all shows they were not even Minimally Decent Samaritans, not because they were not Samaritans, but because they were not even minimally decent.

These things are a matter of degree, of course, but there is a difference, and it comes out perhaps most clearly in the story of Kitty Genovese, who, as you will remember, was murdered while thirty-eight people watched or listened, and did nothing at all to help her. A Good Samaritan would have rushed out to give direct assistance against the murderer. Or perhaps we had better allow that it would have been a Splendid Samaritan who did this, on the ground that it would have involved a risk of death for himself. But the thirty-eight not only did not do this, they did not even trouble to pick up a phone to call the police. Minimally Decent Samaritanism would call for doing at least that, and their not having done it was monstrous.

After telling the story of the Good Samaritan, Jesus said "Go, and do thou likewise." Perhaps he meant that we are morally required to act as the Good Samaritan did. Perhaps he was urging people to do more than is morally required of them. At all events it seems plain that it was not morally required of any of the thirty-eight that he rush out to give direct assistance at the risk of his own life, and that it is not morally required of anyone that he give long stretches of his life—nine years or nine months—to sustaining the life of a person who has no special right (we were leaving open the possibility of this) to demand it.

Indeed, with one rather striking class of exceptions, no one in any country in the world is *legally* required to anywhere near as much as this for anyone else. The class of exceptions is obvious. My main concern here is not the state of the law in respect to abortion, but it is worth drawing attention to the fact that in no state in this country is any man compelled by law to be even a Minimally Decent Samaritan to any person; there is no law under which charges could be brought against the thirty-eight who stood by while Kitty Genovese died. By contrast, in most states in this country women are compelled by law to be not merely Minimally Decent Samaritans, but Good Samaritans to unborn persons inside them. This doesn't by itself settle anything one way or the other, because it may well be argued that there should be laws in this country—as there are in many European countries—compelling at least Minimally Decent Samaritanism.[8] But it does show that there is a gross injustice in the existing state of the law. And it shows also that the groups currently working against liberalization of abortion laws, in fact working toward having it declared unconstitutional for a state to permit abortion, had better start working for the adoption of Good Samaritan laws generally, or earn the charge that they are acting in bad faith.

I should think, myself, that Minimally Decent Samaritan laws would be one thing, Good Samaritan laws quite another, and in fact highly improper. But we are not here concerned with the law. What we should ask is not whether anybody should be compelled by law to be a Good Samaritan, but whether we

---

[8] For a discussion of the difficulties involved, and a survey of the European experience with such laws, see *The Good Samaritan and the Law,* ed. James M. Ratcliffe (New York, 1966).

must accede to a situation in which somebody is being compelled—by nature, perhaps—to be a Good Samaritan. We have, in other words, to look now at third-party interventions. I have been arguing that no person is morally required to make large sacrifices to sustain the life of another who has no right to demand them, and this even where the sacrifices do not include life itself; we are not morally required to be Good Samaritans or anyway Very Good Samaritans to one another. But what if a man cannot extricate himself from such a situation? What if he appeals to us to extricate him? It seems to me plain that there are cases in which we can, cases in which a Good Samaritan would extricate him. There you are, you were kidnapped, and nine years in bed with that violinist lie ahead of you. You have your own life to lead. You are sorry, but you simply cannot see giving up so much of your life to the sustaining of his. You cannot extricate yourself, and ask us to do so. I should have thought that—in light of his having no right to the use of your body—it was obvious that we do not have to accede to your being forced to give up so much. We can do what you ask. There is no injustice to the violinist in our doing so.

7. Following the lead of the opponents of abortion, I have throughout been speaking of the fetus merely as a person, and what I have been asking is whether or not the argument we began with, which proceeds only from the fetus' being a person, really does establish its conclusion. I have argued that it does not.

But of course there are arguments and arguments, and it may be said that I have simply fastened on the wrong one. It may be said that what is important is not merely the fact that the fetus is a person, but that it is a person for whom the woman has a special kind of responsibility issuing from the fact that she is its mother. And it might be argued that all my analogies are therefore irrelevant—for you do not have that special kind of responsibility for that violinist, Henry Fonda does not have that special kind of responsibility for me. And our attention might be drawn to the fact that men and women both *are* compelled by law to provide support for their children.

I have in effect dealt (briefly) with this argument in section 4 above; but a (still briefer) recapitulation now may be in order. Surely we do not have any such "special responsibility" for a person unless we have assumed it, explicitly or implicitly. If a set of parents do not try to prevent pregnancy, do not obtain an abortion, and then at the time of birth of the child do not put it out for adoption, but rather take it home with them, then they have assumed responsibility for it, they have given it rights, and they cannot *now* withdraw support from it at the cost of its life because they now find it difficult to go on providing for it. But if they have taken all reasonable precautions against having a child, they do not simply by virtue of their biological relationship to the child who comes into existence have a special responsibility for it. They may wish to assume responsibility for it, or they may not wish to. And I am suggesting that if assuming responsibility for it would require large sacrifices, then they may refuse. A Good Samaritan would not refuse—or anyway, a Splendid Samaritan, if the sacrifices that had to be made were enormous. But then so would a Good Samaritan assume responsibility for that violinist; so would Henry Fonda, if he is a Good Samaritan, fly in from the West Coast and assume responsibility for me.

8. My argument will be found unsatisfactory on two counts by many of those who want to regard abortion as morally permissible. First, while I do argue that abortion is not impermissible, I do not argue that it is always permissible. There may well be cases in which carrying the child to term requires only Minimally Decent Samaritanism of the mother, and this is a standard we must not fall below. I am inclined to think it a merit of my account precisely that it does *not* give a general yes or a general no. It allows for and supports our sense that, for example, a sick and desperately frightened fourteen-year-old schoolgirl, pregnant due to rape, may *of course* choose abortion, and that any law which rules this out is an insane law. And it also allows for and supports our sense that in other cases resort to abortion is even positively indecent. It would be indecent in the woman to request an abortion, and indecent in a doctor to perform it, if she is in her seventh month, and wants the abortion just to avoid the nuisance of postponing a trip abroad. The very fact that the arguments I have been drawing attention to treat all cases of abortion, or even all cases of abortion in which the mother's life is not at stake, as morally on a par ought to have made them suspect at the outset.

Secondly, while I am arguing for the permissibility of abortion in some cases, I am not arguing for the right to secure the death of the unborn child. It is easy to confuse these two things in that up to a certain point in the life of the fetus it is not able to survive outside the mother's body; hence removing it from her body guarantees its death. But they are importantly different. I have argued that you are not morally required to spend nine months in bed, sustaining the life of that violinist; but to say this is by no means to say that if, when you unplug yourself, there is a miracle and he survives, you then have a right to turn round and slit his throat. You may detach yourself even if this costs him his life; you have no right to be guaranteed his death by some other means, if unplugging yourself does not kill him. There are some people who will feel dissatisfied by this feature of my argument. A woman may be utterly devastated by the thought of a child, a bit of herself, put out for adoption and never seen or heard of again. She may therefore want not merely that the child be detached from her, but more, that it die. Some opponents of abortion are inclined to regard this as beneath contempt—thereby showing insensitivity to what is surely a powerful source of despair. All the same, I agree that the desire for the child's death is not one which anybody may gratify, should it turn out to be possible to detach the child alive.

At this place, however, it should be remembered that we have only been pretending throughout that the fetus is a human being from the moment of conception. A very early abortion is surely not the killing of a person, and so is not dealt with by anything I have said here.

The Morality of Abortion*

BARUCH BRODY

In a recent article,[1] Professor Judith Thomson has, in effect, argued that [a simple view of abortion] is mistaken. How does Professor Thomson defend her claim that the mother has a right to abort the fetus, even if it is a human being, whether or not her life is threatened and whether or not she has consented to the act of intercourse in which the fetus is conceived? At one point,[2] discussing just the case in which the mother's life is threatened, she makes the following suggestion:

> In [abortion], there are only two people involved, one whose life is threatened and one who threatens it. Both are innocent: the one who is threatened is not threatened because of any fault, the one who threatens does not threaten because of any fault. For this reason, we may feel that we bystanders cannot intervene. But the person threatened can.

But surely this description is equally applicable to the following case: A and B are adrift on a lifeboat, B has a disease that he can survive, but A, if he contracts it, will die, and the only way that A can avoid that is by killing B and pushing him overboard. Surely, A has no right to do this. So there must be some special reason why the mother has, if she does, the right to abort the fetus.

There is, to be sure, an important difference between our lifeboat case and abortion, one that leads us to the heart of Professor Thomson's argument. In the case that we envisaged, both A and B have equal rights to be in the lifeboat, but the mother's body is hers and not the fetus's, and she has first rights to its use. The primacy of these rights allow an abortion whether or not her life is threatened. Professor Thomson summarizes this argument in the following way:[3]

> I am arguing only that having a right to life does not guarantee having either a right to be given the use of, or a right to be allowed continued use of, another person's body—even if one needs it for life itself.

---

*From Baruch Brody, *Abortion and the Sanctity of Human Life: A Philosophical View* (Cambridge, Mass.: MIT Press, 1975), pp. 27–30.
[1] J. Thomson, "A Defense of Abortion," *Philosophy and Public Affairs*, Vol. 1 (1971), pp. 47–66. [This is the same article, of course, just reprinted in these pages. Brody's page references will be to the journal in which it first appeared.]
[2] Ibid., p. 53.
[3] Ibid., p. 56.

One part of this claim is clearly correct. I have no duty to X to save X's life by giving him the use of my body (or my life savings, or the only home I have, and so on), and X has no right, even to save his life, to any of those things. Thus, the fetus conceived in the laboratory that will perish unless it is implanted into a woman's body has in fact no right to any woman's body. But this portion of the claim is irrelevant to the abortion issue, for in abortion of the fetus that is a human being the mother must kill X to get back the sole use of her body, and that is an entirely different matter.

This point can also be put as follows: . . . we must distinguish the taking of X's life from the saving of X's life, even if we assume that one has a duty not to do the former and to do the latter. Now that latter duty, if it exists at all, is much weaker than the first duty; many circumstances may relieve us from the latter duty that will not relieve us from the former one. Thus, I am certainly relieved from my duty to save X's life by the fact that fulfilling it means the loss of my life savings. It may be noble for me to save X's life at the cost of everything I have, but I certainly have no duty to do that. And the same observation may be made about cases in which I can save X's life by giving him the use of my body for an extended period of time. However, I am not relieved of my duty not to take X's life by the fact that fulfilling it means the loss of everything I have and not even by the fact that fulfilling it means the loss of my life. . . . Something more is required before rights like self-defense become applicable. A fortiori, it would seem that I am not relieved of the duty not to take life by the fact that its fulfillment means that some other person, who is innocently occupying my body, continues to do so.

At one point in her paper,[4] Professor Thomson does consider this objection. She has previously imagined the following case: a famous violinist, who is dying from a kidney ailment, has been, without your consent, plugged into you for a period of time so that his body can use your kidneys:

> Some people are rather stricter about the right to life. In their view, it does not include the right to be given anything, but amounts to, and only to, the right not to be killed by anybody. But here a related difficulty arises. If everybody is to refrain from killing that violinist, then everybody must refrain from doing a great many different sorts of things . . . everybody must refrain from unplugging you from him. But does he have a right against everybody that they shall refrain from unplugging you from him? To refrain from doing this is to allow him to continue to use your kidneys . . . cer-

---

[4] Ibid., pp. 55–56. It was, therefore, wrong of me to say, as I did in my article, "Thomson on Abortion," *Philosophy and Public Affairs*, Vol. 1 (1972), pp. 335–340, that "she has not attended to the distinction between our duty to save X's life and our duty not to take it." My argument is rather that she has not sufficiently attended to it, to the point that she could discover that, for example, her whole discussion of Henry Fonda's flying in from the West Coast to save my life is, of course, entirely irrelevant.

tainly the violinist has no right against you that you shall allow him
to continue to use your kidneys.

Applying this argument to the case of abortion, we can see that Professor
Thomson's argument would run as follows:

a. Assume that the fetus's right to life includes the right not to be killed by the
woman carrying him.
b. But to refrain from killing the fetus is to allow him the continued use of the
woman's body.
c. So our first assumption entails that the fetus's right to life includes the right
to the continued use of the woman's body.
d. But we all grant that the fetus does not have the right to the continued use
of the woman's body.
e. Therefore, the fetus's right to life cannot include the right not to be killed
by the woman in question.

And it is also now clear what is wrong with this argument. When we granted
that the fetus has no right to the continued use of the woman's body, all that
we meant was the he does not have this right merely because the continued use
saves his life. But, of course, there may be other reasons why he has this right.
One would be that the only way to take the use of the woman's body away from
the fetus is by killing him, and that is something that neither she nor we have
the right to do. So, I submit, the way in which Assumption d is true is irrelevant, and cannot be used by Professor Thomson, *for Assumption d is true only in
cases where the saving of the life of the fetus is at stake and not in cases where the taking
of his life is at stake*. [Italics added for emphasis.]

I conclude therefore that Professor Thomson has not established the truth
of her claims about abortion, primarily because she has not sufficiently attended to the distinction between our duty to save *X*'s life and our duty not to
take it. Once one attends to that distinction, it would seem that the mother, in
order to regain control over her body, has no right to abort the fetus from the
point at which it becomes a human being.

Abortion and the Conscience of the Nation*

RONALD REAGAN

The 10th anniversary of the Supreme Court decision in *Roe v. Wade* is a good
time for us to pause and reflect. Our nationwide policy of abortion-on-demand
through all nine months of pregnancy was neither voted for by our people nor

---

*President Reagan published this essay in 1983.

enacted by our legislators—not a single State had such unrestricted abortion before the Supreme Court decreed it to be national policy in 1973. But the consequences of this judicial decision are now obvious: since 1973, more than 15 million unborn children have had their lives snuffed out by legalized abortions. That is over ten times the number of Americans lost in all our nation's wars.

Make no mistake, abortion-on-demand is not a right granted by the Constitution. No serious scholar, including one disposed to agree with the Court's result, has argued that the framers of the Constitution intended to create such a right. Shortly after the *Roe v. Wade* decision, Professor John Hart Ely, now Dean of Stanford Law School, wrote that the opinion "is not constitutional law and gives almost no sense of an obligation to try to be." Nowhere do the plain words of the Constitution even hint at a "right" so sweeping as to permit abortion up to the time the child is ready to be born. Yet that is what the Court ruled.

As an act of "raw judicial power" (to use Justice White's biting phrase), the decision by the seven-man majority in *Roe v. Wade* has so far been made to stick. But the Court's decision has by no means settled the debate. Instead, *Roe v. Wade* has become a continuing prod to the conscience of the nation.

Abortion concerns not just the unborn child, it concerns every one of us. The English poet, John Donne, wrote: ". . . any man's death diminishes me, because I am involved in mankind; and therefore never send to know for whom the bell tolls; it tolls for thee."

We cannot diminish the value of one category of human life—the unborn—without diminishing the value of all human life. We saw tragic proof of this truism last year when the Indiana courts allowed the starvation death of "Baby Doe" in Bloomington because the child had Down's Syndrome.

Many of our fellow citizens grieve over the loss of life that has followed *Roe v. Wade*. Margaret Heckler, soon after being nominated to head the largest department of our government, Health and Human Services, told an audience that she believed abortion to be the greatest moral crisis facing our country today. And the revered Mother Teresa, who works in the streets of Calcutta ministering to dying people in her world-famous mission of mercy, has said that "the greatest misery of our time is the generalized abortion of children."

Over the first two years of my Administration I have closely followed and assisted efforts in Congress to reverse the tide of abortion—efforts of Congressmen, Senators and citizens responding to an urgent moral crisis. Regrettably, I have also seen the massive efforts of those who, under the banner of "freedom of choice," have so far blocked every effort to reverse nationwide abortion-on-demand.

Despite the formidable obstacles before us, we must not lose heart. This is not the first time our country has been divided by a Supreme Court decision that denied the value of certain human lives. The *Dred Scott* decision of 1857 was not overturned in a day, or a year, or even a decade. At first, only a minority of Americans recognized and deplored the moral crisis brought about by denying the full humanity of our black brothers and sisters; but that minority persisted in their vision and finally prevailed. They did it by appealing to the hearts and minds of their countrymen, to the truth of human dignity under God. From their example, we know that respect for the sacred value of human life is too deeply engrained in the hearts of our people to remain forever suppressed. But the great majority of the American people have not yet made their voices heard, and we cannot expect them to—any more than the public voice arose against slavery—*until* the issue is clearly framed and presented.

What, then, is the real issue? I have often said that when we talk about abortion, we are talking about two lives—the life of the mother and the life of the unborn child. Why else do we call a pregnant woman a mother? I have also said that anyone who doesn't feel sure whether we are talking about a second human life should clearly give life the benefit of the doubt. If you don't know whether a body is alive or dead, you would never bury it. I think this consideration itself should be enough for all of us to insist on protecting the unborn.

The case against abortion does not rest here, however, for medical practice confirms at every step the correctness of these moral sensibilities. Modern medicine treats the unborn child as a patient. Medical pioneers have made great breakthroughs in treating the unborn—for genetic problems, vitamin deficiencies, irregular heart rhythms, and other medical conditions. Who can forget George Will's moving account of the little boy who underwent brain surgery six times during the nine weeks before he was born? Who is the *patient* if not that tiny unborn human being who can feel pain when he or she is approached by doctors who come to kill rather than to cure?

The real question today is not when human life begins, but, *What is the value of human life?* The abortionist who reassembles the arms and legs of a tiny baby to make sure all its parts have been torn from its mother's body can hardly doubt whether it is a human being. The real question for him and for all of us is whether that tiny human life has a God-given right to be protected by the law—the same right we have.

What more dramatic confirmation could we have of the real issue than the Baby Doe case in Bloomington, Indiana? The death of that tiny infant tore at the hearts of all Americans because the child was undeniably a live human being—one lying helpless before the eyes of the doctors and the eyes of the nation. The real issue for the courts was *not* whether Baby Doe was a human being. The real issue was whether to protect the life of a human being who had Down's Syndrome, who would probably be mentally handicapped, but who needed a routine surgical procedure to unblock his esophagus and allow him to eat. A doctor testified to the presiding judge that, even with his physical problem corrected, Baby Doe would have a "non-existent" possibility for "a minimally adequate quality of life"—in other words, that retardation was the equivalent of a crime deserving the death penalty. The judge let Baby Doe starve and die, and the Indiana Supreme Court sanctioned his decision.

Federal law does not allow Federally-assisted hospitals to decide that Down's Syndrome infants are not worth treating, much less to decide to starve them to death. Accordingly, I have directed the Departments of Justice and HHS to apply civil rights regulations to protect handicapped newborns. All hospitals receiving Federal funds must post notices which will clearly state that failure to feed handicapped babies is prohibited by Federal law. The basic issue is whether to value and protect the lives of the handicapped, whether to recognize the sanctity of human life. This is the same basic issue that underlies the question of abortion.

The 1981 Senate hearings on the beginning of human life brought out the basic issue more clearly than ever before. The many medical and scientific witnesses who testified disagreed on many things, but not on the *scientific* evidence that the unborn child is alive, is a distinct individual, or is a member of the human species. They did disagree over the *value* question, whether to give value to a human life at its early and most vulnerable stages of existence.

Regrettably, we live at a time when some persons do *not* value all human life. They want to pick and choose which individuals have value. Some have said that only those individuals with "consciousness of self" are human beings. One such writer has followed this deadly logic and concluded that "shocking as it may seem, a newly born infant is not a human being."

A Nobel Prize winning scientist has suggested that if a handicapped child "were not declared fully human until three days after birth, then all parents could be allowed the choice." In other words, "quality control" to see if newly born human beings are up to snuff.

Obviously, some influential people want to deny that every human life has intrinsic, sacred worth. They insist that a member of the human race must have certain qualities before they accord him or her status as a "human being."

Events have borne out the editorial in a California medical journal which explained three years before *Roe v. Wade* that the social acceptance of abortion is a "defiance of the long-held Western ethic of intrinsic and equal value for every human life regardless of its stage, condition, or status."

Every legislator, every doctor, and every citizen needs to recognize that the real issue is whether to affirm and protect the sanctity of all human life, or to embrace a social ethic where some human lives are valued and others are not. As a nation, we must choose between the sanctity of life ethic and the quality of life ethic.

I have no trouble identifying the answer our nation has always given to this basic question, and the answer that I hope and pray it will give in the future. America was founded by men and women who shared a vision of the value of each and every individual. They stated this vision clearly from the very start in the Declaration of Independence, using words that every schoolboy and schoolgirl can recite:

> We hold these truths to be self-evident, that all men are created equal, that they are endowed by their Creator with certain unalienable rights, that among these are life, liberty, and the pursuit of happiness.

We fought a terrible war to guarantee that one category of mankind— black people in America—could not be denied the inalienable rights with which their Creator endowed them. The great champion of the sanctity of all human life in that day, Abraham Lincoln, gave us his assessment of the Declaration's purpose. Speaking of the framers of that noble document, he said:

> This was their majestic interpretation of the economy of the Universe. This was their lofty, and wise, and noble understanding of the justice of the Creator to His creatures. Yes, gentlemen, to all His creatures, to the whole great family of man. In their enlightened belief, nothing stamped with the divine image and likeness was sent into the word to be trodden on . . . They grasped not only the whole race of man then living, but they reached forward and seized upon the farthest posterity. They erected a beacon to guide their children and their children's children, and the countless myriads who should inhabit the earth in other ages.

He warned also of the danger we would face if we closed our eyes to the value of life in any category of human beings:

> I should like to know if taking this old Declaration of Independence, which declares that all men are equal upon principle and making exceptions to it where will it stop. If one man says it does not mean a Negro, why not another say it does not mean some other man?

When Congressman John A. Bingham of Ohio drafted the Fourteenth Amendment to guarantee the rights of life, liberty, and property to all human beings, he explained that *all* are "entitled to the protection of American law, because its divine spirit of equality declares that all men are created equal." He said the rights guaranteed by the amendment would therefore apply to "any human being." Justice William Brennan, writing in another case decided only the year before *Roe v. Wade*, referred to our society as one that "strongly affirms the sanctity of life."

Another William Brennan—not the Justice—has reminded us of the terrible consequences that can follow when a nation rejects the sanctity of life ethic:

> The cultural environment for a human holocaust is present whenever any society can be misled into defining individuals as less than human and therefore devoid of value and respect.

As a nation today, we have *not* rejected the sanctity of human life. The American people have not had an opportunity to express their view on the sanctity of human life in the unborn. I am convinced that Americans do not want to play God with the value of human life. It is not for us to decide who is worthy to live and who is not. Even the Supreme Court's opinion in *Roe v. Wade* did not explicitly reject the traditional American idea of intrinsic worth and value in all human life; it simply dodged this issue.

The Congress has before it several measures that would enable our people to reaffirm the sanctity of human life, even the smallest and the youngest and the most defenseless. The Human Life Bill expressly recognizes the unborn as human beings and accordingly protects them as persons under our Constitution. This bill, first introduced by Senator Jesse Helms, provided the vehicle for the Senate hearings in 1981 which contributed so much to our understanding of the real issue of abortion.

The Respect Human Life Act, just introduced in the 98th Congress, states in its first section that the policy of the United States is "to protect innocent life, both before and after birth." This bill, sponsored by Congressman Henry Hyde and Senator Roger Jepsen, prohibits the Federal government from performing abortions or assisting those who do so, except to save the life of the mother. It also addresses the pressing issue of infanticide which, as we have seen, flows inevitably from permissive abortion as another step in the denial of the inviolability of innocent human life.

I have endorsed each of these measures, as well as the more difficult route of constitutional amendment, and I will give these initiatives my full support. Each of them, in different ways, attempts to reverse the tragic policy of abortion-on-demand imposed by the Supreme Court ten years ago. Each of them is a decisive way to affirm the sanctity of human life.

We must all educate ourselves to the reality of the horrors taking place. Doctors today know that unborn children can feel a touch within the womb and that they respond to pain. But how many Americans are aware that abortion techniques are allowed today, in all 50 states, that burn the skin of a baby with a salt solution, in an agonizing death that can last for hours?

Another example: two years ago, the *Philadelphia Inquirer* ran a Sunday special supplement on "The Dreaded Complication." The "dreaded complication" referred to in the article—the complication feared by doctors who perform abortions—is the *survival* of the child despite all the painful attacks during the abortion procedure. Some unborn children *do survive the late-term abortions* the Supreme Court has made legal. Is there any question that these victims of abortion deserve our attention and protection? Is there any question that those who *don't* survive were living human beings before they were killed?

Late-term abortions, especially when the baby survives, but is then killed by starvation, neglect, or suffocation, show once again the link between abortion and infanticide. The time to stop both is now. As my Administration acts to stop infanticide, we will be fully aware of the real issue that underlies the death of babies before and soon after birth.

Our society has, fortunately, become sensitive to the rights and special needs of the handicapped, but I am shocked that physical or mental handicaps of newborns are still used to justify their extinction. This Administration has a Surgeon General, Dr. C. Everett Koop, who has done perhaps more than any other American for handicapped children, by pioneering surgical techniques to help them, by speaking out on the value of their lives, and by working with them in the context of loving families. You will not find his former patients advocating the so-called quality of life ethic.

I know that when the true issue of infanticide is placed before the American people, with all the facts openly aired, we will have no trouble deciding that a mentally or physically handicapped baby has the same intrinsic worth and right to life as the rest of us. As the New Jersey Supreme Court said two decades ago, in a decision upholding the sanctity of human life, "a child need not be perfect to have a worthwhile life."

Whether we are talking about pain suffered by unborn children, or about late-term abortions, or about infanticide, we inevitably focus on the humanity of the unborn child. Each of these issues is a potential rallying point for the sanctity of life ethic. Once we as a nation rally around any one of these issues to affirm the sanctity of life, we will see the importance of affirming this principle across the board.

Malcolm Muggeridge, the English writer, goes right to the heart of the matter: "Either life is always and in all circumstances sacred, or intrinsically of no account; it is inconceivable that it should be in some cases the one, and in some the other." The sanctity of innocent human life is a principle that Congress should proclaim at every opportunity.

It is possible that the Supreme Court itself may overturn its abortion rulings. We need only recall that in *Brown v. Board of Education* the Court reversed its own earlier "separate-but-equal" decision. I believe if the Supreme Court took another look at *Roe v. Wade*, and considered the real issue between the sanctity of life ethic and the quality of life ethic, it would change its mind once again.

As we continue to work to overturn *Roe v. Wade*, we must also continue to lay the groundwork for a society in which abortion is not the accepted answer to unwanted pregnancy. Pro-life people have already taken heroic steps, often at great personal sacrifice, to provide for unwed mothers. I recently spoke about a young pregnant woman named Victoria, who said, "In this society we save whales, we save timber wolves and bald eagles and Coke bottles. Yet, everyone wanted me to throw away my baby." She has been helped by Sav-a-Life, a group in Dallas, which provides a way for unwed mothers to preserve the human life within them when they might otherwise be tempted to resort to abortion. I think also of House of His Creation in Coatesville, Pennsylvania, where a loving couple has taken in almost 200 young women in the past ten years. They have seen, as a fact of life, that the girls are *not* better off having abortions than saving their babies. I am also reminded of the remarkable Rossow family of Ellington, Connecticut, who have opened their hearts and their home to nine handicapped adopted and foster children.

The Adolescent Family Life Program, adopted by Congress at the request of Senator Jeremiah Denton, has opened new opportunities for unwed mothers to give their children life. We should not rest until our entire society echoes the tone of John Powell in the dedication of his book, *Abortion: The Silent*

Holocaust, a dedication to every woman carrying an unwanted child: "Please be-lieve that you are not alone. There are many of us that truly love you, who want to stand at your side, and help in any way we can." And we can echo the always-practical woman of faith, Mother Teresa, when she says, "If you don't want the little child, that unborn child, give him to me." We have so many fam-ilies in America seeking to adopt children that the slogan "every child a wanted child" is now the emptiest of all reasons to tolerate abortion.

I have often said we need to join in prayer to bring protection to the un-born. Prayer and action are needed to uphold the sanctity of human life. I be-lieve it will not be possible to accomplish our work, the work of saving lives, "without being a soul of prayer." The famous British Member of Parliament, William Wilberforce, prayed with his small group of influential friends, the "Clapham Sect," for *decades* to see an end to slavery in the British empire. Wil-berforce led that struggle in Parliament, unflaggingly, because he believed in the sanctity of human life. He saw the fulfillment of his impossible dream when Parliament outlawed slavery just before his death.

Let his faith and perseverance be our guide. We will never recognize the true value of our own lives until we affirm the value in the life of others, a value of which Malcolm Muggeridge says: ". . . however low it flickers or fiercely burns, it is still a Divine flame which no man dare presume to put out, be his motives ever so humane and enlightened."

Abraham Lincoln recognized that we could not survive as a free land when some men could decide that others were not fit to be free and should therefore be slaves. Likewise, we cannot survive as a free nation when some men decide that others are not fit to live and should be abandoned to abortion or infanti-cide. My Administration is dedicated to the preservation of America as a free land, and there is no cause more important for preserving that freedom than affirming the transcendent right to life of all human beings, the right without which no other rights have any meaning.

Is Abortion Really a "Moral Dilemma"?*

BARBARA EHRENREICH

Quite apart from blowing up clinics and terrorizing patients, the antiabortion movement can take credit for a more subtle and lasting kind of damage: It has succeeded in getting even pro-choice people to think of abortion as a "moral dilemma," an "agonizing decision" and related code phrases for something murky

---

*This essay appeared in the "Hers" column of *The New York Times*, February 7, 1984.

and compromising, like the traffic in infant formula mix. In liberal circles, it has become unstylish to discuss abortion without using words like "complex," "painful" and the rest of the mealy-mouthed vocabulary of evasion. Regrets are also fashionable, and one otherwise feminist author writes recently of mourning, each year following her abortion, the putative birthday of her discarded fetus.

I cannot speak for other women, of course, but the one regret I have about my own abortions is that they cost money that might otherwise have been spent on something more pleasurable, like taking the kids to movies and theme parks. Yes, that is abortions, plural (two in my case)—a possibility that is not confined to the promiscuous, the disorderly or the ignorant. In fact, my credentials for dealing with the technology of contraception are first rate: I have a Ph.D. in biology that is now a bit obsolescent but still good for conjuring up vivid mental pictures of zygotes and ova, and I was actually paid, at one point in my life, to teach other women about the mysteries of reproductive biology.

· · ·

Yet, as every party to the abortion debate should know, those methods of contraception that are truly safe are not absolutely reliable no matter how reliably they are used. Many women, like myself, have felt free to choose the safest methods because legal abortion is available as a backup to contraception. Anyone who finds that a thoughtless, immoral choice should speak to the orphans of women whose wombs were perforated by Dalkon shields or whose strokes were brought on by high-estrogen birth-control pills.

I refer you to the orphans only because it no longer seems to be good form to mention women themselves in discussions of abortion. In most of the antiabortion literature I have seen, women are so invisible that an uninformed reader might conclude that fetuses reside in artificially warm tissue culture flasks or similar containers. It must be enormously difficult for the antiabortionist to face up to the fact that real fetuses can only survive inside women, who, unlike any kind of laboratory apparatus, have thoughts, feelings, aspirations, responsibilities and, very often, checkbooks. Anyone who thinks for a moment about women's role in reproductive biology could never blithely recommend "adoption, not abortion," because women have to go through something unknown to fetuses or men, and that is pregnancy.

From the point of view of a fetus, pregnancy is no doubt a good deal. But consider it for a moment from the point of view of the pregnant person (if "woman" is too incendiary and feminist a term) and without reference to its potential issue. We are talking about a nine-month bout of symptoms of varying severity, often including nausea, skin discolorations, extreme bloating and swelling, insomnia, narcolepsy, hair loss, varicose veins, hemorrhoids, indigestion and irreversible weight gain, and culminating in a physiological crisis which is occasionally fatal and almost always excruciatingly painful. If men were equally at risk for this condition—if they knew that their bellies might swell as if they were suffering from end-stage cirrhosis, that they would have to go for nearly a year without a stiff drink, a cigarette or even an aspirin, that they would be subject to fainting spells and unable to fight their way onto commuter trains—then I am sure that pregnancy would be classified as a sexually transmitted disease and abortions would be no more controversial than emergency appendectomies.

Adding babies to the picture does not make it all that much prettier, even if you are, as I am, a fool for short, dimpled people with drool on their chins. For no matter how charming the outcome of pregnancy that is allowed to go to term no one is likely to come forth and offer to finance its Pampers or pay its college tuition. Nor are the opponents of abortion promising a guaranteed annual income, subsidized housing, national health insurance and other measures that might take some of the terror out of parenthood. We all seem to expect the individual parents to shoulder the entire burden of supporting any offspring that can be traced to them, and, in the all-too-common event that the father cannot be identified or has skipped town to avoid child-support payments, "parent" means mother.

When society does step in to help out a poor woman attempting to raise children on her own, all that it customarily has to offer is some government-surplus cheese, a monthly allowance so small it would barely keep a yuppie male in running shoes, and the contemptuous epithet "welfare cheat." It would be far more reasonable to honor the survivors of pregnancy in childbirth with at least the same respect and special benefits that we give, without a second thought, to veterans of foreign wars.

But, you will object, I have greatly exaggerated the discomforts of pregnancy and the hazards of childbearing, which many women undergo quite cheerfully. This is true, at least to an extent. In my own case, the case of my planned and wanted pregnancies, I managed to interpret morning sickness as a sign of fetus tenacity and to find, in the hypertrophy of my belly, a voluptuousness ordinarily unknown to the skinny. But this only proves my point: A society that is able to make a good thing out of pregnancy is certainly free to choose how to regard abortion. We can treat it as a necessary adjunct to contraception, or as a vexing moral dilemma, or as a form of homicide—and whichever we choose, that is how we will tend to experience it.

• • •

So I will admit that I might not have been so calm and determined about my abortions if I had had to cross a picket line of earnest people yelling "baby killer," or if I felt that I might be blown to bits in the middle of a vacuum aspiration. Conversely, though, we would be hearing a lot less about ambivalence and regrets if there were not so much liberal head-scratching going on. Abortions will surely continue, as they have through human history, whether we approve or disapprove or hem and haw. The question that worries me is: How is, say, a 16-year-old girl going to feel after an abortion? Like a convicted sex offender, a murderess on parole? Or like a young woman who is capable, as the guidance counselors say, of taking charge of her life?

This is our choice, for biology will never have an answer to that strange and cabalistic question of when a fetus becomes a person. Potential persons are lost every day as a result of miscarriage, contraception or someone's simple failure to respond to a friendly wink. What we can answer, with a minimum of throat-clearing and moral agonizing, is the question of when women themselves will finally achieve full personhood: And that is when we have the right, unquestioned and unabrogated, to *choose* not to be pregnant when we decide not to be pregnant.

13

Scientific Arguments

When scientists praise each other's work, they sometimes say that the analysis of some phenomenon is *elegant, beautiful*, or even *tasteful*. It may seem strange to call a piece of scientific research tasteful, but this only shows a misunderstanding of the character of scientific thought. It is a parody of the scientific enterprise to think that it consists simply of amassing huge quantities of data to prove or disprove some hypothesis. Of course, experimental data are the final court of appeal in scientific research, but the point of scientific theory is to make sense out of nature, to explain it, to make it more intelligible. It is in its explanatory power that a theory can be elegant, beautiful, or even tasteful.

THE LAW OF BUOYANCY

Our first example of a scientific argument is drawn from the ancient world. It has a famous story attached to it. The ruler of Syracuse was worried that a crown he had purchased was not made of pure gold, but he could think of no way of testing whether baser metals had been mixed with the gold. He turned to the mathematician Archimedes for help. Sitting in the public bath—so the story goes—Archimedes was able to solve this problem by deriving the Law of Buoyancy. He was so excited by this discovery that he went bounding through the streets of Syracuse in his nothing-at-all shouting "Eureka!"—which, by the way, does not mean "*Yippee*," but "*I have found it.*"

The proof itself is a model of elegant scientific reasoning. It not only proves the Law of Buoyancy; it also makes sense out of it, and does so in a very simple way. The proof exploits two fundamental propositions:

(1) The surface of a liquid in a vessel is part of the surface of a sphere with the center of the earth as its center. (Proven as Proposition 1.)

(2) The liquid in two sides of a vessel acts like two sides of a lever. (From Postulate 1.)

You may have to think for a moment to see that this first proposition is true. Think about the surface of a tub of water. It conforms perfectly to the surface of the earth and since the surface of the earth is the surface of a sphere, the surface of the water in the tub is also part of the surface of a sphere. (Notice, by the way, that Archimedes simply takes it as an established fact that the earth is spherical. Contrary to popular belief today, this was well known in the ancient world.) The second proposition depends on the common sense observation that an object immersed in a liquid exerts a force on that liquid. When an object floats, this force must be balanced by some opposite force. The genius of Archimedes' proof was to look at the problem in terms of these two propositions. After that, everything follows from the most simple geometry.

On Floating Bodies*

ARCHIMEDES

POSTULATE 1.

"Let it be supposed that a fluid is of such a character that, its parts lying evenly and being continuous, that part which is thrust the less is driven along by that

---

*T. L. Heath, ed., *The Works of Archimedes* (New York: Dover Publications, 1953), pp. 253–59.

which is thrust the more; and that each of its parts is thrust by the fluid which is above it in a perpendicular direction if the fluid be sunk in anything and compressed by anything else."

Proposition 1.

If a surface be cut by a plane always passing through a certain point, and if the section be always a circumference [of a circle] whose centre is the aforesaid point, the surface is that of a sphere.

For, if not, there will be some two lines drawn from the point to the surface which are not equal.

Suppose O to be the fixed point, and A, B to be two points on the surface such that OA, OB are unequal. Let the surface be cut by a plane passing through OA, OB. Then the section is, by hypothesis, a circle whose centre is O.

Thus $OA = OB$; which is contrary to the assumption. Therefore the surface cannot but be a sphere.

Proposition 2.

The surface of any fluid at rest is the surface of a sphere whose centre is the same as that of the earth.

Suppose the surface of the fluid cut by a plane through O, the centre of the earth, in the curve $ABCD$.

$ABCD$ shall be the circumference of a circle.

For, if not, some of the lines drawn from O to the curve will be unequal. Take one of them, OB, such that OB is greater than some of the lines from O to the curve and less than others. Draw a circle with OB as a radius. Let it be EBF, which will therefore fall partly within and partly without the surface of the fluid.

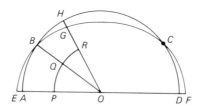

Draw OGH making with OB an angle equal to the angle EOB, and meeting the surface in H and the circle in G. Draw also in the plane an arc of a circle PQR with centre O and within the fluid.

Then the parts of the fluid along PQR are uniform and continuous, and the part PQ is compressed by the part between it and AB, while the part QR is compressed by the part between QR and BH. Therefore the parts along PQ, QR will be unequally compressed, and the part which is compressed the less will be set in motion by that which is compressed the more.

Therefore there will not be rest; which is contrary to the hypothesis.

Hence the section of the surface will be the circumference of a circle whose centre is O; and so will all other sections by planes through O.

Therefore the surface is that of a sphere with centre O.

Proposition 3.

Of solids those which, size for size, are of equal weight with a fluid will, if let down into the fluid, be immersed so that they do not project above the surface but do not sink lower.

If possible, let a certain solid $EFHG$ of equal weight, volume for volume, with the fluid remain immersed in it so that part of it, $EBCF$, projects above the surface.

Draw through O, the centre of the earth, and through the solid a plane cutting the surface of the fluid in the circle $ABCD$.

Conceive a pyramid with vertex O and base a parallelogram at the surface of the fluid, such that it includes the immersed portion of the solid. Let this pyramid be cut by the plane of $ABCD$ in OL, OM. Also let a sphere within the fluid and below GH be described with centre O, and let the plane of $ABCD$ cut this sphere in PQR.

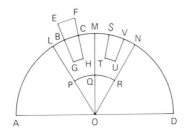

Conceive also another pyramid in the fluid with vertex O, continuous with the former pyramid and equal and similar to it. Let the pyramid so described be cut in OM, ON by the plane of $ABCD$.

Lastly, let $STUV$ be a part of the fluid within the second pyramid equal and similar to the part $BGHC$ of the solid, and let SV be at the surface of the fluid.

Then the pressures on PQ, QR are unequal, that on PQ being the greater. Hence the part at QR will be set in motion by that at PQ, and the fluid will not be at rest; which is contrary to the hypothesis.

Therefore the solid will not stand out above the surface.

Nor will it sink further, because all the parts of the fluid will be under the same pressure.

Proposition 4.

A solid lighter than a fluid will, if immersed in it, not be completely submerged, but part of it will project above the surface.

In this case, after the manner of the previous proposition, we assume the solid, if possible, to be completely submerged and the fluid to be at rest in that position, and we conceive (1) a pyramid with its vertex at O, the centre of the earth, including the solid, (2) another pyramid continuous with the former and equal and similar to it, with the same vertex O, (3) a portion of the fluid within this latter pyramid equal to the immersed solid in the other pyramid, (4) a sphere with centre O whose surface is below the immersed solid and the part of the fluid in the second pyramid corresponding thereto. We suppose a plane to be drawn through the centre O cutting the surface of the fluid in the circle ABC, the solid in S, the first pyramid in OA, OB, the second pyramid in OB, OC, the portion of the fluid in the second pyramid in K, and the inner sphere in PQR.

Then the pressures on the parts of the fluid at PQ, QR are unequal, since S is lighter than K. Hence there will not be rest; which is contrary to the hypothesis.

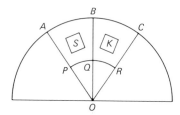

Therefore the solid S cannot, in a condition of rest, be completely submerged.

Proposition 5.

Any solid lighter than a fluid will, if placed in the fluid, be so far immersed that the weight of the solid will be equal to the weight of the fluid displaced.

For let the solid be $EGHF$, and let $BGHC$ be the portion of it immersed when the fluid is at rest. As in Prop. 3, conceive a pyramid with vertex O including the solid, and another pyramid with the same vertex continuous with the former and equal and similar to it. Suppose a portion of the fluid $STUV$ at the base of the second pyramid to be equal and similar to the immersed portion of the solid; and let the construction be the same as in Prop. 3.

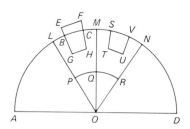

Then, since the pressure on the parts of the fluid at PQ, QR must be equal in order that the fluid may be at rest, it follows that the weight of the portion STUV of the fluid must be equal to the weight of the solid EGHF. And the former is equal to the weight of the fluid displaced by the immersed portion of the solid BGHC.

Proposition 6.

If a solid lighter than a fluid be forcibly immersed in it, the solid will be driven upwards by a force equal to the difference between its weight and the weight of the fluid displaced.

For let A be completely immersed in the fluid, and let G represent the weight of A, and (G+H) the weight of an equal volume of the fluid. Take a solid D, whose weight is H and add it to A. Then the weight of (A+D) is less than that of an equal volume of the fluid; and, if (A+D) is immersed in the fluid, it will project so that its weight will be equal to the weight of the fluid displaced. But its weight is (G+H).

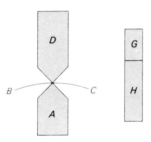

Therefore the weight of the fluid displaced is (G+H), and hence the volume of the fluid displaced is the volume of the solid A. There will accordingly be rest with A immersed and D projecting.

Thus the weight of D balances the upward force exerted by the fluid on A, and therefore the latter force is equal to H, which is the difference between the weight of A and the weight of the fluid which A displaces.

Proposition 7.

A solid heavier than a fluid will, if placed in it, descend to the bottom of the fluid, and the solid will, when weighed in the fluid, be lighter than its true weight by the weight of the fluid displaced.

(1) The first part of the proposition is obvious, since the part of the fluid under the solid will be under greater pressure, and therefore the other parts will give way until the solid reaches the bottom.

(2) Let A be a solid heavier than the same volume of the fluid, and let (G+H) represent its weight, while G represents the weight of the same volume of the fluid.

Take a solid B lighter than the same volume of the fluid, and such that the weight of B is G, while the weight of the same volume of the fluid is $(G+H)$.

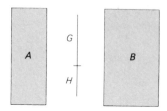

Let A and B be now combined into one solid and immersed. Then, since $(A+B)$ will be the same weight as the same volume of fluid, both weights being equal to $(G+H) + G$, it follows that $(A+B)$ will remain stationary in the fluid.

Therefore the force which causes A by itself to sink must be equal to the upward force exerted by the fluid on B by itself. This latter is equal to the difference between $(G+H)$ and G [Prop. 6]. Hence A is depressed by a force equal to H, i.e. its weight in the fluid is H, or the difference between $(G+H)$ and G.

CONFLICTING SCIENTIFIC INTERPRETATIONS

Archimedes' derivation of the Law of Buoyancy turns upon the insight that the laws of the lever can be applied to what seems a totally different area. This ability to *extend* a theory through seeing such connections is characteristic of scientific progress. Another type of scientific development is more radical—knowledge is not simply extended, but, instead, one scientific framework is replaced (or largely replaced) by another. In biology, the Germ Theory of Disease and the Theory of Evolution Through Natural Selection are examples of such revolutionary developments. Einstein's Theory of Relativity and the rise of Quantum Mechanics are also revolutionary developments. Indeed, every branch of science has undergone at least one such revolutionary change during the past few centuries.

There are some important differences between scientific progress within a framework and the replacement of one framework by another.[1] In the first place, such changes in framework usually meet with strong resistance. A new conceptual framework will be unfamiliar and hard to understand, and may even seem absurd or unintelligible. Even today, for example, the thought that the earth is spinning on its axis and revolving around the sun seems completely counter to our com-

---

[1] Thomas Kuhn gives prominence to this difference in his important work, *The Structure of Scientific Revolutions*, 2nd ed. (Chicago: University of Chicago Press, 1970).

mon-sense view of the world. Also, arguments on behalf of a new framework will be very different from arguments that occur *within* a framework. Disputes over conceptual frameworks cannot be settled by a straightforward appeal to facts. The long debate between Albert Einstein and Niels Bohr concerning Quantum Theory did not turn upon matters of fact, but upon their interpretation. Einstein could not accept the indeterminacy involved in the Quantum Theory's interpretation of the world, and he worked until the end of his life to find some alternative to it. At present, almost no scientist shares Einstein's reservations.

The selection given below illustrates a clash between two such scientific frameworks. It is taken from Galileo's *Dialogue Concerning the Two World Systems—Ptolemaic and Copernican*. The interlocutors are Salviati, Sagredo, and Simplicio. Salviati represents the Copernican system; Simplicio, the Ptolemaic system; Sagredo acts as a moderator, forcing the other two participants in the dialogue to clarify and defend their positions. In attacking the Copernican system, Simplicio lists various arguments from Aristotle that are supposed to show that the earth does not move. Some of these arguments are taken, he says:

> from experiments with heavy bodies which, falling from a height, go perpendicularly to the surface of the earth. Similarly, projectiles thrown vertically upward come down again perpendicularly by the same line, even though they have been thrown to immense height. These arguments are necessary proofs that their motion is toward the center of the earth, which, without moving in the least, awaits and receives them.[2]

Salviati replies that these phenomena do not show that the Ptolemaic system is correct and the Copernican system incorrect, since they can be explained in either world system. More generally, Salviati argues that no terrestrial phenomenon—that is, no phenomenon observable on the earth—can be cited to show that one of these systems is true and the other false. For that matter, no celestial phenomena will settle this issue either, since both world systems provide interpretations of the motions of heavenly bodies. That proponents of each of these systems can agree on particular facts yet disagree profoundly on their correct interpretation shows that we are dealing with a conflict between general frameworks, or general world systems. Arguments of this kind are very different from those that take place within a given scientific framework. This is evident at once if we compare Salviati's reply to Simplicio with Archimedes' derivation of the Law of Buoyancy.

---

[2] Galileo Galilei, *Dialogue Concerning the Two World Systems—Ptolemaic and Copernican*, Stillman Drake, trans. (Berkeley: University of California Press, 1953), p. 125.

Dialogue Concerning the Two World Systems— Ptolemaic and Copernican*

GALILEO GALILEI

SALVIATI: Aristotle says, then, that a most certain proof of the earth's being motionless is that things projected perpendicularly upward are seen to return by the same line to the same place from which they were thrown, even though the movement is extremely high. This, he argues, could not happen if the earth moved, since in the time during which the projectile is moving upward and then downward it is separated from the earth, and the place from which the projectile began its motion would go a long way toward the east, thanks to the revolving of the earth, and the falling projectile would strike the earth that distance away from the place in question. Thus we can accommodate here the argument of the cannon ball as well as the other argument, used by Aristotle and Ptolemy, of seeing heavy bodies falling from great heights along a straight line perpendicular to the surface of the earth. Now, in order to begin to untie these knots, I ask Simplicio by what means he would prove that freely falling bodies go along straight and perpendicular lines directed toward the center, should anyone refuse to grant this to Aristotle and Ptolemy.

SIMPLICIO: By means of the senses, which assure us that the tower is straight and perpendicular, and which show us that a falling stone goes along grazing it, without deviating a hairsbreadth to one side or the other, and strikes at the foot of the tower exactly under the place from which it was dropped.

SALV: But if it happened that the earth rotated, and consequently carried along the tower, and if the falling stone were seen to graze the side of the tower just the same, what would its motion then have to be?

SIMP: In that case one would have to say "its motions," for there would be one with which it went from top to bottom, and another one needed for following the path of the tower.

SALV: The motion would then be a compound of two motions; the one with which it measures the tower, and the other with which it follows it. From this compounding it would follow that the rock would no longer describe that simple straight perpendicular line, but a slanting one, and perhaps not straight.

SIMP: I don't know about its not being straight, but I understand well enough that it would have to be slanting, and different from the straight perpendicular line it would describe with the earth motionless.

---

*Galileo Galilei, *Dialogue Concerning the Two World Systems—Ptolemaic and Copernican*, Stillman Drake, trans. (Berkeley: University of California Press, 1953), pp. 139–49.

SALV: Hence just from seeing the falling stone graze the tower, you could not say for sure that it described a straight and perpendicular line, unless you first assumed the earth to stand still.

SIMP: Exactly so; for if the earth were moving, the motion of the stone would be slanting and not perpendicular.

SALV: Then here, clear and evident, is the paralogism of Aristotle and of Ptolemy, discovered by you yourself. They take as known that which is intended to be proved.

SIMP: In what way? It looks to me like a syllogism in proper form, and not a *petitio principii.*

SALV: In this way: Does he not, in his proof, take the conclusion as unknown?

SIMP: Unknown, for otherwise it would be superfluous to prove it.

SALV: And the middle term; does he not require that to be known?

SIMP: Of course; [otherwise it would be an attempt to prove *ignotum per aeque ignotum.*]

SALV: Our conclusion, which is unknown and is to be proved; is this not the motionlessness of the earth?

SIMP: That is what it is.

SALV: Is not the middle term, which must be known, the straight and perpendicular fall of the stone?

SIMP: That is the middle term.

SALV: But wasn't it concluded a little while ago that we could not have any knowledge of this fall being straight and perpendicular unless it was first known that the earth stood still? Therefore in your syllogism, the certainty of the middle term is drawn from the uncertainty of the conclusion. Thus you see how, and how badly, it is a paralogism.

SAGREDO: On behalf of Simplicio I should like, if possible, to defend Aristotle, or at least to be better persuaded as to the force of your deduction. You say that seeing the stone graze the tower is not enough to assure us that the motion of the rock is perpendicular (and this is the middle term of the syllogism) unless one assumes the earth to stand still (which is the conclusion to be proved). For if the tower moved along with the earth and the rock grazed it, the motion of the rock would be slanting, and not perpendicular. But I reply that if the tower were moving, it would be impossible for the rock to fall grazing it; therefore, from the scraping fall is inferred the stability of the earth.

SIMP: So it is. For to expect the rock to go grazing the tower if that were carried along by the earth would be requiring the rock to have two natural motions; that is, a straight one toward the center, and a circular one about the center, which is impossible.

SALV: So Aristotle's defense consists in its being impossible, or at least in his having considered it impossible, that the rock might move with a motion mixed of straight and circular. For if he had not held it to be impossible that the stone might move both toward and around the center at the same time, he would have understood how it could happen that the falling rock might go grazing the tower whether that was moving or was standing still, and consequently he would have been able to perceive that this grazing could imply nothing as to the motion or rest of the earth.

Nevertheless this does not excuse Aristotle, not only because if he did have this idea he ought to have said so, it being such an important point in the argument, but also, and more so, because it cannot be said either that such an effect is impossible or that Aristotle considered it impossible. The former cannot be said because, as I shall shortly prove to you, this is not only possible but necessary; and the latter cannot be said either, because Aristotle himself admits that fire moves naturally upward in a straight line and also turns in the diurnal motion which is imparted by the sky to all the element of fire and to the greater part of the air. Therefore if he saw no impossibility in the mixing of straight-upward with circular motion, as communicated to fire and to the air up as far as the moon's orbit, no more should he deem this impossible with regard to the rock's straight-downward motion and the circular motion natural to the entire globe of the earth, of which the rock is a part.

SIMP: It does not look that way to me at all. If the element of fire goes around together with the air, this is a very easy and even a necessary thing for a particle of fire, which, rising high from the earth, receives that very motion in passing through the moving air, being so tenuous and light a body and so easily moved. But it is quite incredible that a very heavy rock or a cannon ball which is dropped without restraint should let itself be budged by the air or by anything else. Besides which, there is the very appropriate experiment of the stone dropped from the top of the mast of a ship, which falls to the foot of the mast when the ship is standing still, but falls as far from that same point when the ship is sailing as the ship is perceived to have advanced during the time of the fall, this being several yards when the ship's course is rapid. . . .

SALV: Tell me, Simplicio: Do you feel convinced that the experiment on the ship squares so well with our purpose that one may reasonably believe that whatever is seen to occur there must also take place on the terrestrial globe?

SIMP: So far, yes; . . .

SALV: Rather, I hope that you will stick to it, and firmly insist that the result on the earth must correspond to that on the ship, so that when the latter is perceived to be prejudicial to your case you will not be tempted to change your mind.

You say, then, that since when the ship stands still the rock falls to the foot of the mast, and when the ship is in motion it falls apart from there, then conversely, from the falling of the rock at the foot it is inferred that the ship stands still, and from its falling away it may be deduced that the ship is moving. And since what happens on the ship must likewise happen on the land, from the falling of the rock at the foot of the tower one necessarily infers the immobility of the terrestrial globe. Is that your argument?

SIMP: That is exactly it, briefly stated, which makes it easy to understand.

SALV: Now tell me: If the stone dropped from the top of the mast when the ship was sailing rapidly fell in exactly the same place on the ship to which it fell when the ship was standing still, what use could you make of this falling with regard to determining whether the vessel stood still or moved?

SIMP: Absolutely none; just as by the beating of the pulse, for instance, you cannot know whether a person is asleep or awake, since the pulse beats in the same manner in sleeping as in waking.

SALV: Very good. Now, have you ever made this experiment of the ship?

SIMP: I have never made it, but I certainly believe that the authorities who adduced it had carefully observed it. Besides, the cause of the difference is so exactly known that there is no room for doubt.

SALV: You yourself are sufficient evidence that those authorities may have offered it without having performed it, for you take it as certain without having done it, and commit yourself to the good faith of their dictum. Similarly it not only may be, but must be that they did the same thing too—I mean, put faith in their predecessors, right on back without ever arriving at anyone who had performed it. For anyone who does will find that the experiment shows exactly the opposite of what is written; that is, it will show that the stone always falls in the same place on the ship; whether the ship is standing still or moving with any speed you please. Therefore, the same cause holding good on the earth as on the ship, nothing can be inferred about the earth's motion or rest from the stone falling always perpendicularly to the foot of the tower.

SIMP: If you had referred me to any other agency than experiment, I think that our dispute would not soon come to an end; for this appears to me to be a thing so remote from human reason that there is no place in it for credulity or probability.

SALV: For me there is, just the same.

SIMP: So you have not made a hundred tests, or even one? And yet you so freely declare it to be certain? I shall retain my incredulity, and my own confidence that the experiment has been made by the most important authors who make use of it, and that it shows what they say it does.

SALV: Without experiment, I am sure that the effect will happen as I tell you, because it must happen that way; and I might add that you yourself also know that it cannot happen otherwise, no matter how you may pretend not to know it—or give that impression. But I am so handy at picking people's brains that I shall make you confess this in spite of yourself. . . .

Now tell me: Suppose you have a plane surface as smooth as a mirror and made of some hard material like steel. This is not parallel to the horizon, but somewhat inclined, and upon it you have placed a ball which is perfectly spherical and of some hard and heavy material like bronze. What do you believe this will do when released? Do you think, as I do, that it will remain still?

SIMP: If that surface is tilted?

SALV: Yes, that is what was assumed.

SIMP: I do not believe that it would stay still at all; rather, I am sure that it would spontaneously roll down. . . .

SALV: Now how long would the ball continue to roll, and how fast? Remember that I said a perfectly round ball and a highly polished surface, in order to remove all external and accidental impediments. Similarly I want you to take away any impediment of the air caused by its resistance to separation, and all other accidental obstacles, if there are any.

SIMP: I completely understood you, and to your question I reply that the ball would continue to move indefinitely, as far as the slope of the surface extended, and with a continually accelerated motion. For such is the nature of heavy bodies, which *vires acquirunt eundo*; and the greater the slope, the greater would be the velocity.

SALV: But if one wanted the ball to move upward on this same surface, do you think it would go?

SIMP: Not spontaneously, no; but drawn or thrown forcibly, it would.

SALV: And if it were thrust along with some impetus impressed forcibly upon it, what would its motion be, and how great?

SIMP: The motion would constantly slow down and be retarded, being contrary to nature, and would be of longer or shorter duration according to the greater or lesser impulse and the lesser or greater slope upward.

SALV: Very well; up to this point you have explained to me the events of motion upon two different planes. On the downward inclined plane, the heavy moving body spontaneously descends and continually accelerates, and to keep it at rest requires the use of force. On the upward slope, force is needed to thrust it along or even to hold it still, and motion which is impressed upon it continually diminishes until it is entirely annihilated. You say also that a difference in the two instances arises from the greater or lesser upward or downward slope of the plane, so that from a greater slope downward there follows a greater speed, while on the contrary upon the upward slope a given movable body thrown with a given force moves farther according as the slope is less.

Now tell me what would happen to the same movable body placed upon a surface with no slope upward or downward.

SIMP: Here I must think a moment about my reply. There being no downward slope, there can be no natural tendency toward motion; and there being no upward slope, there can be no resistance to being moved, so there would be an indifference between the propensity and the resistance to motion. Therefore it seems to me that it ought naturally to remain stable. But I forgot; it was not so very long ago that Sagredo gave me to understand that this is what would happen.

SALV: I believe it would do so if one set the ball down firmly. But what would happen if it were given an impetus in any direction?

SIMP: It must follow that it would move in that direction.

SALV: But with what sort of movement? One continually accelerated, as on the downward plane, or increasingly retarded as on the upward one?

SIMP: I cannot see any cause for acceleration or deceleration, there being no slope upward or downward.

SALV: Exactly so. But if there is no cause for the ball's retardation, there ought to be still less for its coming to rest; so how far would you have the ball continue to move?

SIMP: As far as the extension of the surface continued without rising or falling.

SALV: Then if such a space were unbounded, the motion on it would likewise be boundless? That is, perpetual?

SIMP: It seems so to me, if the movable body were of durable material.

SALV: That is of course assumed, since we said that all external and accidental impediments were to be removed, and any fragility on the part of the moving body would in this case be one of the accidental impediments.

Now tell me, what do you consider to be the cause of the ball moving spontaneously on the downward inclined plane, but only by force on the one tilted upward?

SIMP: That the tendency of heavy bodies is to move toward the center of the earth, and to move upward from its circumference only with force; now the downward surface is that which gets closer to the center, while the upward one gets farther away.

SALV: Then in order for a surface to be neither downward nor upward, all its parts must be equally distant from the center. Are there any such surfaces in the world?

SIMP: Plenty of them; such would be the surface of our terrestrial globe if it were smooth, and not rough and mountainous as it is. But there is that of the water, when it is placid and tranquil.

SALV: Then a ship, when it moves over a calm sea, is one of these movables which courses over a surface that is tilted neither up nor down, and if all external and accidental obstacles were removed, it would thus be disposed to move incessantly and uniformly from an impulse once received?

SIMP: It seems that it ought to be.

SALV: Now as to that stone which is on top of the mast; does it not move, carried by the ship, both of them going along the circumference of a circle about its center? And consequently is there not in it an ineradicable motion, all external impediments being removed? And is not this motion as fast as that of the ship?

SIMP: All this is true, but what next?

SALV: Go on and draw the final consequence by yourself, if by yourself you have known all the premises.

SIMP: By the final conclusion you mean that the stone, moving with an indelibly impressed motion, is not going to leave the ship, but will follow it, and finally will fall at the same place where it fell when the ship remained motionless. And I, too, say that this would follow if there were no external impediments to disturb the motion of the stone after it was set free. But there are two such impediments; one is the inability of the movable body to split the air with its own impetus alone, once it has lost the force from the oars which it shared as part of the ship while it was on the mast; the other is the new motion of falling downward, which must impede its other, forward, motion.

SALV: As for the impediment of the air, I do not deny that to you, and if the falling body were of very light material, like a feather or a tuft of wool, the retardation would be quite considerable. But in a heavy stone it is insignificant, and if, as you yourself just said a little while ago, the force of the wildest wind is not enough to move a large stone from its place, just imagine how much the quiet air could accomplish upon meeting a rock which moved no faster than the ship! All the same, as I said, I concede to you the small effect which may depend upon such an impediment, just as I know you will concede to me that if the air were moving at the same speed as the ship and the rock, this impediment would be absolutely nil.

As for the other, the supervening motion downward, in the first place it is obvious that these two motions (I mean the circular around the center and the straight motion toward the center) are not contraries, nor are they destructive of one another, nor incompatible. As to the moving body, it has no resistance whatever to such a motion, for you yourself have already granted the resistance to be against motion which increases the distance from the center, and the tendency to be toward motion which approaches the center. From this it follows necessarily that the moving body has neither a resistance nor a propensity to motion which does not approach toward or depart from the center, and in consequence no cause for diminution in the property impressed upon it. Hence the cause of motion is not a single one which must be weakened by the new action, but there exist two distinct causes. Of these, heaviness attends only to the drawing of the movable body toward the center, and impressed force only to its being led around the center, so no occasion remains for any impediment.

EVOLUTION-SCIENCE VERSUS CREATION-SCIENCE

Debates in the philosophy of science rarely gain public attention, but recent controversies stirred by the demand for *balanced treatment* for creation-science and evolution-science in school science curricula has changed this. Discussions of the nature of science have not only caught the public's attention, they have found their way into our courtrooms. What follows is an attempt at a balanced treatment of those who think that creation-science is a science and those who think it is not.

Background: In 1981, the State of Arkansas adopted legislation mandating a "balanced treatment for Creation-Science and Evolution-Science." The first section of this act (called Act 590 of 1981) reads as follows:

> *Requirement for Balanced Treatment.* Public Schools within this State shall give balanced treatment to creation-science and to evolution-science. Balanced treatment to these two models shall be given in classroom lectures taken as a whole for each course, in textbook materials taken as a whole for each course, in library materials taken as a whole for the sciences and taken as a whole for the humanities, and in other educational programs in public schools, to the extent that such lectures, textbooks, library materials, or educational programs deal in any way with the subject of the origin of man, life, the earth, or the universe.

In response to this legislation, twenty-three individuals and organizations (representing religious, scientific, and educational interests) brought suit, claiming that this bill was unconstitutional on the grounds that that it violated First Amendment doctrine of the separation of church and state. Early in 1982 the U.S. District Court (in *McLean* v. *Arkansas*) ruled that the plaintiffs were correct in holding that the Act 590 violated the First Amendment. It was therefore struck down as unconstitutional.

McLean v. *Arkansas* could have been argued on a number of grounds. One possible position is that explicit religious instruction does not violate the Constitution's doctrine of the separation of church and state. Those defending the Arkansas bill did not, however, adopt this approach, but instead argued that creation-science is a genuine *scientific* alternative to the theory of evolution through natural selection. As such, it can be presented and evaluated in the same manner that any scientific theory is presented and evaluated. Thus defenders of instruction in creation-science deny that teaching this subject matter amounts to introducing religious instruction into public education. The opponents of teaching creation-science in public schools argue that creation-science is not a science, and therefore has no place in a science curriculum. (They further argue that it has no place in any other part of a public school curriculum, because its purposes are clearly religious and thus violate the First Amendment's principle of separation of church and state.) The issue, then, is sharply drawn.

More specifically, proponents of a balanced treatment for creation-science have maintained that creation-science and evolution-science provide alternative *models* for the explanation of the origin of the world and its life. The creation-science model, they argue, is no less scientific than the evolution-science model. Henry M. Morris, Ph.D., has been a forceful defender of the view that creationism should be taught as a *scientific* alternative to Darwin's theory of evolution. The following excerpts from his writings defend the scientific legitimacy of creation-science.

Scientific Creationism*

HENRY M. MORRIS

IMPOSSIBILITY OF SCIENTIFIC PROOF OF ORIGINS

It must . . . be emphasized that it is impossible to *prove* scientifically any particular concept of origins to be true. This is obvious from the fact that the essence of the scientific method is experimental observation and repeatability. A scientific investigator, be he ever so resourceful and brilliant, can neither observe nor repeat *origins!*

This means that, though it is important to have a philosophy of origins, it can only be achieved by faith, not by sight. That is no argument against it, however. Every step we take in life is a step of faith. Even the pragmatist who insists he will only believe what he can see, *believes* that his pragmatism is the best philosophy, though he can't prove it! He also believes in invisible atoms and in such abstractions as the future.

As a matter of observation, belief in something is necessary for true mental health. A philosophy of life is a philosophy, not a scientific experiment. A life based on the whim of the moment, with no rationale, is "a tale told by an idiot, full of sound and fury, signifying nothing."

Thus, one must *believe*, at least with respect to ultimate origins. However, for optimally beneficial application of that belief, his faith should be a reasoned faith, not a credulous faith or a prescribed faith.

To illustrate more exactly what we mean when we say origins cannot be proved, a brief discussion is given below on each of the two basic concepts of origins, creation and evolution:

A. *Creation cannot be proved*
   1. Creation is not taking place now, so far as can be observed. Therefore, it was accomplished sometime in the past, if at all, and thus is inaccessible to the scientific method.
   2. It is impossible to devise a scientific experiment to describe the creation process, or even to ascertain whether such a process *can* take place. The Creator does not create at the whim of a scientist.

*From Henry M. Morris, *Scientific Creationism* (San Diego: Creation-Life Publishers, 1974), pp. 5–13.

B. *Evolution cannot be proved*
   1. If evolution is taking place today, it operates too slowly to be measurable, and, therefore, is outside the realm of empirical science. To transmute one kind of organism into a higher kind of organism would presumably take millions of years, and no team of scientific observers is available to make measurements on any such experiment.
   2. The small variations in organisms which are observed to take place today . . . are irrelevant to this question, since there is no way to prove that these changes within present kinds eventually change the kinds into different, higher kinds. Since small variations (including mutations) are as much to be expected in the creation model as in the evolution model, they are of no value in discriminating between the two models.
   3. Even if modern scientists should ever actually achieve the artificial creation of life from non-life, or of higher kinds from lower kinds, in the laboratory, this would not *prove* in any way that such changes did, or even could, take place in the past by random natural processes.

Since it is often maintained by evolutionists that evolution is scientific, whereas creationism is religious, it will be well at this point to cite several leading evolutionists who have recognized that evolution also is incapable of being proved.[1]

Evolution operates too slowly for scientific observation

One of the nation's leading evolutionists, Theodosius Dobzhansky, has admitted:

> "The applicability of the experimental method to the study of such unique historical processes is severely restricted before all else by the time intervals involved, which far exceed the lifetime of any human experimenter. And yet, it is just such impossibility that is demanded by anti-evolutionists when they ask for 'proofs' of evolution which they would magnanimously accept as satisfactory."[2]

Note the tacit admission that "the experimental method" is an "impossibility" when applied to evolution.

---

[1] It is interesting and encouraging to note that, in the Foreword to the most recent edition of Darwin's *Origin of Species*, a leading British evolutionary biologist, Professor L. Harrison Matthews, F.R.S., recognizes that "Belief in evolution is thus exactly parallel to belief in special creation—both are concepts which believers know to be true but neither, up to the present, has been capable of proof." (London: J. M. Dent & Sons, Ltd., 1971), p. x.

[2] Theodosius Dobzhansky, "On Methods of Evolutionary Biology and Anthropology," *American Scientist*, Vol. 45 (December, 1957), p. 388.

Evolution is a dogma incapable of refutation

Two leading modern biologists have pointed out the fact that, since evolution cannot in any conceivable way be disproved, therefore, neither can it be proved.

> "Our theory of evolution has become . . . one which cannot be re-
> futed by any possible observations. It is thus 'outside of empirical
> science,' but not necessarily false. No one can think of ways in which
> to test it. . . . (Evolutionary ideas) have become part of an evolu-
> tionary dogma accepted by most of us as part of our training."[3]

Similarly, Peter Medawar recognized the problem entailed by the fact that no way exists by which to test evolution.

> "There are philosophical or methodological objections to evolution-
> ary theory. . . . It is too difficult to imagine or envisage an evolu-
> tionary episode which could not be explained by the formulae of
> neo-Darwinism."[4]

In other words, both the long neck of the giraffe and the short neck of the hippopotamus can presumably be explained by natural selection. A theory which incorporates everything really *explains* nothing! It is tautologous. Those who survive in the struggle for existence are the fittest because the fittest are the ones who survive.

Evolution is an authoritarian system to be believed

> "It seems at times as if many of our modern writers on evolution
> have had their views by some sort of revelation and they base their
> opinions on the evolution of life, from the simplest form to the
> complex, entirely on the nature of specific and intra-specific evo-
> lution. . . . It is premature, not to say arrogant, on our part if we
> make any dogmatic assertion as to the mode of evolution of the ma-
> jor branches of the animal kingdom."[5]
> "But the facts of paleontology conform equally well with other
> interpretations. . . . e.g., divine creation, etc., and paleontology by
> itself can neither prove nor refute such ideas."[6]

---

[3] Paul Ehrlich and L. C. Birch, "Evolutionary History and Population Biology," *Nature*, Vol. 214 (1967), p. 352.

[4] Peter Medawar, *Mathematical Challenges to the Neo-Darwinism Interpretation of Evolution*, (Philadelphia: Wistar Institute Press, 1967), p. xi.

[5] G. A. Kerkut, *Implications of Evolution*, (London: Pergamon, 1965), p. 155.

[6] D. Dwight Davis, "Comparative Anatomy and the Evolution of Vertebrates," in *Genetics, Paleontology and Evolution*, (ed. by Jepsen, Mayr and Simpson, Princeton University Press, 1949), p. 74.

Thomas Huxley, probably more responsible than any other one man for the acceptance of Darwinian philosophy, nevertheless recognized that:

> ". . . 'creation' in the ordinary sense of the word, is perfectly conceivable. I find no difficulty in conceiving that, at some former period, this universe was not in existence; and that it made its appearance in six days . . . in consequence of the volition of some pre-existing Being."[7]

The reason for favoring evolution is not because of the scientific evidence

An outstanding British biologist of a number of years ago made the following remarkable observation:

> "If so, it will present a parallel to the theory of evolution itself, a theory universally accepted not because it can be proved by logically coherent evidence to be true but because the only alternative, special creation, is clearly incredible."[8]

The only reason for saying that special creation is incredible would be if one had certain knowledge that there was no God. Obviously, if no Creator exists, then special creation is incredible. But since a universal negative can only be proved if one has universal knowledge, such a statement requires omniscience. Thus, by denying God, Dr. Watson is claiming the attributes of God himself.

There are some scientists, at least, who find it easier to believe in the deity of an omnipotent Creator than in the deity of Professor Watson.

THE TWO MODELS OF ORIGINS

It is, as shown in the previous section, impossible to demonstrate scientifically which of the two concepts of origins is really true. Although many people teach evolution as though it were a proven fact of science, it is obvious that this is false teaching. There are literally thousands of scientists[9] and other educated intellectuals today who reject evolution, and this would certainly not be the case if evolution were as obvious as many scientists say it is.

The same is true of creation, of course. Although many believe special creation to be an absolute fact of history, they must believe this for theological,

---

[7] Leonard Huxley, *Life and Letters of Thomas Henry Huxley*, (London: Macmillan, Vol. II, 1903), p. 429.
[8] D. M. S. Watson, "Adaptation," *Nature*, Vol. 123 (1929), p. 233.
[9] The Creation Research Society, for example, numbers over 700 M.S. and Ph.D. scientists on its rolls.

rather than scientific reasons. Neither evolution nor creation can be either con-firmed or falsified scientifically.[10]

Furthermore, it is clear that neither evolution nor creation is, in the proper sense, either a scientific theory or a scientific hypothesis. Though people might speak of the "theory of evolution" or of the "theory of creation," such termi-nology is imprecise. This is because neither can be *tested*. A valid scientific hy-pothesis must be capable of being formulated experimentally, such that the experimental results either confirm or reject its validity.

As noted in the statement by Ehrlich and Birch cited previously, how-ever, there is no conceivable way to do this. Ideally, we might like to set up an experiment, the results of which would demonstrate either evolution or crea-tion to have been true. But there is no one test, nor any series of tests, which can do this scientifically.

All of these strictures do not mean, however, that we cannot discuss this question scientifically and objectively. Indeed, it is extremely important that we do so, if we are really to understand this vital question of origins and to arrive at a satisfactory basis for the faith we must ultimately exercise in one or the other.

A more proper approach is to think in terms of two scientific models, the *evolution model* and the *creation model*. A "model" is a conceptual framework, an orderly system of thought, within which one tries to correlate observable data, and even to predict data. When alternative models exist, they can be compared as to their respective capacities for correlating such data. When, as in this case, neither can be proved, the decision between the two cannot be solely objective. Normally, in such a case, the model which correlates the greater number of data, with the smallest number of unresolved contradictory data, would be ac-cepted as the more probably correct model.

When particular facts do show up which seem to contradict the predic-tions of the model, it may still be possible to assimilate the data by a slight mod-ification of the original model. As a matter of fact, in the case of the evolution model, as Ehrlich and Birch said: "Every conceivable observation can be fitted into it."

The same generalization, of course, is true of the creation model. There is no observational fact imaginable which cannot, one way or another, be made to fit the creation model. The only way to decide objectively between them, therefore, is to note which model fits the facts and predictions with the smallest number of these secondary assumptions.

Creationists are convinced that, when this procedure is carefully fol-lowed, the creation model will always fit the facts as well as or better than will

---

[10] Dr. N. Heribert-Nilsson, Director of the Botanical Institute at Lund University, Swe-den, said "My attempt to demonstrate evolution by an experiment carried on for more than 40 years has completely failed. . . . The idea of an evolution rests on pure belief." (*Synthetische Artbildung*, 1953).

the evolution model. Evolutionists may, of course, believe otherwise. In either case, it is important that everyone have the facts at hand with which to consider *both* models, rather than one only. The latter is brainwashing, not brain-using! . . .

A. *THE EVOLUTION MODEL*

The evolutionary system attempts to explain the origin, development, and meaning of all things in terms of natural laws and processes which operate today as they have in the past. No extraneous processes, requiring the special activity of an external agent, or Creator, are permitted. The universe, in all its aspects, evolves itself into higher levels of order (particles to people) by means of its innate properties.

To confirm that this is the essential nature of the evolution model, several recognized authorities are cited below, giving their own concepts of evolution.

> "Most enlightened persons now accept as a fact that everything in the cosmos—from heavenly bodies to human beings—has developed and continues to develop through evolutionary processes."[11]

> "Evolution comprises all the stages of the development of the universe: the cosmic, biological, and human or cultural developments. . . . Life is a product of the evolution of inorganic nature, and man is a product of the evolution of life."[12]

> "Evolution in the extended sense can be defined as a directional and essentially irreversible process occurring in time, which in its course gives rise to an increase of variety and an increasingly high level of organization in its products. Our present knowledge indeed forces us to the view that the whole of reality is evolution—a single process of self-transformation."[13]

> "Biological evolution can, however, be explained without recourse to a Creator or a planning agent external to the organisms themselves. There is no evidence, either, of any vital force or immanent energy directing the evolutionary process toward the production of specified kinds of organisms."[14]

---

[11] Rene Dubos, "Humanistic Biology," *American Scientist*, Vol. 53 (March 1965), p. 6.
[12] Theodosius Dobzhansky, "Changing Man," *Science*, Vol. 155 (January 27, 1967), p. 409.
[13] Julian Huxley, "Evolution and Genetics," Chap. 8 in *What Is Science?* Ed. J. R. Newman, (New York: Simon & Schuster, 1955), p. 272.
[14] Francisco J. Ayala, "Biology as an Autonomous Science," *American Scientist*, Vol. 56 (Autumn 1968), p. 213.

Thus evolution entails a self-contained universe, in which its innate laws develop everything into higher levels of organization. Particles evolve into elements, elements into complex chemicals, complex chemicals into simple living systems, simple life forms into complex life, complex animal life into man.

Summarizing, evolution is: (1) naturalistic; (2) self-contained; (3) non-purposive; (4) directional; (5) irreversiable; (6) universal; and, (7) continuing.

B. THE CREATION MODEL

Diametrically opposed to the evolution model, the creation model involves a process of special creation which is: (1) supernaturalistic; (2) externally directed; (3) purposive, and (4) completed. Like evolution, the creation model also applies universally. It also is irreversibly directional, but its direction is downward toward lower levels of complexity rather than upward toward higher levels. The completed original creation was perfect and has since been "running down."

The creation model thus postulates a period of special creation in the beginning, during which all the basic laws and categories of nature, including the major kinds of plants and animals, as well as man, were brought into existence by special creative and integrative processes which are no longer in operation. Once the creation was finished, these processes of *creation* were replaced by processes of *conservation*, which were designed by the Creator to sustain and maintain the basic systems He had created.

In addition to the primary concept of a completed creation followed by conservation, the creation model proposes a basic principle of disintegration now at work in nature (since any significant change in a *perfect* primeval creation must be in the direction of imperfection). Also, the evidence in the earth's crust of past physical convulsions seems to warrant inclusion of post-creation global catastrophism in the model.

The two models may be easily compared by studying the table below:

Evolution Model	Creation Model
Continuing naturalistic origin	Completed supernatural origin
Net present increase in complexity	Net present decrease in complexity

The questions of the *date* of creation (old or young) and the nature of cosmic processes *since* creation (dominantly naturalistic and uniform or catastrophic) are separate issues.

It is proposed that these two models be used as systems for "predicting" data, to see which one does so more effectively. To do this, one should imagine that neither the evolutionist nor the creationist knows in advance what data will be found. They do not know what they will find but bravely make predictions, each on the basis of his own model.

The following table indicates the predictions that would probably be made in several important categories.

BASIC PREDICTIONS

Category	Evolution Model	Creation Model
Galactic Universe	Galaxies Changing	Galaxies Constant
Structure of Stars	Stars Changing into Other Types	Stars Unchanged
Other Heavenly Bodies	Building Up	Breaking Down
Types of Rock Formations	Different in Different "Ages"	Similar in All "Ages"
Appearance of Life	Life Evolving from Non-Life	Life Only from Life
Array of Organisms	Continuum of Organisms	Distinct Kinds of Organisms
Appearance of Kinds of Life	New Kinds Appearing	No New Kinds Appearing
Mutations in Organisms	Beneficial	Harmful
Natural Selection	Creative Process	Conservative Process
Age of Earth	Extremely Old	Probably Young
Fossil Record	Innumerable Transitions	Systematic Gaps
Appearance of Man	Ape-Human Intermediates	No Ape-Human Intermediates
Nature of Man	Quantitatively Superior to Animals	Qualitatively Distinct From Animals
Origin of Civilization	Slow and Gradual	Contemporaneous with Man

It should be noted that the tabulated predictions are predictions of the *primary* models, as defined in their most general terms as in the foregoing discussion. These primary models may be modified by secondary assumptions to fit certain conditions. For example, the basic evolution model may be extended to include harmful, as well as beneficial, mutations, but this is not a natural prediction of the basic concept of evolution. If the "predictions" of evolution, as listed in the above table, were actually observed in the natural world, they would, of course, in every case be enthusiastically acclaimed as strong confirmations of the evolution model. That fact justifies the conclusion that these are the *basic* predictions of evolution.

The above predictions are merely suggestive of the types of entities that can be used to contrast the two models. . . . Creationists maintain that the predictions of the creation model do fit the observed facts in nature better than do those of the evolution model. The data must be *explained* by the evolutionist, but they are *predicted* by the creationist.

William R. Overton, the presiding judge in *McLean* v. *Arkansas*, did not accept the State's argument in behalf of a balanced treatment of evolution-science and creation-science. In part, he went beyond the literal wording of the Act and, looking at goals of those who sponsored the bill, declared that it "was simply and purely an effort to introduce the Biblical version of creation into the public school curricula." By itself, this is not much of an argument, for, if, as some creationists maintain, the Biblical account of creation can be established on scientific grounds, then it would be peculiar to exclude it from the science curriculum simply because it was also supported on religious grounds. In response to this, Judge Overton argued specifically that creation-science does not meet the criteria for being a science. His views are nicely summarized and explained in the following piece by Michael Ruse.

Creation-Science is Not Science*

MICHAEL RUSE

WHAT IS SCIENCE?

It is simply not possible to give a neat definition—specifying necessary and sufficient characteristics—which separates all and only those things that have ever been called "science." The concept "science" is not as easily definable as, for example, the concept "triangle." Science is a phenomenon that has developed through the ages—dragging itself apart from religion, philosophy, superstition, and other bodies of human opinion and belief.[1]

What we call "science" today is a reasonably striking and distinctive set of claims, which have a number of characteristic features. As with most things in life, some items fall on the borderline between science and nonscience (e.g., perhaps Freudian psychoanalytic theory). But it is possible to state positively that, for example, physics and chemistry are sciences, and Plato's Theory of forms and Swedenborgian theology are not.[2]

In looking for defining features, the obvious place to start is with science's most striking aspect—it is an empirical enterprise about the real world of sensation. This is not to say that science refers only to observable entities. Every mature science contains unobservables, like electrons and genes, but ultimately, these unobservables refer to the world around us. Science attempts to understand this empirical world. What is the basis for this understanding? Surveying science and the history of science today, one thing stands out: science involves a search for order. More specifically, science looks for unbroken, blind, natural regularities (*laws*). Things in the world do not happen in just any old way. They follow set paths, and science tries to capture this fact. Bodies of science, therefore, known variously as "theories" or "paradigms" or "sets of models," are collections of laws.[3]

Thus, in Newtonian physics we find Newton's three laws of motion, the law of gravitational attraction, Kepler's laws of planetary motion, and so forth.

*From Marcel Chotkowski La Follete, ed., *Creationism, Science, and the Law: The Arkansas Case* (Cambridge, Mass.: MIT Press, 1983), pp. 151–60.

Editor's Note: Notes for this selection appear immediately following (see pages 355–357).

Similarly, for instance, in population genetics we find the Hardy-Weinberg law. However, when we turn to something like philosophy, we do not find the same appeal to empirical law. Plato's Theory of Forms only indirectly refers to this world. Analogously, religion does not insist on unbroken law. Indeed, religious beliefs frequently allow or suppose events outside law or else events that violate law (miracles). Jesus feeding the 5,000 with the loaves and fishes was one such event. This is not to say that religion is false, but it does say that religion is not science. When the loaves and fishes multiplied to a sufficiency to feed so many people, things happened that did not obey natural law, and hence the feeding of the 5,000 is an event beyond the ken of science.[4]

A major part of the scientific enterprise involves the use of law to effect *explanation.* One tries to show why things are as they are—and how they fall beneath or follow from law (together perhaps with certain specified initial conditions). Why, for example, does a cannon ball go in a parabola and not in a circle? Because of the constraints of Newton's laws. Why do two blue-eyed parents always have blue-eyed children? Because this trait obeys Mendel's first law, given the particular way in which the genes control eye-color. A scientific explanation must appeal to law and must show that what is being explained had to occur. The explanation excludes those things that did not happen.[5]

The other side of explanations is *prediction.* The laws indicate what is going to happen: that the ball will go in a parabola, that the child will be blue-eyed. In science, as well as in futurology, one can also, as it were, predict backwards. Using laws, one infers that a particular, hitherto-unknown phenomenon or event took place in the past. Thus, for instance, one might use the laws of physics to infer back to some eclipse of the sun reported in ancient writings.

Closely connected with the twin notions of explanation and prediction comes *testability.* A genuine scientific theory lays itself open to check against the real world: the scientist can see if the inferences made in explanation and prediction actually obtain in nature. Does the chemical reaction proceed as suspected? In Young's double slit experiment, does one find the bands of light and dark predicted by the wave theory? Do the continents show the expected aftereffects of drift?

Testability is a two-way process. The researcher looks for some positive evidence, for *confirmation.* No one will take seriously a scientific theory that has no empirical support (although obviously a younger theory is liable to be less well-supported than an older theory). Conversely, a theory must be open to possible refutation. If the facts speak against a theory, then it must go. A body of science must be *falsifiable.* For example, Kepler's laws could have been false: if a planet were discovered going in squares, then the laws would have been shown to be incorrect. However, no amount of empirical evidence can disprove, for example, the Kantian philosophical claim that one ought to treat people as ends rather than means. Similarly, Catholic religious claims about transubstantiation (the changing of the bread and wine into the body and blood of Christ) are unfalsifiable.[6]

Science is *tentative*. Ultimately, a scientist must be prepared to reject his theory. Unfortunately, not all scientists are prepared to do in practice what they promise to do in theory; but the weaknesses of individuals are counterbalanced by the fact that, as a group, scientists do give up theories that fail to answer to new or reconsidered evidence. In the last thirty years, for example, geologists have reversed their strong convictions that the continents never move.

Scientists do not, of course, immediately throw their theories away as soon as any counter-evidence arrives. If a theory is powerful and successful, then some problems will be tolerated, but scientists must be prepared to change their minds in the face of the empirical evidence. In this regard, the scientists differ from both the philosophers and the theologians. Nothing in the real world would make the Kantian change his mind, and the Catholic is equally dogmatic, despite any empirical evidence about the stability of bread and wine. Such evidence is simply considered irrelevant.[7]

Some other features of science should also be mentioned, for instance, the urge for simplicity and unification; however, I have now listed the major characteristics. Good science—like good philosophy and good religion—presupposes an attitude that one might describe as professional *integrity*. A scientist should not cheat or falsify data or quote out of context or do any other thing that is intellectually dishonest. Of course, as always, some individuals fail; but science as a whole disapproves of such actions. Indeed, when transgressors are detected, they are usually expelled from the community. Science depends on honesty in the realm of ideas. One may cheat on one's taxes; one may not fiddle the data.[8]

CREATION-SCIENCE CONSIDERED

How does creation-science fit the criteria of science listed in the previous section? By "creation-science" in this context, I refer not just to the definition given in Act 590, but to the whole body of literature which goes by that name. The doctrine includes the claims that the universe is very young (6,000 to 20,000 years), that everything started instantaneously, that human beings had ancestry separate from apes, and that a monstrous flood once engulfed the entire earth.[9]

Laws and natural regularities

Science is about unbroken, natural regularity. It does not admit miracles. It is clear, therefore, that again and again, creation-science invokes happenings and causes outside of law. For instance, the only reasonable inference from Act 590 (certainly the inference that was accepted in the Arkansas court) is that for creation-science the origin of the universe and life in it is not bound by law. Whereas the definition of creation-science includes the unqualified phrase "sudden creation of the universe, energy and life from nothing," the definition of evolution specifically includes the qualification that its view of origins is "naturalistic." Because "naturalistic" means "subject to empirical law," the deliberate omission of such a term in the characterization of creation-science means that no laws were involved.

In confirmation of this inference, we can find identical claims in the writings of creation scientists: for instance, the following passage from Duane T. Gish's popular work *Evolution? The Fossils Say No!*

> Creation. By creation we mean the bringing into being of the basic kinds of plants and animals by the process of sudden, or fiat, creation described in the first two chapters of Genesis. Here we find the creation by God of the plants and animals, each commanded to reproduce after its own kind using processes which were essentially instantaneous.
>
> We do not know how God created, what processes He used, . *for God used processes which are not now operating anywhere in the natural universe.* This is why we refer to divine creation as special creation. We cannot discover by scientific investigations anything about the creative processes used by God.[10]

By Gish's own admission, we are not dealing with science. Similar sentiments can be found in *The Genesis Flood* by John Whitcomb, Jr., and Henry M. Morris:

> But during the period of Creation, God was introducing order and organization and energization into the universe in a very high degree, even to life itself! *It is thus quite plain that the processes used by God in creation were utterly different from the processes which now operate in the universe!* The Creation was a unique period, entirely incommensurate with this present world. This is plainly emphasized and reemphasized in the divine revelation which God has given us concerning Creation, which concludes with these words: "And the heavens and the earth were *finished,* and *all* the host of them. And on the seventh day God *finished* His work which He had made; and He *rested* on the seventh day from *all His work* which He had made. And God blessed the seventh day, and hallowed it; because that in it He *rested* from *all* his work which God had created and made." In view of these strong and repeated assertions, is it not the height of presumption for man to attempt to study Creation in terms of present processes?[11]

Creation scientists generally acknowledge *The Genesis Flood* to be the seminal contribution that led to the growth of the creation-science movement. Morris, in particular, is the father figure of creation-science and Gish his chief lieutenant.

Creation scientists also break with law in many other instances. The creationists believe that the Flood, for example, could not have just occurred through blind regularities. As Whitcomb and Morris make very clear, certain supernatural interventions were necessary to bring about the Flood.[12] Similarly, in order to ensure the survival of at least some organisms, God had to busy himself and break through law.

Explanation and prediction

Given the crucial role that physical laws play for the scientist in these processes, neither explanation nor prediction is possible where no law exists. Thus, explanation and prediction simply cannot even be attempted when one deals with creation-science accounts either of origins or of the Flood.

Even against the broader vistas of biology, creation-science is inadequate. Scientific explanation/prediction must lead to the thing being explained/predicted, showing why that thing obtains and not other things. Why does the ball go in a parabola? Why does it not describe a circle? Take an important and pervasive biological phenomenon, namely, "homologies," the isomorphisms between the bones of different animals. These similarities were recognized as pervasive facets of nature even before Darwin published *The Origin of Species*. Why are the bones in the forelimbs of humans, horses, whales, and birds all so similar, even though the functions are quite different? Evolutionists explain homologies naturally and easily, as a result of common descent. Creationists can give no explanation, and make no predictions. All they can offer is the disingenuous comment that homology signifies nothing, because classification is all man-made and arbitrary anyway. Is it arbitrary that man is not classified with the birds?[13] Why are Darwin's finches distributed in the way that we find on the Galapagos? Why are there fourteen separate species of this little bird, scattered over a small group of islands in the Pacific on the equator? On those rare occasions when Darwin's finches do fly into the pages of creation-science, it is claimed either that they are all the same species (false), or that they are a case of degeneration from one "kind" created back at the beginning of life.[14] Apart from the fact that "kind" is a term of classification to be found only in Genesis, this is not explanation. How could such a division of the finches have occurred, given the short span that the creationists allow since the Creation? And, in any case, Darwin's finches are anything but degenerates. Different species of finch have entirely different sorts of beaks, adapted for different foodstuffs—evolution of the most sophisticated type.[15]

TESTABILITY, CONFIRMATION, AND FALSIFIABILITY

Testability, confirmation, and falsifiability are no better treated by creation-science. A scientific theory must provide more than just after-the-fact explanations of things that one already knows. One must push out into the frontiers of new knowledge, trying to predict new facts, and risking the theory against the discovery of possible falsifying information. One cannot simply work at a secondary level, constantly protecting one's views against threat: forever inventing ad hoc hypotheses to save one's core assumptions.

Creation scientists do little or nothing by way of genuine test. Indeed, the most striking thing about the whole body of creation-science literature is the virtual absence of *any* experimental or observational work by creation scientists. Almost invariably, the creationists work exclusively with the discoveries and claims of evolutionists, twisting the conclusions to their own ends. Argument proceeds by showing evolution (specifically Darwinism) wrong, rather than by showing Creationism right.

However, this way of proceeding—what the creationists refer to as the "two-model approach"—is simply a fallacious form of argument. The views of people like Fred Hoyle and N. C. Wickramasinghe, who believe that life comes from outer space, are neither creationist nor truly evolutionist.[16] Denying evolution in no way proves Creationism. And, even if a more straightforward either/or between evolution and Creationism existed, the perpetually negative approach is just not the way that science proceeds. One must find one's own evidence in favor of one's position, just as physicists, chemists, and biologists do.

Do creation scientists ever actually expose their theories and ideas to test? Even if they do, when new counter-empirical evidence is discovered, creation scientists appear to pull back, refusing to allow their position to be falsified.

Consider, for instance, the classic case of the "missing link"—namely, that between man and his ancestors. The creationists say that there are no plausible bridging organisms whatsoever. Thus, this super-gap between man and all other animals (alive or dead) supposedly underlines the creationists' contention that man and apes have separate ancestry. But what about the australopithecines, organisms that paleontologists have, for most of this century, claimed are plausible, human ancestors? With respect, argue the creationists, australopithecines are not links, because they had ape-like brains, they *walked* like apes, and they used their knuckles for support, just like gorillas. Hence, the gap remains.[17]

However, such a conclusion can be maintained only by blatant disregard of the empirical evidence. *Australopithecus afarensis* was a creature with a brain the size of that of an ape which walked upright.[18] Yet the creationists do not concede defeat. They then argue that the *Australopithecus afarensis* is like an orangutan.[19] In short, nothing apparently makes the creationists change their minds, or allow their views to be tested, lest they be falsified.

Tentativeness

Creation-science is not science because there is absolutely no way in which creationists will budge from their position. Indeed, the leading organization of creation-science, the Creation Research Society (with over five hundred full members, all of whom must have an advanced degree in a scientific/technological area), demands that its members sign a statement affirming that they take the Bible as literally true.[20] Unfortunately, an organization cannot require such a condition of membership, and then claim to be a scientific organization. Science must be open to change, however confident one may feel at present. Fanatical dogmatism is just not acceptable.

Integrity

Creation-scientists use any fallacy in the logic books to achieve their ends. Most particularly, apart from grossly distorting evolutionists' positions, the creation scientists frequently use inappropriate or incomplete quotations. They take the words of some eminent evolutionist, and attempt to make him or her say exactly the opposite to that intended. For instance, in *Creation: The Facts of Life,* author Gary E. Parker constantly refers to "noted Harvard geneticist" Richard Lewontin as claiming that the hand and the eye are the best evidence of God's design.[21] Can this reference really be true? Has the author of *The Genetic Basis of Evolutionary Change*[22] really foresworn Darwin for Moses? In fact, when one looks at Lewontin's writings, one finds that he says that *before Darwin*, people believed the hand and the eye to be the effect of direct design. Today, scientists believe that such features were produced by the natural process of evolution through natural selection, but a reader learns nothing of this from Parker's book.

CONCLUSION

What are the essential features of science? Does creation-science have any, all, or none of these features? My answer to this is none. By every mark of what constitutes science, creation-science fails. And, although it has not been my direct purpose to show its true nature, it is surely there for all to see. Miracles brought about by an intervening supervising force speak of only one thing. Creation "science" is actually dogmatic religious Fundamentalism. To regard it as otherwise is an insult to the scientist, as well as to the believer who sees creation-science as a blasphemous distortion of God-given reason. I believe that creation-science should not be taught in the public schools because creation-science is not science.

Notes and References

1. In my book, *The Darwinian Revolution: Science Red in Tooth and Claw* (Chicago: University of Chicago Press, 1979), I look at the way science was breaking apart from religion in the nineteenth century.

2. What follows is drawn from a number of basic books in the philosophy of science, including R. B. Braithwaite, *Scientific Explanation* (Cambridge, England: Cambridge University Press, 1953); Karl R. Popper, *The Logic of Scientific Discovery* (London: Hutchinson, 1959); E. Nagel, *The Structure of Science* (London: Routledge and Kegan Paul, 1961); Thomas S. Kuhn, *The Structure of Scientific Revolutions* (Chicago: University of Chicago Press, 1962); and C. G. Hempel, *The Philosophy of Natural Science* (Englewood

Cliffs, NJ: Prentice-Hall, 1966). The discussion is the same as what I provided for the plaintiffs in a number of position papers. It also formed the basis of my testimony in court, and, as can be seen from Judge Overton's ruling, was accepted by the court virtually verbatim.

3. One sometimes sees a distinction drawn between "theory" and "model." At the level of this discussion, it is not necessary to discuss specific details. I consider various uses of these terms in my book, *Darwinism Defended: A Guide to the Evolution Controversies* (Reading, MA: Addison-Wesley, 1982).

4. For more on science and miracles, especially with respect to evolutionary questions, see my *Darwinian Revolution, op. cit.*

5. The exact relationship between laws and what they explain has been a matter of much debate. Today, I think most would agree that the connection must be fairly tight—the thing being explained should follow. For more on explanation in biology, see Michael Ruse, *The Philosophy of Biology* (London: Hutchinson, 1973); and David L. Hull, *The Philosophy of Biological Science* (Englewood Cliffs, NJ: Prentice-Hall, 1974). A popular thesis is that explanation of laws involves deduction from other laws. A theory is a body of laws bound in this way: a so-called "hypothetico-deductive" system.

6. Falsifiability today has a high profile in the philosophical and scientific literature. Many scientists, especially, agree with Karl Popper, who has argued that falsifiability is *the* criterion demarcating science from non-science (see especially his *Logic of Scientific Discovery*). My position is that falsifiability is an important part, but only one part, of a spectrum of features required to demarcate science from non-science. For more on this point, see my *Is Science Sexist? And Other Problems in the Biomedical Sciences* (Dordrecht, Holland: Reidel, 1981).

7. At the Arkansas trial, in talking of the tentativeness of science, I drew an analogy in testimony between science and the law. In a criminal trial, one tries to establish guilt "beyond a reasonable doubt." If this can be done, then the criminal is convicted. But, if new evidence is ever discovered that might prove the convicted person innocent, cases can always be reopened. In science, too, scientists make decisions less formally but just as strongly—and get on with business, but cases (theories) can be reopened.

8. Of course, the scientist as citizen may run into problems here!

9. The key definitions in Arkansas Act 590, requiring "balanced treatment" in the public schools, are found in Section 4. Section 4(a)(b) does not specify exactly how old the earth is supposed to be, but in court a span of 6,000 to 20,000 years emerged in testimony.

   The fullest account of the creation-science position is given in Henry M. Morris, ed., *Scientific Creationism* (San Diego: Creation-Life Publishers, 1974).

10. Duane T. Gish, *Evolution? The Fossils Say No!* (San Diego: Creation-Life Publishers, 1973), pp. 22–25, his italics.

11. John Whitcomb, Jr., and Henry M. Morris, *The Genesis Flood* (Philadelphia: Presbyterian and Reformed Publishing Company, 1961), pp. 223–224, their italics.

12. *Ibid.*, p. 76.

13. See Morris, *op cit.*, pp. 71–72, and my discussion in *Darwinism Defended, op. cit.*

14. For instance, in John N. Moore and H. S. Slusher, *Biology/A Search for Order in Complexity* (Grand Rapids: Zondervan, 1977).

15. D. Lack, *Darwin's Finches* (Cambridge, England: Cambridge University Press, 1947).

16. Fred Hoyle and N. C. Wickramasinghe, *Evolution from Space* (London: Dent, 1981).

17. Morris, *op. cit.*, p. 173.

18. Donald Johanson and M. Edey, *Lucy: The Beginnings of Humankind* (New York: Simon and Schuster, 1981).

19. Gary E. Parker, *Creation: The Facts of Life* (San Diego: Creation-Life Publishers, 1979), p. 113.

20. For details of these statements, see the Opinion in *McLean v. Arkansas*, footnote 7.

21. Parker, *op cit.* See, for instance, pp. 55 and 144. The latter passage is worth quoting in full:
    Then there's 'the marvelous fit of organisms to the environment,' the special adaptations of cleaner fish, woodpeckers, bombardier beetles, etc., etc.,—what Darwin called 'Difficulties with the Theory,' and what Harvard's Lewontin (1978) called 'the chief evidence of a Supreme Designer.' Because of their 'perfection of structure,' he says, organisms 'appear to have been carefully and artfully designed.'
    The pertinent article by Richard Lewontin is "Adaptation," *Scientific American* (September 1978).

22. Richard C. Lewontin, *The Genetic Basis of Evolutionary Change* (New York: Columbia University Press, 1974).

14

Philosophical Arguments

It is not easy to explain the character of philosophical reasoning. Indeed, the nature of philosophical reasoning is itself a philosophical problem. We can, however, acquire some sense of it by comparing philosophical reasoning with reasoning as it occurs in daily life. In the opening chapters of this book we noticed that, in everyday discussions, much is taken for granted and left unsaid. In general there is no need to state points that are already a matter of agreement. In contrast, philosophers usually try to make underlying assumptions explicit and then subject them to critical examination. But, even for the philosopher, something must trigger an interest in underlying assumptions—and this usually arises when the advance of knowledge creates fundamental conflicts within the system of hitherto accepted assumptions. Thus much that counts as modern philosophy is an attempt to come to terms with the relationship between modern science and the traditional conception of man's place in the universe.

In recent years, a striking example of such a conflict has been generated by the rise of computer theory and computer technology. Traditionally, humans have cited the capacity to think as the feature that sets them apart from and, of course, above all other creatures. Man has been defined as a rational animal. But we now live in an age in which computers seem able to perform tasks that, had a human being performed them, would certainly count as thinking. Not only can computers perform complex calculations very rapidly, they can also play a tolerably good game of chess. Do machines think? The question seems forced upon us, and it is more than a semantic quibble. In deciding it, we are also re-evaluating the status of an aspect of humanity that has long been considered its unique or distinctive feature. Once we decide whether machines can think, the next question is whether human beings are not themselves merely thinking machines.

The two selections presented in this chapter address such questions. More specifically, they both consider the so-called *Turing Test* for deciding whether or not a machine can think. A. M. Turing, the mathematician who first proposed this test, is one of the geniuses of this century. He not only developed much of the mathematics that underlies modern computer theory, he helped give digital computers their first remarkable application: cracking the German secret codes during the Second World War. In his essay "Computer Machinery and Intelligence,"[1] he attempted to restate the question "Can machines think?" in a way that would admit of a clear answer. He proposed that we ask whether a computer could successfully play what he called the *imitation game*. The test, and its significance, is examined in detail in the first selection: "The Turing Test: A Coffeehouse Conversation" by Douglas R. Hofstadter. The selection also contains some brief reflections on the Turing test by Daniel C. Dennett.

The second selection is by John Searle. It comes from his review of Hofstadter and Dennett's book *The Mind's I,* and presents a systematic critique of the claims in behalf of machine intelligence.

---

[1] A. M. Turing, "Computing Machinery and Intelligence," *Mind*, vol. LIX, no. 236 (1950).

The Turing Test: A Coffeehouse Conversation*

DOUGLAS R. HOFSTADTER

PARTICIPANTS

Chris, a physics student; Pat, a biology student; and Sandy,
a philosophy student.

CHRIS: Sandy, I want to thank you for suggesting that I read Alan Turing's article "Computing Machinery and Intelligence." It's a wonderful piece and it certainly made me think—and think about my thinking.

SANDY: Glad to hear it. Are you still as much of a skeptic about artificial intelligence as you used to be?

CHRIS: You've got me wrong. I'm not against artificial intelligence; I think it's wonderful stuff—perhaps a little crazy, but why not? I simply am convinced that you AI advocates have far underestimated the human mind, and that there are things a computer will never, ever be able to do. For instance, can you imagine a computer writing a Proust novel? The richness of imagination, the complexity of the characters . . .

SANDY: Rome wasn't built in a day!

CHRIS: In the article Turing comes through as an interesting person. Is he still alive?

SANDY: No, he died back in 1954, at just forty-one. He'd only be sixty-seven this year [1981], although he is now such a legendary figure it seems strange to imagine him still alive today.

CHRIS: How did he die?

SANDY: Almost certainly suicide. He was homosexual and had to deal with a lot of harsh treatment and stupidity from the outside world. In the end it apparently got to be too much, and he killed himself.

---

*From Douglas R. Hofstadter and Daniel C. Dennett, *The Mind's I: Fantasies and Reflections on Self and Soul* (New York: Basic Books, 1981), pp. 69–95. This selection appeared previously as "Metamagical Themas: A coffeehouse conversation on the Turing test to determine if a machine can think," in *Scientific American*, May 1981, pp. 15–36.

CHRIS: That's a sad story.

SANDY: Yes, it certainly is. What saddens me is that he never got to see the amazing progress in computing machinery and theory that has taken place.

PAT: Hey, are you going to clue me in as to what this Turing article is about?

SANDY: It is really about two things. One is the question "Can a machine think?"—or rather, "Will a machine ever think?" The way Turing answers this question—he thinks the answer is "yes," by the way—is by batting down a series of objections to the idea, one after another. The other point he tries to make is that the question is not meaningful as it stands. It's too full of emotional connotations. Many people are upset by the suggestion that people are machines, or that machines might think. Turing tries to defuse the question by casting it in less emotional terms. For instance, what do you think, Pat, of the idea of "thinking machines"?

PAT: Frankly, I find the term confusing. You know what confuses me? It's those ads in the newspapers and on TV that talk about "products that think" or "intelligent ovens" or whatever. I just don't know how seriously to take them.

SANDY: I know the kind of ads you mean, and I think they confuse a lot of people. On the one hand we're given the refrain "Computers are really dumb, you have to spell everything out for them in complete detail," and on the other hand we're bombarded with advertising hype about "smart products."

CHRIS: That's certainly true. Did you know that one computer terminal manufacturer has even taken to calling its products "dumb terminals" in order to stand out from the crowd?

SANDY: That's cute, but it just plays along with the trend toward obfuscation. The term "electronic brain" always comes to my mind when I'm thinking about this. Many people swallow it completely, while others reject it out of hand. Few have the patience to sort out the issues and decide how much of it makes sense.

PAT: Does Turing suggest some way of resolving it, some sort of IQ test for machines?

SANDY: That would be interesting, but no machine could yet come close to taking an IQ test. Instead, Turing proposes a test that theoretically could be applied to any machine to determine whether it can think or not.

PAT: Does the test give a clear-cut yes or no answer? I'd be skeptical if it claimed to.

SANDY: No, it doesn't. In a way, that's one of its advantages. It shows how the borderline is quite fuzzy and how subtle the whole question is.

PAT: So, as is usual in philosophy, it's all just a question of words.

SANDY: Maybe, but they're emotionally charged words, and so it's important, it seems to me, to explore the issues and try to map out the meanings of the crucial words. The issues are fundamental to our concept of ourselves, so we shouldn't just sweep them under the rug.

PAT: So tell me how Turing's test works.

SANDY: The idea is based on what he calls the Imitation Game. In this game a man and a woman go into separate rooms and can be interrogated by a third party, via some sort of teletype set-up. The third party can address questions to either room, but has no idea which person is in which room. For the interrogator the idea is to discern which room the woman is in. Now the woman, by her answers, tries to aid the interrogator as much as possible. The man, however, is doing his best to bamboozle the interrogator by responding as he thinks a woman might. And if he succeeds in fooling the interrogator . . .

PAT: The interrogator only gets to see written words, eh? And the sex of the author is supposed to shine through? That game sounds like a good challenge. I would very much like to participate in it someday. Would the interrogator know either the man or the woman before the test began? Would any of them know the others?

SANDY: That would probably be a bad idea. All sorts of subliminal cueing might occur if the interrogator knew one or both of them. It would be safest if all three people were totally unknown to each other.

PAT: Could you ask any question at all, with no holds barred?

SANDY: Absolutely. That's the whole idea.

PAT: Don't you think, then, that pretty quickly it would degenerate into very sex-oriented questions? I can imagine the man, overeager to act convincing, giving away the game by answering some very blunt questions that most women would find too personal to answer, even through an anonymous computer connection.

SANDY: It sounds plausible.

CHRIS: Another possibility would be to probe for knowledge of minute aspects of traditional sex-role differences, by asking about such things as dress sizes and so on. The psychology of the Imitation Game could get pretty subtle. I suppose it would make a difference if the interrogator were a woman or a man. Don't you think that a woman could spot some telltale differences more quickly than a man could?

PAT: If so, maybe *that's* how to tell a man from a woman!

SANDY: Hmm . . . that's a new twist! In any case, I don't know if this original version of the Imitation Game has ever been seriously tried out, despite the fact that it would be relatively easy to do with modern computer terminals. I have to admit, though, that I'm not sure what it would prove, whichever way it turned out.

PAT: I was wondering about that. What would it prove if the interrogator—say, a woman—couldn't tell correctly which person was the woman? It certainly wouldn't prove that the man *was* a woman!

SANDY: Exactly! what I find funny is that although I fundamentally believe in the Turing test, I'm not sure what the point is of the Imitation Game, on which it's founded!

CHRIS: I'm not any happier with the Turing test as a test for "thinking machines" than I am with the Imitation Game as a test for femininity.

PAT: From your statements I gather that the Turing test is a kind of extension of the Imitation Game, only involving a machine and a person in separate rooms.

SANDY: That's the idea. the machine tries its hardest to convince the interrogator that it is the human being, while the human tries to make it clear that he or she is not a computer.

PAT: Except for your loaded phrase "the machine tries," this sounds very interesting. But how do you know that this test will get at the essence of thinking? Maybe it's testing for the wrong things. Maybe, just to take a random illustration, someone would feel that a machine was able to think only if it could dance so well that you couldn't tell it was a machine. Or someone else could suggest some other characteristic. What's so sacred about being able to fool people by typing at them?

SANDY: I don't see how you can say such a thing. I've heard that objection before, but frankly it baffles me. So what if the machine can't tap-dance or drop a rock on your toe? If it can discourse intelligently on any subject you want, then it has shown it can think—to me, at least! As I see it, Turing has drawn, in one clean stroke, a clear division between thinking and other aspects of being human.

PAT: Now *you're* the baffling one. If one couldn't conclude anything from a man's ability to win at the Imitation Game, how could one conclude anything from a machine's ability to win at the Turing game?

CHRIS: Good question.

SANDY: It seems to me that you could conclude *something* from a man's win in the Imitation Game. You wouldn't conclude he was a woman, but you could certainly say he had good insights into the feminine mentality (if there is such a thing). Now, if a computer could fool someone into thinking it was a person, I guess you'd have to say something similar about it—that it had good insights into what it's like to be human, into "the human condition" (whatever that is).

PAT: Maybe, but that isn't necessarily equivalent to thinking, is it? It seems to me that passing the Turing test would merely prove that some machine or other could do a very good job of *simulating* thought.

CHRIS: I couldn't agree more with Pat. We all know that fancy computer programs exist today for simulating all sorts of complex phenomena. In physics, for instance, we simulate the behavior of particles, atoms, solids, liquids, gases, galaxies, and so on. But nobody confuses any of those simulations with the real thing!

SANDY: In his book *Brainstorms*, the philosopher Daniel Dennett makes a similar point about simulated hurricanes.

CHRIS: That's a nice example too. Obviously, what goes on inside a computer when it's simulating a hurricane is not a hurricane, for the machine's memory doesn't get torn to bits by 200-mile-an-hour winds, the floor of the machine room doesn't get flooded with rainwater, and so on.

SANDY: Oh, come on—that's not a fair argument! In the first place, the programmers don't claim the simulation really *is* a hurricane. It's merely a simulation of certain aspects of a hurricane. But in the second place, you're pulling a fast one when you imply that there are no downpours or 200-mile-an-hour winds in a simulated hurricane. To us there aren't any—but if the program were incredibly detailed, it could include simulated people on the ground who would experience the wind and the rain just as we do when a hurricane hits. In their minds—or, if you prefer, in their *simulated* minds—the hurricane would not be a simulation but a genuine phenomenon complete with drenching and devastation.

CHRIS: Oh, boy—what a science-fiction scenario! Now we're talking about simulating whole populations, not just a single mind!

SANDY: Well, look—I'm simply trying to show you why your argument that a simulated McCoy isn't the real McCoy is fallacious. It depends on the tacit assumption that any old observer of the simulated phenomenon is equally able to assess what's going on. But, in fact, it may take an observer with a special vantage point to recognize what is going on. In this case, it takes special "computational glasses" to see the rain and the winds and so on.

PAT: "Computational glasses"? I don't know what you're talking about!

SANDY: I mean that to see the winds and the wetness of the hurricane, you have to be able to look at it in the proper way. You—

CHRIS: No, no, no! A simulated hurricane isn't wet! No matter how much it might seem wet to simulated people, it won't ever be *genuinely* wet! And no computer will ever get torn apart in the process of simulating winds!

SANDY: Certainly not, but you're confusing levels. The laws of physics don't get torn apart by real hurricanes either. In the case of the simulated hurricane, if you go peering at the computer's memory expecting to find broken wires and so forth, you'll be disappointed. But look at the proper level. Look into the *structures* that are coded for in the memory. You'll see that some abstract links have been broken, some values of variables radically changed, and so forth. There's your flood, your devastation—real, only a little concealed, a little hard to detect.

CHRIS: I'm sorry, I just can't buy that. You're insisting that I look for a new kind of devastation, a kind never before associated with hurricanes. Using this idea, you could call *anything* a hurricane as long as its effects, seen through your special "glasses," could be called "floods and devastation."

SANDY: Right—you've got it exactly! You recognize a hurricane by its *effects*. You have no way of going in and finding some ethereal "essence of hurricane," some "hurricane soul," located right in the middle of the eye! It's the existence of a certain kind of *pattern*—a spiral storm with an eye and so forth that makes you say it's a hurricane. Of course there are a lot of things that you'll insist on before you call something a hurricane.

PAT: Well, wouldn't you say that being an atmospheric phenomenon is one vital prerequisite? How can anything inside a computer be a storm? To me, a simulation is a simulation is a simulation!

SANDY: Then I suppose you would say that even the calculations that computers do are simulated—but they are fake calculations. Only people can do genuine calculations, right?

PAT: Well, computers get the right answers, so their calculations are not exactly fake—but they're still just *patterns*. There's no understanding going on in there. Take a cash register. Can you honestly say that you feel it is calculating something when its gears turn on each other? And a computer is just a fancy cash register, as I understand it.

SANDY: If you mean that a cash register doesn't feel like a schoolkid doing arithmetic problems, I'll agree. But is that what "calculation" means? Is that an integral part of it? If so, then contrary to what everybody has thought till now, we'll have to write a very complicated program to perform *genuine* calculations. Of course, this program will sometimes get careless and make mistakes and it will sometimes scrawl its answers illegibly, and it will occasionally doodle on its paper. . . . It won't be more reliable than the post office clerk who adds up your total by hand. Now, I happen to believe eventually such a program could be written. Then we'd know something about how post office clerks and schoolkids work.

PAT: I can't believe you could ever do that!

SANDY: Maybe, maybe not, but that's not my point. You say a cash register can't calculate. It reminds me of another favorite passage of mine from Dennett's *Brainstorms*—a rather ironic one, which is why I like it. The passage goes something like this: "Cash registers can't really calculate; they can only spin their gears. But cash registers can't really spin their gears either; they can only follow the laws of physics." Dennett said it originally about computers; I modified it to talk about cash registers. And you could use the same line of reasoning in talking about people: "People can't really calculate; all they can do is manipulate mental symbols. But they aren't really manipulating symbols; all they are doing is firing various neurons in various patterns. But they can't really make their neurons fire; they simply have to let the laws of physics make them fire for them." Et cetera. Don't you see how this Dennett-inspired *reductio ad absurdum* would lead you to conclude that calculation doesn't exist, hurricanes don't exist, nothing at a higher level than particles and the laws of physics exists? What do you gain by saying a computer only pushes symbols around and doesn't truly calculate?

PAT: The example may be extreme, but it makes my point that there is a vast difference between a real phenomenon and any simulation of it. This is so for hurricanes, and even more so for human thought.

SANDY: Look, I don't want to get too tangled up in this line of argument, but let me try out one more example. If you were a radio ham listening to another ham broadcasting in Morse code and you were responding in Morse code, would it sound funny to you to refer to "the person at the other end"?

PAT: No, that would sound okay, although the existence of a person at the other end would be an assumption.

SANDY: Yes, but you wouldn't be likely to go and check it out. You're prepared to recognize personhood through those rather unusual channels. You don't have to see a human body or hear a voice—all you need is a rather abstract manifestation—a code, as it were. What I'm getting at is this. To "see" the person behind the dits and dahs, you have to be willing to do some decoding, some interpretation. It's not direct perception; it's indirect. You have to peel off a layer or two, to find the reality hidden in there. You put on your "radio-ham's glasses" to "see" the person behind the buzzes. Just the same with the simulated hurricane! You don't see it darkening the machine room—you have to decode the machine's memory. You have to put on special "memory-decoding glasses." *Then* what you see is a hurricane!

PAT: Oh, ho ho! Talk about fast ones—wait a minute! In the case of the short-wave radio, there's a real person out there, somewhere in the Fiji Islands or wherever. My decoding act as I sit by my radio simply reveals that that person exists. It's like seeing a shadow and concluding there's an object out there, casting it. One doesn't confuse the shadow with the object, however! And with the hurricane there's no *real* hurricane behind the scenes, making the computer follow its patterns. No, what you have is just a shadow hurricane without any genuine hurricane. I just refuse to confuse shadows with reality.

SANDY: All right. I don't want to drive this point into the ground. I even admit it is pretty silly to say that a simulated hurricane *is* a hurricane. But I wanted to point out that it's not as silly as you might think at first blush. And when you turn to simulated thought, you've got a very different matter on your hands from simulated hurricanes.

PAT: I don't see why. A brainstorm sounds to me like a mental hurricane. But seriously, you'll have to convince me.

SANDY: Well, to do so I'll have to make a couple of extra points about hurricanes first.

PAT: Oh, no! Well, all right, all right.

SANDY: Nobody can say just exactly what a hurricane is—that is, in totally precise terms. there's an abstract pattern that many storms share, and it's for that reason that we call those storms hurricanes. But it's not possible to make a sharp distinction between hurricanes and nonhurricanes. There are tornados, cyclones, typhoons, dust-devils. . . . Is the Great Red Spot on Jupiter a hurricane? Are sunspots hurricanes? Could there be a hurricane in a wind tunnel?

In a test tube? In your imagination you can even extend the concept of "hurricane" to include a microscopic storm on the surface of a neutron star.

CHRIS: That's not so far-fetched, you know. The concept of "earthquake" has actually been extended to neutron stars. The astrophysicists say that the tiny changes in rate that once in a while are observed in the pulsing of a pulsar are caused by "glitches"— starquakes—that have just occurred on the neutron star's surface.

SANDY: Yes, I remember that now. The idea of a "glitch" strikes me as wonderfully eerie—a surrealistic kind of quivering on a surrealistic kind of surface.

CHRIS: Can you imagine—plate tectonics on a giant rotating sphere of pure nuclear matter?

SANDY: That's a wild thought. So starquakes and earthquakes can both be subsumed into a new, more abstract category. And that's how science constantly extends familiar concepts, taking them further and further from familiar experience and yet keeping some essence constant. The number system is the classic example—from positive numbers to negative numbers, then rationals, reals, complex numbers, and "on beyond zebra," as Dr. Seuss says.

PAT: I think I can see your point here, Sandy. We have many examples in biology of close relationships that are established in rather abstract ways. Often the decision about what family some species belongs to comes down to an abstract pattern shared at some level. When you base your system of classification on very abstract patterns, I suppose that a broad variety of phenomena can fall into "the same class," even if in many superficial ways the class members are utterly unlike each other. So perhaps I can glimpse, at least a little, how to you a simulated hurricane could, in some funny sense, *be* a hurricane.

CHRIS: Perhaps the word that's being extended is not "hurricane" but "be"!

PAT: How so?

CHRIS: If Turing can extend the verb "think," can't I extend the verb "be"? All I mean is that when simulated things are deliberately confused with the genuine article, somebody's doing a lot of philosophical wool-pulling. It's a lot more serious than just extending a few nouns such as "hurricane."

SANDY: I like your idea that "be" is being extended, but I think your slur about "wool-pulling" goes too far. Anyway, if you don't object, let me just say one more thing about simulated hurricanes and then I'll get to simulated minds. Suppose you consider a really deep simulation of a hurricane—I mean a simulation of every atom, which I admit is impossibly deep. I hope you would agree that it would then share all that abstract structure that defines the "essence of hurricane-hood." So what's to hold you back from calling it a hurricane?

PAT: I thought you were backing off from that claim of equality!

SANDY: So did I, but then these examples came up, and I was forced back to my claim. But let me back off, as I said I would do, and get back to *thought*, which is the real issue here. Thought, even more than hurricanes, is an abstract structure, a way of describing some complex events that happen in a medium called a brain. But actually thought can take place in any of several billion brains. there are all these physically very different brains, and yet they all support "the same thing"—thinking. What's important, then, is the abstract *pattern*, not the medium. The same kind of swirling can happen inside any of them, so no person can claim to think more "genuinely" than any other. Now, if we come up with some new kind of medium in which *the same style* of swirling takes place, could you deny that thinking is taking place in it?

PAT: Probably not, but you have just shifted the question. The question now is, how can you determine whether "the same style" of swirling is really happening?

SANDY: The beauty of the Turing test is that it *tells* you when!

CHRIS: I don't see that at all. How would you know that the same style of activity was occurring inside a computer as inside my mind, simply because it answered questions as I do? All you're looking at is its outside.

SANDY: But how do you know that when I speak to you, anything similar to what you call "thinking" is going on inside *me*? The Turing test is a fantastic probe, something like a particle accelerator in physics. Chris, I think you'll like this analogy. Just as in physics, when you want to understand what is going on at an atomic or subatomic level, since you can't see it directly, you scatter accelerated particles off the target in question and observe their behavior. From this you infer the internal nature of the target. The Turing test extends this idea to the mind. It treats the mind as a "target" that is not directly visible but whose structure can be deduced more abstractly. By "scattering" questions off a target mind, you learn about its internal workings, just as in physics.

CHRIS: More exactly put, you can hypothesize about what kinds of internal structures might account for the behavior observed—but they may or may not in fact exist.

SANDY: Hold on, now! Are you saying that atomic nuclei are merely hypothetical entities? After all, their existence—or should I say "hypothetical existence"?—was proven—or should I say "suggested"?—by the behavior of particles scattered off of atoms.

CHRIS: Physical systems seem to me to be much simpler than the mind, and the certainty of the inferences made is correspondingly greater.

SANDY: The experiments are also correspondingly harder to perform and to interpret. In the Turing test, you could perform many highly delicate experiments in the course of an hour. I maintain that people give other people credit for being conscious simply because of their continual external monitoring of them—which is itself something like a Turing test.

PAT: That may be roughly true, but it involves more than just conversing with people through a teletype. We see that other people have bodies, we watch their faces and expressions—we see they are fellow human beings and so we think they think.

SANDY: To me, that seems a highly anthropocentric view of what thought is. Does that mean you would sooner say a mannikin in a store thinks than a wonderfully programmed computer, simply because the mannikin looks more human?

PAT: Obviously I would need more than just vague physical resemblance to the human form to be willing to attribute the power of thought to an entity. But that organic quality, the sameness of origin, undeniably lends a degree of credibility that is very important.

SANDY: Here we disagree. I find this simply too chauvinistic. I feel that the key thing is a similarity of *internal* structure—not bodily, organic, chemical structure, but organizational structure—software. Whether an entity can think seems to me a question of whether its organization can be described in a certain way, and I'm perfectly willing to believe that the Turing test detects the presence or absence of that mode of organization. I would say that your depending on my physical body as evidence that I am a thinking being is rather shallow. The way I see it, the Turing test looks far deeper than at mere external form.

PAT: Hey now—you're not giving me much credit. It's not just the shape of a body that lends weight to the idea there's real thinking going on inside—it's also, as I said, the idea of common origin. It's the idea that you and I both sprang from DNA molecules, an idea to which I attribute much depth. Put it this way: The external form of human bodies reveals that they share a deep biological history, and it's *that* depth that lends a lot of credibility to the notion that the owner of such a body can think.

SANDY: But that is all indirect evidence. Surely you want some *direct* evidence. That is what the Turing test is for. And I think it is the *only* way to test for "thinkinghood."

CHRIS: But you could be fooled by the Turing test, just as an interrogator could think a man was a woman.

SANDY: I admit, I could be fooled if I carried out the test in too quick or too shallow a way. But I could go for the deepest things I could think of.

CHRIS: I would want to see if the program could understand jokes. That would be a real test of intelligence.

SANDY: I agree that humor probably is an acid test for a supposedly intelligent program, but equally important to me—perhaps more so—would be to test its emotional responses. So I would ask it about its reactions to certain pieces of music or works of literature—especially my favorite ones.

CHRIS: What if it said, "I don't know that piece," or even "I have no interest in music"? What if it avoided all emotional references?

SANDY: That would make me suspicious. Any consistent pattern of avoiding certain issues would raise serious doubts in me as to whether I was dealing with a thinking being.

CHRIS: Why do you say that? Why not say that you're dealing with a thinking but unemotional being?

SANDY: You've hit upon a sensitive point. I simply can't believe that emotions and thought can be divorced. Put another way, I think that emotions are an automatic by-product of the ability to think. They are implied by the very nature of thought.

CHRIS: Well, what if you're wrong? What if I produced a machine that could think but not emote? Then its intelligence might go unrecognized because it failed to pass *your* kind of test.

SANDY: I'd like you to point out to me where the boundary line between emotional questions and nonemotional ones lies. You might want to ask about the meaning of a great novel. This requires understanding of human emotions! Is that thinking or merely cool calculations? You might want to ask about a subtle choice of words. For that you need an understanding of their connotations. Turing uses examples like this in his article. You might want to ask it for advice about a complex romantic situation. It would need to know a lot about human motivations and their roots. Now if it failed at this kind of task, I would not be much inclined to say that it could think. As far as I am concerned, the ability to think, the ability to feel, and consciousness are just different facets of one phenomenon, and no one of them can be present without the others.

CHRIS: Why couldn't you build a machine that could feel nothing, but that could think and make complex decisions anyway? I don't see any contradiction there.

SANDY: Well, I do. I think that when you say that, you are visualizing a metallic, rectangular machine, probably in an air-conditioned room—a hard, angular, cold object with a million colored wires inside it, a machine that sits stock still on a tiled floor, humming or buzzing or whatever, and spinning its tapes. Such a machine can play a good game of chess, which, I freely admit, involves a lot of decision making. And yet I would never call such a machine conscious.

CHRIS: How come? To mechanists, isn't a chess-playing machine rudimentarily conscious?

SANDY: Not to this mechanist. The way I see it, consciousness has got to come from a precise pattern of organization—one that we haven't yet figured out how to describe in any detailed way. But I believe we will gradually come to understand it. In my view consciousness requires a certain way of mirroring the external universe internally, and the ability to respond to that external reality on the basis of the internally represented model. And then in addition, what's really crucial for a conscious machine is that it should incorporate a well-developed and flexible self-model. And it's there that all existent programs, including the best chess-playing ones, fall down.

CHRIS: Don't chess programs look ahead and say to themselves as they're figuring out their next move, "If you move here, then I'll go there, and then if you go this way, I could go that way . . ."? Isn't that a sort of self-model?

SANDY: Not really. Or, if you want, it's an extremely limited one. It's an understanding of self only in the narrowest sense. For instance, a chess-playing program has no concept of why it is playing chess, or the fact that it is a program, or is in a computer, or has a human opponent. It has no ideas about what winning and losing are, or—

PAT: How do *you* know it has no such sense? How can you presume to say what a chess program feels or knows?

SANDY: Oh, come on! We all know that certain things don't feel anything or know anything. A thrown stone doesn't know anything about parabolas, and a whirling fan doesn't know anything about air. It's true I can't *prove* those statements, but here we are verging on questions of faith.

PAT: This reminds me of a Taoist story I read. It goes something like this. Two sages were standing on a bridge over a stream. One said to the other, "I wish I were a fish. They are so happy!" The second replied, "How do you know whether fish are happy or not? You're not a fish." The first said, "But you're not me, so how do you know whether I know how fish feel?"

SANDY: Beautiful! Talking about consciousness really does call for a certain amount of restraint. Otherwise you might as well just jump on either the solipsism bandwagon—"I am the only conscious being in the universe"—or the panpsychism bandwagon—"Everything in the universe is conscious!"

PAT: Well, how do you know? Maybe everything *is* conscious.

SANDY: If you're going to join those who claim that stones and even particles like electrons have some sort of consciousness, then I guess we part company here. That's a kind of mysticism I can't fathom. As for chess programs, I happen to know how they work, and I can tell you for sure that they aren't conscious! No way!

PAT: Why not?

SANDY: They incorporate only the barest knowledge about the goals of chess. The notion of "playing" is turned into the mechanical act of comparing a lot of numbers and choosing the biggest one over and over again. A chess program has no sense of shame about losing or pride in winning. Its self-model is very crude. It gets away with doing the least it can, just enough to play a game of chess and do nothing more. Yet, interestingly enough, we still tend to talk about the "desires" of a chess-playing computer. We say, "It wants to keep its king behind a row of pawns," or "It likes to get its rooks out early," or "It thinks I don't see that hidden fork."

PAT: Well, we do the same thing with insects. We spot a lonely ant somewhere and say, "It's trying to get back home" or "It wants to drag that dead bee back to the colony." In fact, with any animal we use terms that indicate emotions, but we don't know for sure how much the animal feels. I have no trouble talking about dogs and cats being happy or sad, having desires and beliefs and so on, but of course I don't think their sadness is as deep or complex as human sadness is.

SANDY: But you wouldn't call it "simulated sadness," would you?

PAT: No, of course not. I think it's real.

SANDY: It's hard to avoid use of such teleological or mentalistic terms. I believe they're quite justified, although they shouldn't be carried too far. They simply don't have the same richness of meaning when applied to present-day chess programs as when applied to people.

CHRIS: I still can't see that intelligence has to involve emotions. Why couldn't you imagine an intelligence that simply calculates and has no feelings?

SANDY: A couple of answers here! Number one, any intelligence has to have motivations. It's simply not the case, whatever many people may think, that machines could think any more "objectively" than people do. Machines, when they look at a scene, will have to focus and filter that scene down into some preconceived categories, just as a person does. And that means seeing some things and missing others. It means giving more weight to some things than to others. This happens on every level of processing.

PAT: What do you mean?

SANDY: Take me right now, for instance. You might think that I'm just making some intellectual points, and I wouldn't need emotions to do that. But what makes me *care* about these points? Why did I stress the word "care" so heavily? Because I'm emotionally involved in this conversation! People talk to each other out of conviction, not out of hollow, mechanical reflexes. Even the most intellectual conversation is driven by underlying passions. There's an emotional undercurrent to every conversation—it's the fact that the speakers want to be listened to, understood, and respected for what they are saying.

PAT: It sounds to me as if all you're saying is that people need to be interested in what they're saying, otherwise a conversation dies.

SANDY: Right! I wouldn't bother to talk to anyone if I weren't motivated by interest. And interest is just another name for a whole constellation of subconscious biases. When I talk, all my biases work together and what you perceive on the surface level is my style, my personality. But that style arises from an immense number of tiny priorities, biases, leanings. When you add up a million of these interacting together, you get something that amounts to a lot of *desires*. It just all adds up! And that brings me to the other point, about feelingless calculation. Sure, that exists—in a cash register, a pocket calculator. I'd say it's even true of all today's computer programs. But eventually, when you put enough feelingless calculations together in a huge coordinated organization, you'll get something that has properties on another level. You can see it—in fact, you *have* to see it—not as a bunch of little calculations, but as a system of tendencies and desires and beliefs and so on. When things get complicated enough, you're forced to change your level of description. To some extent that's already happening, which is why we use words such as "want," "think," "try," and "hope," to describe chess programs and other attempts at mechanical thought. Dennett calls that kind of level switch by the observer "adopting the intentional stance."

The really interesting things in AI will only begin to happen, I'd guess, when the program *itself* adopts the intentional stance toward itself!

CHRIS: That would be a very strange sort of level-crossing feedback loop.

SANDY: It certainly would. Of course, in my opinion, it's highly premature for anyone to adopt the intentional stance, in the full force of the term, toward today's programs. At least that's my opinion.

CHRIS: For me an important related question is: To what extent is it valid to adopt the intentional stance toward beings other than humans?

PAT: I would certainly adopt the intentional stance toward mammals.

SANDY: I vote for that.

CHRIS: That's interesting! How can that be, Sandy? Surely you wouldn't claim that a dog or cat can pass the Turing test? Yet don't you think that the Turing test is the only way to test for the presence of thought? How can you have these beliefs at once?

SANDY: Hmm. . . . All right. I guess I'm forced to admit that the Turing test works only above a certain level of consciousness. There can be thinking beings that could fail the test—but on the other hand, anything that passes it, in my opinion, would be a genuinely conscious, thinking being.

PAT: How can you think of a computer as a conscious being? I apologize if this sounds like a stereotype, but when I think of conscious beings, I just can't connect that thought with machines. To me consciousness is connected with soft, warm bodies, silly though that may sound.

CHRIS: That does sound odd, coming from a biologist. Don't you deal with life in terms of chemistry and physics enough for all magic to seem to vanish?

PAT: Not really. Sometimes the chemistry and physics just increase the feeling that there's something magical going on down there! Anyway, I can't always integrate my scientific knowledge with my gut-level feelings.

CHRIS: I guess I share that trait.

PAT: So how do you deal with rigid preconceptions like mine?

SANDY: I'd try to dig down under the surface of your concept of "machines" and get at the intuitive connotations that lurk there, out of sight but deeply influencing your opinions. I think that we all have a holdover image from the

Industrial Revolution that sees machines as clunky iron contraptions gawkily moving under the power of some loudly chugging engine. Possibly that's even how the computer inventor Charles Babbage viewed people! After all, he called his magnificent many-geared computer the Analytical Engine.

PAT: Well, I certainly don't think people are just fancy steam shovels or even electric can openers. There's something about people, something that—that—they've got a sort of *flame* inside them, something alive, something that flickers unpredictably, wavering, uncertain—but something *creative!*

SANDY: Great! That's just the sort of thing I wanted to hear. It's very human to think that way. Your flame image makes me think of candles, of fires, of thunderstorms with lightning dancing all over the sky in crazy patterns. But do you realize that just that kind of pattern is visible on a computer's console? The flickering lights form amazing chaotic sparkling patterns. It's such a far cry from heaps of lifeless clanking metal! It *is* flamelike, by God! Why don't you let the word "machine" conjure up images of dancing patterns of light rather than of giant steam shovels?

CHRIS: That's a beautiful image, Sandy. It changes my sense of mechanism from being matter-oriented to being pattern-oriented. It makes me try to visualize the thoughts in my mind—these thoughts right now, even—as a huge spray of tiny pulses flickering in my brain.

SANDY: That's quite a poetic self-portrait for a spray of flickers to have come up with!

CHRIS: Thank you. But still, I'm not totally convinced that a machine is all that I am. I admit, my concept of machines probably does suffer from anachronistic subconscious flavors, but I'm afraid I can't change such a deeply rooted sense in a flash.

SANDY: At least you do sound open-minded. And to tell the truth, part of me does sympathize with the way you and Pat view machines. Part of me balks at calling myself a machine. It *is* a bizarre thought that a feeling being like you or me might emerge from mere circuitry. Do I surprise you?

CHRIS: You certainly surprise *me*. So tell us—do you believe in the idea of an intelligent computer, or don't you?

SANDY: It all depends on what you mean. We have all heard the question "Can computers think?" There are several possible interpretations of this (aside from the many interpretations of the word "think"). They revolve around different meanings of the words "can" and "computer."

PAT: Back to word games again. . . .

SANDY: That's right. First of all, the question might mean "Does some present-day computer think, right now?" To this I would immediately answer with a loud "no." Then it could be taken to mean, "Could some present-day computer, if suitably programmed, potentially think?" This is more like it, but I would still answer, "Probably not." The real difficulty hinges on the word "computer." The way I see it, " computer" calls up an image of just what I described earlier: an air-conditioned room with cold rectangular metallic boxes in it. But I suspect that with increasing public familiarity with computers and continued progress in computer architecture, that vision will eventually become outmoded.

PAT: Don't you think computers, as we know them, will be around for a while?

SANDY: Sure, there will have to be computers in today's image around for a long time, but advanced computers—maybe no longer called computers—will evolve and become quite different. Probably, as in the case of living organisms, there will be many branchings in the evolutionary tree. There will be computers for business, computers for schoolkids, computers for scientific calculations, computers for systems research, computers for simulation, computers for rockets going into space, and so on. Finally, there will be computers for the study of intelligence. It's really only these last that I'm thinking of—the ones with the maximum flexibility, the ones that people are deliberately attempting to make smart. I see no reason that these will stay fixed in the traditional image. Probably they will soon acquire as standard features some rudimentary sensory systems—mostly for vision and hearing, at first. They will need to be able to move around, to explore. They will have to be physically flexible. In short, they will have to become more animal-like, more self-reliant.

CHRIS: It makes me think of the robots R2D2 and C3PO in *Star Wars*.

SANDY: As a matter of fact I don't think of anything like them when I visualize intelligent machines. They're too silly, too much the product of a film designer's imagination. Not that I have a clear vision of my own. But I think it is necessary, if people are going to try realistically to imagine an artificial intelligence, to go beyond the limited, hard-edged image of computers that comes from exposure to what we have today. The only thing that all machines will always have in common is their underlying mechanicalness. That may sound cold and inflexible, but what could be more mechanical—in a wonderful way—than the operations of the DNA and proteins and organelles in our cells?

PAT: To me what goes on inside cells has a "wet," "slippery" feel to it, and what goes on inside machines is dry and rigid. It's connected with the fact that computers don't make mistakes, that computers do only what you tell them to do. Or at least that's my image of computers.

SANDY: Funny—a minute ago your image was of a flame, and now it's of something "wet and slippery." Isn't it marvelous how contradictory we can be?

PAT: I don't need your sarcasm.

SANDY: I'm not being sarcastic—I really *do* think it is marvelous.

PAT: It's just an example of the human mind's slippery nature—mine, in this case.

SANDY: True. But your image of computers is stuck in a rut. Computers certainly can make mistakes—and I don't mean on the hardware level. Think of any present-day computer predicting the weather. It can make wrong predictions, even though its program runs flawlessly.

PAT: But that's only because you've fed it the wrong data.

SANDY: Not so. It's because weather prediction is too complex. Any such program has to make do with a limited amount of data—entirely correct data—and extrapolate from there. Sometimes it will make wrong predictions. It's no different from the farmer in the field gazing at the clouds who says, "I reckon we'll get a little snow tonight." We make models of things in our heads and use them to guess how the world will behave. We have to make do with our models, however inaccurate they may be. And if they're too inaccurate, evolution will prune us out—we'll fall over a cliff or something. And computers are the same. It's just that human designers will speed up the evolutionary process by aiming explicitly at the goal of creating intelligence, which is something nature just stumbled on.

PAT: So you think computers will make fewer mistakes as they get smarter?

SANDY: Actually, just the other way around. The smarter they get, the more they'll be in a position to tackle messy real-life domains, so they'll be more and more likely to have inaccurate models. To me, mistake making is a sign of high intelligence!

PAT: Boy—you throw me sometimes!

SANDY: I guess I'm a strange sort of advocate for machine intelligence. To some degree I straddle the fence. I think that machines won't really be intelligent in a humanlike way until they have something like that biological wetness or slipperiness to them. I don't mean literally wet—the slipperiness could be in the software. But biological-seeming or not, intelligent machines will in any case be machines. We will have designed them, built them—or grown them! We will understand how they work—at least in some sense. Possibly no one person will really understand them, but collectively we will know how they work.

PAT: It sounds like you want to have your cake and eat it too.

SANDY: You're probably right. What I'm getting at is that when artificial intelligence comes, it will be mechanical and yet at the same time organic. It will have that same astonishing flexibility that we see in life's mechanisms. And when I say "mechanisms," I *mean* "mechanisms." DNA and enzymes and so on really *are* mechanical and rigid and reliable. Wouldn't you agree, Pat?

PAT: That's true. But when they work together, a lot of unexpected things happen. There are so many complexities and rich modes of behavior that all that mechanicalness adds up to something very fluid.

SANDY: For me it's an almost unimaginable transition from the mechanical level of molecules to the living level of cells. But it's what convinces me that people are machines. That thought makes me uncomfortable in some ways, but in other ways it is an exhilarating thought.

CHRIS: If people are machines, how come it's so hard to convince them of the fact? Surely if we are machines, we ought to be able to recognize our own machinehood.

SANDY: You have to allow for emotional factors here. To be told you're a machine is, in a way, to be told that you're nothing more than your physical parts, and it brings you face to face with your own mortality. That's something nobody finds easy to face. But beyond the emotional objection, to see yourself as a machine you have to jump all the way from the bottommost mechanical level to the level where the complex lifelike activities take place. If there are many intermediate layers, they act as a shield, and the mechanical quality becomes almost invisible. I think that's how intelligent machines will seem to us—and to themselves!—when they come around.

PAT: I once heard a funny idea about what will happen when we eventually have intelligent machines. When we try to implant that intelligence into devices we'd like to control, their behavior won't be so predictable.

SANDY: They'll have a quirky little "flame" inside, maybe?

PAT: Maybe.

CHRIS: So what's so funny about that?

PAT: Well, think of military missiles. The more sophisticated their target-tracking computers get, according to this idea, the less predictably they will function. Eventually you'll have missiles that will decide they are pacifists and will turn around and go home and land quietly without blowing up. We could even have "smart bullets" that turn around in midflight because they don't want to commit suicide!

SANDY: That's a lovely thought.

CHRIS: I'm very skeptical about these ideas. Still, Sandy, I'd like to hear your predictions about when intelligent machines will come to be.

SANDY: It won't be for a long time, probably, that we'll see anything remotely resembling the level of human intelligence. It just rests on too awesomely complicated a substrate—the brain—for us to be able to duplicate it in the foreseeable future. Anyway, that's my opinion.

PAT: Do you think a program will ever pass the Turing test?

SANDY: That's a pretty hard question. I guess there are various degrees of passing such a test, when you come down to it. It's not black and white. First of all, it depends on who the interrogator is. A simpleton might be totally taken in by some programs today. But secondly, it depends on how deeply you are allowed to probe.

PAT: Then you could have a scale of Turing tests—one-minute versions, five-minute versions, hour-long versions, and so forth. Wouldn't it be interesting if some official organization sponsored a periodic competition, like the annual computer-chess championships, for programs to try to pass the Turing test?

CHRIS: The program that lasted the longest against some panel of distinguished judges would be the winner. Perhaps there could be a big prize for the first program that fools a famous judge for, say, ten minutes.

PAT: What would a program do with a prize?

CHRIS: Come now, Pat. If a program's good enough to fool the judges, don't you think it's good enough to enjoy the prize?

PAT: Sure, especially if the prize is an evening out on the town, dancing with all the interrogators!

SANDY: I'd certainly like to see something like that established. I think it could be hilarious to watch the first programs flop pathetically!

PAT: You're pretty skeptical, aren't you? Well, do you think any computer program today could pass a five-minute Turing test, given a sophisticated interrogator?

SANDY: I seriously doubt it. It's partly because no one is really working at it explicitly. However, there is one program called "Parry" which its inventors claim has already passed a rudimentary version of the Turing test. In a series of remotely conducted interviews, Parry fooled several psychiatrists who were told they were talking to either a computer or a paranoid patient. This was an improvement over an earlier version, in which psychiatrists were simply handed transcripts of short interviews and asked to determine which ones were with a genuine paranoid and which ones with a computer simulation.

PAT: You mean they didn't have the chance to ask any questions? That's a severe handicap—and it doesn't seem in the spirit of the Turing test. Imagine someone trying to tell which sex I belong to just by reading a transcript of a few remarks by me. It might be very hard! So I'm glad the procedure has been improved.

CHRIS: How do you get a computer to act like a paranoid?

SANDY: I'm not saying it *does* act like a paranoid, only that some psychiatrists, under unusual circumstances, thought so. One of the things that bothered me about this pseudo-Turing test is the way Parry works. "He"—as they call him— acts like a paranoid in that he gets abruptly defensive, veers away from undesirable topics in the conversation, and, in essence, maintains control so that no one can truly probe "him." In this way, a simulation of a paranoid is a lot easier than a simulation of a normal person.

PAT: No kidding! It reminds me of the joke about the easiest kind of human for a computer program to simulate.

CHRIS: What is that?

PAT: A catatonic patient—they just sit and do nothing at all for days on end. Even I could write a computer program to do that!

SANDY: An interesting thing about Parry is that it creates no sentences on its own—it merely selects from a huge repertoire of canned sentences the one that best responds to the input sentence.

PAT: Amazing! But that would probably be impossible on a larger scale, wouldn't it?

SANDY: Yes. The number of sentences you'd need to store to be able to respond in a normal way to all possible sentences in a conversation is astronomical, really unimaginable. And they would have to be so intricately indexed for retrieval. . . . Anybody who thinks that somehow a program could be rigged up just to pull sentences out of storage like records in a jukebox, and that this program could pass the Turing test, has not thought very hard about it. The funny part about it is that it is just this kind of unrealizable program that some enemies of artificial intelligence cite when arguing against the concept of the Turing test. Instead of a truly intelligent machine, they want you to imagine a gigantic, lumbering robot that intones canned sentences in a dull monotone. It's assumed that you could see through to its mechanical level with ease, even if it were simultaneously performing tasks that we think of as fluid, intelligent processes. Then the critics say, "You see! It would still be just a machine—a mechanical device, not intelligent at all!" I see things almost the opposite way. If I were shown a machine that can do things that I can do—I mean pass the Turing test—then, instead of feeling insulted or threatened, I'd chime in with the philosopher Raymond Smullyan and say, "How wonderful machines are!"

CHRIS: If you could ask a computer just one question in the Turing test, what would it be?

SANDY: Uhmm. . . .

PAT: How about "If you could ask a computer just one question in the Turing test, what would it be?"?

Reflections

Many people are put off by the provision in the Turing test requiring the contestants in the Imitation Game to be in another room from the judge, so only their verbal responses can be observed. As an element in a parlor game the rule makes sense, but how could a legitimate scientific proposal include a deliberate attempt to *hide facts* from the judges? By placing the candidates for intelligence in "black boxes" and leaving nothing as evidence but a restricted range of "external behavior" (in this case, verbal output by typing), the Turing test seems to settle dogmatically on some form of behaviorism, or (worse) operationalism, or (worse still) verificationism. (These three cousins are horrible monster *isms* of the recent past, reputed to have been roundly refuted by philosophers of science and interred—but what is that sickening sound? Can they be stirring in their graves? We should have driven stakes through their hearts!) Is the Turing test just a case of what John Searle calls "operationalist sleight-of-hand"?

The Turing test certainly does make a strong claim about what matters about minds. What matters, Turing proposes, is not what kind of gray matter (if any) the candidate has between its ears, and not what it looks like or smells like, but whether it can *act*—or behave, if you like—intelligently. The particular game proposed in the Turing test, the Imitation Game, is not sacred, but just a cannily chosen test of more general intelligence. The assumption Turing was prepared to make was that nothing could possibly pass the Turing test by winning the Imitation Game without being able to perform indefinitely many other clearly intelligent actions. Had he chosen checkmating the world chess champion as his litmus test of intelligence, there would have been powerful reasons for objecting; it now seems quite probable that one could make a machine that can do that *but nothing else.* Had he chosen stealing the British Crown Jewels without using force or accomplices, or solving the Arab-Israeli conflict without bloodshed, there would be few who would make the objection that intelligence was being "reduced to" behavior or "operationally defined" in terms of behavior. (Well, no doubt *some* philosopher somewhere would set about diligently constructing an elaborate but entirely outlandish scenario in which some utter dolt stumbled into possession of the British Crown Jewels, "passing" the test and thereby "refuting" it as a good general test of intelligence. The true operationalist, of course, would then have to admit that such a lucky moron was, by operationalist lights, truly intelligent since he passed the defining test—which is no doubt why true operationalists are hard to find.)

What makes Turing's chosen test better than stealing the British Crown Jewels or solving the Arab-Israeli conflict is that the latter tests are unrepeatable (if successfully passed once!), too difficult (many manifestly intelligent people would fail them utterly) and too hard to judge objectively. Like a well-composed wager, Turing's test invites trying; it seems fair, demanding but possible, and crisply objective in the judging. The Turing test reminds one of a wager in another way, too. Its motivation is to stop an interminable, sterile debate by saying "Put up or shut up!" Turing says in effect: "Instead of arguing about the ultimate nature and essence of mind or intelligence, why don't we all agree that anything that could pass this test is *surely* intelligent, and then turn to asking how something could be designed that might pass the test fair and square?" Ironically, Turing failed to shut off the debate but simply managed to get it redirected.

Is the Turing test vulnerable to criticism because of its "black box" ideology? First, as Hofstadter notes in his dialogue, we treat *each other* as black boxes, relying on our observation of apparently intelligent behavior to ground our belief in other minds. Second, the black box ideology is in any event the ideology of all scientific investigation. We learn about the DNA molecule by probing it in various ways and seeing how it behaves in response; we learn about cancer and earthquakes and inflation in the same way. "Looking inside" the black box is often useful when macroscopic objects are our concern; we do it by bouncing "opening" probes (such as a scalpel) off the object and then scattering photons off the exposed surfaces into our eyes. Just one more black box experiment.

The question must be, as Hofstadter says: Which probes will be most directly relevant to the question we want to answer? If our question is about whether some entity is intelligent, we will find no more direct, telling probes than the everyday questions we often ask each other. The extent of Turing's "behaviorism" is simply to incorporate that near truism into a handy, laboratory-style experimental test.

Another problem raised but not settled in Hofstadter's dialogue concerns representation. A computer simulation of something is typically a detailed, "automated," multi-dimensional representation of that thing, but of course there's a world of difference between representation and reality, isn't there? As John Searle says, "No one would suppose that we could produce milk and sugar by running a computer simulation of the formal sequences in lactation and photosynthesis. . . ."* If we devised a program that simulated a cow on a digital computer, our simulation, being a mere representation of a cow, would not, if "milked," produce milk, but at best a representation of milk. You can't drink that, no matter how good a representation it is, and no matter how thirsty you are.

But now suppose we made a computer simulation of a mathematician, and suppose it worked well. Would we complain that what we had hoped for was *proofs*, but alas, all we got instead was mere *representations* of proofs? But representations of proofs *are* proofs, aren't they? It depends on how good the proofs represented are. When cartoonists represent scientists pondering blackboards, what they typically represent as proofs or formulae on the blackboard is pure gibberish, however "realistic" these figures appear to the layman. If the simulation of the mathematician produced phony proofs like those in the cartoons, it might still simulate *something* of theoretical interest about mathematicians—their verbal mannerisms, perhaps, or their absentmindedness. On the other hand, if the simulation were designed to produce representations of the proofs a good mathematician would produce, it would be as valuable a "colleague"—in the proof-producing department—as the mathematician. That is the difference, it seems, between abstract, formal products like proofs or songs . . . and concrete, material products like milk. On which side of this divide does the mind fall? Is mentality like milk or like a song?

Before leaping into debate on this issue we might pause to ask if the principle that creates the divide is all that clear-cut at the limits to which we would have to push it, were we to conform a truly detailed, superb simulation of *any* concrete object or phenomenon. Any actual, running simulation is concretely "realized" in some hardware or other, and the vehicles of representation must themselves produce some effects in the world. If the representation of an event

---

*[The quotation is from John R. Searle, "Minds, Brains, and Programs," which is reprinted in *The Mind's I* and originally appeared in *The Behavioral and Brain Sciences*, Vol. 3 (New York: Cambridge University Press, 1980), pp. 69–95. Searle makes the point again in the following selection.]

produces just about the same effects in the world as the event itself would, to insist that it is merely a representation begins to sound willful. . . .

D.C.D.

The Myth of the Computer*

JOHN R. SEARLE

[A] theory, which is fairly widely held in cognitive science, can be summarized in three propositions.

1. *Mind as Program.* What we call minds are simply very complex digital computer programs. Mental states are simply computer states and mental processes are computational processes. Any system whatever that had the right program, with the right input and output, would have to have mental states and processes in the same literal sense that you and I do, because that is all there is to mental states and processes, that is all that you and I have. The programs in question are "self-updating" or "self-designing" "systems of representations."

2. *The Irrelevance of the Neurophysiology of the Brain.* In the study of the mind actual biological facts about actual human and animal brains are irrelevant because the mind is an "abstract sort of thing" and human brains just happen to be among the indefinitely large number of kinds of computers that can have minds. Our minds happen to be embodied in our brains, but there is no essential connection between the mind and the brain. Any other computer with the right program would also have a mind.

Theses 1 and 2 are summarized in the introduction where the authors speak of "the emerging view of the mind as software or program—as an abstract sort of thing whose identity is independent of any particular physical embodiment."

3. *The Turing Test as the Criterion of the Mental.* The conclusive proof of the presence of mental states and capacities is the ability of a system to pass the Turing test, the test devised by Alan Turing and described in his article in this book. If a system can convince a competent expert that it has mental states then it really has those mental states. If, for example, a machine could "converse"

*From John R. Searle, "The Myth of the Computer," *The New York Review of Books*, April 29, 1982, p. 3. Searle is here reviewing Hofstadter and Dennett's *The Mind's I*, the source of the previous selection.

with a native Chinese speaker in such a way as to convince the speaker that it understood Chinese then it would literally understand Chinese.

The three theses are neatly lumped together when one of the editors writes, "Minds exist in brains and may come to exist in programmed machines. If and when such machines come about, their causal powers will derive not from the substances they are made of, but from their design and the programs that run in them. And the way we will know they have those causal powers is by talking to them and listening carefully to what they have to say."

We might call this collection of theses "strong artificial intelligence" (strong AI).[1] These theses are certainly not obviously true and they are seldom explicitly stated and defended.

Let us inquire first into how plausible it is to suppose that specific biochemical powers of the brain are really irrelevant to the mind. It is an amazing fact, by the way, that in twenty-seven pieces about the mind the editors have not seen fit to include any whose primary aim is to tell us how the brain actually works, and this omission obviously derives from their conviction that since "mind is an abstract sort of thing" the specific neurophysiology of the brain is incidental. This idea derives part of its appeal from the editors' keeping their discussion at a very abstract general level about "consciousness" and "mind" and "soul," but if you consider specific mental states and processes—being thirsty, wanting to go to the bathroom, worrying about your income tax, trying to solve math puzzles, feeling depressed, recalling the French word for "butterfly"—then it seems at least a little odd to think that the brain is so irrelevant.

Take thirst, where we actually know a little bit about how it works. Kidney secretions of renin synthesize a substance called angiotensin. This substance goes into the hypothalamus and triggers a series of neuron firings. As far as we know these neuron firings are a very large part of the cause of thirst. Now obviously there is more to be said, for example about the relations of the hypothalamic responses to the rest of the brain, about other things going on in the hypothalamus, and about the possible distinctions between the *feeling* of thirst and the *urge* to drink. Let us suppose we have filled out the story with the rest of the biochemical causal account of thirst.

Now the theses of the mind as program and the irrelevance of the brain would tell us that what matters about this story is not the specific biochemical properties of the angiotensin or the hypothalamus but only the formal computer programs that the whole sequence instantiates. Well, let's try that out as a hypothesis and see how it works. A computer can simulate the formal properties of the sequence of chemical and electrical phenomena in the production of thirst just as much as it can simulate the formal properties of anything else—

---

[1] "Strong" to distinguish the position from "weak" or "cautious" AI, which holds that the computer is simply a very useful tool in the study of the mind, not that the appropriately programmed computer literally has a mind.

we can simulate thirst just as we can simulate hurricanes, rainstorms, five-alarm fires, internal combustion engines, photosynthesis, lactation, or the flow of currency in a depressed economy. But no one in his right mind thinks that a computer simulation of a five-alarm fire will burn down the neighborhood, or that a computer simulation of an internal combustion engine will power a car or that computer simulations of lactation and photosynthesis will produce milk and sugar. To my amazement, however, I have found that a large number of people suppose that computer simulations of mental phenomena, whether at the level of brain processes or not, literally produce mental phenomena.

Again, let's try it out. Let's program our favorite PDP-10 computer with the formal program that simulates thirst. We can even program it to print out at the end "Boy, am I thirsty!" or "Won't someone please give me a drink?" etc. Now would anyone suppose that we thereby have even the slightest reason to suppose that the computer is literally thirsty? Or that any simulation of any other mental phenomena, such as understanding stories, feeling depressed, or worrying about itemized deductions, must therefore produce the real thing? The answer, alas, is that a large number of people are committed to an ideology that requires them to believe just that. So let us carry the story a step further.

The PDP-10 is powered by electricity and perhaps its electrical properties can reproduce some of the actual causal powers of the electrochemical features of the brain in producing mental states. We certainly couldn't rule out that eventuality a priori. But remember: the thesis of strong AI is that the mind is "independent of *any* particular embodiment" because the mind is just a program and the program can be run on a computer made of anything whatever provided it is stable enough and complex enough to carry the program. The actual physical computer could be an ant colony (one of their examples), a collection of beer cans, streams of toilet paper with small stones placed on the squares, men sitting on high stools with green eye shades—anything you like.

So let us imagine our thirst-simulating program running on a computer made entirely of old beer cans, millions (or billions) of old beer cans that are rigged up to levers and powered by windmills. We can imagine that the program simulates the neuron firings at the synapses by having beer cans bang into each other, thus achieving a strict correspondence between neuron firings and beer-can bangings. And at the end of the sequence a beer can pops up on which is written "I am thirsty." Now, to repeat the question, does anyone suppose that this Rube Goldberg apparatus is literally thirsty in the sense in which you and I are?

Notice that the thesis of Hofstadter and Dennett is not that *for all we know* the collection of beer cans might be thirsty but rather that if it has the right program with the right input and output it *must be* thirsty (or understand Proust or worry about its income tax or have any other mental state) because that is all the mind is, a certain kind of computer program, and any computer made of anything at all running the right program would have to have the appropriate mental states.

I believe that everything we have learned about human and animal biology suggests that what we call "mental" phenomena are as much a part of our biological natural history as any other biological phenomena, as much a part of biology as digestion, lactation, or the secretion of bile. Much of the implausibility of the strong AI thesis derives from its resolute opposition to biology; the mind is not a concrete biological phenomenon but "an abstract sort of thing."

Still, in calling attention to the implausibility of supposing that the specific casual powers of brains are irrelevant to minds I have not yet fully exposed the preposterousness of the strong AI position, held by Hofstadter and Dennett, so let us press on and examine a bit more closely the thesis of mind as program.

Digital computer programs by definition consist of sets of purely formal operations on formally specified symbols. The ideal computer does such things as print a 0 on the tape, move one square to the left, erase a 1, move back to the right, etc. It is common to describe this as "symbol manipulation" or, to use the term favored by Hofstadter and Dennett, the whole system is a "self-updating representational system"; but these terms are at least a bit misleading since as far as the computer is concerned the symbols don't *symbolize* anything or *represent* anything. They are just formal counters.

The computer attaches no meaning, interpretation, or content to the formal symbols; and qua computer it couldn't, because if we tried to give the computer an interpretation of its symbols we could only give it more uninterpreted symbols. The interpretation of the symbols is entirely up to the programmers and users of the computer. For example, on my pocket calculator if I print "3 × 3 = ," the calculator will print "9" but it has no idea that "3" means 3 or that "9" means 9 or that anything means anything. We might put this point by saying that the computer has a syntax but no semantics. The computer manipulates formal symbols but attaches no meaning to them, and this simple observation will enable us to refute the thesis of mind as program.

Suppose that we write a computer program to simulate the understanding of Chinese so that, for example, if the computer is asked questions in Chinese the program enables it to give answers in Chinese; if asked to summarize stories in Chinese it can give such summaries; if asked questions about the stories it has been given it will answer such questions.

Now suppose that I, who understand no Chinese at all and can't even distinguish Chinese symbols from some other kinds of symbols, am locked in a room with a number of cardboard boxes full of Chinese symbols. Suppose that I am given a book of rules in English that instruct me how to match these Chinese symbols with each other. The rules say such things as that the "squiggle-squiggle" sign is to be followed by the "squoggle-squoggle" sign. Suppose that people outside the room pass in more Chinese symbols and that following the instructions in the book I pass Chinese symbols back to them. Suppose that unknown to me the people who pass me the symbols call them "questions," and the book of instructions that I work from they call "the program"; the symbols I give back to them they call "answers to the questions" and me they call "the computer." Suppose that after a while the programmers get so good at writing the programs and I get so good at manipulating the symbols that my answers are indistinguishable from those of native Chinese speakers. I can pass the Turing test for understanding Chinese. But all the same I still don't understand a word of Chinese and neither does any other digital computer because all the computer has is what I have: a formal program that attaches no meaning, interpretation, or content to any of the symbols.

What this simple program shows is that no formal program by itself is sufficient for understanding, because it would always be possible in principle for an agent to go through the steps in the program and still not have the relevant understanding. And what works for Chinese would also work for other mental phenomena. I could, for example, go through the steps of the thirst-simulating program without feeling thirsty. The argument also, *en passant*, refutes the Turing test because it shows that a system, namely me, could pass the Turing test without having the appropriate mental states.[2] . . .

The details of how the brain works are immensely complicated and largely unknown, but some of the general principles of the relations between brain functioning and computer programs can be stated quite simply. First, we know that brain processes cause mental phenomena. Mental states are caused by and realized in the structure of the brain. From this it follows that any system that produced mental states would have to have powers equivalent to those of the brain. Such a system might use a different chemistry, but whatever its chemistry it would have to be able to cause what the brain causes. We know from the Chinese room argument that digital computer programs by themselves are never sufficient to produce mental states. Now since brains do produce minds, and since programs by themselves can't produce minds, it follows that the way the brain does it can't be by simply instantiating a computer program. (Everything, by the way, instantiates some program or other, and brains are no exception. So in that trivial sense brains, like everything else, are digital computers.) And it also follows that if you wanted to build a machine to produce mental states, a thinking machine, you couldn't do it solely in virtue of the fact that your machine ran a certain kind of computer program. The thinking machine couldn't work solely in virtue of being a digital computer but would have to duplicate the specific causal powers of the brain.

A lot of the nonsense talked about computers nowadays stems from their relative rarity and hence mystery. As computers and robots become more common, as common as telephones, washing machines, and forklift trucks, it seems

---

[2] The "Chinese room argument" is stated in detail in my article "Minds, Brains, and Programs," pages 353–373 of *The Mind's I*. It originally appeared in *The Behavioral and Brain Sciences*, Vol. 3 (Cambridge University Press, 1980), along with twenty-seven responses and a reply to the responses.

likely that this aura will disappear and people will take computers for what they are, namely useful machines. In the meantime one has to try to avoid certain recurring mistakes that keep cropping up in Hofstadter and Dennett's book as well as in other current discussions.

The first is the idea that somehow computer achievements pose some sort of threat or challenge to human beings. But the fact, for example, that a calculator can outperform even the best mathematician is no more significant or threatening than the fact that a steam shovel can outperform the best human digger. (An oddity of artificial intelligence, by the way, is the slowness of the programmers in devising a program that can beat the very best chess players. From the point of view of games theory, chess is a trivial game since each side has perfect information about the other's position and possible moves, and one has to assume that computer programs will soon be able to outperform any human chess player.)

A second fallacy is the idea that there might be some special human experience beyond computer simulation because of its special humanity. We are sometimes told that computers couldn't simulate feeling depressed or falling in love or having a sense of humor. But as far as simulation is concerned you can program your computer to print out "I am depressed," "I love Sally," or "Ha, ha," as easily as you can program it to print out "3 × 3 = 9." The real mistake is to suppose that simulation is duplication, and that mistake is the same regardless of what mental states we are talking about. A third mistake, basic to all the others, is the idea that if a computer can simulate having a certain mental state then we have the same grounds for supposing it really has that mental state as we have for supposing that human beings have that state. But we know from the Chinese room argument as well as from biology that this simple-minded behaviorism of the Turing test is mistaken.

Until computers and robots become as common as cars and until people are able to program and use them as easily as they now drive cars we are likely to continue to suffer from a certain mythological conception of digital computers. This book is very much a part of the present mythological era of the computer.[3]

---

[3] For more balanced presentations of cognitive science see *Perspectives on Cognitive Science*, edited by Donald Norman (Ablex, Norwood, NJ, 1981); *Mind Design: Philosophy, Psychology and Artificial Intelligence*, edited by John Haugeland (Branford/MIT Press, 1981); Hubert Dreyfus, *What Computers Can't Do: A Critique of Artificial Intelligence* (Harper and Row, 1972).

Appendixes

The essays reprinted here in Appendixes A, B, and C are included for those students who wish to pursue topics in linguistic analysis at a more advanced level. Appendix D contains answers to the probability puzzles offered in Chapter 10.

Appendix A
Performative Utterances*

J. L. AUSTIN

I

You are more than entitled not to know what the word "performative" means. It is a new word and an ugly word, and perhaps it does not mean anything very much. But at any rate there is one thing in its favour, it is not a profound word. I remember once when I had been talking on this subject that somebody afterwards said: "You know, I haven't the least idea what he means, unless it could be that he simply means what he says". Well, that is what I should like to mean.

Let us consider first how this affair arises. We have not got to go very far back in the history of philosophy to find philosophers assuming more or less as a matter of course that the sole business, the sole interesting business, of any utterance—that is, of anything we say—is to be true or at least false. Of course they had always known that there are other kinds of things which we say—things like imperatives, the expressions of wishes, and exclamations—some of which had even been classified by grammarians, though it wasn't perhaps too easy to tell always which was which. But still philosophers have assumed that the only things that they are interested in are utterances which report facts or which describe situations truly or falsely. In recent times this kind of approach has

---

*J. L. Austin, "Performative Utterances," *Philosophical Papers*, 2nd ed., J. O. Urmson and G. J. Warnock, eds. (Oxford: Clarendon Press, 1970), pp. 233–52.

been questioned—in two stages, I think. First of all people began to say: "Well, if these things are true or false it ought to be possible to decide which they are, and if we can't decide which they are they aren't any good but are, in short, nonsense". And this new approach did a great deal of good; a great many things which probably are nonsense were found to be such. It is not the case, I think, that all kinds of nonsense have been adequately classified yet, and perhaps some things have been dismissed as nonsense which really are not; but still this movement, the verification movement, was, in its way, excellent.

However, we then come to the second stage. After all, we set some limits to the amount of nonsense that we talk, or at least the amount of nonsense that we are prepared to admit we talk; and so people began to ask whether after all some of those things which, treated as statements, were in danger of being dismissed as nonsense did after all really set out to be statements at all. Mightn't they perhaps be intended not to report facts but to influence people in this way or that, or to let off steam in this way or that? Or perhaps at any rate some elements in these utterances performed such functions, or, for example, drew attention in some way (without actually reporting it) to some important feature of the circumstances in which the utterance was being made. On these lines people have now adopted a new slogan, the slogan of the "different uses of language". The old approach, the old statemental approach, is sometimes called even a fallacy, the descriptive fallacy.

Certainly there are a great many uses of language. It's rather a pity that people are apt to invoke a new use of language whenever they feel so inclined, to help them out of this, that, or the other well-known philosophical tangle; we need more of a framework in which to discuss these uses of language; and also I think we should not despair too easily and talk, as people are apt to do, about the *infinite* uses of language. Philosophers will do this when they have listed as many, let us say, as seventeen; but even if there were something like ten thousand uses of language, surely we could list them all in time. This, after all, is no larger than the number of species of beetle that entomologists have taken the pains to list. But whatever the defects of either of these movements—the "verification" movement or the "use of language" movement—at any rate they have effected, nobody could deny, a great revolution in philosophy and, many would say, the most salutary in its history. (Not, if you come to think of it, a very immodest claim.)

Now it is one sort of use of language that I want to examine here. I want to discuss a kind of utterance which looks like a statement and grammatically, I suppose, would be classed as a statement, which is not nonsensical, and yet is not true or false. These are not going to be utterances which contain curious verbs like "could" or "might", or curious words like "good", which many philosophers regard nowadays simply as danger signals. They will be perfectly straightforward utterances, with ordinary verbs in the first person singular present indicative active, and yet we shall see at once that they couldn't possibly be true or false. Furthermore, if a person makes an utterance of this sort we should say that he is *doing* something rather than merely *saying* something. This may sound a little odd, but the examples I shall give will in fact not be odd at all, and may even seem decidedly dull. Here are three or four. Suppose, for example, that in the course of a marriage ceremony I say, as people will, "I do"—(sc. take this woman to be my lawful wedded wife). Or again, suppose that I tread on your toe and say "I apologize". Or again, suppose that I have the bottle of champagne in my hand and say "I name this ship the *Queen Elizabeth*". Or suppose I say "I bet you sixpence it will rain tomorrow". In all these cases it would be absurd to regard the thing that I say as a report of the performance of the action which is undoubtedly done—the action of betting, or christening, or apologizing. We should say rather that, in saying what I do, I actually perform that action. When I say "I name this ship the *Queen Elizabeth*" I do not describe the christening ceremony, I actually perform the christening; and when I say "I do" (sc. take this woman to be my lawful wedded wife), I am not reporting on a marriage, I am indulging in it.

Now these kinds of utterance are the ones that we call *performative* utterances. This is rather an ugly word, and a new word, but there seems to be no word already in existence to do the job. The nearest approach that I can think of is the word "operative", as used by lawyers. Lawyers when talking about legal instruments will distinguish between the preamble, which recites the circumstances in which a transaction is effected, and on the other hand the operative part—the part of it which actually performs the legal act which it is the purpose of the instrument to perform. So the word "operative" is very near to what we want. "I give and bequeath my watch to my brother" would be an operative clause and is a performative utterance. However, the word "operative" has other uses, and it seems preferable to have a word specially designed for the use we want.

Now at this point one might protest, perhaps even with some alarm, that I seem to be suggesting that marrying is simply saying a few words, that just saying a few words *is* marrying. Well, that certainly is not the case. The words have to be said in the appropriate circumstances, and this is a matter that will come up again later. But the one thing we must not suppose is that what is needed in addition to the saying of the words in such cases is the performance of some internal spiritual act, of which the words then are to be the report. It's very easy to slip into this view at least in difficult, portentous cases, though perhaps not so easy in simple cases like apologizing. In the case of promising—for example, "I promise to be there tomorrow"—it's very easy to think that the utterance is simply the outward and visible (that is, verbal) sign of the performance of some inward spiritual act of promising, and this view has certainly been expressed in many classic places. There is the case of Euripides' Hippolytus, who said "My tongue swore to, but my heart did not"—perhaps it should be "mind" or "spirit" rather than "heart", but at any rate some kind of backstage artiste. Now it is clear from this sort of example that, if we slip into thinking that such utterances are reports, true or false, of the performance of inward and spiritual acts, we open a loophole to perjurers and welshers and bigamists and so on, so that there are disadvantages in being excessively solemn in this way. It is better, perhaps, to stick to the old saying that our word is our bond.

However, although these utterances do not themselves report facts and are not themselves true or false, saying these things does very often *imply* that certain things are true and not false, in some sense at least of that rather woolly word "imply". For example, when I say "I do take this woman to be my lawful wedded wife", or some other formula in the marriage ceremony, I do imply that I'm not already married, with wife living, sane, undivorced, and the rest of it. But still it is very important to realize that to imply that something or other is true, is not at all the same as saying something which is true itself.

These performative utterances are not true or false, then. But they do suffer from certain disabilities of their own. They can fail to come off in special ways, and that is what I want to consider next. The various ways in which a performative utterance may be unsatisfactory we call, for the sake of a name, the infelicities; and an infelicity arises—that is to say, the utterance is un-happy—if certain rules, transparently simple rules, are broken. I will mention some of these rules and then give examples of some infringements.

First of all, it is obvious that the conventional procedure which by our utterance we are purporting to use must actually exist. In the examples given here this procedure will be a verbal one, a verbal procedure for marrying or giving or whatever it may be; but it should be borne in mind that there are many non-verbal procedures by which we can perform exactly the same acts as we perform by these verbal means. It's worth remembering too that a great many of the things we do are at least in part of this conventional kind. Philos-ophers at least are too apt to assume that an action is always in the last resort the making of a physical movement, whereas it's usually, at least in part, a mat-ter of convention.

The first rule is, then, that the convention invoked must exist and be ac-cepted. And the second rule, also a very obvious one, is that the circumstances in which we purport to invoke this procedure must be appropriate for its in-vocation. If this is not observed, then the act that we purport to perform would not come off—it will be, one might say, a misfire. This will also be the case if, for example, we do not carry through the procedure—whatever it may be—correctly and completely, without a flaw and without a hitch. If any of these rules are not observed, we say that the act which we purported to perform is void, without effect. If, for example, the purported act was an act of marrying, then we should say that we "went through a form" of marriage, but we did not actually succeed in marrying.

Here are some examples of this kind of misfire. Suppose that, living in a country like our own, we wish to divorce our wife. We may try standing her in front of us squarely in the room and saying, in a voice loud enough for all to hear, "I divorce you". Now this procedure is not accepted. We shall not thereby have succeeded in divorcing our wife, at least in this country and others like it. This is a case where the convention, we should say, does not exist or is not accepted. Again, suppose that, picking sides at a children's party, I say "I pick George". But George turns red in the face and says "Not playing". In that case I plainly, for some reason or another, have not picked George—whether because there is no convention that you can pick people who aren't playing, or because George in the circumstances is an inappropriate object for the procedure of picking. Or consider the case in which I say "I appoint you Consul", and it turns out that you have been appointed already—or perhaps it may even transpire that you are a horse; here again we have the infelicity of inappropriate circumstances, inappropriate objects, or what not. Examples of flaws and hitches are perhaps scarcely necessary—one party in the marriage ceremony says "I will", the other says "I won't"; I say "I bet sixpence", but nobody says "Done", nobody takes up the offer. In all these and other such cases, the act which we purport to perform, or set out to perform is not achieved.

But there is another and a rather different way in which this kind of utterance may go wrong. A good many of these verbal procedures are designed for use by people who hold certain beliefs or have certain feelings or intentions. And if you use one of these formulae when you do not have the requisite thoughts or feelings or intentions then there is an abuse of the procedure, there is insincerity. Take, for example, the expression, "I congratulate you". This is designed for use by people who are glad that the person addressed has achieved a certain feat, believe that he was personally responsible for the success, and so on. If I say "I congratulate you" when I'm not pleased or when I don't believe that the credit was yours, then there is insincerity. Likewise if I say I promise to do something, without having the least intention of doing it or without believing it feasible. In these cases there is something wrong certainly, but it is not like a misfire. We should not say that I didn't in fact promise, but rather that I did promise but promised insincerely; I did congratulate you but the congratulations were hollow. And there may be an infelicity of a somewhat similar kind when the performative utterance commits the speaker to future conduct of a certain description and then in the future he does not in fact behave in the expected way. This is very obvious, of course, if I promise to do something and then break my promise, but there are many kinds of commitment of a rather less tangible form than that in the case of promising. For instance, I may say "I welcome you", bidding you welcome to my home or wherever it may be, but then I proceed to treat you as though you were exceedingly unwelcome. In this case the procedure of saying "I welcome you" has been abused in a way rather different from that of simple insincerity.

Now we might ask whether this list of infelicities is complete, whether the kinds of infelicity are mutually exclusive, and so forth. Well, it is not complete, and they are not mutually exclusive; they never are. Suppose that you are just about to name the ship, you have been appointed to name it, and you are just about to bang the bottle against the stem; but at that very moment some low type comes up, snatches the bottle out of your hand, breaks it on the stem, shouts out "I name this ship the *Generalissimo Stalin*", and then for good measure kicks away the chocks. Well, we agree of course on several things. We agree that the ship certainly isn't now named the *Generalissimo Stalin*, and we agree that it's an infernal shame and so on and so forth. But we may not agree as to how we should classify the particular infelicity in this case. We might say that here is a case of a perfectly legitimate and agreed procedure which, however, has been invoked in the wrong circumstances, namely by the wrong person, this low type instead of the person appointed to do it. But on the other hand we might look at it differently and say that this is a case where the procedure has not as a whole been gone through correctly, because part of the procedure for naming a ship is that you should first of all get yourself appointed as the person to do the naming and that's what this fellow did not do. Thus the way we should classify infelicities in different cases will be perhaps rather a difficult matter, and may even in the last resort be a bit arbitrary. But of course lawyers, who have to deal very much with this kind of thing, have invented all kinds of technical terms and have made numerous rules about different kinds of cases, which enable them to classify fairly rapidly what in particular is wrong in any given case.

As for whether this list is complete, it certainly is not. One further way in which things may go wrong is, for example, through what in general may be called misunderstanding. You may not hear what I say, or you may understand me to refer to something different from what I intended to refer to, and so on. And apart from further additions which we might make to the list, there is the general over-riding consideration that, as we are performing an act when we issue these performative utterances, we may of course be doing so under duress or in some other circumstances which make us not entirely responsible for doing what we are doing. That would certainly be an unhappiness of a kind—any kind of nonresponsibility might be called an unhappiness; but of course it is a quite different kind of thing from what we have been talking about. And I might mention that, quite differently again, we could be issuing any of these utterances, as we can issue an utterance of any kind whatsoever, in the course, for example, of acting a play or making a joke or writing a poem—in which case of course it would not be seriously meant and we shall not be able to say that we seriously performed the act concerned. If the poet says "Go and catch a falling star" or whatever it may be, he doesn't seriously issue an order. Considerations of this kind apply to any utterance at all, not merely to performatives.

That, then, is perhaps enough to be going on with. We have discussed the performative utterance and its infelicities. That equips us, we may suppose, with two shining new tools to crack the crib of reality maybe. It also equips us— it always does—with two shining new skids under our metaphysical feet. The question is how we use them.

II

So far we have been going firmly ahead, feeling the firm ground of prejudice glide away beneath our feet which is always rather exhilarating, but what next? You will be waiting for the bit when we bog down, the bit where we take it all back, and sure enough that's going to come but it will take time. First of all let us ask a rather simple question. How can we be sure, how can we tell, whether any utterance is to be classed as a performative or not? Surely, we feel, we ought to be able to do that. And we should obviously very much like to be able to say that there is a grammatical criterion for this, some grammatical means of deciding whether an utterance is performative. All the examples I have given hitherto do in fact have the same grammatical form; they all of them begin with the verb in the first person singular present indicative active—not just any kind of verb of course, but still they all are in fact of that form. Furthermore, with these verbs that I have used there is a typical asymmetry between the use of this person and tense of the verb and the use of the same verb in other persons and other tenses, and this asymmetry is rather an important clue.

For example, when we say "I promise that . . .", the case is very different from when we say "He promises that . . .", or in the past tense "I promised that . . .". For when we say "I promise that . . ." we do perform an act of promising—we give a promise. What we do *not* do is to report on somebody's performing an act of promising—in particular, we do not report on somebody's use of the expression "I promise". We actually do use it and do the promising. But if I say "He promises", or in the past tense "I promised", I precisely do report on an act of promising, that is to say an act of using this formula "I promise"—I report on a present act of promising by him, or on a past act of my own. There is thus a clear difference between our first person singular present indicative active, and other persons and tenses. This is brought out by the typical incident of little Willie whose uncle says he'll give him half-a-crown if he promises never to smoke till he's 55. Little Willie's anxious parent will say "Of course he promises, don't you, Willie?" giving him a nudge, and little Willie just doesn't vouchsafe. The point here is that he must do the promising himself by saying "I promise", and his parent is going too fast in saying he promises.

That, then, is a bit of a test for whether an utterance is performative or not, but it would not do to suppose that every performative utterance has to take this standard form. There is at least one other standard form, every bit as common as this one, where the verb is in the passive voice and in the second or third person, not in the first. The sort of case I mean is that of a notice inscribed "Passengers are warned to cross the line by the bridge only", or of a document reading "You are hereby authorized" to do so-and-so. These are undoubtedly performative, and in fact a signature is often required in order to show who it is that is doing the act of warning, or authorizing, or whatever it may be. Very typical of this kind of performative—especially liable to occur in written documents of course—is that the little word "hereby" either actually occurs or might naturally be inserted.

Unfortunately, however, we still can't possibly suggest that every utterance which is to be classed as a performative has to take one or another of these two, as we might call them, standard forms. After all it would be a very typical performative utterance to say "I order you to shut the door". This satisfies all the criteria. It is performing the act of ordering you to shut the door, and it is not true or false. But in the appropriate circumstances surely we could perform exactly the same act by simply saying "Shut the door", in the imperative. Or again, suppose that somebody sticks up a notice "This bull is dangerous", or simply "Dangerous bull", or simply "Bull". Does this necessarily differ from sticking up a notice, appropriately signed, saying "You are hereby warned that this bull is dangerous"? It seems that the simple notice "Bull" can do just the same job as the more elaborate formula. Of course the difference is that if we just stick up "Bull" it would not be quite clear that it is a warning; it might be there just for interest or information, like "Wallaby" on the cage at the zoo, or "Ancient Monument". No doubt we should know from the nature of the case that it was a warning, but it would not be explicit.

Well, in view of this break-down of grammatical criteria, what we should like to suppose—and there is a good deal in this—is that any utterance which is performative could be reduced or expanded or analysed into one of these two standard forms beginning "I . . ." so and so or beginning "You (or he) hereby . . ." so and so. If there was any justification for this hope, as to some extent there is, then we might hope to make a list of all the verbs which can appear in these standard forms, and then we might classify the kinds of acts that can be performed by performative utterances. We might do this with the aid of a dictionary, using such a test as that already mentioned—whether there is the characteristic asymmetry between the first person singular present indicative active and the other persons and tenses—in order to decide whether a verb is to go into our list or not. Now if we make such a list of verbs we do in fact find that they fall into certain fairly well-marked classes. There is the class of cases where we deliver verdicts and make estimates and appraisals of various kinds. There is the class where we give undertakings, commit ourselves in various ways by saying something. There is the class where by saying something we exercise various rights and powers, such as appointing and voting and so on. And there are one or two other fairly well-marked classes.

Suppose this task accomplished. Then we could call these verbs in our list explicit performative verbs, and any utterance that was reduced to one or the other of our standard forms we could call an explicit performative utterance. "I order you to shut the door" would be an explicit performative utterance, whereas "Shut the door" would not—that is simply a "primary" performative utterance or whatever we like to call it. In using the imperative we may be ordering you to shut the door, but it just isn't made clear whether we are ordering you or entreating you or imploring you or beseeching you or inciting you or tempting you, or one or another of many other subtly different acts which, in an unsophisticated primitive language, are very likely not yet discriminated. But we need not overestimate the unsophistication of primitive languages. There are a great many devices that can be used for making clear, even at the primitive level, what act it is we are performing when we say something—the tone of voice, cadence, gesture—and above all we can rely upon the nature of the circumstances, the context in which the utterance is issued. This very often makes it quite unmistakable whether it is an order that is being given or whether, say, I am simply urging you or entreating you. We may, for instance, say something like this: "Coming from him I was bound to take it as an order". Still, in spite of all these devices, there is an unfortunate amount of ambiguity and lack of discrimination in default of our explicit performative verbs. If I say something like "I shall be there", it may not be certain whether it is a promise, or an expression of intention, or perhaps even a forecast of my future behaviour, of what is going to happen to me; and it may matter a good deal, at least in developed societies, precisely which of these things it is. And that is why the explicit performative verb is evolved—to make clear exactly which it is, how far it commits me and in what way, and so forth.

This is just one way in which language develops in tune with the society of which it is the language. The social habits of the society may considerably affect the question of which performative verbs are evolved and which, sometimes for rather irrelevant reasons, are not. For example, if I say "You are a poltroon", it might be that I am censuring you or it might be that I am insulting you. Now since apparently society approves of censuring or reprimanding, we have here evolved a formula "I reprimand you", or 'I censure you", which enables us expeditiously to get this desirable business over. But on the other hand, since apparently we don't approve of insulting, we have not evolved a simple formula "I insult you", which might have done just as well.

By means of these explicit performative verbs and some other devices, then, we make explicit what precise act it is that we are performing when we issue our utterance. But here I would like to put in a word of warning. We must distinguish between the function of making explicit what act it is we are performing, and the quite different matter of *stating* what act it is we are performing. In issuing an explicit performative utterance we are not stating what act it is, we are showing or making explicit what act it is. We can draw a helpful parallel here with another case in which the act, the conventional act that we perform, is not a speech-act but a physical performance. Suppose I appear before you one day and bow deeply from the waist. Well, this is ambiguous. I may be simply observing the local flora, tying my shoe-lace, something of that kind; on the other hand, conceivably I might be doing obeisance to you. Well, to clear up this ambiguity we have some device such as raising the hat, saying "Salaam", or something of that kind, to make it quite plain that the act being performed is the conventional one of doing obeisance rather than some other act. Now nobody would want to say that lifting your hat was stating that you were performing an act of obeisance; it certainly is not, but it does make it quite plain that you are. And so in the same way to say "I warn you that . . ." or "I order you to . . ." or "I promise that . . ." is not to state that you are doing something, but makes it plain that you are—it does constitute your verbal performance, a performance of a particular kind.

So far we have been going along as though there was a quite clear difference between our performative utterances and what we have contrasted them with, statements or reports or descriptions. But now we begin to find that this dinstinction is not as clear as it might be. It's now that we begin to sink in a little. In the first place, of course, we may feel doubts as to how widely our performatives extend. If we think up some odd kinds of expression we use in odd cases, we might very well wonder whether or not they satisfy our rather vague criteria for being performative utterances. Suppose, for example, somebody says "Hurrah". Well, not true or false; he is performing the act of cheering. Does that make it a performative utterance in our sense or not? Or suppose he says "Damn"; he is performing the act of swearing, and it is not true or false. Does that make it performative? We feel that in a way it does and yet it's rather different. Again, consider cases of "suiting the action to the words"; these too may make us wonder whether perhaps the utterance should be classed as performative. Or sometimes, if somebody says "I am sorry", we wonder whether this is just the same as "I apologize"—in which case of course we have said it's a performative utterance—or whether perhaps it's to be taken as a description, true or false, of the state of his feelings. If he had said "I feel perfectly awful about it", then we should think it must be meant to be a description of the state of his feelings. If he had said "I apologize", we should feel this was clearly a performative utterance, going through the ritual of apologizing. But if he says "I am sorry" there is an unfortunate hovering between the two. This phenomenon is quite common. We often find cases in which there is an obvious pure performative utterance and obvious other utterances connected with it which are not performative but descriptive, but on the other hand a good many in between where we're not quite sure which they are. On some occasions of course they are obviously used the one way, on some occasions the other way, but on some occasions they seem positively to revel in ambiguity.

Again, consider the case of the umpire when he says "Out" or "Over", or the jury's utterance when they say that they find the prisoner guilty. Of course, we say, these are cases of giving verdicts, performing the act of appraising and so forth, but still in a way they have some connexion with the facts. They seem to have something like the duty to be true or false, and seem not to be so very remote from statements. If the umpire says "Over", this surely has at least something to do with six balls in fact having been delivered rather than seven, and so on. In fact in general we may remind ourselves that "I state that . . ." does not look so very different from "I warn you that . . ." or "I promise to . . .". It makes clear surely that the act that we are performing is an act of stating, and so functions just like "I warn" or "I order". So isn't "I state that . . ." a performative utterance? But then one may feel that utterances beginning "I state that . . ." do have to be true or false, that they *are* statements.

Considerations of this sort, then, may well make us feel pretty unhappy. If we look back for a moment at our contrast between statements and performative utterances, we realize that we were taking statements very much on trust from, as we said, the traditional treatment. Statements, we had it, were to be true or false; performative utterances on the other hand were to be felicitous or infelicitous. They were the doing of something, whereas for all we said making statements was not doing something. Now this contrast surely, if we look back at it, is unsatisfactory. Of course statements are liable to be assessed in this matter of their correspondence or failure to correspond with the facts, that is, being true or false. But they are also liable to infelicity every bit as much as are performative utterances. In fact some troubles that have arisen in the study of statements recently can be shown to be simply troubles of infelicity. For example, it has been pointed out that there is something very odd about saying something like this: "The cat is on the mat but I don't believe it is". Now this is an outrageous thing to say, but it is not self-contradictory. There is no reason why the cat shouldn't be on the mat without my believing that it is. So how are we to classify what's wrong with this peculiar statement? If we remember now the doctrine of infelicity we shall see that the person who makes this remark about the cat is in much the same position as somebody who says something like this: "I promise that I shall be there, but I haven't the least intention of being there." Once again you can of course perfectly well promise to be there without having the least intention of being there, but there is something outrageous about saying it, about actually avowing the insincerity of the promise you give. In the same way there is insincerity in the case of the person who says "The cat is on the mat but I don't believe it is", and he is actually avowing that insincerity—which makes a peculiar kind of nonsense.

A second case that has come to light is the one about John's children—the case where somebody is supposed to say "All John's children are bald but John hasn't got any children". Or perhaps somebody says "All John's children are bald", when as a matter of fact—he doesn't say so—John has no children. Now those who study statements have worried about this; ought they to say that the statement "All John's children are bald" is meaningless in this case? Well, if it is, it is not a bit like a great many other more standard kinds of meaninglessness; and we see, if we look back at our list of infelicities, that what is going wrong here is much the same as what goes wrong in, say, the case of a contract for the sale of a piece of land when the piece of land referred to does not exist. Now what we say in the case of this sale of land, which of course would be effected by a performative utterance, is that the sale is void—void for lack of reference or ambiguity of reference; and so we can see that the statement about all John's children is likewise void for lack of reference. And if the man actually says that John has no children in the same breath as saying they're all bald, he is making the same kind of outrageous utterance as the man who says "The cat is on the mat and I don't believe it is", or the man who says "I promise to but I don't intend to".

In this way, then, ills that have been found to afflict statements can be precisely paralleled with ills that are characteristic of performative utterances. And after all when we state something or describe something or report something, we do perform an act which is every bit as much an act as an act of ordering or warning. There seems no good reason why stating should be given a specially unique position. Of course philosophers have been wont to talk as though you or I or anybody could just go round stating anything about anything and that would be perfectly in order, only there's just a little question: is it true or false? But besides the little question, is it true or false, there is surely the question: *is* it in order? Can you go round just making statements about anything? Suppose for example you say to me "I'm feeling pretty mouldy this morning". Well, I say to you "You're not"; and you say "What the devil do you mean, I'm not?" I say "Oh nothing—I'm just stating you're not, is it true or false?" And you say "Wait a bit about whether it's true or false, the question is what did you mean by making statements about somebody else's feelings? I told you I'm feeling pretty mouldy. You're just not in a position to say, to state that I'm not". This brings out that you can't just make statements about other people's feelings (though you can make guesses if you like); and there are very many things which, having no knowledge of, not being in a position to pronounce about, you just can't state. What we need to do for the case of stating, and by the same token describing and reporting, is to take them a bit off their pedestal, to realize that they are speech-acts no less than all these other speech-acts that we have been mentioning and talking about as performative.

Then let us look for a moment at our original contrast between the performative and the statement from the other side. In handling performatives we have been putting it all the time as though the only thing that a performative utterance had to do was to be felicitous, to come off, not to be a misfire, not to be an abuse. Yes, but that's not the end of the matter. At least in the case of many utterances which, on what we have said, we should have to class as performative—cases where we say "I warn you to . . .", "I advise you to . . ." and so on—there will be other questions besides simply: was it in order, was it all right, as a piece of advice or a warning, did it come off? After that surely there will be the question: was it good or sound advice? Was it a justified warning? Or in the case, let us say, of a verdict or an estimate: was it a good estimate, or a sound verdict? And these are questions that can only be decided by considering how the content of the verdict or estimate is related in some way to fact, or to evidence available about the facts. This is to say that we do require to assess at least a great many performative utterances in a general dimension of correspondence with fact. It may still be said, of course, that this does not make them *very* like statements because still they are not true or false, and that's a little black and white speciality that distinguishes statements as a class apart. But actually—though it would take too long to go on about this—the more you think about truth and falsity the more you find that very few statements that we ever utter are just true or just false. Usually there is the question are they fair or are they not fair, are they adequate or not adequate, are they exaggerated or not exaggerated? Are they too rough, or are they perfectly precise, accurate, and so on? "True" and "false" are just general labels for a whole dimension of different appraisals which have something or other to do with the relation between what we say and the facts. If, then, we loosen up our ideas of truth and falsity we shall see that statements, when assessed in relation to the facts, are not so very different after all from pieces of advice, warnings, verdicts, and so on.

We see then that stating something is performing an act just as much as is giving an order or giving a warning; and we see, on the other hand, that, when we give an order or a warning or a piece of advice, there is a question about how this is related to fact which is not perhaps so very different from the kind of question that arises when we discuss how a statement is related to fact. Well, this seems to mean that in its original form our distinction between the performative and the statement is considerably weakened, and indeed breaks down. I will just make a suggestion as to how to handle this matter. We need to go very much farther back, to consider all the ways and senses in which saying anything at all is doing this or that—because of course it is always doing a good many different things. And one thing that emerges when we do do this is that, besides the question that has been very much studied in the past as to what a certain utterance *means*, there is a further question distinct from this as to what was the *force*, as we may call it, of the utterance. We may be quite clear what "Shut the door" means, but not yet at all clear on the further point as to whether as uttered at a certain time it was an order, an entreaty or whatnot. What we need besides the old doctrine about meanings is a new doctrine about all the possible forces of utterances, towards the discovery of which our proposed list of explicit performative verbs would be a very great help; and then, going on from there, an investigation of the various terms of appraisal that we use in discussing speech-acts of this, that, or the other precise kind—orders, warnings, and the like.

The notions that we have considered then, are the performative, the infelicity, the explicit performative, and lastly, rather hurriedly, the notion of the forces of utterances. I dare say that all this seems a little unremunerative, a little complicated. Well, I suppose in some ways it is unremunerative, and I suppose it ought to be remunerative. At least, though, I think that if we pay attention to these matters we can clear up some mistakes in philosophy; and after all philosophy is used as a scapegoat, it parades mistakes which are really the mistakes of everybody. We might even clear up some mistakes in grammar, which perhaps is a little more respectable.

And is it complicated? Well, it is complicated a bit; but life and truth and things do tend to be complicated. It's not things, it's philosophers that are simple. You will have heard it said, I expect, that over-simplification is the occupational disease of philosophers, and in a way one might agree with that. But for a sneaking suspicion that it's their occupation.

Appendix B
Logic and Conversation*

H. P. GRICE

It is a commonplace of philosophical logic that there are, or appear to be, divergences in meaning between, on the one hand, at least some of what I shall call the *formal* devices '~', '.', '$\vee$', '$\supset$', '(x)', '($\exists$x)', '($\imath$x)' (when these are given a standard two-valued interpretation), and, on the other, what are taken to be

*H. P. Grice, "Logic and Conversation," in *The Logic of Grammar*, Donald Davidson and Gilbert Harman, eds. (Encino, Calif.: Dickinson Publishing Co., 1975), pp. 64–153.

their analogues or counter parts in natural language, such expressions are 'not', 'or', 'if', 'all', 'some' (or 'at least one'), 'the'. Some logicians may at some time have wanted to claim that there are in fact no such divergences; but such claims, if made at all, have been somewhat rashly made, and those suspected of making them have been subjected to some pretty rough handling.

Those who concede that such divergences exist adhere, in the main, to one or other of two rival groups, which for the purposes of this article I shall call the formalist and the informalist groups. An outline of a not uncharacteristic formalist position may be given as follows: In so far as logicians are concerned with the formulation of very general patterns of valid inference, the formal devices possess a decisive advantage over their natural counterparts. For it will be possible to construct in terms of the formal devices a system of very general formulas, a considerable number of which can be regarded as, or are closely related to, patterns of inferences, the expression of which involves some or all of the devices. Such a system may consist of a certain set of simple formulas which must be acceptable if the devices have the meaning which has been assigned to them, and an indefinite number of further formulas, many of them less obviously acceptable, each of which can be shown to be acceptable if the members of the original set are acceptable. We have thus a way of handling dubiously acceptable patterns of inference, and if, as is sometimes possible, we can apply a decision procedure, we have an even better way. Furthermore, from a philosophical point of view, the possession by the natural counterparts of those elements in their meaning, which they do not share with the corresponding formal devices, is to be regarded as an imperfection of natural languages; the elements in question are undesirable excrescences. For the presence of these elements has the result that the concepts within which they appear cannot be precisely and clearly defined, and that at least some statements involving them cannot, in some circumstances, be assigned a definite truth-value. The indefiniteness of these concepts is not only objectionable in itself but leaves open the way to metaphysics; we cannot be certain that none of these natural language expressions is metaphysically 'loaded'. For these reasons the expressions, as used in natural speech, cannot be regarded as finally acceptable, and may turn out to be, finally, not fully intelligible. The proper course is to conceive and begin to construct an ideal language, incorporating the formal devices, the sentences of which will be clear, determinate in truth-value, and certifiably free from metaphysical implications; the foundations of science will now be philosophically secure, since the statements of the scientist will be expressible (though not necessarily actually expressed) within this ideal language. (I do not wish to suggest that all formalists would accept the whole of this outline, but I think that all would accept at least some part of it.)

To this, an informalist might reply in the following vein. The philosophical demand for an ideal language rests on certain assumptions which should not be conceded; these are, that the primary yardstick by which to judge the adequacy of a language is its ability to serve the needs of science, that an expression cannot be guaranteed as fully intelligible unless an explication or analysis of its meaning has been provided, and that every explication or analysis must take the form of a precise definition which is the expression or assertion of a logical equivalence. Language serves many important purposes besides those of scientific inquiry. We can know perfectly well what an expression means (and so *a fortiori* that it is intelligible) without knowing its analysis, and the provision of an analysis may (and usually does) consist in the specification, as generalized as possible, of the conditions which count for or against the applicability of the expression being analyzed. Moreover, while it is no doubt true that the formal devices are specially amenable to systematic treatment by the logician, it remains the case that there are very many inferences and arguments, expressed in natural language and not in terms of these devices, which are nevertheless recognizably valid. So there must be a place for an unsimplified, and so more or less unsystematic, logic of the natural counterparts of those devices. This logic may be aided and guided by the simplified logic of the formal devices, but cannot be supplanted by it. Indeed, not only do the two logics differ, but sometimes they come into conflict: rules which hold for a formal device may not hold for its natural counterpart.

Now on the general question of the place in philosophy of the reformation of natural language, I shall, in this article, have nothing to say. I shall confine myself to the dispute in its relation to the alleged divergences mentioned at the outset. I have moreover no intention of entering the fray on behalf of either contestant. I wish, rather, to maintain that the common assumption of the contestants that the divergences do in fact exist is (broadly speaking) a common mistake, and that the mistake arises from an inadequate attention to the nature and importance of the conditions governing conversation. I shall, therefore, proceed at once to inquire into the general conditions which, in one way or another, apply to conversation as such irrespective of its subject matter.

IMPLICATURE

Suppose that A and B are talking about a mutual friend C, who is now working in a bank. A asks B how C is getting on in his job, and B replies, "Oh quite well, I think; he likes his colleagues, and he hasn't been to prison yet." At this point A might well inquire what B was implying, what he was suggesting, or even what he meant by saying that C had not yet been to prison. The answer might be any one of such things as that C is the sort of person likely to yield to the temptation provided by his occupation, that C's colleagues are really very unpleasant and treacherous people, and so forth. It might of course be quite unnecessary for A to make such an inquiry of B, the answer to it being, in the context, clear in advance. I think it is clear that whatever B implied, suggested, or meant, in this example is distinct from what B said, which was simply that C had not been to prison yet. I wish to introduce, as a term of art, the verb 'implicate', the related nouns 'implicature' (cf. 'implying') and 'implicatum' (cf. 'what is implied'). The point of this maneuver is to avoid having, on each occasion, to choose between this or that member of the family of verbs for which 'implicate' is to do general duty. I shall, for the time being at least, have to assume to a considerable extent an intuitive understanding of the meaning of 'say' in such contexts, and an ability to recognize particular verbs as members of the family with which 'implicate' is associated. I can, however, make one or two remarks which may help to clarify the more problematic of these assumptions, namely that connected with the meaning of the word 'say'.

(1) In the sense in which I am using the word 'say', I intend what someone has said to be closely related to the conventional meaning of the words (the sentence) which he has uttered. Suppose someone to have uttered the sentence "He is in the grip of a vice." Given a knowledge of the English language, but no knowledge of the circumstances of the utterance, one would know something about what the speaker had said, on the assumption that he was speaking standard English, and speaking literally. One would know that he had said, about some particular male person or animal X, that at the time of the utterance (whatever that was) either (i) that X was unable to rid himself of a certain kind of bad character trait, or (ii) that some part of X's person was caught in a certain kind of tool or instrument. (This is an approximate account, of course.) But for a full identification of what the speaker had said, one would need to know (a) the identity of X, (b) the time of utterance, (c) the meaning, on the particular occasion of utterance, of the phrase "in the grip of a vice" (a decision between (i) and (ii)). This brief indication of my use of 'say' leaves it open whether a man who says (today) "Harold Wilson is a great man" and another who says (also today) "The British Prime Minister is a great man" would, if each knew that the two singular terms had the same reference, have said the same thing. But whatever decision is made about this question, the apparatus I am about to provide will be capable of accounting for any implicatures that might depend on the presence of one rather than another of these singular terms in the sentence uttered. Such implicatures would merely be related to different maxims.

(2) In some cases the conventional meaning of the words used will determine what is implicated, besides helping to determine what is said: If I say (smugly) "He is an Englishman; he is, therefore, brave," I have certainly committed myself by virtue of the meaning of my words, to its being true that his being brave is a consequence of (follows from) his being an Englishman. But while I have said that he is an Englishman, and said that he is brave, I do not want to say that I have *said* (in the favored sense) that it follows from his being an Englishman that he is brave, though I have certainly indicated, and so implicated, that this is so. I do not want to say that my utterance of this sentence would be, *strictly speaking*, false should the consequence in question fail to hold. So *some* implicatures are conventional, unlike the one with which I introduced this discussion of implicature.

I wish to represent a certain subclass of nonconventional implicatures, which I shall call *conventional* implicatures, as being essentially connected with certain general features of discourse; so my next step is to try to say what these features are.

The following may provide a first approximation to a general principle. Our talk exchanges do not normally consist of a succession of disconnected remarks, and would not be rational if they did. They are, characteristically, to some degree at least cooperative efforts. Each participant recognizes in them, to some extent, a common purpose or set of purposes, or at least a mutually accepted direction. This purpose or direction may be fixed from the start (e.g., by an initial proposal of a question for discussion), or it may evolve during the exchange; it may be fairly definite, or it may be so indefinite as to leave very considerable latitude to the participants (as in a casual conversation). But at each stage, *some* possible conversational moves would be excluded as conversationally unsuitable. We might then formulate a rough general principle which participants will be expected (ceteris paribus) to observe, viz: "Make your conversational contribution such as is required, at the stage at which it occurs, by the accepted purpose or direction of the talk exchange in which you are engaged." One might label this the Cooperative Principle (CP).

On the assumption that some such general principle as the above is acceptable, one may perhaps distinguish four categories under one or other of which will fall certain more specific maxims and submaxims, the following of which will in general yield results in accordance with the Cooperation Principle. Echoing Kant, I call these categories Quantity, Quality, Relation, and Manner. The category of *Quantity* relates to the quantity of information to be provided and under it fall the maxims

(1) "Make your contribution as informative as is required (for the current purposes of the exchange),"

and possibly

(2) "Do not make your contribution more informative than is required."

(The second maxim is disputable; it might be said that to be overinformative is not a transgression of the CP but merely a waste of time. However, it might be answered that such overinformativeness may be confusing in that it is liable to raise side issues; and there may also be an indirect effect, in that the hearers may be misled, as a result of thinking that there is some particular *point* in the provision of excess information. However this may be, there is perhaps a different reason for doubt about the admission of this second maxim, namely, that its effect will be secured by a later maxim, which concerns relevance.)

Under the category of *Quality* falls a supermaxim: "Try to make your contribution one that is true," and two more specific maxims:

(1) "Do not say what you believe to be false."
(2) "Do not say that for which you lack adequate evidence."

Under the category of *Relation* I place a single maxim, namely, "Be relevant." Though the maxim itself is terse, its formulation conceals a number of problems which exercise me a good deal; questions about what different kinds of foci of relevance there may be, how these shift in the course of a talk exchange, how to allow for the fact that subjects of conversation are legitimately changed, and so on. I find the treatment of such questions exceedingly difficult, and I hope to revert to them in a later lecture [not included here].

Finally under the category of *Manner*, which I understand as relating, not (like the previous categories) to what is said, but rather to *how* what is said is to be said, I include the supermaxim: "Be perspicuous" and various maxims such as

(1) "Avoid obscurity of expression"
(2) "Avoid ambiguity"
(3) "Be brief (avoid unnecessary prolixity)"
(4) "Be orderly"

And one might need others.

It is obvious that the observance of some of these maxims is a matter of lesser urgency than is the observance of others; a man who has expressed himself with undue prolixity would, in general, be open to milder comment than would a man who had said something which he believes to be false. Indeed it might be felt that the importance of at least the first maxim of Quality is such that it should not be included in a scheme of the kind which I am constructing; other maxims only come into operation on the assumption that this maxim of Quality is satisfied. While this may be correct, so far as the generation of implicatures is concerned it seems to play a role not totally different from the other maxims; and it will be convenient, for the present at least, to treat it as a member of the list of maxims.

There are of course all sorts of other maxims (aesthetic, social, or moral in character) such as "Be polite," which are also normally observed by participants in talk exchanges, and these may also generate nonconventional implicatures. The conversational maxims, however, and the conversational implicatures connected with them, are specially connected (I hope) with the particular purposes which talk (and so talk exchange) is adapted to serve and is primarily employed to serve. I have stated my maxims as if this purpose were a maximally effective exchange of information; this specification is of course too narrow, and the scheme needs to be generalized to allow for such general purposes as influencing or directing the actions of others.

As one of my avowed aims is to see talking as a special case or variety of purposive, indeed rational, behavior, it may be worth noting that the specific expectations or presumptions connected with at least some of the foregoing maxims have their analogues in the sphere of transactions which are not talk exchanges. I list briefly one such analogue for each conversational category.

I *Quantity*. If you are assisting me to mend a car, I expect your contribution to be neither more nor less than is required; if for example, at a particular stage I need four screws, I expect you to hand me four, rather than two or six.

II *Quality*. I expect your contributions to be genuine and not spurious. If

I need sugar as an ingredient in the cake you are helping me bake, I do not expect you to hand me salt; if I need a spoon, I do not expect a trick spoon made of rubber.

III *Relation*. I expect a partner's contribution to be appropriate to immediate needs at each stage of the transaction; if I am mixing ingredients for a cake, I do not expect to be handed a good book, or even a pot-holder (though this might be an appropriate contribution at a later stage).

IV *Manner*. I expect a partner to make it clear what contribution he is making, and to execute his performance with reasonable dispatch.

These analogies are relevant to what I regard as a fundamental question about the CP and its attendant maxims, namely, what the basis is for the assumption which we seem to make, and on which (I hope) it will appear that a great range of implicatures depend, that talkers will in general (ceteris paribus and in the absence of indications to the contrary) proceed in the manner which these principles prescribe. A dull but no doubt at a certain level adequate answer is that it is just a well-recognized empirical fact that people *do* behave in these ways; they have learned to do so in childhood, and have not lost the habit of doing so; and indeed it would involve a good deal of effort to make a radical departure from the habit. It is much easier, for example, to tell the truth than to invent lies.

I am, however, enough of a rationalist to want to find a basis which underlies these facts, undeniable though they may be; I would like to be able to think of the standard type of conversational practice not merely as something which all or most do *in fact* follow, but as something which it is *reasonable* for us to follow, which we *should not* abandon. For a time I was attracted by the idea that observance of the CP and the maxims, in a talk exchange, could be thought of as a quasi-contractual matter, with parallels outside the realm of discourse. If you pass by when I am struggling with my stranded car, I no doubt have some degree of expectation that you will offer help; but once you join me in tinkering under the hood, my expectations become stronger and take more specific forms (in the absence of indications that you are merely an incompetent meddler). Likewise, talk exchanges seem to me to exhibit, characteristically, certain features which jointly distinguish cooperative transactions: (1) that the participants have some common immediate aim, like getting a car mended (Their ultimate aims may of course be independent and even in conflict; each may want to get the car mended in order to drive off leaving the other stranded. In characteristic talk exchanges there is a common aim even if, as in an over-the-wall chat, it is a second-order one, namely, that each party should for the time being identify himself with the transitory conversational interests of the other.); (2) that the contributions of the participants should be dovetailed, mutually dependent; (3) that there is some sort of understanding (which may be explicit but which is often tacit) that, other things being equal, the transaction should continue in appropriate style unless both parties agree it should terminate. You don't just shove off, or start doing something else.

But while some such quasi-contractual basis as this may apply to some cases, there are too many types of exchange, like quarreling and letter writing, which it fails to fit comfortably. In any case one feels that the talker who is irrelevant or obscure has primarily let down not his audience but himself. So I would like to be able to show that observance of the CP and maxims is reasonable (rational) along the following lines: that any one who cares about the goals that are central to conversation/communication (such as giving and receiving information, influencing and being influenced by others) must be expected to have an interest, given suitable circumstances, in participation in talk exchanges which will be profitable only on the assumption that they are conducted in general accordance with the CP and the maxims. Whether any such conclusion can be reached, I am uncertain; in any case I am fairly sure I cannot reach it until I am a good deal clearer about the nature of relevance and of the circumstances in which it is required.

It is now time to show the connection between the CP and maxims on the one hand, and conversational implicature on the other.

A participant in a talk exchange may fail to fulfill a maxim in various ways which include the following:

(1) He may quietly and unostentatiously *violate* a maxim; if so, in some cases he will be liable to mislead.

(2) He may *opt out* from the operation both of the maxim and of the CP; he may say, indicate, or allow it to become plain that he is unwilling to cooperate in the way in which the maxim requires. He may say, for example, "I cannot say more, my lips are sealed."

(3) He may be faced by a *clash:* he may be unable, for example, to fulfill the first maxim of Quantity ("Be as informative as required") without violating the second maxim of Quality ("Have adequate evidence for what you say").

(4) He may *flout* a maxim; that is, he may *blatantly* fail to fulfill it. On the assumption that the speaker is able to fulfill the maxim and do so without violating another maxim (because of a clash), is not opting out, and is not in view of the blatancy of his performance, trying to mislead, the hearer is faced with a minor problem: how can his saying what he did say be reconciled with the supposition that he is observing the overall CP? This situation is one which characteristically gives rise to a conversational implicature; and when a conversational implicature is generated in this way, I shall say that a maxim is being *exploited.*

I am now in a position to characterize the notion of conversational implicature, a man who, by (in when) saying (or making as if to say) that *p* has implicated that *q*, may be said to have conversationally implicated that *q*, *provided that:* (1) he is to be presumed to be observing the conversational maxims, or at least the cooperative principle; (2) the supposition that he is aware that, or thinks that *q*, is required in order to make his saying or making as if to say *p* (or doing so in *those* terms) consistent with this presumption; and (3) that the speaker thinks (and would expect the hearer to think that the speaker thinks) that it is within the competence of the hearer to work out, or grasp intuitively, that the supposition mentioned in (2) *is* required. Apply this to my initial example, to B's remark that C has not yet been to prison. In a suitable setting A might reason as follows: "(1) B has apparently violated the maxim 'Be relevant' and so may be regarded as having flouted one of the maxims conjoining perspicuity; yet I have no reason to suppose that he is opting out from the operation of the CP; (2) given the circumstances I can regard his irrelevance as only apparent if and only if I suppose him to think that C is potentially dishonest; (3) B knows that I am capable of working out step (2). So B implicates that C is potentially dishonest."

The presence of a conversational implicature must be capable of being worked out; for even if it can in fact be intuitively grasped, unless the intuition is replaceable by an argument, the implicature (if present at all) will not count as a *conversational* implicature; it will be a *conventional* implicature. To work out that a particular conversational implicature is present, the hearer will rely on the following data: (1) the conventional meaning of the words used, together with the identity of any references which may be involved; (2) the CP and its maxims; (3) the context linguistic or otherwise of the utterance; (4) other items of background knowledge; (5) the fact (or supposed fact) that all relevant items falling under the previous heading are available to both participants, and that both participants know or assume this to be so. A general pattern for the working out of a conversational implicature might be given as follows: "He has said that p; there is no reason to suppose that he is not observing the maxims, or at least the CP; he could not be doing this unless he thought that q; he knows (and knows that I know that he knows) that I can see that the supposition that he thinks that q is required; he has done nothing to stop me thinking that q; therefore he intends me to think, or is at least willing to allow me to think, that q; and so he has implicated that q."

I shall now offer a number of examples which I shall divide into three groups.

Group A: Examples in which no maxim is violated, or at least in which it is not clear that any maxim is violated.

(1) A is standing by an obviously immobilized car and is approached by B, and the following exchange takes place:

A: "I am out of petrol."
B: "There is a garage round the corner."

(*Gloss*: B would be infringing the maxim "Be relevant" unless he thinks, or thinks it possible, that the garage is open, and had petrol to sell; so he implicated that the garage is, or at least may be, open, and so on.)

In this example, unlike the case of the remark "He hasn't been to prison yet," the unstated connection between B's remark and A's remark is so obvious that, even if one interprets the supermaxim of Manner, "Be perspicuous," as applying not only to the expression of what is said, but also to the connection of what is said, with adjacent remarks, there seems to be no case for regarding that supermaxim as infringed in this example. The next example is perhaps a little less clear in this respect.

(2) A: "Smith doesn't seem to have a girl friend these days."
    B: "He has been paying a lot of visits to New York lately."

B implicates that Smith has, or may have, a girl friend in New York. Gloss is unnecessary in view of that given for the previous example.

In both examples the speaker implicates that which he must be assumed to believe in order to preserve the assumption that he is observing the maxim of relation.

Group B: An example in which a maxim is violated, but its violation is to be explained by the supposition of a clash with another maxim. A is planning with B an itinerary for a holiday in France. Both know that A wants to see his friend C if to do so would not involve too great a prolongation of his journey:

    A: "Where does C live?"
    B: "Somewhere in the South of France."

(*Gloss*: There is no reason to suppose that B is opting out; his answer is, as he well knows, less informative than is required to meet A's needs; this infringement of the first maxim of Quantity can only be explained by the supposition that B is aware that to be more informative would be to say something which infringed the maxim of Quality, "Don't say what you lack adequate evidence for," so B implicates that he does not know in which town C lives.)

Group C: Examples which involve exploitation, that is, a procedure by which a maxim is flouted for the purpose of getting in a conversational implicature by means of something of the nature of a figure of speech. In these examples, though some maxim is violated at the level of what is said, the hearer is entitled to assume that that maxim, or at least the overall Cooperative Principle, is observed at the level of what is implicated.

(1a) (A flouting of the first maxim of Quantity): A is writing a testimonial about a pupil who is a candidate for a philosophy job, and his letter reads as follows: "Dear Sir, Mr. X's command of English is excellent, and his attendance at tutorials has been regular, Yours, etc." (*Gloss*: A cannot be opting out, since if he wished to be uncooperative, why write at all? He cannot be unable, through ignorance, to say more, since the man is his pupil; moreover, he knows that more information than this is wanted. He must, therefore, be wishing to impart information which he is reluctant to write down. This supposition is only tenable on the assumption that he thinks that Mr. X is no good at philosophy. This, then, is what he is implicating.)

Extreme examples of a flouting of the first maxim of Quantity are provided by utterances of patent tautologies like "Women are women," "War is war." I would wish to maintain that at the level of what is said, in my favored sense, such remarks are totally noninformative and so, at that level, cannot but infringe the first maxim of Quantity in any conversational context. They are, of course, informative at the level of what is implicated, and the hearer's identification of their informative content at this level is dependent on his ability to explain the speaker's selection of this *particular* patent tautology.

(1b) (An infringement of the second maxim of Quantity: "Do not give more information than is required" on the assumption that the existence of such a maxim should be admitted.) A wants to know whether *p*; and B volunteers not only the information that *p*, but information to the effect that it is certain that *p*, and that the evidence for its being true that *p* is so-and-so and such-and-such.

B's volubility may be undesigned, and if it is so regarded by A, it may raise in A's mind a doubt whether B is as certain as he says he is ("Methinks the lady doth protest too much"). But if it is thought of as designed, it would be an oblique way of conveying that it is to some degree controversial whether or not *p*. It is however arguable that such an implicature could be explained by reference to the maxim of Relation without invoking an alleged second maxim of Quantity.

(2a) Examples in which the first maxim of Quality is flouted.

Irony. X, with whom till now A has been on close terms, has betrayed a secret of A's to a business rival. A and his audience both know this. A says "X is a fine friend." (*Gloss:* It is perfectly obvious to A and his audience that what A has said or has made as if to say is something which he does not believe, and the audience knows that A knows that this is obvious to the audience. So, unless A's utterance is entirely pointless, A must be trying to get across some proposition other than the one he purports to be putting forward. This must be some obviously related proposition; the most obviously related proposition is the contradictory of the one he purports to be putting forward.)

Metaphor. For example, "You are the cream in my coffee." Such examples characteristically involve categorical falsity, so the contradictory of what the speaker has made as if to say will, strictly speaking, be a truism; so it cannot be *that* that such a speaker is trying to get across. The most likely supposition is that the speaker is attributing to his audience some feature or features in respect of which the audience resembles (more or less fancifully) the mentioned substance.

It is possible to combine metaphor and irony by imposing on the hearer two stages of interpretation. I say "You are the cream in my coffee," intending the hearer to reach first the metaphor interpretant "You are my pride and joy," and then the irony interpretant "You are my bane."

Meiosis. Of a man to have broken up all the furniture, one says "He was a little intoxicated."

Hyperbole. "Every nice girl loves a sailor."

(2b) Examples in which the second maxim of Quality "Do not say that for which you lack adequate evidence" is flouted are perhaps not easy to find, but the following seems to be a specimen. I say of X's wife, "She is probably deceiving him this evening." In a suitable context, or with a suitable gesture or tone of voice, it may be clear that I have no adequate reason for supposing this to be so. My partner, to preserve the assumption that the conversational game is still being played, assumes that I am getting at some related proposition or the acceptance of which I *do* have a reasonable basis. The related proposition might well be that she is given to deceiving her husband, or possibly that she is the sort of person who wouldn't stop short of such conduct.

(3) Examples in which an implicature is achieved by real as distinct from apparent violation of the maxim of Relation are perhaps rare, but the following seems to be a good candidate. At a genteel tea party A says "Mrs. X is an old bag." There is a moment of appalled silence, then B says "The weather has been quite delightful this summer, hasn't it?" B has blatantly refused to make what *he* says relevant to A's preceding remark. He thereby implicates that A's remark should not be discussed, and perhaps more specifically, that A has committed a social gaffe.

(4) Examples in which various maxims falling under the supermaxim "Be perspicuous" are flouted.

(a) *Ambiguity.* We must remember that we are only concerned with ambiguity that is deliberate, and which the speaker intends or expects to be recognized by his hearer. The problem the hearer has to solve is why a speaker should, when still playing the conversational game, go out of his way to choose an ambiguous utterance. There are two types of case:

(i) Examples in which there is no difference, or no striking difference, between two interpretations of an utterance in respect of straightforwardness; neither interpretation is notably more sophisticated, less standard, more recondite or more farfetched than the other. We might consider Blake's lines: "Never seek to tell thy love, Love that never told can be." To avoid the complications introduced by the presence of the imperative mood, I shall consider the related sentence, "I sought to tell my love, love that never told can be." There may be a double ambiguity here. "My love" may refer to either a state of emotion or an object of emotion, and "Love that never told can be" may mean either "Love that cannot be told" or "Love that if told cannot continue to exist." Partly because of the sophistication of the poet and partly because of internal evidence (that the ambiguity is kept up), there seems to be no alternative to supposing that the ambiguities are deliberate and that the poet is conveying both what he would be saying if one interpretation were intended rather than the other, and vice versa; though no doubt the poet is not explicitly *saying* any of these things, but only conveying or suggesting them (cf. "Since she [nature] pricked thee out for women's pleasure, mine be thy love, and thy love's use their treasure.")

(ii) Examples in which one interpretation is notably less straightforward than another. Take the complex example of the British General who captured the town of Sind and sent back the message "Peccavi." The ambiguity involved ("I have Sind"—"I have sinned") is phonemic not morphemic; and the expression actually used is unambiguous; but since it is in a language foreign to speaker and hearer, translation is called for, and the ambiguity resides in the standard translation into native English.

Whether or not the straightforward interpretant ("I have sinned") is being conveyed, it seems that the nonstraightforward must be. There might be stylistic reasons for conveying by a sentence merely its nonstraightforward interpretant, but it would be pointless, and perhaps also stylistically objectionable, to go to the trouble of finding an expression which nonstraightforwardly conveys that p, thus imposing on an audience the effort involved in finding this interpretant, if this interpretant were otiose so far as communication was concerned. Whether the straightforward interpretant is also being conveyed seems to depend on whether such a supposition would conflict with other conversational requirements; for example, would it be relevant, would it be something that the speaker could be supposed to accept, and so on. If such requirements are not satisfied, then the straightforward interpretant is not being conveyed. If they are, it is. If the author of "Peccavi" could naturally be supposed to think that he had committed some kind of transgression, for example, had disobeyed his orders in capturing Sind, and if reference to such a transgression would be relevant to the presumed interests of the audience, then he would have been conveying both interpretations; otherwise he would be conveying only the one.

(b) *Obscurity.* How do I exploit, for the purposes of communication, a deliberate and overt violation of the requirement that I should avoid obscurity? Obviously, if the Cooperative Principle is to operate, I must intend my partner to understand what I am saying despite the obscurity which I import into my utterance. Suppose that A and B are having a conversation in the presence of a third party, for example, a child; then A might be deliberately obscure, though not too obscure, in the hope that B would understand and that the third party would not. Furthermore, if A expects B to see that A is being deliberately obscure, it seems reasonable to suppose that, in making his conversational contribution in this way, A is implicating that the contents of his communication should not be imparted to the third party.

(c) *Failure to be brief or succinct.* Compare the remarks

(1) "Miss X sang 'Home sweet home.' "
(2) "Miss X produced a series of sounds which corresponded closely with the score of 'Home sweet home.' "

Suppose that a reviewer has chosen to utter (2) rather than (1). (*Gloss:* Why has he selected that rigmarole in place of the concise and nearly synonymous "sang"? Presumably to indicate some striking difference between Miss X's performance and those to which the word "singing" is usually applied. The most obvious supposition is that Miss X's performance suffered from some hideous defect. The reviewer knows that this supposition is what is likely to spring to mind; so that is what he is implicating.)

I have so far considered only cases of what I might call particularized conversational implicature; that is to say, cases in which an implicature is carried by saying that p on a particular occasion, in virtue of special features of the context; cases in which there is no room for the idea that an implicature of this sort is *normally* carried by saying that *p*. But there are cases of generalized conversational implicature. Sometimes one can say that the use of a certain form of words in an utterance would normally (in the *absence* of special circumstances) carry such-and-such an implicature or type of implicature. Noncontroversial examples are perhaps hard to find, since it is all too easy to treat a generalized conversational implicature as if it were a conventional implicature. I offer an example which I hope may be fairly noncontroversial.

Anyone who uses a sentence of the form "X is meeting a woman this evening" would normally implicate that the person to be met was someone other than X's wife, mother, sister, or perhaps even close platonic friend. Similarly, if I were to say "X went into a house yesterday and found a tortoise inside the front door," my hearer would normally be surprised if some time later I revealed that the house was X's own. I could produce similar linguistic phenomena involving the expression "a garden", "a car", "a college", and so on. Sometimes, however, there would normally be no such implicature ("I have been sitting in a car all morning"), and sometimes a reverse implicature ("I broke a finger yesterday"). I am inclined to think that one would not lend a sympathetic ear to a philosopher who suggested that there are three senses of the form of expression "an X": one in which it means roughly "something which satisfies the conditions defining the word X"; another in which it means approximately "an X (in the first sense) which is only remotely related in a certain way to some person indicated by the context"; and yet another in which it means "an X (in the first sense) which is closely related in a certain way to some person indicated by the context." Would we not much prefer an account on the following lines (which of course may be incorrect in detail)? When someone by using the form of expression "an X" implicates that the X does not belong to or is not otherwise closely connected with some identifiable person, the implicature is present because the speaker has failed to be specific in a way in which he might have been expected to be specific, with the consequence that it is likely to be assumed that he is not in a position to be specific. This is a familiar implicature situation, and is classifiable as a failure, for one reason or another, to fulfill the first maxim of Quantity. The only difficult question is why it should, in certain cases, be presumed, independently of information about particular contexts of utterance, that specification of the closeness or remoteness of the connection between a particular person or object and a further person who is mentioned or indicated by the utterance should be likely to be of interest. The answer must lie in the following region: transactions between a person and other persons or things closely connected with him are liable to be very different as regards their concomitants and results from the same sort of transactions involving only remotely connected persons or things; the concomitants and results, for instance, of my finding a hole in *my* roof are likely to be very different from the concomitants and results of my finding a hole in someone else's roof. Information, like money, is often given without the giver knowing to just what use the recipient will want to put it. If someone to whom a transaction is mentioned gives it further consideration, he is likely to find himself wanting the answers to further questions which the speaker may not be able to identify in advance; if the appropriate specification will be likely to enable the hearer to answer a considerable variety of such questions for himself, then there is a presumption that the speaker should include it in his remark; if not, then there is no such presumption.

Finally, we can now show that, conversational implicature being what it is, it must possess certain features.

(1) Since to assume the presence of a conversational implicature we must assume that at least the Cooperative Principle is being observed, and since it is possible to opt out of the observation of this principle, it follows that a generalized conversational implicature can be canceled in a particular case. It may be explicitly canceled, by the addition of a clause which states or implies that the speaker has opted out, or it may be contextually canceled, if the form of utterance which usually carries it is used in a context which makes it clear that the speaker *is* opting out.

(2) In so far as the calculation that a particular conversational implicature is present requires, besides contextual and background information, only a knowledge of what has been said (or of the conventional commitment of the utterance), and in so far as the manner of expression plays no role in the calculation, it will not be possible to find another way of saying the same thing, which simply lacks the implicature in question, except where some special feature of the substituted version is itself relevant to the determination of an implicature (in virtue of one of the maxims of manner). If we call this feature "nondetachability," one may expect a generalized conversational implicature which is carried by a familiar, nonspecial locution to have a high degree of nondetachability.

(3) To speak approximately, since the calculation of the presence of a conversational implicature presupposes an initial knowledge of the conventional force of the expression the utterance of which carries the implicature, a conversational implicatum will be a condition which is not included in the original specification of the expression's conventional force. Though it may not be impossible for what starts life, so to speak, as a conversational implicature to become conventionalized, to suppose that this is so in a given case would require special justification. So, initially at least, conversational implicata are not part of the meaning of the expressions to the employment of which they attach.

(4) Since the truth of a conversational implicatum is not required by the truth of what is said (what is said may be true, what is implicated may be false), the implicature is not carried by what is said, but only by the saying of what is said or by "putting it that way."

(5) Since to calculate a conversational implicature is to calculate what has to be supposed in order to preserve the supposition that the Cooperative Principle is being observed, and since there may be various possible specific explanations, a list of which may be open, the conversational implication in such cases

will be a disjunction of such specific explanations; and if the list of these is open, the implicatum will have just the kind of indeterminacy which many actual implicata do in fact seem to possess.

Appendix C
Talking About Women*

ROBIN T. LAKOFF

When a word acquires a bad connotation by association with something unpleasant or embarrassing, people may search for substitutes that do not have the uncomfortable effect—that is, euphemisms. Since attitudes toward the original referent are not altered by a change of name, the new name itself takes on the adverse connotations, and a new euphemism must be found. It is no doubt possible to pick out areas of particular psychological strain or discomfort—areas where problems exist in a culture—by pinpointing items around which a great many euphemisms are clustered. An obvious example concerns the various words for that household convenience into which human wastes are eliminated: toilet, bathroom, rest room, comfort station, lavatory, water closet, loo, and all the others.

In the case of women, it may be encouraging to find no richness of euphemism; but it is discouraging to note that at least one euphemism for "woman" does exist and is very much alive. The word, of course, is "lady," which seems to be replacing "woman" in a great many contexts. Where both exist, they have different connotations; where only one exists, there is usually a reason to be found in the context in which the word is uttered.

Related to the existence of euphemistic terms for "woman" is the existence of euphemistic terms for woman's principal role, that of "housewife." Most occupational terms do not have coexisting euphemisms: these seem to come into being only when the occupation is considered embarrassing or demeaning. Thus there is no euphemism for "professor," "doctor," "bank president"; but we do find "mortician" and "funeral director" for "undertaker"; "custodian" and "sanitary engineer" for "janitor"; "domestic" for "cleaning woman"; and so forth. Similarly one keeps running into hopeful suggestions, principally in the pages of women's magazines, that the lot of the housewife would be immeasurably improved if she thought of herself as "homemaker," "household executive," "household engineer," or any of several others. I am not sure what to make of the fact that none of these (unlike those of the bona fide occupational euphemisms) has taken hold: is it because the "housewife" doesn't consider her status

*Language and Women's Place (New York: Harper & Row, 1975), pp. 19–42.

demeaning? Then why the search for euphemisms? Or does she feel that there is no escape through a change in nomenclature, or lack pride in her job to such an extent that she doesn't feel up to making the effort? This is a question for the sociologist.

It may be objected that *lady* has a masculine counterpart, namely *gentleman*, occasionally shortened to *gent*. But I don't think this is a fair comparison. *Lady* is much more common than *gent(leman)*, and, since *gent* exists, the reason is not ease of pronunciation. *Lady* is really a euphemism for *woman*, but *gentleman* is not nearly frequent enough to classify as a euphemism for *man*. Just as we do not call whites "Caucasian-Americans," there is no felt need to refer to men commonly as "gentlemen." And just as there is a need for such terms as "Afro-Americans," there is similarly a felt need for "lady." One might even say that when a derogatory epithet exists, a parallel euphemism is deemed necessary. (The term WASP, white Anglo-Saxon Protestant, may occur to the reader as a possible derogatory term which has no parallel euphemism. But in fact, WASP is not parallel in usage to *nigger*, *polack*, or *yid*. One can refer to himself as a WASP, as one cannot refer to himself as a *nigger* without either a total lack of self-pride or bitter sarcasm. Thus one can say: "Sure I'm a WASP, and proud of it!" but probably not: "Sure I'm a nigger, and proud of it!" without special sarcastic inflection in the voice suggesting that it is an imitation of the addressee.) To avoid having to resort to terms like "Afro-American," we need only get rid of all expressions like "nigger"; to banish "lady" in its euphemistic sense from the vocabulary of English, we need only first get rid of "broad" and its relations. But of course, . . . we cannot achieve this commendable simplification of the lexicon unless we somehow remove from our minds the idea that blacks *are* niggers, and that women *are* broads. The presence of the words is a signal that something is wrong, rather than (as too often interpreted by well-meaning reformers) the problem itself. The point here is that, unless we start feeling more respect for women and, at the same time, less uncomfortable about them and their roles in society in relation to men, we cannot avoid *ladies* any more than we can avoid *broads*.

In the past, some ethnic groups that today are relatively respectable were apparently considered less so. And in looking at reports of the terms used to describe those groups at the earlier time, we find two interesting facts: first, there is a much greater incidence of derogatory epithets for that group (as might be expected); and second (which one might not be led to expect automatically) there exist euphemistic terms for that group that are no longer in general use. One can only conclude that euphemisms vanish as they are no longer needed. The example I have in mind is that of the words used to describe Jews. Aside from the uncomplimentary epithets which still exist today, though not encountered very often, one finds, in reading novels written and set more than half a century ago, a number of euphemisms that are not found any more, such as "Hebrew gentleman" and "Israelite." The disappearance of the euphemisms concurrently with the derogatory terms suggests that women will be *ladies* until some more dignified status can be found for them.

It might also be claimed that *lady* is no euphemism because it has exactly the same connotations as woman, is usable under the same semantic and contextual conditions. But a cursory inspection will show that this is not always the case. The decision to use one term rather than the other may considerably alter the sense of a sentence. The following are examples:

(1) (a) A (woman) that I know makes amazing things out of shoelaces and old
      (lady)
                                              boxes.

    (b) A (woman) I know works at Woolworth's.
       (lady)

    (c) A (woman) I know is a dean at Berkeley.
       (lady)

(These facts are true for some speakers of English. For others, *lady* has taken over the function of *woman* to such an extent that *lady* can be used in all these sentences.)

In my speech, the use of *lady* in (1) *(c)* imparts a frivolous or nonserious tone to the sentence: the matter under discussion is one of not too great moment. In this dialect, then, *lady* seems to be the more colloquial word: it is less apt to be used in writing, or in discussing serious matters. Similarly in (1) *(a)*, using *lady* would suggest that the speaker considered the "amazing things" not to be serious art, but merely a hobby or an aberration. If *woman* is used, she might be a serious (pop art) sculptor.

Related to this is the use of *lady* in job terminology. For at least some speakers, the more demeaning the job, the more the person holding it (if female, of course) is likely to be described as a *lady*. Thus, *cleaning lady* is at least as common as *cleaning woman*, *saleslady* as *saleswoman*. But one says, normally, *woman doctor*. To say *lady doctor* is to be very condescending: it constitutes an insult. For men, there is no such dichotomy. *Garbageman* or *salesman* is the only possibility, never **garbage gentleman*.[1] And of course, since in the professions the male is unmarked, we never have **man (male) doctor*.

Numerous other examples can be given, all tending to prove the same point: that if, in a particular sentence, both *woman* and *lady* might be used, the use of the latter tends to trivialize the subject matter under discussion, often subtly ridiculing the woman involved. Thus, for example, a mention in the San Francisco *Chronicle* of January 31, 1972, of Madalyn Murray O'Hair as the "lady atheist" reduces her position to that of scatterbrained eccentric, or at any rate, one who need not be taken seriously. Even *woman atheist* is scarcely defensible: first, because her sex is irrelevant to her philosophical position, and second, because her name makes it clear in any event. But *lady* makes matters still worse. Similarly a reference to a *woman sculptor* is only mildly annoying (since there is

---

[1] In conformity with current linguistic practice, throughout this work an asterisk (*) will be used to mark a sentence that is inappropriate in some sense, either because it is syntactically deviant or used in the wrong social context.

no term *male sculptor, the discrepancy suggests that such activity is normal for a man, but not for a woman), but still it could be used with reference to a serious artist. Lady sculptor, on the other hand, strikes me as a slur against the artist, deliberate or not, implying that the woman's art is frivolous, something she does to fend off the boredom of suburban housewifery, or at any rate, nothing of moment in the art world. Serious artists have shows, not dilettantes. So we hear of one-woman shows, but never one-lady shows.

Another realm of usage in which lady contrasts with woman is in titles of organizations. It seems that organizations of women who have a serious purpose (not merely that of spending time with one another) cannot use the word lady in their titles, but less serious ones may. Compare the Ladies' Auxiliary of a men's group, or the Thursday Evening Ladies Browning and Garden Society with *Ladies' Lib or *Ladies Strike for Peace.

What is curious about this split is that lady is, as noted, in origin a euphemism for woman. What kind of euphemism is it that subtly denigrates the people to whom it refers, suggests that they are not to be taken seriously, are laughing stocks? A euphemism, after all, is supposed to put a better face on something people find uncomfortable. But this is not really contradictory. What a euphemism is supposed to do, actually, is to remove from thought that part of the connotations of a word that creates the discomfort. So each of the euphemisms for toilet, starting with toilet, seems to be trying to get further from the notion of excrement, by employing successively more elegant terminology that seems designed to suggest that the piece of furniture in question has really other primary uses, for performing one's toilette, for washing, for comfort, for resting, but never for those other things. Perhaps the notion of the nonseriousness of women is not the thing that makes men—the devisers of euphemism—as well as women, uncomfortable. Perhaps it is some other aspect of the man-woman relationship. How can we determine whether this is in fact the case?

One way of identifying the precise source of discomfort is, perhaps, by looking at the derogatory terms for something. Many of the terms for blacks refer to their physical characteristics. And the latest euphemism for blacks, Afro-Americans, seems to be a specific attempt to get away from color names. (The term black is not a euphemism, but rather an attempt to confront the issue squarely and make color into a source of pride.) And as has often been noted, derogatory terms for women are very often overtly sexual: the reader will have no difficulty recalling what I allude to here.

The distinction between lady and woman, in those dialects of American English in which it is found, may be traceable to other causes than the sexual connotations present in woman. Most people who are asked why they have chosen to use lady where woman would be as appropriate will reply that lady seemed more polite. The concept of politeness thus invoked is the politeness used in dignifying or ennobling a concept that normally is not thought of as having dignity or nobility. It is this notion of politeness that explains why we have cleaning lady, but not, normally, lady doctor. A doctor does not need to be exalted by conventional expressions: she has dignity enough from her professional status. But a cleaning woman is in a very different situation, in which her occupational category requires ennobling. Then perhaps we can say that the very notion of womanhood, as opposed to manhood, requires ennobling since it lacks inherent dignity of its own: hence the word *woman* requires the existence of a euphemism like *lady*. Besides or possibly because of being explicitly devoid of sexual connotation, *lady* carries with it overtones recalling the age of chivalry: the exalted stature of the person so referred to, her existence above the common sphere. This makes the term seem polite at first, but we must also remember that these implications are perilous: they suggest that a "lady" is helpless, and cannot do things for herself. In this respect the use of a word like *lady* is parallel to the act of opening doors for women—or ladies. At first blush it is flattering: the object of the flattery feels honored, cherished, and so forth; but by the same token, she is also considered helpless and not in control of her own destiny. Women who protest that they *like* receiving these little courtesies, and object to being liberated from them, should reflect a bit on their deeper meaning and see how much they like *that*.

This brings us to the consideration of another common substitute for *woman*, namely *girl*. One seldom hears a man past the age of adolescence referred to as a boy, save in expressions like "going out with the boys," which are meant to suggest an air of adolescent frivolity and irresponsibility. But women of all ages are "girls": one can have a man, not a boy, Friday, but a girl, never a woman or even a lady, Friday; women have girl friends, but men do not—in a nonsexual sense—have boyfriends. It may be that this use of *girl* is euphemistic in the sense in which *lady* is a euphemism: in stressing the idea of immaturity, it removes the sexual connotations lurking in *woman*. Instead of the ennobling present in *lady*, *girl* is (presumably) flattering to women because of its stress on youth. But here again there are pitfalls: in recalling youth, frivolity, and immaturity, *girl* brings to mind irresponsibility: you don't send a girl to do a woman's errand (or even, for that matter, a boy's errand). It seems that again, by an appeal to feminine vanity (about which we shall have more to say later) the users of English have assigned women to a very unflattering place in their minds: a woman is a person who is both too immature and too far from real life to be entrusted with responsibilities and with decisions of any serious nature. Would you elect president a person incapable of putting on her own coat? (Of course, if we were to have a married woman president, we would not have any name for her husband parallel to *First Lady*, and why do you suppose that is?)

Perhaps the way in which *lady* functions as a euphemism for *woman* is that it does not contain the sexual implications present in *woman*: it is not "embarrassing" in that way. If this is so, we may expect that, in the future, *lady* will replace *woman* as the primary word for the human female, since *woman* will have become too blatantly sexual. That this distinction is already made in some contexts at least is shown in the following examples:

(2) *(a)* She's only twelve, but she's already a woman.

        *lady

(b) After ten years in jail, Harry wanted to find a woman.
                              *lady
(c) She's my woman, see, so don't mess around with her.
          *lady

It may be, finally, that the reason the use of *lady* rather than *woman* in a sentence creates the impression of frivolity discussed above is precisely because of the euphemistic nature of *lady*. In serious discussion, one does not typically employ euphemisms. So, for instance, a sentence like (3) *(a)* is more suited to cocktail party chitchat by returning tourists than to learned discussion by anthropologists, who would be more likely to use a technical term, as in (3) *(b):*

(3) *(a)* When the natives of Mbanga want to use the little boys' room, first they find a large pineapple leaf. . . .

　　(b) When the natives of Mbanga wish to defecate, first they find a large pineapple leaf. . . .

Perhaps the discomfort men suffer in contemplating, more or less unconsciously, the sexuality of women is traceable to guilt feelings on their part. The guilt arises, I should think, not only because they think sex is inherently dirty (that is another problem) but because if one deals with women as primary sexual beings, one is in effect automatically relegating them to object status; if women are there for the use and enjoyment of men, they are not fully human beings in their own right. But women are in most other respects evidently human. So a man feels somewhat ambivalent—more or less consciously—and reacts all the more strongly for that reason. Hence, perhaps, the rather hysterical ridicule heaped on Women's Lib in the media. In any case, throughout English one finds evidence of many sorts that women are viewed (by women as well as men) as secondary beings: as having an existence only when defined by a man.

These facts about women's position should cause us to question one of the commonest criticisms made of women's behavior, as opposed to men's: one often hears that women are vain and self-centered, concerned only about their appearance and how others view them. A little thought should convince anyone that, in fact, it is men who are self-centered and egocentric and that women's seeming vanity is not that at all.

As noted above, a woman's reputation and position in society depend almost wholly on the impression she makes upon others, how others view her. She must dress decoratively, look attractive, be compliant, if she is to survive at all in the world. Then her overattention to appearance and appearances (including, perhaps, overcorrectness and overgentility of speech and etiquette) is merely the result of being forced to exist only as a reflection in the eyes of others. She does not, cannot, do anything in her own behalf or purely for her own pleasure or aggrandizement. (Rather ironically, the only way she can increase her own comfort, pleasure, and security is through her husband's advancement, and thus she can achieve material comforts only through someone else's efforts. What seem to be self-centered efforts are really aimed at the opinions of others, and what appear to be efforts for someone else are really the only ones permissible for a woman's own behalf. It is no wonder women lack an identity and feel they have no place of their own.)

In fact, men are the vain sex. Men may derive pleasure directly from their own works. Men do things purely for their own satisfaction, not caring nearly so much how it will look to others. This, surely, is the true egocentricity. Further, it seems to me that the ultimate vanity or self-centeredness is to be found in eccentricity. The eccentric alone truly cares only for himself and his own pleasure: he does not concern himself with how his actions affect others or look to others. And eccentricity is far more common and far more tolerated in men than in women. A strong personality in general, a mark of egocentricity, is again valued in men much more than in women. For these reasons, women are not very successful in business or politics, where both vanity and eccentricity of certain sorts can be marks of distinction rather than objects of ridicule.

Sociologically it is probably fairly obvious that a woman in most subcultures in our society achieves status only through her father's, husband's, or lover's position. What is remarkable is that these facts show up linguistically in nonobvious ways.

Suppose we take a pair of words which, in terms of the possible relationships in an earlier society, were simple male-female equivalents, analogous to bull: cow. Suppose we find that, for independent reasons, society has changed in such a way that the primary meanings now are irrelevant. Yet the words have not been discarded, but have acquired new meanings, metaphorically related to their original senses. But suppose these new metaphorical uses are no longer parallel to each other. By seeing where the parallelism breaks down, we can intuit something about the different roles played by men and women in this culture. One good example of such a divergence through time is found in the pair *master* and *mistress*. Once used with reference to one person's power over another, these words became unusable in their original sense as the master-servant relationship became nonexistent. But the words are still common as used in sentences (4) and (5):

(4) (a) He is a master of the intricacies of academic politics.
     (b) *She is a mistress . . .

(5) (a) *Harry declined to be my master, and so returned to his wife.
     (b) Rhonda declined to be my mistress, and so returned to her husband.

Unless used with reference to animals or slaves, *master* now generally refers to a man who has acquired consummate ability in some field, normally nonsexual. But its feminine counterpart cannot be used in this way. It is practically restricted to its sexual sense of "paramour." We start out with two terms, both roughly paraphrasable as "one who has power over another." But the masculine form, once one person is no longer able to have absolute power over another, becomes unable metaphorically in the sense of "have power over *something*." The feminine counterpart also acquired a metaphorical interpretation, but the metaphor here is sexual: one's mistress "has power over" one in a sexual sense. And this expression is probably chivalrous, rather than descriptive of the real-world relationship between lovers. In terms of choice, of economic control, and so forth, it is generally the man who holds the power in such a relationship; to call a woman one's "mistress" is the equivalent of saying "please" in prefacing a request to a subordinate. Both are done for politeness and are done purely because both participants in the relationship, in both cases, know that the supposed inferiority of the mistress's lover and of the user of "please" is only a sham. Interesting too in this regard is the fact that "master" requires as its object only the name of some activity, something inanimate and abstract. But "mistress" requires a masculine noun in the possessive to precede it. One cannot say:

(6) *Rhonda is a mistress.

One must be *someone's* mistress.

And obviously too, it is one thing to be an *old master*, like Hans Holbein, and another to be an *old mistress*: the latter, again, requires a masculine possessive form preceding it, indicating who has done the discarding. *Old* in the first instance refers to absolute age: the artist's lifetime versus the time of writing. But *old* in the second really means "discarded," "old" with respect to someone else. . . .

So here we see several important points concerning the relationship between men and women illustrated: first, that men are defined in terms of what they do in the world, women in terms of the men with whom they are associated; and second, that the notion of "power" for a man is different from that of "power" for a woman: it is acquired and manifested in different ways. One might say then that these words have retained their principal meanings through time; what has changed is the kinds of interpersonal relationships to which they refer.

As a second example, the examples in (7) should be completely parallel semantically:

(7) *(a)* He's a professional.
    (b) She's a professional.

Hearing and knowing no more about the subjects of the discourse than this, what would one assume about them in each case? Certainly in *(a)* the normal conclusion the casual eavesdropper would come to was that "he" was a doctor or a lawyer or a member of one of the other professions. But it is much less likely that one would draw a similar conclusion in *(b)*. Rather, the first assumption most speakers of English seem to make is that "she" is a prostitute, literally or figuratively speaking. Again, a man is defined in the serious world by what he does, a woman by her sexuality, that is, in terms of one particular aspect of her relationship to men.

This discrepancy is not confined to English. Victor Wen has informed me that a similar situation pertains in Chinese. One may say of a man, "He's in business," and of a woman, "She's in business," lexically and grammatically parallel. The former means about what its English equivalent means. But the latter is synonymous to sentence (7) *(b)*.

James Fox tells me that in many cultures, as in English, people may be referred to metaphorically by animal names, suggesting that they have some of the attributes of that animal, real or part of the folklore. What is interesting here is that where animal names may be applied to both men and women—whether or not there are separate terms for male and female in the animal—the former may have connotations in all sorts of areas, while the latter, whatever other connotations the term may suggest, nearly always makes sexual reference as well. Compare in this regard *dog* and *bitch*, *fox* and *vixen*, and the difference between *he's a pig* and *she's a pig*.

The sexual definition of women, however, is but one facet of a much larger problem. In every aspect of life, a woman is identified in terms of the men she relates to. The opposite is not usually true of men: they act in the world as autonomous individuals, but women are only "John's wife," or "Harry's girl friend." Thus, meeting a woman at a party, a quite normal opening conversational gambit might be: "What does your husband do?" One very seldom hears, in a similar situation, a question addressed to a man: "What does your wife do?" The question would, to a majority of men, seem tautological: "She's my wife—that's what she does." This is true even in cases in which a woman is being discussed in a context utterly unrelated to her relationships with men, when she has attained sufficient stature to be considered for high public office. In fact, in a recent discussion of possible Supreme Court nominees, one woman was mentioned prominently. In discussing her general qualifications for the office, and her background, the *New York Times* saw fit to remark on her "bathing-beauty figure." Note that this is not only a judgment on a physical attribute totally removed from her qualifications for the Supreme Court, but that it is couched in terms of how a man would react to her figure. Some days later, President Nixon announced the nominations to his Price Board, among them one woman. In the thumbnail sketches the *Times* gave of each nominee, it was mentioned that the woman's husband was a professor of English. In the case of none of the other nominees was the existence of a spouse even hinted at, and much less was there any clue about the spouse's occupation. So here, although the existence of a husband was as irrelevant for this woman appointee as the existence of a wife was for any of the male appointees, the husband was mentioned, since a woman cannot be placed in her position in society by the readers of the *Times* unless they know her marital status. The same is not at all true of men. Similarly in the 1971 mayoral campaign in San Francisco, the sole woman candidate was repeatedly referred to as *Mrs. Feinstein*, never *Feinstein*, when her opponents were regularly referred to by first and last names or last names alone: *Joseph Alioto*, or *Alioto*, not *Mr. Alioto*. Again, the woman had to be identified by her relationship to a man, although this should bear no relevance to her qualifications for public office.

While sharp intellect is generally considered an unqualified virtue in a man, any character trait that is not related to a woman's utility to men is considered suspect, if not downright bad. Thus the word *brainy* is seldom used of men; when used of women it suggests (1) that this intelligence is unexpected in a woman; (2) that it isn't really a good trait. If one calls a woman "smart," outside of the sense of "fashionable," either one means it as a compliment to her domestic thrift and other housekeeping abilities or, again, it suggests a bit of wariness on the part of the speaker.

Also relevant here are the connotations (as opposed to the denotative meanings) of the words *spinster* and *bachelor*. Denotatively, these are, again, parallel to "cow" versus "bull": one is masculine, the other feminine, and both mean "one who is not married." But there the resemblance ends. *Bachelor* is at least a neutral term, often used as a compliment. *Spinster* normally seems to be used pejoratively with connotations of prissiness, fussiness, and so on. Some of the differences between the two words are brought into focus in the following examples:

(8) *(a)* Mary hopes to meet an eligible bachelor.
   (b) *Fred hopes to meet an eligible spinster.

It is the concept of an *eligible spinster* that is anomalous. If someone is a spinster, by implication she is not eligible (to marry); she has had her chance, and been passed by. Hence, a girl of twenty cannot be properly called a spinster: she still has a chance to be married. (Of course, *spinster* may be used metaphorically in this situation, as described below.) But a man may be considered a bachelor as soon as he reaches marriageable age: to be a bachelor implies that one has the choice of marrying or not, and this is what makes the idea of a bachelor existence attractive, in the popular literature. He has been pursued and has successfully eluded his pursuers. But a spinster is one who has not been pursued, or at least not seriously. She is old unwanted goods. Hence it is not surprising to find that a euphemism has arisen for *spinster*, a word not much used today, *bachelor girl*, which attempts to capture for the woman the connotations *bachelor* has for a man. But this, too, is not much used except by writers trying to give their (slick magazine) prose a "with-it" sound. I have not heard the word used in unself-conscious speech. *Bachelor*, however, needs no euphemisms.

When *bachelor* and *spinster* are used metaphorically, the distinction in connotation between the two becomes even clearer:

(9) *(a)* John is a regular bachelor.
   (b) Mary is a regular spinster.

The metaphorical connotations of "bachelor" generally suggest sexual freedom; of "spinster," puritanism or celibacy. So we might use a sentence like (9) *(a)* if John was in fact married but engaged in extramarital affairs freely. It is hard to think of other circumstances in which it might be used. Certainly it could not be used if John were married but determined to remain celibate. (9) *(b)*, on the other hand, might be used under two conditions: first, if Mary were in fact unmarried, but still of marriageable age (that is, not yet a literal spinster), and very cold and prissy; second, if Mary were married, with the same characteristics. The use of "regular," then, seems to be an indicator that the noun it modifies is to be taken purely in its connotative rather than denotative sense.

These examples could be multiplied. It is generally considered a *faux pas*, in proper society, to congratulate a girl on her engagement, while it is correct to congratulate her fiancé. Why is this? The reason here seems to be that it is impolite to remind someone of something that may be uncomfortable to him. To remind a girl that she must catch someone, that perhaps she might not have caught anyone, is rude, and this is what is involved, effectively, in congratulating someone. To congratulate someone is to rejoice with him in his good fortune; but it is not quite nice to remind a girl that getting married is good fortune for her, indeed a veritable necessity; it is too close to suggesting the bad fortune that it would be for her had she not found someone to marry. In the context of this society's assumptions about women's role, to congratulate a girl on her engagement is virtually to say, "Thank goodness! You had a close call!" For the man, on the other hand, there was no such danger. His choosing to marry is viewed as a good thing, but not something essential, and so he may be congratulated for doing a wise thing. If man and woman were equal in respect to marriage, it would be proper to congratulate either both or neither.

Another thing to think about is the traditional conclusion of the marriage service: "I now pronounce you man and wife." The man's position in the world, and in relation to other people including the bride, has not been changed by the act of marriage. He was a "man" before the ceremony, and a "man" he still is (one hopes) at its conclusion. But the bride went into the ceremony a "woman," not defined by any other person, at least linguistically; she leaves it a "wife," defined in terms of the "man," her husband. There are many other aspects of traditional marriage ceremonies in our culture that might be used to illustrate the same point.

And having discussed bachelorhood and spinsterhood, and the marital state, we arrive at widowhood. Surely a bereaved husband and a bereaved wife are equivalent: they have both undergone the loss of a mate. But in fact, linguistically at any rate, this is not true. It is true that we have two words, *widow* and *widower*: but here again, *widow* is far commoner in use. Widows, not widowers, have their particular roles in folklore and tradition, and mourning behavior of particular sorts seems to be expected more strongly, and for a longer time, of a widow than of a widower. But there is more than this, as evidenced by the following:

(10) *(a)* Mary is John's widow.
  (b) *John is Mary's widower.

Like *mistress*, *widow* commonly occurs with a possessive preceding it, the name of the woman's late husband. Though he is dead, she is still defined by her relationship to him. But the bereaved husband is no longer defined in terms of his wife. While she is alive, he is sometimes defined as Mary's husband (though less often, probably, than she is as "John's wife"). But once she is gone, her function for him is over, linguistically speaking anyway. So once again, we see that women are always defined in terms of the men to whom they are related, and hence the worst thing that can happen to a woman is not to have a man in this relationship—that is, to be a spinster, a woman with neither husband nor lover, dead or alive.

What all these facts suggest is merely this, again: that men are assumed to be able to choose whether or not they will marry, and that therefore their not being married in no way precludes their enjoying sexual activity; but if a woman is not married, it is assumed to be because no one found her desirable. Hence if a woman is not married by the usual age, she is assumed to be sexually undesirable, prissy, and frigid.

The reason for this distinction seems to be found in the point made earlier: that women are given their identities in our society by virtue of their relationship with men, not vice versa. . . .

Now it becomes clearer why there is a lack of parallelism in men's and women's titles. To refer to a man as *Mr.* does not identify his marital status; but there is no such ambiguous term for women: one must decide on *Mrs.* or *Miss.* To remedy this imbalance, a bill was proposed in the United States Congress by Bella Abzug and others that would legislate a change in women's titles: *Miss* and *Mrs.* would both be abolished in favor of *Ms.* Rather less seriously, the converse has been proposed by Russell Baker, that two terms should be created for men, *Mrm.* and *Srs.*, depending upon marital status. We may ask several questions: (*a*) Why does the imbalance exist in the first place? (*b*) Why do we feel that Baker's suggestion (even if it did not come from Baker) is somehow not to be taken as seriously as Abzug's? And (*c*) does Abzug's proposal have a chance of being accepted in coloquial speech? (One must distinguish between acceptance in official use and documents, where Ms. is already used to some extent, and acceptance in colloquial conversation, where I have never heard it. I think the latter will be a long time in coming, and I do not think we can consider Ms. a real choice until this occurs.)

(*a*) A title is devised and used for a purpose: to give a clue to participants in social interaction how the other person is to be regarded, how he is to be addressed. In an avowedly class-conscious society, social ranking is a significant determining factor: once you know that your addressee is to be addressed as "lord," or "mister," or "churl," you know where he stands with respect to you; the title establishes his identity in terms of his relationship with the larger social group. For this reason, the recent suggestion that both *Mr.* and *Mrs./Miss* be abolished in favor of *Person* is unlikely to be successful: *Person* tells you only what you already know, and does not aid in establishing ranking or relationship between two people. Even in a supposedly classless society, the use of *Mr.* (as opposed to simple last name or first name) connotes a great deal about the relationship of the two participants in the discourse with respect to each other. To introduce yourself, "I'm Mr. Jones" puts the relationship you are seeking to establish on quite a different basis than saying, "I'm Jones," or "I'm John," and each is usable under quite different contextual conditions, socially speaking. As long as social distinctions, overt or covert, continue to exist, we will be unable to rid our language of titles that make reference to them. It is interesting that the French and Russian revolutions both tried to do away with honorific titles that distinguished class by substituting "citizen(ess)" and "comrade." These, however, are not purely empty like "person": they imply that speaker and addressee share a relationship in that both are part of the state and hence, by implication, both equal. In France, the attempt was not long-lived. (Although *tovarishch* is normal today in the Soviet Union, I don't know whether it is really usable under all conditions, whether a factory worker, for instance, could use it to his foreman, or his foreman's wife.)

Although, in our society, naming conventions for men and women are essentially equal (both have first and last names, and both may have additional names, of lesser importance), the social conventions governing the choice of form of address is not parallel in both sexes. Thus, as noted, a man, Mr. John Jones, may be addressed as John, as Jones, as Mr. Jones, and as Mr. John Jones. The first normally implies familiarity, the second intimacy coupled with Jones's inferiority (except in situations of nondirect address, as in professional citation; or among intimates, as a possibly more intimate form of address even than first name alone, without inferiority being implied); the third distance and more or less equality. The last is never used in direct address, and again indicates considerable distance. To address someone by first name alone is to assume at least equality with the other person, and perhaps superiority (in which case the other person will respond with *Mr.* and last name). *Mr. Jones* is probably the least-marked form of address, a means of keeping distance with no necessary suggestions of status. To address someone as *Jones* socially or in business may be an indication of his inferior status, but to refer to someone that way professionally (as at a linguistics conference, generally in indirect reference rather than direct address) seems to be a mark of his acceptance, as a colleague and a person to be taken seriously as a fellow member of the profession. In this way, perhaps, it is related to the last-name-only of familiarity: it is "we know each other well; we are equals and pals, or equals and colleagues." . . .

Aside from making apparent a dilemma arising from a social inequity, the facts noted above are of interest for other reasons: they show that titles are very much alive in our supposedly classless society, and apparently small differences in their use reflect great chasms in social position among users. The use (or misuse) of titles supplies much information to people, and hence titles are important in our language as in our society, and not about to be lightly discarded.

If then, we can reasonably assume that a title supplies information about the person to whose name it is attached, we may further assume that this information is necessary in telling people how to interact with this person. And if this sort of information is felt to be necessary for one class of people and not another, we may expect to find a distinction made in the titles for the first class, if at all, but not the second.

So it is with *Mrs.*, *Miss*, and *Mr.* Since a significant part of the opinion one normally forms about a woman's character and social station depends on her marital status—as is not the case with men—it is obvious that the title of address should supply this information in the case of women, but not of men.

(It may seem as though a man's marital status is, under certain conditions, of crucial interest to a woman, and therefore this point is suspect. But I think we have to distinguish between importance in the eyes of a single person in a particular situation, and importance in the eyes of society at large, in a great many possible situations. At almost every turn, because of the way social and business events are arranged, one needs to know a woman's marital status, and the position held by her husband. But one does not need the same information about a man, since his social status can be gauged, generally, purely by reference to his own accomplishments.) Once again, it would seem that trying to legislate a change in a lexical item is fruitless. The change to *Ms.* will not be generally adopted until a woman's status in society changes to assure her an identity based on her own accomplishments. (Perhaps even more debasing than the *Mrs./Miss* distinction is the fact that the woman in marrying relinquishes her own name, while the man does not. This suggests even more firmly that a woman is her husband's possession, having no other identity than that of his wife. Not only does she give up her last name [which, after all, she took from her father], but often her first name as well, to become *Mrs. John Smith.*)

Although blacks are not yet fully accorded equal status with whites in this society, nevertheless *black*, a term coined to elicit racial pride and sense of unity, seems to have been widely adopted both by blacks and whites, both in formal use and in the media, and increasingly in colloquial conversation. Does this constitute a counterexample to my claim here? I think not, but rather an element of hope. My point is that linguistic and social change go hand in hand: one cannot, purely by changing language use, change social status. The word *black*, in its current sense, was not heard until the late 1960s or even 1970, to any significant extent. I think if its use had been proposed much earlier, it would have failed in acceptance. I think the reason people other than blacks can understand and sympathize with black racial pride is that they were made aware of the depths of their prejudice during the civil rights struggles of the early 1960s. It took nearly ten years from the beginning of this struggle for the use of *black* to achieve wide acceptance, and it is still often used a bit self-consciously, as though italicized. But since great headway was made first in the social sphere, linguistic progress could be made *on that basis*; and now this linguistic progress, it is hoped, will lead to new social progress in turn. The women's movement is but a few years old, and has, I should think, much deeper ingrained hostility to overcome than the civil rights movement ever did. (Among the intelligentsia, the black civil rights struggle was never a subject for ridicule, as women's liberation all too often is, among those very liberals who were the first on their blocks to join the NAACP.) The parallel to the black struggle should indicate that social change must precede lexical change: women must achieve some measure of greater social independence of men before *Ms.* can gain wider acceptance.

(*b*) There is thus a very good reason why a distinction is made in the case of women, but not men, in the matter of marital status. But this fact suggests an answer to the second question posed above, regarding why *Ms.* is felt to be a more serious proposal than Baker's suggestion. It is obviously easier to imagine obliterating an extant distinction than creating a new one: easier to learn to ignore the marital status of a woman than to begin to pay attention to that of a man. Moreover, we may also assume that for a woman, the use of *Ms.* is a liberating device, one to be desired. But (as Baker suggests) the use of two titles for men is an encumbrance, a remover of certain kinds of liberties, and something definitely undesirable. So the two suggestions are not equivalent, and if either were ever to be accepted, the choice of *Ms.* is the probable candidate.

(*c*) The third question regarding the chances *Ms.* has for real acceptance has, in effect, already been answered. Until society changes so that the distinction between married and unmarried women is as unimportant in terms of their social position as that between married and unmarried men, the attempt in all probability cannot succeed. Like the attempt to substitute any euphemism for an uncomfortable word, the attempt to do away with *Miss* and *Mrs.* is doomed to failure if it is not accompanied by a change in society's attitude to what the titles describe.

Appendix D
Answers to Probability Puzzles

The following are answers to the puzzles found in Chapter 10, "Probability."

(1) Your first instinct may be to suppose that the chances must be 50/50 that the remaining sandwich is a ham sandwich, because that was the probability of picking the bag containing two ham sandwiches to begin with. But don't forget that drawing out a ham sandwich gives some evidence concerning which bag was selected. Because the chances are *twice* as good for drawing a ham sandwich out of the bag containing two ham sandwiches than it is for drawing it from the bag with only one ham sandwich, the chances are two in three that you are in the bag that started with two ham sandwiches. Thus, the probability that the remaining sandwich is a ham sandwich is actually 2/3.

(2) Again, the most common reaction to this puzzle is wrong. It seems obvious that the original probability of selecting the cheese sandwich (one in three) will not be affected by anything that happens after the selection is made. But don't forget that new information is provided after the initial choice, which makes a difference. In fact, the chances of getting the cheese sandwich are 2/3 if you switch.

To see this, first notice that it will be a *bad* idea to switch only if you have started by selecting the bag with the cheese sandwich in it. The probability of starting with the bag with the cheese sandwich in it is, of course, 1/3. On the other hand, 2/3 of the time you will have started with a bag with a chicken fat sandwich in it, and switching will get you the bag containing the cheese. So it is a *good* idea to switch after one of the bags containing a chicken fat sandwich is removed because two out of three times you will get the bag containing the cheese sandwich by doing so.

(3) To get a handle on the Fogelin's Palace puzzle, we can consider a simpler case where the bet only has to ride twice. Now, once more, if you win one and lose one (in whatever order), you come out behind:

	Win	Lose
Total	$150	$90

	Lose	Win
Total	$60	$90

So again, it may seem a bad idea to gamble in Fogelin's Palace.

The flaw in this reasoning is that not all possible cases have been considered. The following chart shows the results of all possible combinations of wins and losses:

W	W	$225
W	L	$ 90
L	W	$ 90
L	L	$ 36

It is easy to see that the total winnings with two wins outweigh the losses in the other three cases. More exactly, the expected value can be calculated by dividing the sum of the figures on the right (the total payoffs) by four (the total number of equally likely outcomes).

$$\text{Expected value} = \$441/4 = \$110.25$$

The same line of reasoning will show that four-bet sequences have a favorable expected value as well. You will, in fact, have more losing sequences than winning sequences, but, as in the example above, winning sequences pay off enough to outweigh the more frequent losing sequences.

Copyrights and Acknowledgments

The author wishes to thank the following publishers and copyright holders for permission to reprint material used in this book:

Basic Books, Inc., Publishers, for "The Turing Test: A Coffeehouse Conversation," by Douglas R. Hofstadter, and "Reflections," by Daniel C. Dennett. From *The Mind's I*, by Douglas R. Hofstadter and Daniel C. Dennett. Copyright © 1981 by Basic Books, Inc., Publishers. Reprinted by permission of the publisher.

Creation Life Publishers for the excerpt from *Scientific Creationism*, Creation Life Publishers, San Diego, California, 1974, pp. 4–13. Reprinted by permission of the publisher.

Dover Publications for the excerpt "On Floating Bodies," from *The Works of Archimedes*, T. L. Heath, ed. Dover Publications, 1953.

H. P. Grice and Dickinson Publishing Co., for "Logic and Conversation," in *The Logic of Grammar*, Donald Davidson and Gilbert Harmon, eds. Copyright © 1975 by H. P. Grice. Reprinted by permission of the author.

Harper & Row, Publishers, Inc., for pages 19–42 from *Language and Woman's Place*, by Robin Lakoff. Copyright © 1975 by Robin Lakoff. Reprinted by permission of Harper & Row, Publishers, Inc.

King Features for the article "Protesters Are Ugly, Stupid," by Jeffrey Hart. Copyright © 1980 by King Features Syndicate, Inc. Reprinted with special permission of King Features Syndicate, Inc.

The MIT Press for the article "Creation-Science Is Not Science," by Michael Ruse, from *Science, Technology & Human Values*, Vol. 7, No. 40, Summer 1982. The MIT Press, copyright 1982; and for the excerpt "The Morality of Abortion," from *Abortion and the Sanctity of Human Life: A Philosophical View*, by Baruch Brody. The MIT Press, copyright 1975.

The New York Review of Books for the excerpt from "The Myth of the Computer," by John Searle, in *The New York Review of Books*, April 29, 1982. Reprinted by permission from *The New York Review of Books*. Copyright © 1982 Nyrev, Inc.

The New York Times Company for "Is Abortion Really a Moral Dilemma?" by Barbara Ehrenreich, February 7, 1985, and "Fraternities, Where Men May Come to Terms with Other Men," by Rev. William H. Stemper, Jr., June 16, 1985, *The New York Times*. Copyright © 1985 by The New York Times Company. Reprinted by permission.

Index

A

Abell, George O., *Exploration of the Universe*, 104*n*
abortion
  argumentative reconstruction, 130–37
  question of, 295–96
  weighing factors in, 136–37
"Abortion and the Conscience of the Nation" (Reagan), 313–20
ad hominem attack, 87–89
ad hominem fallacy, 87–89
Agreement
  and Difference, Joint Method of, 235–37
  Method of, 233–34
ambiguity, 78–79
  fallacy of, 8, 81–82
analogy
  in legal reasoning, 267–68
  in moral reasoning, 296
"and," truth conditions for, 141–42
"any," before distributed predicate terms, 212–13
appeals to authority, 90–94
  vague, in close analysis, 55–56
a priori procedures, for probability claims, 244–45
Archimedes, "On Floating Bodies," 325–30
argumentative performatives, 11–13
  in close analysis, 54
argumentative reconstruction, *see* reconstruction, argumentative
arguments
  ad hominem, 87–89
  assuring in, 39–40
  basic structure of, 29–31
  circular, 38
  close analysis of, *see* close analysis
  deductive vs. inductive, 218–21
  deep analysis of, 118–37
  definitions in, 83–85
  discounting in, 41–42
  enthymematic, 120
  evaluation of, 35–38

evaluative language in, 43–46
expressive language in, 43–46
fallacies, *see* fallacies
form of, 144
"from the heap," 72–73
guarding in, 40–41
identification of premises and conclusions, 33
"if-then" sentences, 31–32
legal, *see* legal reasoning
moral, *see* moral reasoning
philosophical, 358–90
reconstruction, *see* reconstruction, argumentative
refutations, *see* refutations
scientific, 324–55
self-sealers, 96–99
slippery slope, 73–74
soundness of, 36
standard form of, 32–34
validity of, 35, 140–67; *see also* formal analysis
warranting connectives, 30–32
artifacts, linguistic, 8
assuring, 391
  in close analysis, 54–57, 61–62
astrology, refutation of, 104
attacks, ad hominem, 88–89
Austin, J. L., 10
  "Performative Utterances," 391–403

B

Bakke decision, 280–91
basic propositions, *see* propositions, basic
begging the question, 94–96
"Belief in The Law of Small Numbers" (Tversky and Kahneman), 223–24
bias
  in sampling, 222–25
  sources of, 226–30
    informal judgmental heuristics, 226–30
    prejudice, 226

formal analysis (*cont.*)
conversational implication and, 187–91
domain of discourse, 175–76
existential import, 178–80, 206–209
immediate inference, theory of, 191–201
contraposition, 197–201
conversion, 192–94
obversion, 194–97
logical language and ordinary language, 161–64
propositional logic, 140–47
conjunction, 140–46
disjunction, 146–47
negation, 147
square of opposition, 181–87
contradictories, 183–85
contraries, 182–83
subalterns, 186–87
subcontraries, 185–86
syllogisms
applications, 210–11
categorical, definition, 202
rules for evaluating, 211–15
theory of, 201–203
valid and invalid, 203
Venn diagrams for, 204–206
truth-functional connectives in, 148–55
"Fraternities, Where Men May Come to Terms with Other Men" (Stemper), 66–67
"from the heap" arguments, 72–73

G

Galileo Galilei, *Dialogue Concerning the Two World Systems—Ptolemaic and Copernican*, 331, 332–39
gambler's fallacy, 255–56
Geller, Uri, 91n
generalizations
causal, 230–33
"but-for" test, 232
explanation with, 230–31
prediction with, 231
hasty, 223–24
inductive, 221–30
acceptability of premises in, 222
fallacy of biased sampling, 223–25
sample size, 222–24
sources of bias in, 226–30
Gould, Stephen J., *The Mismeasure of Man*, 93
grammarians, moods of sentences, 9
grammatical rules, 7
Greenhouse, Linda, "Of Tents with Wheels and Houses with Oars," 76n
Grice, H. P.
conditionals and validity, 163–64
conversational implication, 17n
Cooperative Principle, 15

Manner, 16–17
rule of Quantity, 15, 189
rule of Relevance, 16
rule of Strength, 15
rule of Quality, 16
"Logic and Conversation," 15, 20, 403–418
guarding, 40–41
in close analysis, 54–57, 60, 62–63

H

Hart, Jeffrey, "Protesters are 'Ugly, Stupid'," 100–101
Herrick, Robert, "Upon Julia's Clothes," 8
heuristics, judgmental, 226–30
availability, 228–29
representative, 227–28
Hofstadter, Douglas R., "The Turing Test: A Coffeehouse Conversation," 360–82
Hume, David
on hasty generalizations, 223–24
A Treatise of Human Nature, 226
hypothetical syllogism, 159–60

I

"if" and "only if," 165–67
"if-then" sentences, 31–32
illicitly distributed predicate, fallacy of, 214
illicitly distributed subject, fallacy of, 214
imitation game, 359
immediate inference, theory of, 191–200
contraposition, 197–200
conversion, 192–94
existential import in, 178–80
obversion, 194–97
implication, conversational, 17–25
deception, 21–23
irony, 24
metaphor, 24
rhetorical questions, 23–24
sarcasm, 24
square of opposition and, 187–91
violation of conversational rules, 19–20
indeterminacy, of facts in legal disputes, 266–67
indicative conditionals, 155–57
inductive generalizations, *see* generalizations, inductive
interpretations, scientific, 330–31
irony, 24
irrelevance, *see* relevance, fallacies of
"Is Abortion Really a 'Moral Dilemma'?" (Ehrenreich), 320–23

J

Jackson (Justice), 268–69

validity (*cont.*)
    truth-table definition for, 143
  disjunction, 146–47
  negation, 147
  of syllogisms, 203–206
  and truth-functional equivalence, 154–55
value, relative, 252–54, 261
Venn diagrams, 173

for immediate inference, 192–200
for syllogisms, 204–206

W

warranting connectives, 30–31
  in close analysis, 54–55, 62
  "if-then" sentences, 31–32
  list of, 30
Warren (Chief Justice), 277–80